POETRY INTO SONG

POETRY INTO SONG

Performance and Analysis of *Lieder*

DEBORAH STEIN

ROBERT SPILLMAN

Foreword by Elly Ameling
with Max Deen Larsen

New York   Oxford
OXFORD UNIVERSITY PRESS
1996

To Laurel and George

Oxford University Press

Oxford   New York
Athens   Auckland   Bangkok   Bombay
Calcutta   Cape Town   Dar es Salaam   Delhi
Florence   Hong Kong   Istanbul   Karachi
Kuala Lumpur   Madras   Madrid   Melbourne
Mexico City   Nairobi   Paris   Singapore
Taipei   Tokyo   Toronto

and associated companies in
Berlin   Ibadan

Copyright © 1996 by Oxford University Press, Inc.

Published by Oxford University Press, Inc.,
198 Madison Avenue, New York, New York 10016

Oxford is a registered trademark of Oxford University Press

Library of Congress Cataloging-in-Publication Data
Stein, Deborah J. (Deborah Jane)
   Poetry into song : performance and analysis of lieder / Deborah
Stein and Robert Spillman.
      p.   cm.
   Includes scores for 17 songs.
   Includes bibliographical references (p.   ) and index.
   ISBN 0-19-509328-3
   1. Songs—Analysis, appreciation.   2. Songs—Interpretation
(Phrasing, dynamics, etc.)   3. Songs—19th century—History and
criticism.   4. Songs—20th century—History and criticism.
I. Spillman, Robert.   II. Title.
MT110.S74   1996
782.42168'0943—dc20   95-5398

1 3 5 7 9 8 6 4 2

Printed in the United States America
on acid-free paper

Acknowledgments

We have many to thank for assistance in completing this book. We thank Maribeth Anderson Payne for her interest and enthusiasm for the project and Soo Mee Kwon for her unflagging support and advice as the book went into publication. We are particularly grateful that Oxford University Press made the book financially accessible to those who would benefit from it the most.

There are many other individuals who contributed to the success of this project over the course of several years. For their enthusiasm and their many insights into *Lieder* and performance, we thank Carol and Brady Allred, Hali Fieldman, Cynthia Gonzales, Alan Gosman, Bryon Grohman, Steven Laitz, Ann-Marie Reynolds Laitz, Patrick McCreless, Mary Jane Loizou, Dan McMullin, Janet Schmalfeldt, Loraine Schneider, and Susan Youens. We are extremely grateful to David Lewin and Hali Fieldman, who read portions of the manuscript with great care and offered superb suggestions, and to Cynthia, Alan, Hali, Henny Bordwin, and Peggy Clarke for careful proofreading. Many colleagues sustained us through the final stages of this project; we extend special gratitude to Steven Bruns and Patrick Mason of the University of Colorado, Boulder and Lyle Davidson, Alan Fletcher, D'Anna Fortunato, Helen Greenwald and Veronica Jochum of the New England Conversatory. To Henny Bordwin, Director of the American Schubert Institute in Boston, a special thanks for her generous assistance in ways too varied and numerous to mention here; the Institute has proven to be an immense resource for study of *Lied* performance and scholarship, and has contributed remarkably to the success of this project.

Others who have provided particular inspiration to the authors are a number of extraordinary scholars, musicians, and performers, including Arleen Auger, Robert Bailey, Dalton Baldwin, Wallace T. Berry, Edward T. Cone, David Epstein, Jan DeGaetani, Donald Grobe, Julius Huehn, Sergius Kagan, David B. Lewin, Barry McDaniel, Gerald Moore, Herman Reutter, Carl Schachter, Peter Schreier, Rita Streich, and Fritz Wunderlich.

Finally, a special thanks to Elly Ameling, whose consummate understanding and unparalleled performance of German *Lieder* was an abiding influence and inspiration to the authors and whose Foreword with Max

Deen Larsen graces our work in a way that cannot be suitably expressed. In addition to her enthusiasm for this book, Elly Ameling has, through her recitals, recordings, and masterclasses, provided stunning insight and clarity into the works explored in this volume.

Contents

Foreword

The irresistible beauty of the *Lied* has long cast its spell on listeners around the world. Those distinctive harmonies with which Franz Schubert and Hugo Wolf express intimate ideals and desires speak to people everywhere. No music pierces the heart's mysteries more deeply and no music is more deeply alive with verbal magic . . . a serious challenge indeed for performers and audiences who have little German. For it is the poetry of the Age of Goethe that has made the *Lied* possible, exquisite poetry that cannot be translated into other languages, but only into music.

The book you have in hand is about artistic transformation. It will guide you, and follow you, on your inner journeys as a performer, seeking to turn poems into songs. Here you enter a world where two plus two rarely equals four, a world teeming with latent voices waiting to be called into life, a world of vibrant tonal colors, a world where the very sounds of words must be meaning itself. More than a compendium of analytical concepts, this is a book that enables you to shape individual interpretations through personal encounter with a lively train of provocative questions and creative experiments. Providing abundant exercises for pianist and singer alike, *Poetry into Song* is an invitation to experience metamorphosis.

Elly Ameling
with
Dr. Max Deen Larsen
Franz Schubert-Institut
Baden bei Wien

Preliminary Clarifications

Three different subjects are studied in this volume: poetry, musical performance, and music analysis. While our ultimate goal is to combine the three into a manifold understanding of German art song performance, we begin by separating the subjects from one another and examining each as a separate topic. This approach models how we believe performers need to study a *Lied* in performance preparation: they must study first the poetry, then the performance problems, and then each aspect of the musical structure in turn. By the end of the process, a recombination of the three topics will occur through polished performance, when singer and pianist convey their undertanding of the poetry and the music in the magical act of musical expression.

In Part I, "The Language of Poetry," two chapters offer ways to think about poetry. Chapter One, "Introduction to German Romanticism," provides the historical context of German Romantic poetry and defines recurring themes, images, and metaphors. Chapter Two, "Devices and Delights in Poetry," presents the norms and practices of poetic texts, including use of rhetorical devices, poetic meter, and special forms of word usage. Chapter Two also explains the concept of "persona," or whose voice is speaking, as persona occurs in both German Romantic poetry and in the musical setting.[1] These opening chapters will give readers the resources necessary for examining and understanding all of the verse set by the great *Lied* composers; moreover, they will provide the foundation for all discussions of poetry and related issues of text in this book.

The three chapters that comprise Part II, "The Language of the Performer," address the various issues of technical concern to the singer and pianist. Most of the issues here are familiar to anyone who performs; in Chapter Three, "Texture," and Chapter Four, "Temporality," we review how musicians think about these basic elements and suggest how they influence both singer and pianist in preparing a *Lied* for performance. In Chapter Five, "Elements of Interpretation," we discuss how decisions about use of timbre and dynamics and concerns about ensemble coordination all help shape and articulate the performer's conception of a musical setting. These chapters are not intended to give the performer answers to questions of interpretation; rather, they suggest a process for thinking about decision making. As we discuss these more technical issues of *Lied* performance in Part II, we hope that examination of actual repertory within these chapters will encourage a deepened sensitivity to both the music and the means of conveying poetic ideas through musical expression.

Having set the framework for understanding the *Lied* genre in terms of poetry and general performance concerns, Part III, "The Language of Music," then presents chapters that systematically review the various ways to analyze individual works in preparation for performance. Much of Chapters Six through Nine covers familiar territory. Chapter Six, "Harmony and Tonality," and Chapter Seven, "Melody and Motive," combine a variety of analytical approaches that first define norms of harmonic, tonal, melodic, and motivic usage and then show how composers used deviations in these areas to convey the richness and complexity of the poetry they set. Chapter Eight, "Rhythm and Meter," reviews temporal norms of musical syntax within the beat, the bar, and the phrase, and then shows how composers used rhythmic and metric deviations to convey poetic tensions. Chapter Nine, "Form in the German *Lied*," combines basic formal designs with discussion of more sophisticated formal issues such as poetic and musical repetition and reinterpretation, and the disparities between poetic form and musical form. In order to make the important material in these chapters the most accessible, we offer three additional resources: first, the notes for each chapter cite numerous references for additional study or review; second, Appendix II provides a glossary of all important terms that are defined throughout the book; and third, Appendix III provides an extensive bibliography.

These analytical chapters will assist performers in two complementary ways: on the one hand, the review of musical *norms* sets a foundation for conceptualizing each aspect of a given *Lied,* and on the other hand, the discussion of musical innovation demonstrates how the desire to set poetic texts in the most expressive and imaginative way expands these common-practice norms through *deviations* in every musical dimension: harmony, tonality, melody, rhythm, meter, and form. In addition, our study highlights the unusual performance challenges created by these various musical deviations and discusses how understanding musical innovation helps musicians perform these works with new perceptiveness and, hence, greater confidence.

Finally, Chapter Ten, "Different Settings of a Single Text," brings together the analytical approaches of earlier chapters in studying different settings of the same text. This chapter both models analytical approaches to several different songs and suggests ways to conceptualize the individual styles of the four great *Lied* composers: Schubert, Schumann, Brahms, and Wolf. In addition, a comparison is made between settings of two other, often-neglected groups of important *Lied* composers: Clara Schumann (exemplifying women composers) and Gustav Mahler (representing composers better known for their orchestral work). While students may be tempted to go directly to this chapter for insight into various composers' styles, we urge that readers wait until all the technical concepts and terms in earlier chapters have been presented and absorbed. Without the basic framework from these earlier chapters, the stylistic features suggested at the end of the book will be, at best, hollow and superficial.

Terminology

This book incorporates a number of different types of language and employs technical terms particular to divergent topics: poetry in German and English, concerns and techniques of musical performance, and systems and approaches to music analysis. In order to assist the reader in distinguishing among these languages and to highlight some of the more important terms that recur, we have adopted the following notational devices: all foreign terms (German and Italian)are italicized and titles of poems and songs are enclosed in quotation marks. The numerous technical terms employed are given a special notation: when an important term is introduced, it will be stated in small capitals. All terms so indicated will be redefined for quick reference in Appendix II, and the resourceful reader will adopt these terms immediately and use them in the most careful and thoughtful way.

As an additional aid to the sections on music analysis, major chords and major-mode keys will be notated with uppercase Roman numerals (for example, C major as I) and minor chords and minor-mode keys will be notated in lowercase Roman numerals (for example, c minor as i).

Examples and Exercises

This book uses the poetry and/or music of the glorious *Lied* repertory for three purposes: (1) to demonstrate general points being made; (2) to dramatize different forms of an analytic technique; and (3) to test the reader's comprehension of a given topic. The first two involve either study of the musical score or careful scrutiny of various "figures" in the text. The text must be read with musical scores in hand, and the reader can refer to the Repertory List in Appendix IV to be fully prepared for a concentrated reading of each chapter. Readers also must take the time necessary to study all figures, which offer poetic verse, musical excerpts, or diagrams to exemplify particular points. These figures are not gratuitous examples to be skimmed over, but rather are major components of the exposition.

In order to enhance the usefulness of these explanatory sections either within the classroom setting or as part of an outside reading assignment, we suggest the following procedure. Any discussion of a poem should be prefaced by a dramatic recitation of the verse, preferably in both the original German and the suggested English translation. Literal translations of all poems cited in the text can be found in Appendix I; the suggested sources for other translations should be used only as an alternative.[2] Because most of us are unaccustomed to reading poetry aloud, these readings may at first feel self-conscious and uncomfortable; however, with time and practice such discomfort should abate, and readers will begin to understand more clearly one of the most important features of German Romantic poetry: the special musicality that results from the use of poetic meters and the languages of sound (for example, alliteration, assonance, and onomatopoeia). Such dramatic readings also will simulate how composers approached the poetry they set; most knew poets and heard poetic readings, and many recited poems aloud over and over before composing the musical setting.[3]

When examining a *Lied*, a similar process is encouraged. After the text is read aloud, the piece should be performed. These "performances" are not intended as polished recitals; rather, they are working "readings" that set up a framework for deeper study. Any performance difficulties should be noted not as errors, but as technical challenges to all; any performance confusion or ambiguity likewise will signal issues of interpretive choice that require further discussion and thought. By adopting such a relaxed approach to these performance readings, both performers and listeners will be more able to think about choices rather than remain defensive of hastily drawn or rigidly held interpretations. As a result, a richer, more imaginative understanding of the piece will evolve.

Once the first performance has been heard and the ensuing discussion in the text is understood, then a second "reading" will dramatize the points just considered and show if the initial performance has been altered in any way. The entire process of performing, listening, analyzing, and performing again should yield a new understanding of the reciprocal interaction between performance and analysis: an astute performance can give the listener/analyst a persuasive understanding of a work of art and, in a similar way, an imaginative analysis can give the musician new insights into performance. By constantly challenging one another in this way, the performer and analyst (who may of course be one and the same person!) can develop a deeper understanding of the music, while at the same time remaining open to future reconsiderations.

In addition to using *Lieder* to exemplify various points made throughout the book, we also use the repertory as the basis of a series of exercises at the end of each chapter. These exercises test the reader's understanding of the topics just covered and request diverse answers to a variety of analytical questions. All exercises should be approached with the same procedure adopted for chapter examples: first, the text should be recited, then the piece performed or at least heard on tape or compact disc; only then should the analytical questions be answered. Some answers will involve giving measure numbers or other brief responses; others will require making more detailed charts, diagrams, or musical sketches of various sorts. In all cases, the reader is encouraged to consider the piece in question as repertory being prepared for performance, and to think that answering the questions in these exercises is analogous to preparing in one way to play or sing that piece.

Repertory

Even though this text incorporates some of the most beautiful music ever written by some of the world's most cherished composers, our selection of repertory was constrained by several factors. First, we wanted our study to be immediately relevant and valuable, and thus chose some of the most beloved songs of the greatest masters. Second, we needed to use songs that were readily accessible to performers, that could be sightread relatively easily and could be performed several times over without undue strain on either singer or pianist. Third, in order to keep the repertory limited to a reasonable size, most songs had to have multiple functions within the book.

A fourth consideration that guided our selection of repertory was an overall concern about the size and cost of the study. In order to limit the size of the text itself and to reduce the amount of additional scores needed, we tried to use songs found within the reliable Dover score series for *Lieder.* Thus readers must have either the Dover volumes listed below or appropriate versions of the songs noted in Appendix IV. The necessary Dover scores are: (1) Schubert, *59 Favorite Songs;* (2) *Schubert's Songs to Texts by Goethe;* (3) Schubert's *Complete Song Cycles;* (4) Schumann, *Selected Songs for Solo Voice and Piano* (5) Wolf, *Spanish and Italian Songbooks;* and (6) Strauss, *Fifty-seven Songs for Voice and Piano.* Unfortunately, no one volume of the Dover series for Brahms was sufficient, hence all songs by Brahms, and any other repertory not listed here are included in Appendix V, where scores have been taken from the most reliable editions available.

We end these introductory remarks with some cautions. Our careful choice of repertory (including consideration of the source of score) and text translation has attempted to prevent the unwitting reader from being mislead by uninformed editors, translators, and performers. Any reader who has other scores or translations is warned about the vagaries of text translations, particularly those on record jackets or those inserted directly into the score, and about improperly edited scores that add slurs and other performance indications not notated by the composer.[4] We also warn those who wish to listen to tapes or compact discs rather than live performances to beware the limitations of interpretative judgments when listening to fixed performances, even performances by great *Lied* interpreters. We want the study of this text to be based as much as possible upon *live* performance. Feeling one's way through a song is far more informative than listening to a polished performance, and young musicians need to remain as open as possible to nuances of interpretation and differences in interpretive choices.

Part I
The Language of Poetry

CHAPTER ONE

Introduction to German Romanticism

Und meine Seele spannte	And my soul spread
Weit ihre Flügel aus,	Wide its wings,
Flog durch die stillen Lande,	Flew through the silent land,
Als flöge sie nach Haus.	As if it were flying home.[1]

These lines, from a poem by Joseph Freiherr von Eichendorff, typify the poetry written in the period called German Romanticism, poetry full of rich nature images and vivid poetic sensibilities. In this chapter, we summarize the characteristics of the poetry of this period by identifying the predominant themes and images and by demonstrating those features that gave these poems their unique quality.

We begin by making the same disclaimer found in every other introduction to German Romanticism, that the jumble of ideas and passions called German Romanticism is too complex to be easily described and that any attempt to categorize or explain this historical period risks oversimplification and even misinformation. We nevertheless include a chapter on this difficult topic because it is so important that performers of this quintessentially Romantic genre understand something of the spirit and historical context in which these creative works were shaped. For many students, this may be the beginning of a lifelong study of the German Romantic mind and soul, and we hope to convey an approach to learning about this complex subject that will continue to serve performers for years to come.

While it might seem easiest to define "romanticism" generally as a contrast to "classicism," such labels tend to oversimplify the issues and mask the richness of the two historical periods and the creative forces at work within them. For example, Goethe, a poet most commonly associated with German Romanticism, was actually deeply rooted in "classical" themes and attitudes and only at times adopted some, but not all, so-called "Romantic" ideas. The same also could be said of Beethoven, whose music incorporates both classical and romantic elements. We thus use such "isms" with utmost care, calling the aesthetic movement in nineteenth-century Germany "German Romanticism," but using that designation in the most complex sense of an ever-changing and often contradictory artistic movement.[2]

Historical Context of German Romanticism

German Romanticism arose on the heels of the French Revolution (1789–1799) and within the reaction against the period called the ENLIGHT-ENMENT,[3] a reaction that began in the transitional movement called STURM UND DRANG ("Storm and Stress," 1770s), a movement characterized by increased intensity and emotionalism.[4] The Romantic period proper spans approximately thirty years, from 1796 to c. 1830, but the impact of the movement continued throughout the nineteenth century. The various twists and turns of Romantic philosophical and literary development, along with the activity of some of its major figures, can be divided into three phases. *Early Romanticism* was focused in Berlin and Jena from 1796 to 1804; it included the writers Novalis (pseudonym for Fredrich von Hardenberg, 1772–1801), August Wilhelm Schlegel (1767–1845), Friedrich Schlegel (1772–1829), Ludwig Tieck (1773–1853), and Wilhelm Heinrich Wackenroder (1773–1798); it also included the philosophers Johann Gottlieb Fichte (1762–1814) and F. W. J. Schelling (1775–1854). *Middle Romanticism* was centered primarily around Heidelberg, Dresden, and Vienna from 1804 to 1815; it included the writers Achim von Arnim (1781–1831), Clemens Brentano (1778–1842), Adalbert von Chamisso (1781–1838), Joseph von Eichendorff (1778–1857), Jakob Grimm (1785–1863), Wilhelm Grimm (1786–1859), and E. T. A. Hoffmann (1776–1822); it also included the painters Caspar David Friedrich (1774–1840) and Philipp Otto Runge (1777–1810) and the composers Ludwig von Beethoven (1770–1827) and Franz Schubert (1797–1828). *Late Romanticism*, then, was centered in Dresden and Munich from 1815 to c. 1830; it included the composers Carl Maria von Weber (1786–1826) and Robert Schumann (1810–1856). The movement thus began regionally and swept throughout Germany, the ranks of writers and artists swelling to ever-wider circles of intense artistic interaction and collaboration.[5]

Within the historical development of German Romanticism, the position of the literary giant Johann Wolfgang Goethe (1749–1832) is fittingly complex. Whereas Goethe began within the classical tradition and was a major figure, along with Johann Gottfried Herder (1744–1803), in the *Sturm und Drang* movement of the 1770s, his work held tremendous significance for the Romantics: his hero Werther of *Die Leiden des jungen Werthers* (*The Sorrows of Young Werther,* 1774) came to represent the "new hero" of the times, and his themes in *Faust: Ein Fragment* (*Faust: A Fragment,* 1790), *Wilhelm Meisters Wanderjahre* (*Wilhelm Meister's Years of Travel,* 1795–1796), and much of his poetry reflected many essential elements of the Romantic movement.[6]

The championing of Goethe by the Romantics is ironic, however. He continued to promote the classical themes of orderliness and reason, and he became an outspoken critic of many aspects of Romanticism, repudiating such romantic themes as unbridled subjectivism, yearning for the infinite, and preoccupation with death and otherworldliness.[7] Despite the ambivalent relationship of Goethe and the Romantics, however, his poetry and novels continued to include many elements deemed Romantic, and his poetry was set by most *Lied* composers of the nineteenth century.

German Romantic Themes and Imagery

We begin our summary of German Romantic elements by introducing two fundamental features of the Romantic soul: (1) the insatiable quest to go beyond what is known and (2) the embrace of the contradictory or DICHOTOMOUS, the mingling of two seemingly incompatible, opposing elements into a singular entity.[8]

The desire to extend beyond what is known was a major shift from the self-imposed limitations of the Enlightenment. Romantics wanted to eliminate boundaries, to extend beyond limits, and to enjoy the infinite. This resulted in the desire to escape mundane daily existence through intoxication and through embrace of chaos, through exploration of the mystical and investigation of the abnormal. The poet took us to imaginary lands, often unfamiliar, vague, or murky, and this quest beyond what was known occurred in many guises: in the mysticism of religious belief, in the darkness of the night, and in the amorphous world of dreams.

The celebration of the contradictory also was a reaction against what was considered an oppressive rationality and orderliness during the Enlightenment. Romantics wanted to define their world through opposition and PARADOX: to intensify reality with the imaginary, to emphasize the spiritual through contrast with the material.[9] As German scholar Siegbert S. Prawer states: "The most characteristic art of German Romanticism transports reader, viewer and listener to a frontier between the visible and the invisible, the tangible and the intangible. Something transcendent shines through everyday reality . . ."[10]

This merging of contradictory elements created confusion, bewilderment, and ambiguities of time, place, and persona;[11] instinct collided with reason, and the tortured present mingled with the happy past. The resulting lack of clarity and the multiplicity of meanings all created a rich and meaningful chaos that was cherished by the Romantics, and led, in turn, to a basic axiom of German Romanticism: Romantic irony. By definition, IRONY is "a method of expression in which the intended meaning of words used is the direct opposite of their usual sense,"[12] and the central irony of the Romantic period was that the poet sought the infinite, which by definition was unobtainable. This irony is expressed through different combinations of contradictory elements, for example: Romantic yearning (*romantische Sehnsucht*) for unattainable love; weeping for joy because love is full of pain; or the moon's light creating shadows on the landscape.[13]

The essential elements of German Romanticism can be expressed in four main themes, each theme being captured by a typical Romantic metaphor. The theme of Heightened Individuality is dramatized by the figure of The Wanderer; The Evocative World of Nature is typified by the Lonely Forest; The Seductiveness of Mystery is represented by The Night; and Spiritual Salvation is projected by Yearning for Peaceful Death. All of these themes and metaphors emphasize the characteristic German Romantic need to explore the unknown and the dichotomous.

Heightened Individuality

German Romanticism was, first and foremost, a period of intense emotionalism, introspection, and self-absorption. Poets celebrated the individual and savored every human emotion from ecstatic joy to devastating despair. The German Romantic movement continued the *Sturm und Drang* concentration on the inner life of characters and the vacillations, inner conflicts, and ambiguous passions that ruled them. Goethe's Werther *(Die Leiden des jungen Werthers)* was championed not because of his actions, which were few, but because of the depth and intensity of his emotions; Novalis's Heinrich *(Heinrich von Ofterdingen)* was a Romantic figure caught in his inner world, dreaming and brooding in emotional immobility.

German Romantic literature is full of poems whose very titles highlight feelings and psychological states, for example, Matthäus von Collin's *Wehmut* ("Melancholy"); Eichendorff's *Heimweh* ("Homesickness"); Ludwig Christoph Heinrich Hölty's *Seligkeit* ("Bliss"); and Wilhelm Müller's *Eifersucht und Stolz* ("Jealousy and Pride" from *Die schöne Müllerin*). In addition, the Romantic celebrated sensuousness, savoring the sounds and the aromas of nature and allowing the senses to become intoxicated and the imagination to become imbued with sensory delight:

Hörst du nicht die Quellen gehen	Hear you not the brook's running
Zwischen Stein und Blumen weit	Amongst stones and flowers afar
Nach den stillen Waldesseen,	Toward silent forest lakes,
Wo die Marmorbilder stehen,	Where marble statues stand,
In der schönen Einsamkeit?	In fair solitude?
Von den Bergen sacht hernieder,	From the mountains gently downward,
Weckend die uralten Lieder,	Awakening the ancient songs,
Steigt die wunderbare Nacht,	There rises the wondrous night,
Und die Gründe glänzen wieder,	And the valleys gleam again,
Wie du's oft im Traum gedacht.	As you often imagined in dreams.[14]

Exploration of the complexities of the human psyche also included investigation into the elusive world of the subconscious and dreams (both wish-fulfillment fantasies and nightmares); emotional extremes were sought through intoxication (using wine or drugs, or within the powers of love and nature) and through study of the bizarre and the grotesque.[15] The *Doppelgänger*, a spectral double that so haunted the Romantic, was a particularly vivid figure that confronted the poet with another side of the self and thereby placed the poet within the dichotomy of the soul.[16]

The most powerful Romantic image that conveyed the poet's preoccupation with the themes of the individual and the world of emotion was the figure of the Wanderer, the solitary figure whose travels through the world reflected a similar spiritual journey within. This Romantic protagonist mused and brooded, communed with nature and spoke to God, and experienced Romantic yearning with exquisite sensibility. Indeed, the wanderer symbolized the ironic, Romantic quest for the unattainable, usually for a lost love, that yearning that so trapped the poet within the pain of unfulfillment.

The wanderer image embodied two other elements of German Romanticism: the interest in the common people and the belief that the plight of everyday existence, with the omnipresent difficulties of love, was best expressed by the artist. The wanderer's many guises often were a camouflage for the alienated artist, who wandered about in order to escape unhappiness and to find resolution of inner turmoil. This image incorporated the Romantic paradox of needing human comfort of both family and a beloved, which is transient and unpredictable, and, at the same time, seeking release from the foibles of human interaction through solitude in nature or through the release of death. Müller's protagonist in *Die Winterreise* was such a figure, as were Goethe's poets in the two "Wanderers Nachtlied" lyrics.[17] Eichendorff's wanderers sought release through religious fulfillment, and Heine's wanderers reflected and agonized within the safer world of nature. The opening stanza of Friedrich Schlegel's "Der Wanderer" ("The Wanderer") captures both the wanderer's longing for relief from everyday strife and the sense of homelessness that results:

Wie deutlich des Mondes Licht
Zu mir spricht,
Mich beseelend zu der Reise:
"Folge treu dem alten Gleise,
Wähle keine Heimat nicht.
Ew'ge Plage
Bringen sonst die schweren Tage.
Fort zu andern
Sollst du wechseln, sollst du wandern
Leicht entfliehend jeder Klage."

How clearly the moon's light
Speaks to me,
Inspiring me on my journey:
"Follow faithfully the old track,
Choose no home anywhere,
Lest eternal torment
Otherwise bring bad times.
On to others
You will turn, you will move on
Lightly escaping all grief."[18]

In addition to The Wanderer figure, Romantic poetry also used a myriad of colorful common folk to depict the poet's struggles, for example, Eichendorff's "Der Musikant" ("The Musician"); Goethe's "Der Sänger" ("The Minstrel"); Johann Mayrhofer's "Der Alpenjäger" ("The Alpine Hunter"); Eduard Mörike's "Das verlassene Mägdlein" ("The Forsaken Maiden"); and Müller's "Der Leiermann" ("The Organ Grinder").

The Evocative World of Nature

Just as the luxurious inner world of the human psyche gave the Romantic poet a wealth of themes and images, so the numinous world of nature, with its diverse elements and conflicting forces, provided the poet with an abundance of material. The natural world contained a wide array of natural objects, creatures, and sounds that provided the poet with both an atmosphere in which to feel and sense vividly and a landscape in which to wander and struggle. The opening stanza of Goethe's "An den Mond" ("To the Moon") exemplifies the poet's state within nature:

Füllest wieder Busch und Tal	You fill again wood and vale
Still mit Nebelglanz,	Silently with gleam of mist,
Lösest endlich auch einmal	You set free at last
Meine Seele ganz;	My soul entirely; [19]

In addition to providing the poet with a new dramatic stage, nature's world also embodied the Romantic struggle between dichotomous or ambivalent forces: on the one hand, nature healed with nurturing warmth and soothing breezes; on the other hand, nature destroyed with debilitating cold and menacing storms. The sensitive poet was vulnerable to nature and thus was acutely aware of nature's mysteries and variabilities, including how nature changed with the seasons and the time of day.[20] Further, much poetry centers around moments of change within the day, for example, where the anticipation of night at dusk or the release from night at dawn prompted the poet's sensitivity in heightened form.[21]

In a similar way, nature's richness prompted the poet's sense of the numinous or imminent. The poet's was a small voice within an immense, at times overpowering, natural presence that provoked both awe and dread and that included both the supernatural and the means for transcendence. Eichendorff, whose lyrics combined love of nature with a deep religious devotion, used nature poems to dramatize the conflict between the diabolical sphere that existed below ground, the divine realm high above, and the poet caught between the two, struggling within nature's murmuring landscape.[22]

Pianist and author Charles Rosen combines the world of nature with the notions of time and memory in several ways: "What [Schumann's poets] retain . . . from the tradition of landscape poetry . . . is the complex sense of time in which past, present, and future coexist and interpenetrate each other. Memory and premonition are as immediate and powerful as direct perception— which serves, indeed, for the most part simply to recall and to predict."[23] The elements of dichotomy and ambiguity also come into play: "The ingenious confusion of momentary, seasonal, and millennial time gives one the illusion of grasping the processes of nature from microscopic to macroscopic level, . . . The portrayal of change, the representation of a reality that is fluid, ever in motion, is generally acknowledged as typical of Romantic style . . . the fluidity of style is a manifestation of a more profound change in the way the world was perceived. Instability became a source of inspiration as well as anxiety."[24] Rosen believes that truths about time and nature are understood over time: "it is less the truth of nature than the way of arriving at the truth that interests the artist. The portrayal of the hidden processes of thought, however, is achieved by the images of nature themselves and by the vivacity of the representation. In music, too, composers were often unsatisfied by the static representation of a sentiment by simple musical analogy, but sought to portray the processes of feeling and even [in] the actual functioning of memory."[25] Rosen also maintains that "memory is the central theme of early nineteenth-century lyric poetry"[26] and that "the most signal triumphs of the Romantic portrayal of memory are not those which recall past happiness, but remembrances of those moments when future happiness still seemed possible, when hopes were not yet frustrated. . . . Romantic memories are often those of absence, of that which never was."[27]

The power of nature and the poet's tenuous position within nature led to the vivid image of "Waldeinsamkeit" ("The Loneliness of the Forest"). Within the solitary, lonely forest, the poet experienced the dichotomies within nature and within the psyche; the forest is a place for introspection and a unique communion between internal and external worlds. The opening lines of Mayrhofer's "Nachtstück" ("Nocturne") portray the poet alone in the forest:

Wenn über Berge sich der Nebel breitet,	When over the mountains the mist spreads
Und Luna mit Gewölken kampft,	And Luna with the clouds struggles,
So nimmt der Alte seine Harfe, und schreitet,	So the old man takes his harp and strides,
Und singt waldeinwärts und gedämpft:	And sings into the forest and quietly:
Du heilige Nacht!	O holy night!
Bald ist's vollbracht.	Soon shall it end.[28]

Other nature images recur in German Romantic poetry, including numerous images of flowers and birds.[29] Water images abound: brooks and streams represent nature's comforting side and stormy seas depict nature's menace.[30] Water also represents the origin of life and the resting place of death, as beautifully stated in von Collin's "Leiden der Trennung" ("Sorrows of Separation"), a poem replete with water imagery:

Vom Meere trennt sich die Welle,	From the sea separates the wave,
Und seufzet durch	And sighs its way through the
Blumen im Thal,	Flowers in the valley,
Und fühlet, gewiegt	And feels [whether] cradled
in der Quelle,	in the spring,
Gebannt in dem Brunnen,	[Or] confined in the well,
nur Qual!	only torment!
Es sehnt sich die Welle	Longs the wave
In lispelnder Quelle,	[Whether] in the
	whispering spring,
Im murmelnden Bache,	In the murmuring stream,
Im Brunnengemache,	In the well-chamber,
Zum Meer, zum Meer	[To be] back to the sea
Von dem sie kam,	From whence it came,
Von dem sie Leben nahm,	From which it took its life,
Von dem, des Irrens matt	From which, tired of
und müde,	wandering,
Sie süße Ruh' verhofft und Friede.	It hopes for sweet rest and peace.[30]

The Seductiveness of Mystery

A direct consequence of the reaction against the Enlightenment's orderliness was a savoring of chaos, obscurity, and ambiguity that comprise the theme we call "The Seductiveness of Mystery." The enticement of the mysterious came from every corner of the Romantic's experience, from the mysteries of the inner psychological domain (the unconscious and dreams), to those within nature's vastness, to the mystical side of religious devotion. The poet's inner world was scrutinized through analysis of dreams, study of madness, and interest in hypnosis. The mysterious in nature was captured in dark forests, murmuring brooks, and moonlit landscapes full of diffused light and hushed night rustlings. The mysteries within religious conviction were expressed as both awe and dread, as senses of yearning and premonition. In the contradiction so characteristic of German Romanticism, the poet's spiritual side both revered and feared what remained unknown and unknowable.

The heightened reactions to the mysteries of the psyche, the world of nature, and the spiritual were most vivid at night, when darkness provided an escape from daily life and intensified the unknown, when the poet was solitary and felt more in tune with the mysterious.[32] Two literary examples show the extremes of night's power for the Romantic. The excerpt from Novalis's *Hymnen an die Nacht (Hymns to the Night)* shows a rapturous intensity:

Aside I turn to the holy, ineffable, mysterious Night. Far below lies the world, sunken in a profound pit: waste and solitary is its place. Through the strings of the heart wafts deep sadness. I seek, as drops of dew, to subside and to blend with ashes. Distances of memory, desires of youth, dreams of childhood, the brief joys and futile hopes of the whole of long life, come in gray raiment like evening mists after the sun's setting.[33]

The first stanza of Heine's "Die Lotosblume" ("The Lotus Flower") depicts a more muted response:

Die Lotosblume ängstigt   The lotus-flower fears
Sich vor der Sonne Pracht,   Itself before the sun's glory
Und mit gesenktem Haupte   And with bowed head,
Erwartet sie träumend die Nacht. Awaits, dreaming, the night.[34]

Spiritual Salvation

The theme of religious fervor and devotion, especially within Catholicism, permeates much German Romantic poetry. Religious faith was intimately linked to the German Romantic longing for death (as spiritual salvation) and was expressed most vividly within the context of nature. When combined with nature's benevolence, the notion of spiritual salvation through death offered a release from both external earthly concerns and the poet's innermost torments. In characteristic form, contrasting religious views coexisted comfortably in this period: for example, Novalis, in *Hymnen an die Nacht*, expresses intense ecstatic faith in relationship to both love and death, while in contrast, Eichendorff's novels and lyrics express the poet's more gentle faith within a simpler longing for peace through nature.

As already suggested, the Romantic's religious devotion often was expressed in the context of the love for the mysterious, as religious faith included mystical and supernatural elements, and the concept of a divine presence included an "other world" beyond that known on earth. This then accompanied another important aspect of German Romanticism: the preoccupation with the mysteries of death. In contrast to Goethe's classical portrait of death as evil in "Erlkönig," the Romantics adopted the medieval image of death as a gentle release from life's complexities and a serene return to nature's peaceful domain. For example, in the second stanza of Matthias Claudius's "Der Tod und das Mädchen" ("Death and the Maiden"), death speaks soothingly to the maiden:

Gib deine Hand, du
  schön und zart Gebild!
Bin Freund und komme nicht
  zu strafen.
	Give me your hand, you
	  fair and gentle thing!
	I am a friend and do not
	  come to punish.[35]

The Romantic poet's preoccupation with the spiritual domain of death leads to our fourth characteristic German Romantic image, that of yearning for death. While this yearning often was experienced within the context of traditional religious belief, many German Romantics replaced the customary religious deity with that of nature; nature's infinite mysteriousness also provided solace and inspired worship. The opening stanza of a poem that exemplifies this recurring yearning image was set in one of Schubert's best-loved *Lieder:* Johann Georg Jacobi's "Litanei" ("Litany"):

Ruhn in Frieden alle Seelen,
Die vollbracht ein banges
  Quälen,
Die vollendet süßen Traum,
Lebenssatt,
  geboren kaum,
Aus der Welt hinüberschieden:
Alle Seelen ruhn in Frieden!
	Rest in peace, all souls,
	Who, completed an anxious
	  torment,
	And ended sweet dreams,
	Those weary of life, those
	  scarcely born,
	From this world are departed:
	All souls, rest in peace![36]

The image of yearning for peaceful death recurs throughout the poetry of this period, often in combination with the equally important and recurrent images of lost wanderer, lonely forest, and mysterious night. These typical German Romantic images bring with them the complex issues and emotions so emblematic of the period: the wanderer's preoccupation with the inner world of feelings, dreams, and visions typifies the theme of heightened individuality; the lonely forest within a rich natural world of nurturing and menacing forces connotes The evocative world of nature; the dark world of night, wherein the wanderer feels the most poignantly and the natural landscape shimmers the most vividly, evokes the seductiveness of mystery; and, finally, the image of yearning for peaceful death depicts the Romantic's conviction that release from all earthly torment, including the inescapable pain of lost love, can be attained through spiritual salvation. In all cases, the Romantic both searches beyond what is knowable and, at the same time, savors the dichotomous elements within what is known.

While this brief survey has identified characteristic German Romantic themes within separate categories, these themes and images easily commingle within elaborate poetic expressions. For example, the wanderer image often incorporates elements of all the themes mentioned above: a folk hero wandering about in nature's landscape represents the sensitive artist who is alienated from family and homeland and mourning lost love. This poet roams nature's mysterious world during the darkness of night and identifies with the loneliness of the forest as he yearns for release from life's insufferable torment. While nature soothes the poet, the Romantic also seeks spiritual salvation through peaceful death, a release from earthly torment that beckons from the shadows of the moonlight.

Cultural Influences within German Romanticism

In addition to these recurring German Romantic themes, other elements enriched the poet's Romantic expressivity. In order to convey their ideas and emotions in particularly colorful images, the Romantics turned to the imagery and heritage of several different periods and cultures, including revival of Antiquity and the Middle Ages, assimilation of foreign cultures, and celebration of the present through nationalism and the development of folk culture.

Revival of Interest in Antiquity and the Middle Ages

Along with their longing to escape life's difficulties through death, the Romantics desired to escape the concerns of the present through immersion within a more resonant past. Just as revival of antiquity had been featured in the classical period, where Goethe and Schiller admired ancient Greek and Roman characteristics that bolstered classical tenets, so the Romantics adapted Greek and Roman history (mythological stories and heroes) and culture (architectural structures and Mediterranean ambiance) to dramatize and depict Romantic themes and characteristics. The adventures of such heroes as Orpheus, Ganymede, and Prometheus were described anew,[37] and the spirit of the time was captured in Romantic reveries such as the first stanza of Mörike's "An eine Äolsharfe" ("To an Aeolian Harp"):

Angelehnt an die Efeuwand
Dieser alten Terrasse,
Du, einer luftgebornen

Reclining against the ivy wall
Of this ancient terrace,
You of a zephyr-born

Geheimnisvolles Saitenspiel,	Mysterious string music,
Fang an,	Begin,
Fange wieder an	Begin anew
Deine melodische Klage!	Your melodious plaint![38]

Allusions to Greek and Roman life and myths gave new dimension to such Romantic concerns as poetic torment and despair arising from the foibles of romantic love;[39] images of antiquity such as Greek ruins and ancient musical instruments illustrated nineteenth-century interest in ancient history and the assimilation of antiquity within evolving Romantic ideals and mythologies. The German Romantic image of the Golden Age, for example, refers to the ideal time of happiness in antiquity for which the Romantic poet yearned.[40]

Romantics also loved images from the Middle Ages, recalling and re-shaping stories such as that of Hans Sachs in Wagner's *Die Meistersinger,* and of Tannhäuser, Wagner's sojourner in the Mountain of Venus. Images of crumbling walls and sleeping knights conjured up these ancient days and, as shown in the first stanza of Eichendorff's "Auf einer Burg" ("In a Castle"), shed a filtered light on the present day:

Eingeschlafen auf der Lauer	Asleep at his lookout
Oben ist der alter Ritter;	Up there is the old knight;
Drüber gehen Regenschauer,	Overhead go rain squalls,
Und der Wald rauscht durch	And the forest rustles through
das Gitter.	the lattice.[41]

Translations of English and Oriental Literature

German Romantics also sought new poetic subjects and images by translating English and Oriental literature from different historical periods. Like the use of elements of antiquity and the Middle Ages, these new mate-rials were a rich poetic resource; they provided new contexts for Romantic depictions and offered a particular poetic "distance" through a certain for-eignness. The English repertory included adaptations or translations of pseudo-Gaelic folklore attributed to the fictitious third-century bard, Ossian, Shakespeare's dramas (translated especially by A. W. Schlegel), and more contemporary poets such as Sir Walter Scott and Robert Burns.[42]

A similar investigation into more exotic cultures culled images and scenarios from such remote places as Persia and China, which also evoked a foreignness and distance that intensified poetic mystery. Goethe's study of Persian literature resulted in the *West-östlicher Divan (East-West Book of Love Poetry)* of 1819, an homage to the Persian poet Hafiz written when Goethe was 70 years old. Later poets such as Friedrich Rückert, Professor of Oriental Language at Munich, and August Graf von Platen also incorporated similar oriental references in their poems, Rückert using Persian forms as well as subjects. The following excerpt from Goethe's *Divan,* "Erschaffen und Beleben" ("Creation and Animation"), illustrates the link sought between the world of Hafiz and Goethe's own:

So, Hafis, mag dein holder Sang,	So Hafiz, may your dear song,
Dein heiliges Exempel	Your blessed example
Uns führen, bei der Gläser Klang,	Conduct us at the glasses' clink
Zu unsres Schöpfers Tempel.	To our Creator's temple.[43]

Incorporation of Nationalism and Folk Culture

Finally, German Romantic poetry cultivated the new, post-revolutionary nationalism and the interest in folk culture that began in the *Sturm und Drang* period. The new nationalism provided expression of such common Romantic themes as love of nature and yearning for home, as exemplified in the final stanza of Eichendorff's "Heimweh" ("Homecoming"):

Der Morgen, das ist meine Freude!	But dawn, that's my delight!
Da steig ich in stiller Stund	Then I climb in a peaceful hour
Auf den höchsten Berg in die Weite,	The highest mountain far away,
Grüß dich, Deutschland, aus Herzensgrund!	I greet you, Germany, from my heart's depth![44]

Further, as intimated earlier, the development of Germany's folk culture led in general to the emergence of "the common folk" and in particular to the evolution of a new "folk hero." A wealth of lyrics depicted everyday life of commoners, and poetic portraits of common folk resulted in some of the most famous poetic cycles set by *Lied* composers, for example, Wilhelm Müller's *Die schöne Müllerin* and Adalbert von Chamisso's *Frauenliebe und -leben.*[45] Some of these poetic portraits of everyday people created new folk heroes. While in earlier literature, heroic figures had been kings and conquerors, the new Romantic hero was from the bourgeoisie, for example, students in Goethe's *Wilhelm Meisters Wanderjahre* and Mörike's *Maler Nolten* (1832) and a young musician in Eichendorff's *Aus dem Leben eines Taugenichts* (*Diary of a Good-for-Nothing*, 1826).

The new interest in folk culture also resulted in important collections of folk material, including the *Stimmen der Völker* (*Voices of the Peoples,*

1778–1779) of Johann Gottfried Herder, *Des Knaben Wunderhorn (The Boy's Magic Horn,* 1805–1808) of Clemens Brentano and Achim von Arnim, and *Alte hoch- und niederdeutsche Volkslieder (Old High and Low German Songs,* 1844–1845) of Ludwig Uhland.[46] In addition, folk literature such as the Grimm fairy tales was added to the mythologies from antiquity and the Middle Ages to develop a new Romantic cultural identity. A good example of this is the myth of the "LORELEI" as portrayed by both Heine and Eichendorff.[47]

This review of German Romantic elements and influences captures the multifarious nature of the German Romantic and the rich world in which the poet thrived. Whether gazing at nature's vastness or at a medieval castle, the Romantic poet remained caught in the ironic relationship between the self and the world. Trapped in wanting the unattainable, the poet sought refuge in contradictory arenas: within nature's mystery which both awed and threatened the poet's soul or within a past that remained elusive but yet resonant. These images poured from the Romantic poets and were transformed by the *Lied* composers who set their verse. The *Lieder* that resulted make up a wondrous artistic genre that embodied layers of meaning within a dramatic, previously unknown expressivity, a repertory of miniature masterpieces that has endured to this day.

Exercises

Using the poems below, identify all the German Romantic images and themes you can find, showing how some images and themes work together. As an example, we analyze the first stanza of Joseph von Spaun's "Der Jüngling und der Tod" ("The Young Man and Death") as follows:

Der Jüngling:	*The Young Man:*
Die Sonne sinkt	The sun sinks,
Ach könnt ich mit ihr scheiden	Ah, that I might with it depart,
Mit ihrem letzten Strahl entfliehn!	With its last ray might flee!
Ach diese namenlosen	Ah, these nameless
Qualen meiden	torments escape
Und weit in schönre Welten ziehn!	And afar to finer worlds travel![48]

1. First we summarize the poem: the poet speaks through the young man in terms of *nature* by mentioning the sunset; in response to the setting sun, he expresses a *longing,* first for *release from nameless torments,* then toward *death's "finer world."*

2. We then list and interpret the individual images.
   a. The image of "nameless torments" bespeaks the various difficulties of *love.*

   b. The image of death as "finer world" has *religious* connotations.

   c. The images of departure connect *nature* ("last ray") to *poet's/young man's inner world* ("escape").

3. We conclude the analysis by redefining the verse in terms of thematic combination: the poem combines (1) wanderer expressing *Sehnsucht* in (2) the context of nature, and (3) the appeal for death occurring with the (4) approach of night.

1. "Auf ein altes Bild" (Mörike)

"Inspired by an Old Picture"[49]

In grüner Landschaft
 Sommerflor,
Bei kühlem Wasser, Schilf
 und Rohr,
Schau, wie das Knäblein
 sündelos
Frei spielet auf der Jungfrau
 Schoß!
Und dort in Walde wonnesam,
Ach, grünet schon des Kreuzes
 Stamm!

In a green landscape's
 summer flora,
By cool water, reeds
 and rushes,
See how the little Boy,
 innocent,
Freely plays on the Virgin's
 lap!
And there, in the wood, blissfully,
Ah, grows already the cross's
 trunk!

2. "Er ist's" (Mörike)

"(Spring) It Is"[50]

Veilchen träumen schon,
Wollen balde kommen.
Horch, von fern ein leiser
 Harfenton!
Frühling, ja du bists!
Dich hab ich vernommen!

Violets are dreaming,
Want soon to be here.
Hark, from afar a soft
 harptone!
Spring, yes it is you!
You have I heard!

3. "Iphigenia" (Mayrhofer)

"Iphigenia"[51]

Blüht denn hier an Tauris
 Strande
Keine Blum' aus Hellas Lande,

Weht kein milder Segenshauch
Aus den lieblichen Gefilden,
Wo Geschwister mit mir spielten?—

Ach, mein Leben ist ein Rauch!

Blooms then here on the Tauris
 shore
No flower from my Greek
 homeland,
Blows no gentle breeze
From the blessed fields,
Where my siblings played with
 me?—
Ah, my life is but smoke!

4. "Meeres Stille" (Goethe)

Tiefe Stille herrscht im Wasser,
Ohne Regung ruht das Meer,
Und bekümmert sieht der Schiffer
Glatte Fläche rings umher.
Keine Luft von keiner Seite!
Todesstille fürchterlich!
In der ungeheuern Weite
Reget keine Welle sich.

"Sea Calm"[52]

Deep calm rules the water,
Without motion rests the sea,
And troubled sees the sailor
Smooth levelness all around.
No wind from any quarter!
Deadly calm dreadful!
In the vast expanse
Stirs no wave.

5. "Nachtzauber" (Eichendorff)

Hörst du nicht die Quellen gehen
Zwischen Stein und Blumen weit
Nach den stillen Waldesseen,
Wo die Marmorbilder stehen,
In der schönen Einsamkeit?
Von den Bergen sacht hernieder,

Weckend die uralten Lieder,
Steigt die wunderbare Nacht,
Und die Gründe glänzen wieder,
Wie du's oft im Traum gedacht.

"Night Magic"[53]

Hear you not the brook's running
Amongst stones and flowers afar
Toward silent forest lakes,
Where marble statues stand
In fair solitude?
From the mountains gently
     downward,
Awakening the ancient songs,
There rises the wondrous night,
And the valleys gleam again,
As you often in dreams imagined.

6. "Schöne Fremde" (Eichendorff)

Es rauschen die Wipfel und
     schauern,
Als machten zu dieser Stund
Um die halbversunkenen Mauern
Die alten Götter die Rund.
Hier hinter den Myrtenbäumen
In heimlich dämmernder Pracht,
Was sprichst du wirr wie in
     Träumen
Zu mir, phantastische Nacht?

"Beautiful Foreign Land"[54]

They murmur, the tree-tops, and
     shiver,
As though to make at this hour
Around half-sunken walls
The gods of old, the rounds.
Here, beyond the myrtles,
In secretly darkening splendor,
What whisper you, confused
     as in dreams
To me, fantastic night?

7. "Verklärung" (Alexander Pope,
   trans. Herder)

Lebensfunke, vom Himmel
     entglüht,
Der sich loszuwinden müht,

"Transfiguration"[55]

Spark of life from heaven
     kindled,
That to wrench itself away toils,

Zitternd, kühn, vor Sehnen
   leidend,
Gern und doch mit Schmerzen
   scheidend!

Trembling, brave, longing
   enduring,
Gladly and yet in agony
   departing!

8. "Zwielicht" (Eichendorff)

"Twilight"[56]

Dämmrung will die Flügel spreiten,
Schaurig rühren sich die Bäume,
Wolken ziehn wie schwere
   Träume—
Was will dieses Graun bedeuten?

Dusk will its wings spread,
Awesomely stir the trees,
Clouds come like heavy
   dreams—
What does this dread mean?

CHAPTER TWO

Devices and Delights in Poetry

The essence of song, especially of the Romantic *Lied*, is an equality of music and text, a synthesis of a new art form out of two disparate media. Those who fail to understand the meaning of the poem fail, as well, to understand the meaning of the music that sets it. Indeed, performers who have not thoroughly studied the poetry cannot sing or play the *Lied* with the focus, the imagination, and the vitality that is essential for both the musicians and their audience.

The necessity of studying the poetry in *Lied* performance preparation is not optional; rather, it is a major part of the basic work of both singer and accompanist. We thus begin with a word of encouragement to those who feel intimidated about studying poetry, who feel ill equipped, inexperienced, or even wholly ignorant. Earlier in this century, the study of poetry, and of literature in general, was considered a vital part of a standard secondary education. More recently, however, the spread of specialization and the advancement of technology have preempted the time once dedicated to the study of language and the other arts. Many college music students who are interested in the Art Song, therefore, have never had the opportunity to study language as an art, be it in poetry or in prose.

This chapter offers such individuals a primer of common poetic usage written expressly for the study of German Romantic poetry.[1] Readers are encouraged to use the terminology and concepts offered here as much and as often as possible.[2] With time and practice, study of poetry will become a natural part of performance preparation.

Our introduction to poetry will be restricted to one century and one language: eighteenth- and nineteenth-century German Romantic poetry. The conventions of poetic form and content during the nineteenth century are fairly consistent, giving what could be considered a common practice of poetry parallel to the common practice of music during the same period. As we describe these poetic norms, one must keep in mind that much great nineteenth-century poetry was written in languages other than German, and that despite our restrictions to the German masters of the Romantic period, many of the terms and concepts offered here apply to all poetry, regardless of nationality and historical context.[3]

We separate our discussions of poetry into two fundamental components: poetic content and poetic form. Under the general topic of poetic content, we examine various rhetorical devices such as imagery, metaphor, simile, symbol, irony, pun, and personification, as well as the more general concerns of poetic progression, *Stimmung* (to be defined presently), persona, and mode of address. Within the area of poetic form, we explain meter and scansion, rhyme schemes (including assonance and alliteration), stanzaic division, and line integrity (enjambment and caesura).

In addition to the general concerns of word usage and word/line ordering, we also will examine how words were chosen for the very properties of language that suggest musical setting of verse: words that exploit *sound* and *color.* Choosing certain words because their bright or dark sounds convey particular senses or emotions is one of the poet's most dramatic resources, and recognizing these sonorous and coloristic words is of great concern for both composers setting the poetry and singers enunciating the text. By being sensitive to the color of language and the sounds of spoken —and sung—words, performers will better enunciate the words within both the vocal line and the musical phrase and will, as well, understand the poem's special use of language that is translated into music.

Despite our initial separation of content and form, the two ultimately merge in the art form we call poetry. A poem is both a complex set of diverse parts and an elegant artistic whole that surpasses the sum of the individual elements. Putting a poem back together after analysis is like coordinating a musical performance; both the actual poem and the actual musical composition coalesce into an artistic experience that grows deeper and richer the more we come to understand it.

Poetic Content

The meaning of a poem derives from word choice and combination, and from the use of several poetic devices that give words unusual richness and resonance. While many of the terms and concepts here may be somewhat familiar, we urge the reader to consider the *precise* meaning of such commonly used (and misused) terms as "imagery" and "metaphor." When these terms are used glibly, they lose their capacity to illuminate the nuances of poetic meaning, something we are trying to show here with great care. In general, the use of such rhetorical devices as image, metaphor, symbol, etc. forms the core of the great poems of masters such as Goethe, Heine, and Eichendorff. By examining how these great poets used language, we will understand what Eichendorff said when he spoke in nature images, why Heine treated his subjects with irony, and how Goethe depicted the emotions within his protagonists.

Poetic Representation

According to Webster, the word "rhetoric" connotes "the art of using words effectively . . . to influence or persuade . . . including the use of figures of speech."[4] A "figure of speech" is defined in turn as "an expression using words in an unusual or nonliteral sense to give beauty or vividness of style; [including use of] metaphor, personification, simile. . . ." Poetry is, among other things, the art of speaking rhetorically, of expressing thoughts and feelings in terms that are unusual—delicate, sweet, provocative, intense. Toward that end, poets enhance their expressions first and foremost with the most common rhetorical devices: the image and the symbol. Generally speaking, an IMAGE is a *representation* of something that renders an idea more vivid and that places the idea within a rich and expressive context. In addition, a poem's imagery also connotes a choice of setting and detail of description that further dramatizes the poetic meaning; for example, a hopeful young lover's world is a warm spring day full of nature's beauty and song, all the nurturing elements contributing to a feeling of optimism and happiness. The more complex the imagery, the more vivid the depiction; a shepherd looking from the mountaintop to the valley is different from the shepherd bowed over his staff gazing down to the valley.[5]

Certain images assume heightened form when a comparison is made to a vivid scene or object. For example, the poet may describe the beloved with a METAPHOR: "My love *is* a flower" or a SIMILE: "My love *is like* a red, red rose." In each case, the lover's description through the world of nature enhances the poetic conception and conveys much about the poet's feelings without their having to be stated explicitly.

Another term associated with poetry that is often considered synonymous with "image" is SYMBOL. And while both terms refer essentially to the same thing, a symbolic representation often is more abstract. For example, while the songs of birds generally connote an image of lively nature sounds, the nightingale's song is an actual symbol of the lament for lost love.

Two final devices for concentrated and imaginative poetic depiction are pun and personification. A PUN is the use of a word that has two different meanings, and where the use of such a double meaning heightens the individual meanings in turn. A famous Rückert poem, "Ich atmet' einen linden Duft," uses a pun to evoke the doubleness of sense memory.[6] Figure 2.1 shows the translation.

FIGURE 2.1 Pun in Rückert, "Ich atmet' einen linden Duft."

Ich atmet' einen linden Duft.	I breathed a gentle fragrance.
Im Zimmer stand	In the room stood
Ein Zweig der Linde,	A sprig of lime,
Ein Angebinde	A gift
Von lieber Hand.	Of a dear hand.
Wie lieblich war der Lindenduft!	How lovely was the fragrance!
Wie lieblich ist der Lindenduft!	How lovely is the fragrance!
Das Lindenreis	That lime sprig,

Brachst du gelinde:	You broke tenderly;
Ich atme leis	I breathe softly
Im Duft der Linde	In the fragrance of lime
Der Liebe linden Duft.	Love's gentle fragrance.

The pun exploits the double meaning for the word "linde," which as an adjective (lower case l) means gentle and as a noun (upper case L) means lime or lime tree. This is, of course, not the citrus fruit tree, but a deciduous "Linden" tree of Northern climates. This captures the twofold nature of sense memory, as a *lime scent* evokes a memory of a *gentle* love associated with the fragrance of lime. The use of "linde" as adverb contributes to the poem's exploitation of multiple meanings; in stanza 2, line 3, "gelinde" can be translated as "tenderly" when the poet describes the lover's symbolic breaking of the lime sprig.

This elegant poem demonstrates how double meanings in poetry enhance poetic imagery. Rückert's pun also underscores the complicated temporal changes in sense memory; the scent of lime of the *present* recalls the scent from the *past* (stanza 1, line 1), and prompts the poet's memory of the *past* (the remainder of stanza 1). Stanza 2 then occurs within the present recollection of the *past*, the memory in stanza 1 prompting a return to the present. This is emphasized by the change in tense in the repeated line from the last line of stanza 1 to the beginning of stanza 2: "Wie lieblich *war* der Lindenduft!" becomes "Wie lieblich *ist* der Lindenduft!"

The device of PERSONIFICATION intensifies an image by endowing something with human qualities. For example, a typical German Romantic personification is a brook or other body of water whose existence is given human characteristics. In Wilhelm Müller's famous poetic cycles set by Schubert, the protagonists speak to the brooks as if they were companions. In *Die schöne Müllerin*, for example, the young miller's entire journey occurs with the accompaniment of his friend and teacher, the brook (Figure 2.2). This

FIGURE 2.2 Personification of the brook in *Die Schöne Müllerin*.

Song 1: "Vom Wasser haben wir's gelernt" ("From the water have we learned it")

Song 2: "Ist das denn meine Straße? O Bächlein, sprich, wohin?" ("Is this, then, my path? O brooklet, say, whereto?")

Song 4: "War es also gemeint, mein rauschender Freund?" ("Was it thus meant, my babbling friend?")

Song 6: "O Bächlein meiner Liebe, wie bist du heut' so stumm!" ("O brooklet of my love, how are you today so silent!")

FIGURE 2.3 Personification in *Winterreise.*

Der du so lustig rauschtest,	You who so merrily bubbled
Du heller, wilder Fluß,	You bright, boisterous stream,
Wie still bist du geworden,	How silent have you become;
Gibst keinen Scheidegruß.	(You) give no farewell.

personification enables the youth to muse aloud, his rhetorical questions to the brook, adding a rich dimension to both his ongoing journey and his evolving development as a person. Müller returns to this device in *Winterreise,* where, for example, in Song 7 the poet speaks directly to the stream in "Auf dem Flusse" ("On the Stream," Figure 2.3).

Because of this use of rhetoric, the poetic queries to personified nature elements can be interpreted in several ways. On a more literal level, the questions can be considered "rhetorical," that is, not requiring an answer. In this way, the poet may ask a brook or the moon knowing that the questions really cannot be answered and the personification is just a means of speaking aloud what is thought or felt. When the inquiries are considered on a more metaphorical level, however, personified elements can function as a part of the poet's own being, the "dialogue" between poet and brook representing an internal dialogue between two parts of the poet's inner self. In this way, the imagery of wanderer and personified image in, for example, *Winterreise,* represent a journey within the poet himself, each address to a personified object along the journey (tears, snow, brook, etc.) reflecting a new facet of the poet's inner development.

This potential for dual interpretation is crucial to understanding poetic images and symbols. The literal presentation of descriptive images and personifications also functions metaphorically: how love nourishes or anguish hurts or conflict festers. Each level of expression (literal and metaphorical) enhances the experience of the other: the quest for love is only as vivid as the depiction of the lonely shepherd and the image of the lonely shepherd is only as powerful as the devastating loss it represents.

Our list of poetic devices also includes the more complex usage of IRONY, the expression of one thing to convey something else, often something having an opposite meaning. The power of ironic expression lies in the fact that what is being said is in the form of a dichotomy or duality. Ironic presentations are more complex, richer expressions, and often occur in sarcastic, sardonic, or humorous contexts. In ironic poems, for example, the poet may somehow be at odds with what is being expressed or may use some form of dishonesty. Two poems of Heine, a poet celebrated for his use of irony, demonstrate how this enhances poetic meaning. Figure 2.4 shows the fourth poem of Schumann's *Dichterliebe,* "Wenn ich in deine Augen seh.'"

FIGURE 2.4 Irony: Heine, "Wenn ich in deine Augen seh'," *Dichterliebe.*

Wenn ich in deine Augen seh',	When I gaze into your eyes,
So schwindet all' mein Leid und Weh;	So flees all my hurt and pain;
Doch wenn ich küsse deinen Mund,	But when I kiss your mouth,
So werd' ich ganz und gar gesund.	Then I become wholly healed.
Wenn ich mich lehn' an deine Brust,	When I recline upon your breast,
Kommt's über mich wie Himmelslust;	It steals over me as heavenly bliss;
Doch wenn du sprichst: ich liebe dich!	But when you say: I love you!
So muß ich weinen bitterlich.	Then must I weep bitterly.[7]

While initially this lyric suggests the soothing, healing qualities of love, the final line casts the entire expression into an ironic light: Why cannot the poet enjoy the peacefulness of love? What causes the bitter tears? The irony of the poet's bitterness makes us rethink the joy even as the poem presents the images of love's sweet gentleness.

A similar sentiment is presented in a later poem from *Dichterliebe,* "Ich hab' im Traum geweinet;" see Figure 2.5. Again a portrait of love's power is jarred by an ironic response. While the poem's first two stanzas suggest tears as a reasonable response to lost love, first from the lover's death, then from the lover's rejection, the final stanza ends ironically

FIGURE 2.5 Irony in Heine, "Ich hab' im Traum geweinet," *Dichterliebe.*

Ich hab' im Traum geweinet,	I have wept in my dream,
Mir träumt', du lägest im Grab.	I dreamt you lay in your grave.
Ich wachte auf, und die Träne	I awoke, and the tear
Floß noch von der Wange herab.	Flowed still down my cheek.
Ich hab' im Traum geweinet,	I wept in my dream,
Mir träumt', du verließest mich.	I dreamt you were leaving me.
Ich wachte auf, und ich weinte	I awoke, and I wept
Noch lange bitterlich.	Yet long, bitterly.
Ich hab' im Traum geweinet,	I wept in my dream,
Mir träumte, du wär'st mir noch gut.	I dreamt you loved me still.
Ich wachte auf, und noch immer	I awoke, and still
Strömt meine Tränenflut.	Stream my flood of tears.[8]

when the poet's dream of love fulfillment results in the same "flood of tears." Just as "Wenn ich in deine Augen seh'" ended with ironic bitterness, so "Ich hab' im Traum geweinet" ends ironically with irrational despair.

The irony of both poems results from an *unexpected* poetic response to lost love—be it real, feared, or dreamed. With a bit of reflection, the meaning behind the irony becomes clearer: perhaps it is not the love itself that leads to ironic reactions, but rather it is the anguish over the *loss* of love, actual or feared, that causes the unexpected bitterness and despair. In the first poem, for instance, is the lover actually gone and the initial imagery thus a fantasy or dream? Does the bitterness then occur when the poet awakens to the reality that the sweet love is, in fact, really lost or may soon vanish? In the second poem, is the continued torment based on fear of *future* loss, or is the dream of love fulfillment devastating in fact because when the poet awakens, the love fulfillment no longer exists, had only been within a dream? This interpretation casts a different light on the first and second dreams of lost love. The earlier dreams of loss resulted in tears because the poet remembered *past* love or feared *future* loss. The final dream of achieving love then prompts tears because the poet is without love *in the present.* This second Heine poem uses irony to explore the Romantic preoccupations with the dichotomies of dream and reality, of loss and fulfillment, in addition to the threefold relationship to time: recalling the past, existing in the present, and yearning for or fearing the future.

Poetic Progression and Stimmung

Our discussion of poetic content must include two additional analytical concerns, concepts of poetic meaning called "poetic progression" and *Stimmung.* The concept of poetic progression involves tracing the poet's thoughts or feelings as they evolve over time within one general span or continuum; that of *Stimmung* involves the ascribing, in some but not all poetry, of a single poetic mood or psychological state that pervades the entire poem. Both illuminate how smaller images and rhetorical devices are incorporated into a larger sense of poetic meaning.

The determination of POETIC PROGRESSION involves tracing some form of activity or movement (physical, emotional, psychological) from one place to another, incorporating, usually, several types of motion at the same time. For example, while a Wanderer moves from one location to another, this physical progression also includes emotional changes: the Wanderer who stands among friendly folk in a tavern later finds himself alone beside a solitary tree in a moment of acute loneliness. The determination of poetic progression is best made after all the internal elements have been assessed; individual images and shifts in content all contribute to an overriding poetic progression that evolves from the poem's beginning to its very conclusion.

Our two Heine poems of irony will exemplify how to trace poetic progression. As shown in Figure 2.4, Heine's "Wenn ich in deine Augen seh'" presents sentiments of love in two stanzas. In stanza 1, the poet talks directly to the beloved and describes inner emotional responses to simple interactions (when I look, my sorrow leaves; when I kiss, I am healed). This interaction/response continues for the first two lines of stanza 2 (when I recline, I feel bliss), but changes dramatically in lines 3 and 4, where the poet receives an actual response: the beloved speaks. To this dramatic change, the poet reacts with bitter—ironic—tears, and the poem ends in a wholly different place from its beginning. The poem's activity is emotional and psychological: initial poetic responses of calm and healing (lines 1–6) become ironically bitter (lines 7–8). The poetic progression thus traces the poet's complex relation to love's various ironies; a lengthy expression of happy love turns suddenly—in reaction to words spoken by another—into an ultimate expression of bitter tears.

The Heine poem in Figure 2.5, "Ich hab' im Traum geweinet," also speaks of love, but here the poetic progression is dramatically different. The poem begins and ends in despair, and the progression moves from an initially understandable pain of lost love to a final irrational pain related, seemingly, to attained love. While on the one hand, the image of tears remains constant, the cause of these tears progresses, and the poet who still weeps at the end is in a dramatically different place from the poet's opening tears.

While the first Heine poem conveys a progression from nurturing love to bitter despair, this second poem progresses from the clear pain of lost love to a more complex pain of love fulfillment. In both poems, the poetic progression captures the poem's essential message without conveying every image of the poem. Thus, the notion of poetic progression offers performers an approach to poetry that differs dramatically from immersion into details of poetic expression we have been advocating so far. The two approaches are, in fact, complementary; once performers master the details of poetic meaning, the singer and pianist can place the poetic complexities into their poetic progression: the overarching temporal experience that makes the poem and its setting a coherent whole.

The concept of *STIMMUNG* is more difficult to define. Within the German language the word "*Stimmung*" has several different meanings, but in connection with German Romantic poetry, the term *Stimmung* designates a mood, a pervasive atmosphere within nature that resonates within the poetic soul.[9] The concept of *Stimmung* thus signifies an essence of sympathy between a poet and nature, an empathy that creates a single pervasive mood and/or psychological state within a poem. This technique is most closely associated with Eichendorff, but also is found in other poets, particularly those using extensive nature imagery.

The determination of a poem's *Stimmung*, like the discovery of its poetic progression, is an invaluable resource for the performer, who can anchor the variances of musical expression within a single governing poetic —and musical—mood. Two short poems by Eichendorff demonstrate the concept of *Stimmung*. Figure 2.6 shows the text to "Abends" and "Kurze Fahrt."[10] Both poems speak of the yearning for death, each within a different *Stimmung*. In "Abends," the mood is tranquil, as the poet describes nature's murmuring landscape at twilight (stanza 1) and the Wanderer's yearning for similar peace within his heart (through death in stanza 2). The *Stimmung* combines the peacefulness of nature with the watchful yearning of the Wanderer. In "Kurze Fahrt," on the other hand, the peaceful death sought

FIGURE 2.6 *Stimmung* in "Abends" and "Kurze Fahrt."

"Abends"	"At Eventide"

Abendlich schon rauscht
    der Wald
Aus den tiefsten Gründen,
Droben wird der Herr nun bald,
Bald die Stern anzünden;
Wie so stille in den Gründen
Abendlich nur rauscht
    der Wald.
	At eventide, already murmurs
	    the forest
	From the deepest valleys,
	On high, God now will soon,
	Soon kindle the stars;
	How quiet in the valleys
	At eventide, only murmurs
	    the forest.

Alles geht zu seiner Ruh, Wald und Welt versausen, Schauernd hört der Wandrer zu, Sehnt sich wohl nach Hause, Hier in Waldes grüner Klause, Herz, geh endlich auch zur Ruh.	All goes to its rest, Forest and world cease to stir, In awe, listens the wanderer, Yearning for home, Here, in the forest's green cell, Heart, go at last also to rest.

"Kurze Fahrt"	"Short Journey"
Posthorn, wie so keck und fröhlich Brachst du einst den Morgen an,	Posthorn, how bold and merry Introduced you once the morning,
Vor mir lag's so frühlingsselig, Daß ich still auf Lieder sann.	Lay before me such spring bliss, That I thought silently of songs.

Dunkel rauscht es schon im
    Walde,
Wie so abendkühl wird's heir,
Schwager, stoß ins Horn—
    wie balde
Sind auch wir im
    Nachtquartier!
	Darkly murmurs already the
	    forest,
	How evening-cool it grows here,
	Coachman, sound your horn—
	    how soon
	Will we also be lodged for the
	    night!

in stanza 2 has an eagerness that springs from the memories of youthful mer-
riment ("frühlingsselig") described in stanza 1. The call to the coachman is
not the subdued waiting of the Wanderer, but rather is a happy welcoming
by one ready to join the placid landscape of night.

The different moods of the two poems are reinforced by the sounds of
their poetic languages. In "Abends," the poet addresses his heart (the mono-
syllabic "Herz"), while in "Kurze Fahrt," the poet addresses the coachman
(the complex mixture of sounds in "Schwager"). "Abends" uses darker vowels to sustain a quietness: "a" (Wald, bald, alles); "au" (rauscht, Aus, versausen, Schauernd, Klause, auch); "u" (nun, nur, Ruh, zu, zur, und); and "o"
(schon, Droben, whol). In contrast, "Kurze Fahrt" uses many lighter vowels:
"ie" (wie, Lieder, hier); "e" (keck, den, Morgen, selig, es); "i" (fröhlich, mir,
ich, still, im, wird's, ins, sind, wir). The final word of "Abends" is "Ruh"
("rest"), a dark, drawn-out monosyllable that fits the peacefulness of the
poem. "Kurze Fahrt," which uses lively images throughout, ends with the
consonant-laden syllables of the military resting place: "Nachtquartier"
("night quarters").

The two Eichendorff lyrics show the subtle but important differences
of mood and image in poems that treat the same general theme, and both
singer and pianist must agree upon the *Stimmung* of each poem for a unified
performance. In addition, the nuances of mood and psychological expression that are clarified when *Stimmung* is determined can greatly enhance the
performer's vision and poetic depiction.

Attention to the use of *Stimmung* does require one caveat, however; it
is all too easy to search for a general mood in a poem and lose sight of more
subtle poetic details. In general, ascertaining an underlying mood or psychological state is a complicated process, and young musicians are urged to
consider the issue of *Stimmung* with great care and deliberation.

Persona and Mode of Address

All issues of poetic content and meaning are influenced by our final
concern here: the questions of poetic PERSONA: who is speaking in a poem
(and its setting) and MODE OF ADDRESS: to whom does the persona(s)
speak?[11] A poem may employ one of several general personas or "voices"
depending on the type of poem: in a lyric, the poet may project his or her
own voice or assume that of a protagonist (for example, a wanderer); in a
historical narrative or poetic drama, on the other hand, the poet may adopt
either the voice of a narrator or the voice of an actual character in a drama.
Each of these personas may in turn utilize one of several different modes of
address, or audience being addressed. In a lyric, the poet may speak either
inwardly within a soliloquy or outwardly to another presence, for example,
another person, a spiritual being, or elements within nature. In a narrative

or play, on the other hand, the poet may speak either to an audience, where no response is expected, or to other characters within the drama, whose response occurs within the dramatic presentation.[12]

An additional concern about the poetic mode of address is whether it remains constant or changes during the course of the poem. This is obvious in a drama where distinct characters or personas engage in dialogue, but it is also common in lyrics having only one persona. When, for example, a poet begins by speaking to nature but then shifts to speaking more inwardly, that change in mode of address dramatizes a change within the poet, whose response to nature prompts poetic introspection. Such a shift in mode of address is a dramatic vehicle for poetic development, as an initial poetic statement to, say, flowers or moonlight is transformed by the poet's evolving inner experience of love or melancholy. The great *Lied* composers were extremely sensitive to such changes in mode of address, and responded with some of the most exquisite changes in musical expressivity.

Concerns around poetic persona and mode of address are amplified when poetry is set to music, especially within the intimate *Lied* genre. Edward T. Cone has translated the idea of poetic persona and mode of address into the domain of the musical setting, where the vocal persona literally sings the poet's words, and the accompanists' often several instrumental personas either join the vocal persona or add additional ones.[13] While the role of the vocal persona is relatively straightforward, that of the accompaniment (pianist, chamber group, or full orchestra), can be far more complex. In simpler settings, the accompaniment will double the vocal line and the vocal persona; in more complex settings, however, such as we encounter in much of the great *Lied* repertory, the accompanist or instrumental persona projects several different voices, including those portrayed within instrumental solos such as introductions, interludes, and postludes.[14] In addition, because the accompanist's "voice" does not specifically "speak" the text, accompanimental personas may project a number of other aspects of the poetry. For example, the accompaniment may depict rustling forests or swirling winds, projecting the poetic environment in which the vocal persona "speaks"; or the accompaniment may portray the psychological condition of the vocal persona, for example, using rising musical lines to depict an emotional or spiritual ascent, or ponderous chords to depict a bereaved lover's despair. The instrumental persona also may assume one role within a dichotomous poetic world, for example, the pianist can project the "real world" from which the poet/singer flees through a "fantasy world," for example, as in "Gretchen am Spinnrade," or, the accompaniment may represent the poet's conscience or subconscious that opposes the part of the poet represented by the vocal persona, as in "Im wunderschönen Monat Mai."

Several poetic settings exemplify some of the issues raised here, beginning with Schubert's beloved setting of Goethe's famous "Erlkönig."[15] Goethe's narrative, with its four distinct characters: narrator, father, son, and

Erlking, demonstrates multiple personas within a poem and its setting.[16] Goethe separates the characters from one another with various articulations: the narrator and Erlking each have their own stanzas; the internal dialogues are then separated from the narrator's opening and closing frame; and finally, the struggle between father and son against the Erlking is depicted by an alternation of father/son stanzas with those of the Erlking. In addition, the speeches of the Erlking are enclosed in quotation marks and the intimate dialogues between father and son within stanzas are articulated by dashes.

Goethe's poem also demonstrates several different modes of address. As would be expected, the narrator addresses a general audience, while the other characters speak to each other, the dialogues between father and son having an intimate yet frenzied quality and the evil lures of the Erlking being directed to the boy as if he were already separate from his father.

Both Loewe's strophic and Schubert's more elaborate through-composed setting of this dramatic narrative convey the changes in both persona and modes of address with a variety of musical alterations, from surface changes in texture, rhythm, motivic design, and register to deeper-level changes in key and mode, and such elaborate musical alteration dramatically enhances the characterizations Goethe had indicated through visual means. The performers must convey the unique depictions of the four characters within the ongoing poetic drama, and, as well, maintain the song's overall musical continuity.

While settings of "Erlkönig" demonstrate various composers' responses to a poem featuring multiple personas and modes of address, Wolf's setting of Mörike's lyric "Lebe wohl" exemplifies a composer's approach to a poem where a single persona changes its mode of address midway through the poem (Figure 2.7). The poem divides into two stanzas, the first stanza directed at the rejecting lover and the second shifting its mode of address to a brooding introspection within the poet. In Wolf's setting, the vocal persona

FIGURE 2.7 Persona and mode of address in "Lebe wohl."

"Lebe wohl"—Du fühlest nicht,	"Farewell"—You feel not,
Was es heißt, dies Wort der	What it means, this word of
Schmerzen;	pains;
Mit getrostem Angesicht	With benign expression
Sagtest du's und leichtem Herzen.	You said it and with a light heart.
Lebe wohl!—Ach	"Farewell"—Oh, a
tausendmal	thousand times
Hab' ich mir es vorgesprochen,	Have I spoken it to myself,
Und in nimmersatter Qual	And in insatiable torment
Mir das Herz damit gebrochen!	Broken my heart with it![17]

is unusually disjunct throughout, with the change in mode of address signaled by the measure of silence in bar 9. This significant change to introspection greatly affects the song's second half, which is characterized by
modulatory activity and a vocal line that is sung mostly forte *"immer
gesteigerter"* ("ever intensifying") with a dramatically high climax followed by
a rapidly falling DÉNOUEMENT.[18]

While generally the pianist's persona and mode of address comple-
ment those of the singer, additional personas and modes of address occur
in the accompaniment as well. Wolf's "Lebe wohl" demonstrates. The piano
begins by doubling the vocal line and persona but soon develops a higher
TESSITURA[19] that contains a countermelody expressive of a second persona.
The interlude following the singer's first phrase then develops a lower tessitura within a complex and ambiguous harmonic sequence; this instrumental persona continues in that range in direct contrast to the line of the
singer. When the singer then reenters in the higher register for the rest of
the first stanza, it is clear that the accompaniment continues separately.
The piano's sequence in the lowermost registers suggests that the instrumental persona has perhaps become the subconscious of the despairing
lover, meandering in the depths, as the vocal persona describes the rejecting lover's ironic "getrostem Angesicht" ("indifferent expression") and
"leichtem Herzen" ("light heart").

The differences between vocal and instrumental personas continue in
the setting of stanza 2, where the accompanist alone repeats what had been
projected along with the vocal line. The piano musically reiterates the initial
word "Lebe wohl" that the vocal persona can no longer bear to utter, and the
ensuing change in mode of address leads to the accompaniment's adoption
of yet another persona within the ongoing modulatory sequence. This new
piano persona might be the brooding soul of the poet/singer, and as the
vocal persona speaks new words through the evolving melodic line, the
accompaniment continues to project (through the echo of the "Lebe wohl"
motive) the obsessive ache of rejection.

Wolf's depiction of the poetic shifts in Mörike's poem leads him to end
the song in a different key from that of the opening, a radical tonal design
that corresponds to the dramatic poetic progression. The vocal persona
sings into but not clearly *within* the new key, and the vocal line and persona
conclude in a telling gesture of uncertainty. When the vocal line ceases, the
instrumental persona must complete the setting alone within the new key;
the piano postlude thus dramatizes the difference between vocal and instrumental personas that remains at the song's conclusion.[20]

The concept of poetic and musical personas thus adds several new
dimensions to our study of the *Lied*. Because singer and pianist may project
different personas within the setting, the performance embodies a multiplicity of interpretive "musical voices" that portray the poetic personas in
rich detail. The determination of personas and modes of address thus pre-

sents a great challenge for performers, who are urged to give free reign to interpretations of both the poetry and their roles within the musical settings.

Poetic Form

Formal Divisions

Poetic meaning is organized through unique features of form.[21] Our survey of poetic form will illustrate the formal issues considered by composers who set poetry to music; understanding the translation of poetic form into musical form will greatly enhance the performer's understanding of how the *Lied* conveys the poetry and how to prepare for musical performance.

Poems are divided into sections called STANZAS (sometimes called "strophes"), divisions that are notated in the printed text by empty spaces. A COUPLET is a two-line unit of poetry; it can comprise a complete stanza, or it can be incorporated into a larger stanza.[22] A three-line stanza is called a *tercet*, a four-line stanza a *quatrain*, and a five-line stanza, a *cinquain*.

The length of the lines within stanzas is extremely variable, and differences in line lengths also contribute to the poem's meaning. Shorter lines tend to be more vivid and to convey their content more concisely, with fewer elements. The effect of such verses can vary from pithiness to epigrammatic terseness. In contrast, lengthier lines of poetry convey more information and can express any number of things such as luxuriousness or lugubriousness. The length of poetic line directly affects the composer's setting, and the resulting short or long vocal phrases are accompanied by other musical elements that help to convey the underlying poetic brevity or expansiveness.

Just as line length is inherently significant to the poem's meaning, so are poetic articulations of pause: the comma, semicolon, colon, dash, and period. Such indications of pause vary according to context and occur as well in different places within the stanza. In general, lines within stanzas are articulated in three ways: end-stopped, enjambed, and using caesura. If a line or phrase stops naturally at the right-hand end, it is called END-STOPPED: "Es kennt mich dort keiner mehr." If the first line or phrase does not stop, but flows naturally into the next, the line uses ENJAMBMENT: "Aus der Heimat hinter den Blitzen rot/ Da kommen die Wolken her." This poses a particularly interesting problem for singers, who must decide whether to run two musical phrases together or to pause for a breath, perhaps in a place other than the natural musical phrase-ending; Schumann's setting of Eichendorff's "In der Fremde," from which the above lines are taken, provides a good example of the need to make such decisions.

The third way to separate a line within a stanza is the use of a CAESURA (or cesura), a differently notated pause: "Doch wenn du sprichst: ich liebe dich!" This is by far the most dramatic form of articulation and tends to get a slightly longer pause than any other except the period that ends a stanza. The setting of caesura creates interesting challenges for composer and performer alike. Composers must decide about subdividing such poetic lines into comparable musical phrases, and singers likewise must choose where to breathe within longer musical units, particularly where the musical phrase uses an extension.[23] The determination of "where to breathe" may well change depending upon whether a poem is read silently, spoken out loud, or sung in musical time.

When you read poetry, take a minute to think about the implications of pausing with a comma instead of a semicolon or a dash instead of a period. These articulations suggest nuances of poetic meaning and, of even greater importance for poetic setting, indicate something about the tempo of the poem as either read silently or spoken aloud. Such considerations assisted the composer in both determining musical tempos for *Lied* settings and in actually shaping the lines of poetry into vocal phrases.

Two other factors characterize how lines function and interrelate within stanzas: first, whether lines rhyme with one another and second, whether lines end with the same rhythmic pattern. In general, rhyming lines and those ending with similar rhythms are strongly connected or interrelated. Rhyming lines are clearly connected by sound and lines sharing a common rhythm are linked by rhythmic stress. Line endings fall into two basic types: (1) a line that ends with a stressed syllable has a strong ending; and (2) one that ends with an unstressed syllable has a weak ending.[24] The alternation of strong and weak endings in poetry is a common technique in German (as well as French and Italian) poetry, and this alternation was an important factor in setting poetic lines as musical phrases. We will examine the use of poetic rhythms in the later section, "Poetic Meter"; now we must consider how rhyme schemes effect poetic form.

Rhyme Schemes

Most German Romantic poetry uses some form of END-RHYME, the ending of two lines of a stanza with words having the same vowel sound, for example, P*ein*/All*ein*.[25] The shorter stanzaic forms, such as couplets, quatrains, etc. use end-rhyme schemes to help organize the poem's meaning, lines that rhyme connecting uniquely with one another. In addition, the choice of which lines rhyme affects how quickly or slowly the poem flows.

We diagram end-rhyme using small letters of the alphabet: *aa* signifies a rhymed couplet. Quatrains notated *abba*, *abab*, and *aaba* create other relationships between and among lines.[26] While the alternating rhyme scheme (*abab*) tends to set up a moderate tempo, a pair of lines that rhyme directly, such as the *bb* within the *abba* pattern tends to accelerate the pace within the stanza. A famous example of how rhyme patterns affect the flow of the poem is Dante's use of "terza rima" throughout *The Divine Comedy*. There the continual interlock of the tercets helps to propel the poetry forward: *aba bcb cdc ded*, etc.·

We demonstrate the different effects of end-rhyme patterns by comparing the first stanzas of two poems by Goethe: "Der Musensohn" uses a six-line stanza with the complex end-rhyme pattern: *aabccb*; "Der Sänger" uses a more typical *ababccb* pattern within the uneven seven-line stanza. Figure 2.8 gives the texts.

In "Der Musensohn," the rhyming *b* lines clarify the sentence structure, where each group of three lines comprises a complete sentence. Goethe combines lines 1 and 2 through end-rhyme to complete the first image: a spirit singing through nature. This pairing of lines sets up a brisk rhyme pattern that is then broken by the lack of rhyme between lines 3 and 4, a change in rhyme pattern that signals a change in poetic image. The new end syllable of line 3 completes the idea of the spirit roaming about and provides an emphatic ending. The rhyming lines 4 and 5 then connect the spirit with the external world and line 6, which rhymes with line 3, concludes the first stanza and joins the opening poetic image with the anticipated end-rhyme pairing of lines 3 and 6.

In contrast to the pacing of the "Der Musensohn" stanza, the alternating rhyme pattern in the first part of "Der Sänger" allows the King's query

FIGURE 2.8 Comparison of end-rhyme patterns.

"Der Musensohn"		"Son of the Muses"
Durch Feld und Wald	*a*	Through field and forest
zu schweifen,		to roam,
Mein Liedchen weg zu pfeifen,	*a*	My little song to whistle,
So geht's von Ort zu Ort!	*b*	So it goes from place to place!
Und nach dem Takte reget	*c*	And keeps time,
Und nach dem Maß beweget	*c*	And in rhythm moves
Sich alles an mir fort.	*b*	Everything with me.[27]

"Der Sänger"		"The Minstrel"
"Was hör ich draußen vor dem Tor,	*a*	"What hear I outside the gate,
Was auf der Brücke schallen?	*b*	What on the bridge sounds?
Laß den Gesang vor unserm Ohr	*a*	Let that song for our ears
Im Saale widerhallen!"	*b*	Echo in this hall!"
Der König sprach's, der Page lief;	*c*	So the king said, the page ran;
Der Knabe kam, der König rief:	*c*	The page returned, the king cried:
"Laß mir herein den Alten!"	*b*	"Let the old man be admitted!"[28]

to flow simply through the first four lines. The accelerated rhyming that follows for lines 5 and 6 then conveys the energy of the page's response. This is followed by the weak rhyming of the final line, 7, with the rhyme of lines 2 and 4, that recurring rhyme bringing the episode to its resolution and the complete stanza to a close.

While end-rhyme is the most powerful way to link lines of poetry, other forms of rhyming create additional connections. The use of rhyme *within* a line, using syllables other than final ones, is called INTERIOR RHYME, and such rhyming is a common way to link words through sound as well as meaning, either within individual lines or over the course of several lines. The two well-known poetic devices that exploit such word usage are assonance and alliteration. ASSONANCE connects words through common *vowel* sounds and thus forms internal rhymes: comb*i*ning words that rh*y*me to create a f*i*ne des*i*gn of l*i*ne. ALLITERATION creates similar word connections but uses a repeated initial consonant sound: *c*arefully *c*rafted *c*onsonances *c*reate *c*learer *c*onnections. Here the effect is less a rhyming as we traditionally know it, and more a linking through a different sort of sound reiteration. Both devices connect words through sound, and both thus require special attention from the singer.[29]

Figure 2.9 details some instances of assonance and alliteration from Goethe's "Der Sänger." Figure 2.9a shows how Goethe marks the King's command of stanza 1 with several instances of assonance using the vowel "a" to accompany the *a* end-rhyme of lines 2 and 4. Figure 2.9b shows how the end-rhyme acceleration of lines 5 and 6 is intensified by using alliteration on "K" (*K*önig . . . *K*nabe *k*am") and further assonance on "a." Figure 2.10a offers two additional examples from Goethe that feature both assonance and alliteration; read each aloud slowly. Goethe's first Harper song uses assonance to intensify the pervasive anguish of the poem. The "ein" words of pain, "*Ein*-samk*eit*" and "P*ein*," are echoed by other "ein" usages throughout. In addi-

FIGURE 2.9A Assonance and alliteration in "Der Sänger," lines 1–4.

> W*a*s hör ich draußen vor dem Tor,
> W*a*s auf der Brücke sch*a*llen?
> L*a*ß den Ges*a*ng vor unserm Ohr
> Im S*aa*le widerh*a*llen!"

FIGURE 2.9B Assonance and alliteration in "Der Sänger," lines 5–6.

> Der *K*önig spr*a*ch's, der P*a*ge lief;
> Der *K*n*a*be *k*am, der *K*önig rief:

FIGURE 2.10A Assonance and Alliteration in "Gësange des Harfners."

"Gesänge des Harfners"	"The Minstrel's Songs"
Wer sich der *Ein*samk*ei*t ergibt,	Who himself to loneliness gives,
Ach! der ist bald all*ein*;	Ah, he is soon alone;
Ein jeder lebt, *ein* jeder liebt	Everyone lives, everyone loves
Und läßt ihn s*ei*ner P*ein*.	And leaves him to his pain.[30]

tion, Goethe also uses two repeated "i" vowel sounds to create word connections around verbs: "s*i*ch"/"*i*st" and "erg*i*bt"/"*i*hn". This creates an acceleration of verb activity in conjunction with the intensified anguish of the poem.

A more dramatic form of interior rhyme combines sounds into what may be called a compound alliteration. This occurs in the second Harper song (Figure 2.10b) and increases the repetition so evocative of sustained suffering: "*jeder l*ebt" is followed by "*jeder l*iebt." In "Trost in Tränen," the stanzas alternate between a tormented young poet's *Sehnsucht* and the persona that poses questions. The repeated "d," of stanza 1 emphasizes the heaviness of the young man's sorrow, as do the rhyming "ein" words of stanza 1 reiterated in stanza 2. In fact, the "ein" words convey the poetic progression, as "ersch*ein*t" becomes "gew*ein*t" followed by "*ein*sam" and "m*ein* *ein*gner Schmerz." Goethe also combines the "d" alliteration with "an" assonance in stanza 1: "*d*irs *an* *d*en Augen *an,*/ . . . *d*u h*a*st" and uses a similar combination of consonant and vowel in stanza 2: "Und Tr*än*en fließ*en* gar so süß,/ Erleicht*ern* mir das H*er*z." Here a remarkable progression of alliteration/assonance occurs: the "e" and "n" link the flowing tears image with the notion of "Erleichtern" or "to ease." This then leads to aligment with the most significant word to come, "Herz," where the "n" is replaced by "r." The "ern"

FIGURE 2.10B Assonance and Alliteration in "Trost in Tränen."

"Trost in Tränen"	"Comfort in Tears"
Wie kommts, da*ß d*u so traurig bist,	How is it that you are so sad,
*D*a alles froh erscheint?	When all seems happy?
Man sieht *d*irs an *d*en Augen an,	One can see from your eyes,
Gewiß *d*u hast geweint.	Certainly, you have been weeping.
"Und hab ich *ein*sam auch gew*ein*t	"And I have in solitude also wept,
So ists m*ein* *ein*gner Schmerz,	It is my own distress,
Und Tränen fließen gar so süß,	And tears flow so very sweetly,
Erl*ei*chtern mir das Herz."	Alleviating unto me my heart."[31]

composite thus may "ease" the way for "Herz" to be connected with "Tränen fließen" and the decrease in frequence of the "i" vowel may indicate release from pain.

Two other uses of word rhyming contribute to the flow and content of poetry. First, the use of multiple rhymes between words increases word associations. The words "people" and "steeple," for example, exemplify a double rhyme, and "funnily" and "sunnily" show a triple. Double and triple rhymes can function both as end-rhyme connections and as internal rhymes; such rhyming compounds create a denser pattern of word association and often create poetic acceleration as well.

Another technique of using a word sound to help convey poetic meaning does not involve a rhyme pattern; rather, ONOMATOPOEIA is a word choice wherein the word's meaning is expressed in sound, for example, "buzz" or "soothe" in English, or "Stille" ("quiet" or "silence"), "Ruh" ("peace"), or "zerstückeln" ("cut into little pieces") in German. Understanding the use of onomatopoeia depends entirely upon having an intimate knowledge of the language, and students must be wary of text translations that do not give literal translations.[32]

Poetic Meter

Most poetry written in western civilization is called "accentual-syllabic"; some syllables are accented or stressed and others are not. The pattern of word stress in poetry is called POETIC METER, and the number of stressed syllables in a line also is subject to various traditions and regulations. Adherence to such limitations is part of what makes composing in verse both so difficult and so beautiful, and it is also what made the setting of verse within musical phrases so possible.

Lines of poetry thus are word groupings that form patterns of stressed and unstressed syllables, patterns that organize the poetic stresses into unique designs. A single unit of the pattern is called a FOOT, and the types of meters divide, like musical meters, into duple and triple categories. In all, there are five characteristic patterns, two duple (iambic and trochaic), two triple (anapest and dactylic), and one singleton (spondee). These meters are notated in Figure 2.11 (⌣ = unstressed; / = stressed):[34]

FIGURE 2.11 Poetic meters.

Duple		Triple	
Iambic (iamb)	⌣ /	anapest (anapest)	⌣ ⌣ /
Trochaic (trochee)	/ ⌣	Dactylic (dactyl)	/ ⌣ ⌣

Single or Duple
spondaic (spondee)   /   or   / /

Lines of poetry, then, comprise several feet of one of the above meters. The rare line with only one foot is called a monometer; a dimeter has two feet; a trimeter has three, a tetrameter, four, and a pentameter, five. A line with six feet is a hexameter; lines longer than a hexameter tend to be awkward for musical setting and are usually broken with a caesura.[34]

As we demonstrate poetic meters in some detail, two things should be kept in mind. First, the choice of rhythm and meter influences the speed at which a text can be spoken and consequently how a text can be set to music. Lines with spondees, for example, with their single- or double-stressed syllables, tend to move slowly and can feel labored, while lines with anapests and dactyls, with their several short unstressed syllables, lend themselves to swifter movement. The caesura creates a break of metric flow; during scansion, the caesura is indicated by the sign: ‖. While such considerations were important to all the great *Lied* composers, they were especially so to Schubert and Wolf, who evolved declamatory styles that gave precise enunciations to the rhythms of the words they set in order to preserve the inherent metric structure of the poetry.[35]

A second issue to keep in mind about poetic meter is that the meters are metric norms: they are used, as musical meters are, to set up a metric basis within which the poetry, like the music, comes into shape. In great poetry, metric patterns are often broken in order to create dramatic emphasis or at moments of climax; such changes in meter are called SUBSTITUTIONS and, as we will see presently, these substitutions are as important as the actual meters themselves.

The determination of a poem's poetic meter, including where substitutions might occur, is called SCANSION. In this analytical procedure, we scan a poem to determine where the stresses occur (and by default where the unstressed syllables are) and then choose the meter that best describes the metric pattern. Beginning scanners, particularly those whose knowledge of German is not secure, often get discouraged when they first try to scan a poem. They are surprised at how difficult it is to be certain about both where the stresses occur and what poetic meter prevails, and the possibility of a metric substitution can be even more unsettling. In addition, some may get frustrated when they encounter a poem where there is not necessarily one "correct" scansion, but rather where a choice has to be made between two different but equally feasible meters.

As you begin to do scansion, keep in mind that it is an inexact process and that more than one analysis may have merit. The goals are to be sure about how words are both pronounced individually and spoken within the line (this is especially important for the singer) and to decide carefully what metric pattern seems to predominate. The relative freedom of scansion interpretation is similar to that of the musician facing certain performance decisions; the uncertainty of many options can be overcome by careful thought and hard work.

FIGURE 2.12 Scansion: Eichendorff, "In der Fremde."

1. Aus der Heimat hinter den Blitzen rot   [5]
   / ᵕ / ᵕ / ᵕ ᵕ / ᵕ /
   From the homeland behind the lightening red

2. Da kommen die Wolken her,   [3]
    ᵕ / ᵕ ᵕ / ᵕ /
   There approach clouds,

3. Aber Vater und Mutter sind lange tot,   [5]
   / ᵕ / ᵕ ᵕ / ᵕ ᵕ / ᵕ /
   But father and mother have long been dead,

4. Es kennt mich dort keiner mehr.   [3]
    ᵕ / ᵕ ᵕ / ᵕ /
   No one remembers me there anymore.

5. Wie bald, wie bald kommt die stille Zeit,   [4]
    ᵕ / ᵕ / ᵕ   ᵕ / ᵕ /
   How soon, how soon comes the quiet time,

6. Da ruhe ich auch, und über mir   [4]
    ᵕ / ᵕ ᵕ /   ᵕ / ᵕ /
   There rest I also, and over me

7. Rauschet die schöne Waldeinsamkeit,   [4]
   /   ᵕ ᵕ / ᵕ / ᵕ ᵕ /
   Murmurs the beautiful loneliness of the forest

8. Und keiner mehr kennt mich auch hier.   [4]
    ᵕ / ᵕ ᵕ / ᵕ / /
   And no one anymore knows me also here.

Two examples of scansion demonstrate a clear use of meter and substitution. We begin with Eichendorff's "In der Fremde"; Figure 2.12 presents the poem, translation, and scansion.[36] Remember: while scansion is concerned primarily with rhythm and meter, the choice of meter, together with any substitutions, helps convey nuances of poetic meaning.

On first pass, the poem's meter seems ambiguous and contradictory. Not one, but two patterns seem operative, the strong–weak duple (trochaic, / ᵕ) and strong–weak–weak triple (dactylic, / ᵕ ᵕ). In addition, while lines 1, 3, and 7 begin with stressed syllables (trochees, / ᵕ), the majority begin with weak syllables (iambs, ᵕ /). Does that mean we have a pattern of weak–strong (iambic, ᵕ /) instead of the trochee? The pattern of line endings contributes to the confusion; without exception they end on a stressed syllable. Does that suggest, again, iambic meter, or are the line endings spondees (/)?

The above process of observation and consideration is typical of scansion. Not one but at least two meters are possible. In situations like this, where one meter does not assert itself readily and unambiguously, other factors must be considered. We will address the above questions systematically in order to demonstrate how scansion of complex meter is worked through. While some poems set in *Lieder* may prove more straightforward, many will have the complexity and richness of this Eichendorff lyric.

In choosing whether the meter is duple or triple, the decision rests with which type of meter *predominates*. Here the duple pattern is more prevalent and the triple is more the exception. Another consideration when two sets of meters seem possible, especially those that are opposites like iambic vs. trochaic or anapest vs. dactylic, is to choose the one that most preserves the integrity of the words. Figure 2.13 shows line 1. The trochee (/ ˘) and dactyl (/ ˘ ˘) patterns begin the line and the poem with a stressed syllable and also preserve intact the three 2-syllable words: "Heimat," "hinter," and "Blitzen." This contrasts dramatically with the use of iambs (˘ /) and an anapest (˘ ˘ /), which cuts all such words in half. We determine then that the prevailing meter is trochaic, with dactyls occurring systematically (at least once per line) to accelerate the line.[37]

Having decided upon a meter, we can now count the number of feet per line. These numbers (in square brackets in Figure 2.12) will give further information about the relationship of lines to one another and will identify any changes in line length that might occur. General questions to ask about line length include: Are all lines of equal length or do their lengths vary? Is there a pattern to line lengths? If so, what does that contribute to the progression of the poem?

The lines in fact do vary in length and a pattern of line pairing evolves. An unequal 5 + 3 pairing in stanza 1 creates a certain rhythm (long line followed by short line) that is then altered by a more regular 4 + 4 pairing in stanza 2. The effect of this change in line length pattern reflects the overall meaning of the poem: the nature images of trouble (lightning, clouds) and the poet's brooding of stanza 1 are captured rhythmically by the uneven lines, while the change to thoughts of death's peacefulness in stanza 2 is reflected rhythmically in a more even pattern of line lengths. This interpretation underscores the necessity of considering poetic meaning when determining scansion; the rhythm and meter of the words is deeply connected to the poem's meaning.

FIGURE 2.13 Choosing meter for line 1, "In der Fremde."

Aus der Heimat hinter den Blitzen rot,

/ ˘ / ˘ / ˘ ˘ / ˘ /

Returning to our Eichendorff poem, we consider next the problem of lines beginning with unstressed syllables and ending in a single stressed syllable within a trochaic meter. Looking again at Figure 2.12, lines 1 and 2, we see that the two issues actually are related, as line 1 ends with an incomplete trochee and the next line finishes the foot with a sort of pickup. This recurs between lines 3 and 4, 4 and 5, 5 and 6, and 7 and 8. The two exceptions to this occur when lines 3 and 7 begin with stressed syllables (the complete trochee); the endings of the previous lines 2 and 6 are notated, accordingly, as spondees.

The considerable use of dactyls throughout the poem demonstrates the concept of substitution. In this case, the triple dactyl meter (/ ⌣ ⌣) substitutes for the duple trochee (/ ⌣) in a constant metric shifting that adds variety to each line and thus prevents a singsong quality. While we look for a pattern of dactyl usage, none appears; the seemingly random use contributes thus to a rhythmic vitality and the overall result of the substitution is one of rhythmic variety.

In addition to the constant substitutions of dactyls throughout, two lines (6 and 8) can have several different metric interpretations, depending on decisions of word emphasis. Figure 2.14 details the two options for scanning line 6, "Da ruhe ich auch." In (a), the spondee of the second foot emphasizes "ich," focusing on the poet yearning for peaceful death and in (b), the spondee emphasis is on "Da" the actual place of salvation; either interpretation works fine. Line 8 poses a similar problem, as shown in Figure 2.15.[38] In (a), the avoidance of a dactyl creates a line solely of trochees for an unremitting rhythmic drive to the poem's conclusion; in this case the only word receiving any emphasis is the final designation "hier." In (b), on the other hand, the line includes the ubiquitous dactyl, and the use of a set of spondees at the poem's conclusion creates both an effective deceleration for closure and also the emphasis upon "auch hier": the "hier" refers to the poet's present location, "In der Fremde," and the "auch" links the present solitude with that of the past. In (c), finally, the variety of poetic meters emphasizes the importance of the concluding line: the familiar dactyl is followed by a trochee that emphasizes the verb "kennt," the lack of being "known" underscoring the poet's sense of isolation. The concluding pair of spondees provides, as in reading (b), a strong sense of closure along with emphasis on "auch hier." Again, all interpretations are valid.

FIGURE 2.14 Metric interpretation, "Da ruhe ich auch."

	Da	ruhe	ich	auch
(a)	⌣	/ ⌣	/	/
(b)	/	/ ⌣	⌣	/

FIGURE 2.15 Metric interpretation, "Und Keiner mahr Kennt mich auch."

	Und	Keiner	mehr	kennt	mich	auch	hier
(a)	˘	/ ˘	/	˘	/	˘	/
(b)	˘	/ ˘	/	˘	˘	/	/
(c)	˘	/ ˘	˘	/	˘	/	/

No matter which scansions are chosen for these two lines, the use of spondees as substitutes for trochees creates a pattern of line endings that is consistent throughout. Our second poem demonstrating scansion has a more complex design. Instead of the more typical use of one prevailing meter and some well-chosen substitutions in the Eichendorff, Hölty's "Die Mainacht" eschews a single meter in favor of a metric complex whose pattern is replicated throughout.[39] Figure 2.16 presents the poem, translation, and scansion; while the figure reproduces the poem as printed, the line numbering (1–4) within each stanza helps confirm the repeated metric pattern of the scansion.

FIGURE 2.16 Scansion, Hölty, "Die Mainacht."

Stanza 1

1. Wann der silberne Mond durch   When the silver moon through
   / ˘ / ˘ ˘ / /
   die Gesträuche blinkt,   [6]   the shrubs shines,
   ˘ ˘ / ˘ /

2. Und sein schlummerndes   And its slumbering
   ˘ ˘ / ˘ ˘
   Licht über den Rasen streut,[6]   light over the grass scatters,
   / / ˘ ˘ / ˘ /

3. Und die Nachtigall flötet,   [3 +] And the nightingale flutes,
   / ˘ / ˘ ˘ / ˘

4. Wandl' ich traurig von   Wander I sadly from
   / ˘ / ˘ ˘
   Busch zu Busch.   [4]   bush to bush.
   / ˘ /

Stanza 2

1. Überhüllet von Laub girret ein   Concealed by foliage coo a
   / ˘ / ˘ ˘ / / ˘ ˘
   Taubenpaar   [6]   pair of doves
   / ˘ /

2. Sein Entzücken mir vor;   their ecstasy before me;
 / ˘ / ˘ ˘ /
   aber ich wende mich,   [6]   but I turn away,
   / ˘ ˘ / ˘ /

3. Suche dunklere Schatten,   [3 +] Seek deeper shadows,
 / ˘ / ˘˘ / ˘

4. Und die einsame Träne rinnt. [4] And a solitary fear flows.
   / ˘ / ˘˘ / ˘ /

Stanza 3

1. Wann, o lächelndes Bild,   When, o smiling image,
   / ˘ / ˘ ˘ /
   welches wie Morgenrot   [6]   that like the morning red
   / ˘ ˘ / ˘ /

2. Durch die Seele mir strahlt,   irradiates through my soul,
 / ˘ / ˘ ˘ /
   find' ich auf Erden dich?   [6]   find I on earth you?
   / ˘ ˘ / ˘ /

3. Und die einsame Träne   [3]   And that solitary tear
   / ˘ / ˘˘ / ˘

4. Bebt mir heißer die Wang'   [4]   trembles the hotter down my
   / ˘ / ˘ ˘ /
   herab!   cheek!
   ˘ /

The poem divides into three stanzas of four lines each, and at first
glance neither one length of line (number of feet) nor one meter predominates. However, upon closer inspection, we see that the pattern and number of feet found in stanza 1 is repeated exactly in stanzas 2 and 3, and that
the pattern of metric change in line 1 recurs with some variation in lines 2
through 4. Figure 2.17 shows the metric pattern for stanza 1. Lines 1 and 2
have the same pattern. Lines 3 and 4 begin the same but end differently; line
3 has three feet, whereas line 4 repeats the pattern of line 3 but adds a final
stressed foot. Since all lines of the stanza correspond in part to line 1, we can

FIGURE 2.17 Metric Pattern for Stanza 1, "Die Mainacht."

1.	/˘	/˘˘	/	/˘˘	/˘	/
2.	/˘	/˘˘	/	/˘˘	/˘	/
3.	/˘	/˘˘	/˘			
4.	/˘	/˘˘	/˘	/		

FIGURE 2.18 Metric pattern for line 1, "Die Mainacht."

trochee	dactyl	spondee	dactyl	trochee	spondee
/ ◡	/ ◡ ◡	/	/ ◡◡	/ ◡	/

consider line 1's meter as the generating pattern, as shown in Figure 2.18. In metric terms, line 2 repeats the pattern exactly; line 3 keeps the first two feet but then substitutes a trochee for the spondee and omits the last two feet; line 4 then repeats line 3 exactly and adds a spondee at the end.[40] The line shortenings in lines 3 and 4 along with the various substitutions create rhythmic acceleration through line 3 and into and through line 4. This corresponds to the changes in poetic content: in stanza 1, for example, the poet describes the nocturnal scene in lines 1 and 2; records the nightingale's song in line 3, and then in line 4, actively wanders within the moonlit landscape.

The variety of meters found in each line of "Die Mainacht" allows for an unusual metric variety that then forms a larger metric pattern. The weightiness of the spondees is balanced by the lighter dactyls, and the metric richness helps convey the evolving poetic meaning. The metric diversity conveys how the complex scene shimmers and slumbers above—and within —the wandering poet, and how the poet then turns inward from nature's diffused light to explore the complex internal turmoil of lost love.

Model Analysis: Goethe's "Wanderers Nachtlied I"

We conclude this chapter on poetic content and form by analyzing a masterpiece of Goethe. "Wanderers Nachtlied I" was set by several composers over a span of more than a century; Schubert's setting, D. 224, was written in 1823.[41]

Goethe first notated "Über allen Gipfeln ist Ruh" on the wall of a hut in the mountains of Thüringen on September 6, 1780 (Figure 2.19).[42] The poem demonstrates his mastery over nuances of poetic meaning and design; read the German text aloud slowly, with especially careful pronunciation of all vowel sounds.

FIGURE 2.19 Goethe's "Wanderers Nachtlied I."

Über allen Gipfeln	Over all mountaintops
Ist Ruh,	Is peace.
In allen Wipfeln	In all treetops
Spürest du	Detect you
Kaum einen Hauch;	Scarcely a breath;

Die Vöglein schweigen im Walde.	The little birds are quiet in the woods.
Warte nur, balde	Wait now, soon
Ruhest du auch.	Rest you also.

Turning first to the poem's meaning, we see that the verse begins with a terse description of nature in lines 1–6 that seems a simple setting for the poet, who in lines 7–8 expresses the poem's central issue: the Romantic yearning for peaceful death. While the nature imagery initially seems a backdrop to the drama *within* the poet, this peaceful description of quiet treetops and hushed birds actually functions as more than a poetic setting and ambiance. Rather, the repose, quiet, and darkness of the short, slow-paced opening lines all symbolize the peaceful death that the poet seeks. The finality of the terse "ist Ruh" of line 2 embodies the arrival and completion of peaceful death, and the depiction of small creatures that are "quiet in the woods" of line 6 represents the worldly antithesis to death that the poet prepares to leave. Significantly, line 6, with its luxuriant length and symbols of liveliness, functions both to contrast the finality of line 2 and to provide a pivotal moment wherein the poet turns away from nature and moves inward to the world of introspection.

The poetic images within this terse poem are intensified by the sounds inherent in the poetic language. Goethe limited himself to only ten vowel sounds, with a preference for the darker ones. The word color reflects the poem's overall progression from bright to dark, mirroring the natural progression from twilight to full night. The vowels and their coloristic meanings are given in Figure 2.20.

The only bright sounds (*Über*, "Sp*ü*rest", D*ie*) are at the beginnings of lines 1, 4, and 6, and by line 8, nothing but dark sounds reach the ear. The "u" sound (R*u*h, d*u*, n*u*r), especially, strikes the listener as being restful and dark, and the surrounding dark "a" and "au" sounds (H*au*ch, W*a*lde, b*a*lde, *au*ch) assist in creating a smooth, calming effect. This technical mastery of word sound enabled the poet to construct a linguistic metaphor of color for his poetic message, a use of word timbre that must be faithfully conveyed in the singer's performance.[43]

FIGURE 2.20 Vowels and color: "Wanderers Nachtlied I."

Vowels	Brightness/darkness
ü, ie	bright
i (open I)	semibright
ö, e (schwa), ei	semidark
a, u, au	dark

While the poetic imagery, including the use of word color, seems relatively straightforward, the poetic progression is rich and complex. Rather
than depicting a journey that moves from life to death, the poem opens with
death imagery, moves to images of life, and then returns to an altered sense
of death. This progression captures the rich psychological journey within the
poet. Acknowledgment of the peacefulness of death (lines 1–5) begins the
psychological process of departing life (line 6) and preparing for death
(lines 7–8). The profundity of the poetic progression is in turn reinforced
by the nature imagery, which conveys a similar journey in life forces: the
images progress from the mineral ("Gipfeln") to the vegetable ("Wipfeln")
to the animal ("Vöglein") to, finally, the specifically human ("du"), who
actively prepares for final rest within nature's order. Lines 1–5 thus depict
remote but evolving nature at rest, line 6 recalls the energy of life, and lines
7–8 leave nature altogether and enter the psychological world of the poet.

In a essay written over four decades ago, Elizabeth M. Wilkinson
describes Goethe's use of language and poetic structure with remarkable
clarity and insight that warrants a lengthy quote:

> There is in it not a simile, not a metaphor, not a symbol. Three brief,
> simple statements of fact are followed by a plain assertion for the
> future. . . . the original German exhibits a mysterious and perfect union
> of sound and sense. We point to the immediacy with which language
> here conveys the hush of evening: [lines 1–2] . . . the long *u* of 'R*u*h'
> and in the ensuing pause we detect the perfect stillness that descends
> upon nature with the coming of twilight. . . . the indispensable syllable *e*
> in 'Vög*e*lein' and 'Wald*e*' makes the sixth line a lilting lullaby which
> inevitably evokes the rocking movement of rest 'in the tree-tops'. . .
> here the verse does not describe the stillness of evening, it has become
> the stillness of evening: the language is evening stillness itself. . . . The
> poet-wanderer here is not embracing Nature in the Romantic way. He
> is, of necessity, by the very order of the poem, embraced within it, as
> the last link in the organic scale of being.

Later, Wilkinson concludes:

> What is so amazing about [the poem], is that subjective and objective
> experience are here completely fused. The evocation of mood, the pro-
> jection of man's longing for peace on to nature, the tenderness of the
> diminutive Vögelein with its reminiscence of the folksong, all these are
> not at all at odds with—they are entirely consistent with—the objective
> truth about the evolution of nature. . . . the appearances of Nature are
> rendered, but also the organic relation between them; man's mind is

shown as the final link in the chain of creation. Nature becomes conscious of itself, but it also takes its proper place within nature. . . . A poem such as 'Über allen Gipfeln' has clearly been organized at the deepest levels of the mind. . . the proof lies in the complete assimilation of experience into language without the intervention of conceptual thought. And at the deepest level of Goethe's mind the subjective and objective modes are quite evidently harmonized. One and the same poetic formulation can give expression to both the subjective feeling of the human heart and the objective knowledge of the human mind.[44]

The issues of persona and mode of address add another dimension to the poetic content. As the poem's title indicates, the poet's persona is that of nocturnal wanderer, the Romantic figure symbolizing poignant alienation and loneliness. The question of mode of address has several possibilities. In lines 7–8, if the poet speaks to an actual "listener," to a communal spirit and a compassionate companion, then the poem includes the gentle element of human interaction. If, however, the verse is truly a "Wanderer's Evensong," then the wanderer must be speaking inwardly, the solitude of the soliloquy in turn transforming the poetic images into a true Romantic scene of a solitary figure surrounded by nature's immense landscape. If the poem is indeed a soliloquy, then the meaning of its imagery changes and the element of longing intensifies. The isolation in the quiet evening deepens, especially for the singer, and the persona(s) of the accompanist can be altogether different from that of a sympathetic audience.

It is difficult to capture the poem's essence with a *Stimmung* that incorporates nature's quiet evening with the poet's longing for peaceful death, especially because the quiet energy of nature's hushed stillness contradicts the finality of peaceful death. The notion of quiet expectation does work here; the wanderer's experience of the reticent landscape is charged by anticipation of joining nature in death while, at the same time, the eagerness for death is muted by the suppressed energy in nature's stillness.

The poem's form, of course, supports the poetic content just discussed. The poem divides into two equal stanzas or quatrains (four lines each). This stanzaic symmetry is undermined by two formal irregularities: first, there is no regularity of line length; and second, the pattern of alternating strong and weak endings changes from the first stanza to the second. The pattern of line endings, including the pattern changes, coincides with the end-rhyme structure; Figure 2.21 shows this correspondence between line endings and end-rhyme (S = strong, W = weak). By changing the alternating WSWS and *abab* patterns of the first stanza to the symmetrical SWWS and *cddc* patterns in the second, Goethe avoids any singsong quality inherent is the simple alternation scheme. The result is a short poem of deceptively rich details of

FIGURE 2.21 Line endings and end-rhyme in "Wanderers Nachtlied I."

	Line ending	End-rhyme
Stanza 1	W	*a*
	S	*b*
	W	*a*
	S	*b*
Stanza 2	S	*c*
	W	*d*
	W	*d*
	S	*c*

form and design, characteristics of simplicity and complexity that are captured vividly in Schubert's setting.

The use of end-rhyme is accompanied by much internal rhyming as well. For example, the rhyming of "R*uh*" and "d*u*" in lines 2 and 4 is repeated with the identical two syllables *within* line 8 ("R*uh*est d*u* auch."). Such assonances also are found in lines 5 ("k*aum*/H*auch*"); 6 ("... l*ein*/schw*eig* ..."); and 7 ("w*arte*/B*alde*").

Turning now to the poem's scansion, the number of metrical feet and the prevailing meter are illustrated in Figure 2.22. The meter is essentially trochaic (/ ⌣) with systematic use of spondees for strong endings in lines 2, 4, 5, and 8. The most noticeable irregularities are metric reversal in line

FIGRE 2.22 Scansion for "Wanderers Nachtlied I."

Line/meter	Feet
Über allen Gipfeln / ⌣ / ⌣ / ⌣	3
Ist Ruh, ⌣ /	1.5
In allen Wipfeln ⌣ / ⌣ / ⌣	2.5
Spürest du / ⌣ /	2
Kaum einen Hauch; /? / ⌣ / ⌣?	2.5(?)
Die Vöglein schweigen im Walde. ⌣ / ⌣ / ⌣ ⌣ / ⌣	3.5

FIGURE 2.2 *continued*

Warte nur, balde   3(?)

/ ⌣ /? / ⌣
　　　⌣?

Ruhest du auch.   3

/ ⌣ /? /
　　⌣?

2 (reverses to iamb: ⌣ /), use of half-foot at the beginning of lines 3 and 6, use of an anapest (/ ⌣ ⌣) in line 6, and ambiguous inner feet in lines 7 and 8: either a spondee foot (/) or an extra weak half-foot (⌣). In addition, the beginning syllable of line 5, "kaum" could be considered either a strong spondee that creates symmetry with its rhyming "Hauch" at the line's end, or a weak half-foot (⌣) that dramatizes the word's meaning ("scarcely").

While the varying number of feet suggests a haphazard eight-line verse of irregular line lengths and metric shifts and substitutions, the metric usage becomes clearer when enjambment and rhyming patterns are taken into account. For example, the enjambment of lines 1 and 2 result in four feet, the same number as the rhyming lines 3 and 4. Lines 5 and 6, each of which is endstopped, combine for six feet total, the same number as the final enjambed lines 7–8.[45] A rhythmic pattern thus of 4 + 4 + 6 + 6 feet thus helps propel the poem through uneven line lengths and a varying metric design. In this sense, the progression from stanzas 1 to 2 demonstrates a gradual increase of number of feet, an increase that has tremendous implications for both the composer's setting and the performer's interpretation.

Schubert's interpretation of the poem's complex scansion may be gleaned from his setting. In line 5, he stresses both "kaum" and "ein," while both "Warte nur" in line 7 and "ruhest Du" in line 8 are treated as dactyls (/ ⌣ ⌣). Nevertheless, a singer can stress the "nur" in line 7, despite its being set as a descent from "warte"; it is a quarter note, and could be accented. Interestingly, most listeners will perceive such an accent as false, one that is less natural than the effect found by following Schubert's descending lines and diminuendo.

The various irregularities of metric design demonstrate Goethe's mastery over a complex poetic shape, as the complexities of poetic meter create a metaphor for the poem's theme of the German Romantic wanderer. The relative stability and regularity of lines 1 and 2 are not heard again in the poem until line 8. From the point of view of form, this return to the opening stability at the poem's conclusion has two formal functions: first, formal reprise in any temporal work of art is crucial; and second, with this particular poem, the stability of the beginning and ending frame the poem's unsettled middle section, which creates the effect of starting, journeying, and arriving—a rhythmic depiction of the poem's actual poetic progression.

Exercises

Using the poems suggested, the following exercises test your ability to analyze poetry from a number of perspectives. Remember to read the German aloud, especially before analyzing the meter, use of vowels, and end-rhyme schemes.

1. "An den Schlaf" (Mörike)
2. "Blumengruß" (Goethe)
3. "Der Tod, das ist die kühle Nacht" (Heine)
4. "Einsamkeit" (Goethe)
5. "Er ist's" (Mörike)
6. "Leise zieht durch mein Gemüt" (Heine)
7. "Meeres Stille" (Goethe)
8. "Mondenschein" (Heine)
9. "Nachtzauber" (Eichendorff)
10. "Verschwiegene Liebe" (Eichendorff)
11. "Wanderers Nachtlied II" (Goethe)
12. Wiegenlied" (*Des Knaben Wunderhorn*) (Brentano and Von Arnim)

Exercise 2.1: Use of poetic imagery

Trace the use of poetic imagery (image, symbol, metaphor, simile) in five poems. Give the two levels of meaning: the literal meaning conveyed in images and the deeper meaning being so symbolized (for example, poems 1, 3, 5, 6, 9, 10).

Exercise 2.2: Use of word sounds

Analyze five poems for their use of word sounds, especially vowels. In addition to noting all use of vowels for shades of darkness and lightness, indicate how vowel usage creates assonance and how consonant repetition creates alliteration. State how all uses of word sounds help convey the poem's content (poems 1, 3, 4, 5, 6, 7, 8, 11).

Exercise 2.3: Poetic progression and Stimmung

Trace the poetic progression and determine the *Stimmung* for five poems. In a few sentences, indicate how knowledge of these factors might change your initial poetic interpretation (poems 2, 3, 7, 10, 11).

Exercise 2.4: Use of irony and personification

Find five instances of irony and personification and show how these devices are used in the poetry (poems 1, 3–6).

Exercise 2.5: Poetic meter

Using five poems, notate the scansion beneath each line of poetry, including separation of the lines into feet. Indicate the prevailing meter, any metric substitutions, the pattern of feet per line, and the pattern of line endings (weak/strong) (poems 1, 3, 5, 10, 12).

Exercise 2.6: Rhyming patterns

Choose five poems that use interesting patterns of end-rhyme (i.e., not merely rhyme alternation) and state how the end-rhyme pattern affects the poem's rhythm and flow. Then find five additional instances of interior rhyme, including use of assonances. Indicate how the use of rhyme contributes to portrayal of poetic content (poems 3, 5, 8–10, 12).

Samples of German Romantic Poetry

1. "An den Schlaf" (Mörike)

"To Sleep"[46]

Schlaf! süßer Schlaf! obwohle dem
    Tod wie du nichts
    gleicht,
Auf diesem Lager doch
    willkommen heiss ich dich!
Denn ohne Leben so, wie lieblich
    lebt es sich!
So weit vom Sterben, ach, wie
    stirbt es sich so leicht!

Sleep! sweet sleep, although
    death you as nothing else
    resemble,
upon this couch still
    welcome declare I you!
For without life thus, how
    sweet is living!
So far from dying, oh, how
    dying is so easy!

2. "Blumengruß" (Goethe)

"Flower Greeting"[47]

Der Strauß, den ich
    gepflücket,
Grüße dich vieltausendmal!

(May) the bouquet I have
    plucked,
Greet you many thousands of
    times!

Ich habe mich oft gebücket,
Ach, wohl eintausendmal,
Und ihn ans Herz gedrücket
Wie hunderttausendmal!

I have often bent,
Ah, at least a thousand times,
And it to my heart pressed
As if a hundred thousand times!

3. "Der Tod, das ist die kühle
Nacht" (Heine)

"Death (that) Is the Cool Night"[48]

Der Tod, das ist die kühle Nacht,
Das Leben ist der schwüle Tag.
Es dunkelt schon, mich schläfert,
Der Tag hat mich müd gemacht.
Über mein Bett erhebt sich ein
Baum,
Drin singt die junge
Nachtigall;
Sie singt von lauter Liebe,
Ich hör es, ich hör es sogar im
Traum.

Death is the cool night,
Life is the sultry day.
Falls Dusk already, I am drowsy,
The day has me tired made.
Over my bed rises a tree,

In which sings the young
nightingale;
She sings solely of love,
I hear it, I hear it even in
dreams.

4. "Einsamkeit" (Goethe)

."Solitude"[49]

Die ihr Felsen und Bäume
bewohnt, o heilsame Nymphen,
Gebet jeglichem gern, was er im
stillen begehrt!
Schaffet dem Traurigen Trost, dem
Zweifelhaften Belehrung
Und dem Liebenden gönnt, das
ihm begegne sein Glück.
Denn euch gaben die Götter, was
sie den Menschen versagten,
Jeglichem, der euch vertraut,
tröstlich und hilfreich zu sein.

You who rocks and trees
inhabit, o healing nymphs,
Give to each gladly what he
silently desires!
Bring to the sad, solace, to the
uncertain, counsel,
And to the lover grant, that
he meet his happiness.
For to you gave the gods what
they to men denied:
To each who trust you,
comforting and helpful to be.

5. "Er ist's" (Mörike)

"(Spring) It Is"[50]

Frühling läßt sein blaues Band
Wieder flattern durch die Lüfte;
Süße, wohlbekannte Düfte
Streifen ahnungsvoll
das Land.

Spring lets its blue ribbon
Once more flutter in the breeze;
Sweet, familiar fragrances
Drift full of expectancy through
the land.

Veilchen träumen schon,
Wollen balde kommen.
Horch, von fern ein leiser
Harfenton!

Violets dream already,
Want to soon arrive.
Hark, from afar a soft
harptone!

Frühling, ja du bists!	Spring, yes you it is!
Dich hab ich vernommen!	You have I heard!

6. "Leise zieht durch mein Gemüt" (Heine)   "Gently Moves through my Soul"[51]

Leise zieht durch mein Gemüt	Gently moves through my soul
Liebliches Geläute.	Sweet bells' ringing.
Klinge, kleines Frühlingslied,	Sound, tiny song of spring,
Kling hinaus ins Weite.	Sound out far and wide.
Kling hinaus, bis an das Haus,	Sound out as far as the house
Wo die Blumen sprießen.	Where the flowers bloom.
Wenn du eine Rose schaust,	Should you a rose see,
Sag, ich laß' sie grüßen.	Say (that) I send to it greeting.

7. "Meeres Stille" (Goethe)   "Sea Calm"[52]

Tiefe Stille herrscht im Wasser	Deep calm rules the water,
Ohne Regung ruht das Meer,	Without motion rests the sea,
Und bekümmert sieht der Schiffer	And troubled sees the sailor
Glatte Fläche rings umher.	Smooth levelness all around.
Keine Luft von keiner Seite!	No wind from any quarter!
Todesstille fürchterlich!	Deadly calm dreadful!
In der ungeheuern Weite	In the vast expanse
Reget keine Welle sich.	Stirs no wave.

8. "Mondenschein" (Heine)   "Moonlight"[53]

Nacht liegt auf den fremden Wegen,	Night lies on the unfamiliar ways,
Krankes Herz und müde Glieder;—	Sick heart and tired limbs;—
Ach, da fließt, wie stiller Segen,	Ah, there streams as a silent blessing,
Süßer Mond, dein Licht hernieder.	Sweet moon, your light descending.
Süßer Mond, mit deinen Strahlen	Sweet moon, with your beams
Scheuchest du das nächt'ge Grauen;	Drive you away night's horror;
Es zerrinnen meine Qualen,	Vanish my torments,
Und die Augen übertauen.	And my eyes melt from falling tears.

9. "Nachtzauber" (Eichendorff)   "Night Magic"[54]

Hörst du nicht die Quellen gehen	Hear you not the brooks running
Zwischen Stein und Blumen weit	Amongst stones and flowers afar
Nach den stillen Waldesseen,	Toward silent forest lakes,

Wo die Marmorbilder stehen,
In der schönen Einsamkeit?
Von der Bergen sacht
   hernieder,
Weckend die uralten Lieder,
Steigt die wunderbare Nacht,
Und die Gründe glänzen wieder,
Wie du's oft im Traum gedacht.

Kennst die Blume du, entsprossen
In dem mondbeglänzten Grund?
Aus der Knospe, halb erschlossen,
Junge Glieder blühend sprossen,
Weiße Arme, roter Mund,
Und die Nachtigallen schlagen,
Und rings hebt es an zu klagen,
Ach, for Liebe todeswund,
Von versunknen schönen Tagen—
Komm, o komm zum stillen
   Grund!

Where the marble statues stand,
In fair solitude?
From the mountains softly
   descends,
Stirring the old songs,
Rises the wondrous night
And the valleys gleam again,
As you often in dreams imagined.

Know the flower you, blossomed
In the moonlit valley?
Out from its bud half-open,
Young limbs have blossomed,
White arms, red mouth,
And nightingales warble,
And all around is raised a lament,
Ah, by love wounded mortally,
Of lost lovely days—
come, oh come to the silent
   valley!

10. "Verschwiegene Liebe"
   (Eichendorff)

"Silent Love"[55]

Über Wipfel und Saaten
In den Glanz hinein—
Wer mag sie erraten,
Wer holte sie ein?
Gedanken sich wiegen,
Die Nacht ist verschwiegen,
Gedanken sind frei.

Errät es nur eine,
Wer an sie gedacht
Beim Rauschen der Haine,
Wenn niemand mehr wacht
Als die Wolken, die fliegen—
Mein Lieb ist verschwiegen
Und schön wie die Nacht.

Over treetops and grain fields
Into the gleam—
Who may them guess,
Who retrieve them?
Thoughts sway,
The night is silent,
Thoughts are free.

May guess only one
Who of her has thought
By the murmur of the woods,
When no one more watches
Like the clouds that soar—
My love is silent
And beautiful as the night.

11. "Wanderers Nachtlied II"
   (Goethe)

"Wanderer's Nightsong II"[56]

Der du von dem Himmel bist,
Alles Leid und Schmerzen stillest,
Den, der doppelt elend ist,
Doppelt mit Erquickung füllest,

You who from heaven are,
(who) all pain and sorrow ease,
By whom the doubly wretched is,
Doubly with fresh vigor filled,

Ach, ich bin des Treibens müde!	Ah, I am of restlessness tired!
Was soll all der Schmerz und Lust?	What is all this pain and joy?
Süßer Friede,	Sweet peace,
Komm, ach, komm in meine Brust!	Come, ah come into my breast!

12. "Wiegenlied"   "Cradle Song"[57]
    (Des Knaben Wunderhorn)
    (Brentano and Von Arnim)

Guten Abend, gut Nacht,	Good night, good night,
Mit Rosen bedacht,	with roses covered,
Mit Näglein besteckt,	with carnations adorned,
Schlupf unter die Deck:	slip under your quilt:
Morgen früh, wenn Gott will,	by morning early, if God wills,
Wirst du wieder geweckt.	will you again be awakened.
Guten Abend, gut Nacht,	Good night, good night,
Von Englein bewacht,	with angels keeping watch,
Die zeigen im Traum	they show (you) in dreams
Dir Christkindleins Baum:	the Christ-child's tree:
Schlaf nun selig und süß,	Sleep now happy and sweet,
Schau im Traum's Paradies.	see in your dreams Heaven.

Addendum for Poetry Analysis

These poems may be used for additional practice:

1. "Ablösung im Sommer" (*Des Knaben Wunderhorn*)
   (Brentano and Von Arnim)

2. "An meinen großen Schmerzen" (Heine)

3. "Beherzigung" (Goethe)

4. "Der König bei der Krönung" (Mörike)

5. "Das verlassene Mägdlein" (Mörike)

6. "Ein Sonett" (seventeenth century, trans. Herder)

7. "Geheimes" (Goethe)

8. "Genialisch Treiben" (Goethe)

9. "Gottes Segen" (Eichendorff)

10. "Lehn' deine Wang' " (Heine)

Part II
The Language of the Performer

CHAPTER THREE

Texture

The term TEXTURE refers to the relative density or thickness (as opposed to sparseness or thinness) of a piece. Horizontal or linear density involves how frequently notes or rhythms occur, whether sounds are separated or adjacent, and how far apart pitches are from one another; vertical density involves how many notes are sounding at the same time, including how many *different* pitches occur simultaneously. We begin by examining textural "norms" in *Lieder*, both within the vocal line and in the more complex accompaniment. We then explore textural variations, those given or hinted at by the composer and those which result from a performer's personal decision. Certain textures are used to illuminate the drama of the text, and attention to textural concerns helps the performer to convey the nuances of the poetry. For example, a singer might approach two songs by Brahms very differently. "Vergebliches Ständchen" might be sung with a slender, flexible sound, or vocal color, to convey more precisely the dialogue between the conflicted lovers, while "Sapphische Ode" might be sung with great richness and thickness of tone as a means of conveying that poem's emotional intensity. A pianist, meanwhile, might decide to play Schubert's "Ständchen" with little or no pedal, but pedal heavily in Schubert's "Die Krähe," the variation in pedal effect conveying, once again, different aspects of the poetry. Each decision about tone or sound density adds an interpretive nuance to the vocal line or the accompaniment, which in turn contributes to the composer's expression of the poetic text.

Vocal Styles

In general, the *Lied*'s vocal line is characterized by some of the following variables:

1. Only one note per syllable vs. several notes per syllable

2. Repeated notes (several syllables sung in succession on one pitch) in contrast to a continually rising and falling vocal line

3. Small intervals vs. large ones

4. Notes sung smoothly and closely together (legato-style singing), or more separated and "bouncy" (parlando-style singing)

5. Articulation markings that make pitches distinct (e.g., STACCATO, stress or accent markings), as opposed to slurs connecting two or more pitches.

These diverse vocal characteristics usually fall into one of four different vocal styles, each of which represents a different way to enunciate (syllabic vs. florid) and articulate (parlando vs. legato) the words of the poetry. In the syllabic and parlando styles, words and syllables are emphasized individually, while in the florid and legato styles, words are grouped together within more complex vocal gestures. These styles are easiest to understand in terms of contrasts, and we begin with the difference between syllabic and florid text settings.

Syllabic vs. Florid Text Settings

In the SYLLABIC style, each syllable is sung on one pitch, a technique, popular with Schubert's predecessors such as Zelter, that presents the text with clarity and simplicity. Two exclusively syllabic Schubert *Lieder* illustrate: "Lied eines Schiffers an die Dioskuren," D. 360, and "Der Leiermann," D. 911, no. 24. For each song, read the poem aloud and sing the vocal line. In "Lied eines Schiffers" ("Sailor's Song to the Dioscuri"), the simple presentation of the text demonstrates the straightforward faith of the sailor-narrator and his modesty in the face of his god.[1] "Der Leiermann" ("The Organ Grinder") demonstrates a vastly different effect with this style. The steady eighth-note progress of the text underlines the poignancy of the organ-grinder's dire circumstances, the bitter cold of the atmosphere, and even, in some poetic interpretations, the narrator's insanity.

The syllabic style should not be confused with the RECITATIVE style from the opera repertory, where the singer enjoys considerable rhythmic freedom in singing both words and phrases. Even though in "Der Leiermann" the texture of the vocal line moving over sustained chords looks similar to recitative passages, the singer should refrain from taking rhythmic liberties and emphasize the poetic pathos through a rigid rhythmic regularity. This interpretation is completely at odds with the recitative tradition, and in general, most *Lied* composers exercise more rhythmic control over their material than occurs in opera recitative sections.[2]

The opposite of syllabic style is not recitative, but rather is the FLORID style, where some syllables are stretched out over two or more pitches. Schubert's "Wohin?" D. 795, no. 2, and "Ave Maria," D. 839, demonstrate; again read the poems aloud and sing the vocal phrases. In "Wohin?" DUPLETS, or groups of two notes, set poetic syllables throughout. In phrase 1, the arch of the line begins and ends with duplets; phrase 2 then starts with a duplet on "wohl" and ends with a particularly legato setting of "Felsen-." These figures recur throughout the *Lied*, with an especially ebullient setting of "und immer heller" ("and ever clearer") in mm. 32–33, where the vocal activity depicts both the babbling brook and the poet's eager response to the brook's animation. Schubert's famous "Ave Maria" presents a more elaborate example of florid style; the MORDENTS and trills that embellish the scalar figurations capture both the intensity of the poet and the religious fervor that permeates the text.[3]

As a general rule, *Lied* composers most frequently employ a mixture of syllabic and florid styles, where most of a setting is syllabic, and duplets and more elaborate figures punctuate the texture to emphasize a word or phrase. The richness and complexity of this *mixture* of styles is, in fact, *the* characteristic vocal texture of the German Romantic *Lied*.

Legato and Parlando Vocal Lines

The two other vocal styles, LEGATO and PARLANDO, also provide a clear contrast in vocal expression. In legato singing, the notes are connected as smoothly as possible, with the tone from one syllable meeting seamlessly that of another. In contrast, the syllables in the more buoyant parlando style are more disconnected from one another, and therefore are often more obviously stressed.

While sometimes a performer may prefer one style over another, composers suggest their own stylistic choices in their notation. Consider, for example, whether Schubert suggests legato or parlando styles in "Wohin?" and "Ave Maria." Even though the numerous duplets in "Wohin?" suggest a legato presentation, the use of equal note values and repeated notes within a rapid pace usually indicates a lighter, more parlando singing style. "Ave Maria," in contrast, exhibits many legato style characteristics, where the vocal line combines:

1. A slow tempo
2. Long note values on some syllables
3. Florid setting of other syllables
4. Short, unstressed, connecting notes in a melodic line that emphasize musical effects over word enunciation

Two well-known *Lieder* by Wolf, "Ich hab' in Penna" and "Lebe wohl" also demonstrate the contrast between legato and parlando styles. In "Ich hab' in Penna," the series of short notes within the rapid-tempo syllabic setting illustrate the impertinent text in a vigorous, typically parlando manner. In "Lebe wohl," the alternation of shorter and longer note values, the mixture of large and small intervals, the short phrases in slow tempo, and the intense extremes of dynamics all suggest a more sustained and intense legato vocal style.

Accompanimental Styles

The accompanist supports the singer's line with harmonic progression and other forms of melody, all within several different kinds of textures. The accompaniment also has several typical characteristics, includings:

1. Simple chords

2. Simple chords broken into repeated rhythmic figures

3. Contrapuntal textures with various lines moving along with or against each other

4. A consistent texture throughout or shifts in texture

5. Various markings of articulation that indicate the grouping or separation of notes, and their relative lengths

Accompanimental texture thus combines two different musical ideas: harmonic presentation, including many different kinds of chordal figuration, and melodic presentation, including doubling of the vocal melody and use of countermelodies. This basic accompanimental combination of harmony and melody falls into three traditional categories: (1) melody and accompaniment, (2) HOMOPHONY (or homorhythm), and (3) contrapuntal texture. Each of these general types conveys the poetry differently and each supports the vocal line with different textures.

The variety and range of accompanimental textures spans a continuum of relationships between piano accompaniment and vocal line that ranges from simplest to most complex. The simplest accompanimental texture is the homophonic or chordal texture, where the accompaniment is clearly subservient to the vocal line and provides little more than the harmonic foundation; Schubert's "Meeres Stille" is a classic example of this type. A slightly more animated texture energizes the supporting harmonic progression with a more complicated rhythmic figuration; the opening of Schumann's "In der Fremde" uses sixteenth-note arpeggiation for such an effect, as do the various figurations in Schubert's "Wohin?"[4]

A more complex relationship between vocal line and accompaniment occurs when the accompaniment has a more dominant melodic component. Again there is a range of possibilities. In the simplest case, the piano's right hand (RH) doubles the vocal line, while in more complex instances, the piano offers a countermelody to the vocal line. The technique of doubling the vocal line in the piano accompaniment is demonstrated clearly by two Schumann songs: "Seit ich ihn gesehen" and "In der Fremde." In "Seit ich ihn gesehen," the top note of the piano chords doubles the voice until the third beat of m. 9; at that point, the singer's notes are doubled by the piano's interior voices, a doubling change that has a powerful impact. This contrasts with "In der Fremde," where, beginning in m. 10, the piano RH presents a countermelody that first contrasts with the vocal line in mm. 10–11, wrestles with it for metric clarity in mm. 12–13, and finally doubles the vocal line in mm. 14ff.

The combination of vocal and accompanimental melodies in *Lieder* brings us to the most complex accompanimental texture: the contrapuntal style where the accompaniment has significant melodic independence from the vocal line, including use of several lines of counterpoint within the accompaniment itself. Two Wolf *Lieder* exemplify different contrapuntal textures. In "Ich hab' in Penna," the rhythmically repeated thirds within the harmonic underpinning are accompanied by melodic phrases and punctuations in the piano that alternate with vocal phrases in a rich, complex texture. This contrapuntal weaving of lines also occurs in Wolf's "Mir ward gesagt," where the bass line pulls away from the more stationary vocal line. This makes a wonderful metaphor for the dramatic idea of the poem, where the lover (in the accompaniment) leaves the distressed narrator (in the vocal line) and travels "to a distant place."

An even more elaborate counterpoint occurs in our final example, Wolf's "Lebe wohl," where vocal and instrumental phrases weave in and out, joining, separating, answering one another, sometimes in four-part harmony and sometimes in an even thicker texture. The poem describes the obsession of a poet who is rejected by a seemingly indifferent lover. The poet describes the painful rejection in stanza 1, and then broods over the unbearable pain of loss in stanza 2. The singer's line is dramatically disjunct and chromatic, and the pianist plays a number of different kinds of phrases, some that accompany the singer, some that double the vocal line but add additional countermelodies, some that contrast the vocal line contrapuntally with different melodies in distinct rhythms and textures. The dramatic counterpoint between vocal line and accompaniment richly depicts the anguished poet, as various changes in the accompaniment represent different aspects of the poet's inner turmoil. In this and similar songs, the piano part can almost stand alone, as an independent, musically satisfying work that conveys the poetic progression without the text even being articulated by the vocal line.

Charles Rosen, in *The Romantic Generation,* offers many compelling insights into the relationship of vocal line and piano accompaniment. His most important example is Schumann, whose *Lieder* create a new concept of vocal line and ensemble relationship. According to Rosen, Schumann's "originality . . . radically transforms the traditional relationship of song to accompaniment . . . [Eschewing] the principle [of] the independence of the vocal melody [as] a coherent and satisfying whole in itself even when the prelude, postludes, and echoes are elaborate . . . [Schumann's greatest innovation is] . . . the incomplete destruction of the independence of the vocal form. . . . [the vocal line's] independence is not totally suppressed; Schumann is able to . . . sometimes oppose voice and instrument, to identify them at other moments and finally to have them realize the same musical line, but out of phase with each other."[5]

Models for Study of Texture

We conclude this overview of the role of texture in *Lieder* by posing questions of textural interpretation in five well-known songs: a somewhat detailed comparison of Schubert's "Wanderers Nachtlied I," D. 768, with Schumann's "Seit ich ihn gesehen," op. 42, no. 1, and briefer examinations of three individual masterpieces: Schubert's "Meeres Stille," D. 216, and "Litanei," D. 343, and Brahms's "Ständchen," op. 106, no. 1. In each case, we suggest ways to *think* about texture, either in the context of textural comparisons or by asking—but not necessarily answering—questions about textural usage and how texture conveys the poetic text. In this way, we convey an *approach* to understanding texture and the relationship of texture to poetry that should assist the singer, the pianist, and the ensemble throughout their performance careers. In all cases, read the poetry carefully and perform or listen to the song thoughtfully, paying careful attention to the smallest details of notation.

Comparison of the vocal and accompanimental textures in Schubert's "Wanderers Nachtlied I" and Schumann's "Seit ich ihn gesehen" is very revealing; the two settings initially seem quite similar in texture, but in fact use different textural subtleties to set altogether different poetic ideas. Schubert's "Wanderers Nachtlied I" begins with a piano introduction. The essentially four-part texture of mm. 1–2 creates a serious, somber, slow-paced mood that is both reminiscent of religious chorales and expressive of a poetic richness and warmth. This thick homophonic texture in the piano's dark register thus anticipates the poet's serious contemplation of the comfort of religious salvation through peaceful death. This texture continues when the voice enters in m. 3. However, several small changes in texture create subtle motion within the essentially peaceful phrase: first, the accompaniment's *alto* voice, rather than the soprano, doubles the vocal line; and second, the use of contrary motion within the accompanimental chorale creates a contrapuntal richness within the ongoing poetic contemplation. After six beats of being cradled *within* the piano chords, the doubling of the voice moves up to the soprano position; this subtle but dramatic textural change marks the movement in the text: "allen Wipfeln spürest du kaum" ("every tree-top you feel scarce [a breath]").

Midway through the song, changes in poetic imagery prompt Schubert to alter both piano accompaniment and vocal line. The piano texture changes halfway through m. 5, as the chordal style of the opening is replaced by 3½ bars of rocking sixteenth notes, and the rhythmic figuration of the four-part harmony successfully evokes the slight but significant motion of the trees. A similar shift in vocal color then occurs in mm. 7–8, where most of the syllables are sung as duplets and the line becomes more limpid and mellifluous.[6]

After the middle section's increased complexity, Schubert concludes the song with a return to the opening homophonic style. However, the texture again has been altered significantly. The vocal line and accompaniment move several times in contrary motion and the voice is no longer doubled in the piano. And, because the piano sustains many notes, the texture thins out somewhat and the song's vertical sonorities are both more complex and, at the same time, slightly thinner and less rich. All of this results in a texture of increased transparency that reflects the poet's spiritual transcendence.

The subtleties of texture in this song pose interesting interpretive challenges to performers. While at the outset the vocal line's simplicity displays characteristics of parlando singing, the syllabic setting, use of smaller intervals and repeated notes, and the slow tempo might suggest a more legato manner. Weighing these competing indications, a singer might well opt for a straightforward, simple singing line, neither as choppy and fragmented as parlando nor as connected as legato.

Another interpretive challenge arises from textural changes made to reflect the poetic progression of three atmospheres or moods: (1) an opening nocturnal solemnity and seriousness, mm. 1–5½; (2) musical depiction of gentle life forces (motion of trees and small birds) that move the poet, mm. 5½–8; and (3) spiritual solemnity and serenity that accompany the poetic resolution, mm. 9–end. The musical shifts from one poetic state and musical texture to the next must be smooth, even seamless, just as the poetic progression is gradual and uninterrupted.

Schumann's "Seit ich ihn gesehen" initially shows many similarities to the textural usage in "Wanderers Nachtlied I": homophonic motion, four-part chordal accompaniment, extensive accompanimental doubling of the vocal line, mostly syllabic setting of the text, and a piano introduction and postlude presenting material from the first vocal statement. On closer examination, however, many details of textural articulation demonstrate different textural usage. The first difference is Schumann's consistent use of the initial texture, in contrast to Schubert's textural changes throughout the song. Schumann's consistent, essentially four-part homophony is, however, balanced by a variety of articulations. For example, the musical changes in mm. 6–16 (and again mm. 23–32) pose the performance question of whether to use the legato or parlando style. Once again the song suggests the possibility of both, and the singer and pianist must decide how much connection or separation to use.

The decision of legato vs. parlando is complicated by Schumann's complex uses of rests, staccato markings, and slurs. For example, in mm. 1–3, the chords in the piano are all separated from one another, either by rests or by staccato markings, and these bars are followed by five beats with no staccato markings or rests at all. The separated chords of m. 5 are then followed by the remainder of the first verse (mm. 6–16) with no rests or staccato marks. The second strophe proceeds in a similar fashion and the singer must decide whether or not to parallel the piano articulation: sing parlando in mm. 2, 3, 5, 18, 19, and 21, and then sing legato for the rest of the *Lied*.

The question of legato vs. parlando for both singer and pianist is not clarified by the slur markings in the piano part (mm. 1–3, 5, 17–19, 21, and 33–34) that correspond to those sections with separated chords. Are the chords separated or connected? Does the composer indicate varying degrees of separateness?[7] While we cannot detail the complexities of Schumann's notational nuances, the overall concern about legato vs. parlando style for both singer and pianist remains a vivid reminder of the poem's central poetic idea: the dreamlike state and "love blindness" of the young girl.

Within the complexities of Schumann's notation, performers of "Seit ich ihn gesehen" can use the following guidelines: (1) mm. 1, 2, 3 (beat 1), and 5 are less legato in both voice and piano than the rest of the song; (2) the remainder of the song is to be performed legato; (3) m. 10 with its upbeat is somewhat less legato in the piano than in the voice, and less legato than the piano a bar earlier; and finally, (4) mm. 11–14 are the most legato, with the smoothest and most intense connection between notes of both the piano and the vocal line.

Two additional aspects of the song's texture are noteworthy here. First, the setting of the latter half of each stanza is particularly effective because: (1) the piano stays in a low, rich register; (2) the vocal line moves through its widest intervals, a major seventh and a major sixth, while singing only *one* syllable: "tief" ("deep"); and (3) the notes of the piano part are tied together through a number of slurs and overlapping held notes, creating a rich texture of dissonance and resolution.

Other significant textural factors for the ensemble are that the singer's pitches are always doubled by the piano, now above, now below, sometimes clear and sometimes hidden, and consistently that the piano four- or five-part texture uses, the latter achieved by simple vertical doubling of chord tones. These textural consistencies balance the notational complexities and enable performers to convey a general feeling of textural continuity despite the nuances of touch just detailed.

Turning now to consideration of texture in other settings, we dramatize the importance of texture by posing a series of rhetorical questions, starting with a song of seemingly the simplest accompanimental texture, Schubert's "Meeres Stille." In preparing this song for performance, the singer and pianist will want to ask themselves the following: (1) For what poetic reasons might Schubert have chosen a steady chordal accompaniment? (2) Why did he choose to roll the chords? (3) Why does the pace never vary? (4) Why did he write the small, more rapid vocal MELISMAS in mm. 7 and 11?[8] (5) Why are there no dynamic indications through most of the song? Why is there a CRESCENDO in mm. 26–27? (6) Does this mean that there is no variation in dynamics until then? If so, why? (7) Does the piano texture change anywhere? And, finally, (8) Is the vocal line to be sung more parlando or more legato, and what is your reasoning?

As you can see, questions of texture invariably touch upon other important issues such as tempo and dynamics, issues we will discuss more fully in Chapters Four and Five. This continues to be so in Schubert's "Litanei," where the following questions should be posed: (1) What indications suggest that this vocal style is most probably legato? (2) What indications of legato style are suggested in the piano part? (3) Is there any doubling of the vocal line in the piano? Is there any near-doubling (that is, similar contour)? (4) How many different articulations are there in the piano part? (5) How many rests are there in the vocal line? How often will the singer probably have to breathe? How can the singer take time to breathe? (6) How many rests are there in the piano part? (7) What is the function of the top line in the piano, mm. 11–13? And (8) What in the text does Schubert convey by his choice of vocal *and* accompaniment style?

Our final example of textural queries, Brahms's "Ständchen," employs texture differently from Schubert's characteristic usage, and most of the questions about "Ständchen" arise from Brahms's notation:[9] (1) In the piano introduction, how many different articulations are used and how are they notated? (2) Does the number of voices change within this introduction? (3) Do the dynamics change from one articulation to the next? (4) In mm. 9 and 10, are the phrases articulated the same way in voice and piano? (5) Throughout the first verse, what is the difference in the notation of the RH and left hand (LH) figures? Does this denote a difference in texture? (6) How does the notation in the first interlude (mm. 13–14) differ from similar figures in the introduction? (7) Is there any precedence for the voice and top line of the piano to double each other in the second strophe? (8) How many different articulations are indicated in the accompaniment of the second strophe? Does it sound as if the voice should vary its articulation similarly? (9) In mm. 13–15, 19, and 21, what differences in articulation occur between RH and LH? How and where is the RH legato? (10) For what dramatic effect does Brahms start the arpeggiated figure in m. 22? What is its relation to the rolled chords in measures 18 and 20? (11) When the second interlude (mm. 24–27) parallels mm. 1–4, what is the same, and what is new? (12) Are there any differences in inflection between verse 3 and verse 1? (13) How many different articulations are indicated in the coda (mm. 36–39)? And finally, (14) which musical figures might denote the "singing" suggested by the poem's mention of a flute, violin, and zither?

The questions posed above demonstrate the rich musical context for texture in *Lieder* and the importance of considering the poetic text in making interpretive decisions about texture and related musical issues. The chapters that follow about temporality, dynamics, timbre, and musical accent and stress all build on the foundation of musical texture and reflect the musical means of depicting the poetry being set.

Exercises

All the exercises in Part II, Chapters Three to Five, utilize the repertory listed below; in some cases, try to use a variety of different *Lieder,* and in others, use the same songs for more than one exercise.

Exercise 3.1: Vocal Styles

Determine the predominant vocal style—legato, parlando, florid, syllabic—of five *Lieder,* using the following questions as a guide:

1. Does the vocal style remain constant?
2. If it changes, where and why (look at the text)?
3. Why did the composer choose the particular style(s) used?

Exercise 3.2: Acccompanimental Textures

Decide what accompanimental texture is most prevalent in five *Lieder:* simple chords, chordal figuration, melody plus accompaniment, homophony, counterpoint; if the texture changes, what effect does the composer seek?

Repertory for Exercises in Chapters Three to Five

"Allerseelen"	"Lebe wohl"
"Auch kleine Dinge"	"Lied eines Schiffers"
"Ave Maria"	"Litanei"
"Der Leiermann"	"Meeres Stille"
"Der Lindenbaum"	"Mein Liebster singt"
"Der Neugierige"	"Mir ward gesagt"
"Die Mainacht"	"Mondnacht"
"Die Forelle"	"Morgen!"
"Die Rose, Die Lilie"	"Nähe des Geliebten"
"Erlkönig"	"Seit ich ihn gesehen"
"Gesang Weylas"	"Ständchen (Der Mond steht)"
"Gretchen am Spinnrade"	"Ständchen (Mach auf, doch leise)"
"Ich hab' im Traum geweinet"	"Vergebliches Ständchen"
"Ich hab' in Penna"	"Wanderers Nachtlied I"
"Im Rhein, im heiligen Strome"	"Widmung"
"In dem Schatten"	"Wie Melodien zieht es mir"
"In der Fremde"	"Wohin?"

CHAPTER FOUR

Temporality

Our examination of TEMPORALITY explores how long things last, both the lengths of notes and their relative durations as suggested by notation, and the speed at which something is performed, as determined by consideration of TEMPO. In both cases, the composer's indications may be either straightforward and precise or vague and open to interpretation. We will also consider those *Lieder* that involve significant changes in temporality, where the composer alters a musical pace in response to shifts in poetic progression. This chapter begins a discussion of temporality that continues in Chapters Five and Eight; together the three chapters provide performers with all the tools necessary to understand how music is organized and shaped in order to flow a particular way through time.[1]

Nuances of Notation

Composers indicate their concept of a song's pacing and timing through notation and tempo indications. This topic is difficult at best; while performers can guide their tempo choices by notational conventions, such as the time signature, the notation of an underlying pulse, adherence to rhythmic and metric norms, and use of phrase slurs, these factors do not ensure understanding of the composer's full temporal intent. In addition, two other factors of performance practice influence musical pace: first, performers choose a slower or faster tempo according to their own interpretation of a composer's general tempo indication, and second, performers use a certain amount of RUBATO, where some notes are held a fraction longer than others, as an essential interpretive agent in most nineteenth-century music. Given these subjective performance tendencies, we will not offer specific rules or guidelines about the meaning of a composer's notations; rather, we will suggest ways to *think about* how such notation provides clues about temporality, and how a composer's temporality conveys the poetic text.

We preface our examination of tempo considerations with a caution about three terms that are often used in talking about certain articulations within a given tempo: "accent," "stress," and "agogic accent." These terms will be defined more precisely in Chapter Eight, in the section "Rhythmic, Metric and Phrase Norms," but it is important to realize here that a potential confusion exists in using this terminology when discussing performance and analysis. Essentially the problem is that performers use these terms differently from theorists, and there is no way to speak of accents, stresses, and agogic accents that has the same meaning within the languages of both performers and theorists. We thus clarify the different meanings of these terms for the two groups, noting that the meanings can remain distinct as long as the context is clearly understood.

In general, music theorists debate how to use the terms *accent* and *stress*, and in this book we adopt only one set of several possible definitions. The terms ACCENT and STRESS generally are used in connection with pitch emphasis through metric or rhythmic devices. Accent means emphasis through normal metric emphasis or through unusual forms of rhythmic emphasis, and stress is used more generically as a noun or verb that means emphasis. Thus we can use both terms in describing an accent: accent occurs as a normal metric stress on the downbeat. The term AGOGIC ACCENT is a rhythmic device where a composer emphasizes a pitch by either placing it on a normally weak beat (that is, creating a syncopation) or sustaining it for a relatively long duration, or both. In this way, agogic accent is a musical stress that occurs when a long note occurs and when this long note begins on a weak beat.

To the performer, on the other hand, the terms *accent* and *stress* relate to the concept of attack; an accent is a strong attack and a stress is a softer attack. And the term *agogic accent* relates not to emphasis through unusual metric placement and longer duration, but rather to rubato—a slight hesitation or delay used to emphasize a given pitch.

While the dramatic difference in meanings of these important terms may seem great, the various definitions occur for the most part within the clear contexts of either theoretical/analytical discourse or discussions of performance issues. Where a possibility of confusion arises in a given situation, it is necessary only to state clearly which terminology is being used, for example, "the agogic accent according to the theoretical meaning" or "the accent as performers use the term."[2]

Two songs by Schumann, the seemingly simple "Die Rose, die Lilie, die Taube" from *Dichterliebe,* and the complex setting of Rückert's "Widmung," help dramatize the performer's need to interpret Schumann's notation carefully. The fast-paced, simpler "Die Rose, die Lilie," for example, is over quickly, and it is easy for the pianist to overlook some of the notation's fine tuning. The rich variety in the accompaniment is particularly surprising, since the vocal line has very little articulation and is virtually without rests, the only pause in the vocal line being the short rest in m. 5. This absence of breathing spaces has prompted many singers to take "Die Rose, die Lilie" at a breakneck tempo so that they can perform the entire song in one breath. As we will see, this unduly fast speed results in a neglect of the poetry that is most unfortunate; this song sets a poem full of rhyming devices, and it is careless to rush through the words and sounds too quickly.

The rich detail and variation in the piano accompaniment can be seen with a quick glance at the page. Closer examination reveals that the RH part has three distinct articulations: (1) unmarked separated sixteenths on the offbeat throughout the *Lied;* (2) staccato markings under slurs (compare with Schumann's setting of "Seit ich ihn gesehen") in mm. 17–20; and (3) sustained chords in mm. 16 and 21. The LH part receives even greater attention: (1) unmarked sixteenths on the beat have sixteenth rests in between; (2) the bass line changes to eighth notes in m. 9, but without written eighth-note connecting bars; and (3) the sixteenth rests never return in the left hand. In addition to all this, the bass eighth notes in mm. 10, 11, 17, and 18 are connected by slurs, but the eighths in mm. 17 and 18 are connected by bars.[3] And finally, the last two chords are written as eighths with staccato marks: Are these longer than sixteenth notes without staccato marks?

Attention to the subtle notational changes in the piano accompaniment of "Die Rose, die Lilie" adds more interest and challenge to the pianist's performance and enriches the experience of both performers and audience alike. In addition, these notational variations encourage the ensemble to adopt a more reasonable tempo, one that will help project the subtle rhythms in the accompaniment as well as a clearer vocal presentation of the poetic text.

The first question to pose about the more complex "Widmung" is the choice of meter: Why did Schumann use 3/2 instead of the more customary 3/4 or even 6/4, and what is the effect of this metric difference? Next, we note several recurring dotted rhythms in the song's opening A section, mm. 1–13: the dotted eighth/sixteenth motive recurring throughout, along with the less obvious whole note/half note rhythm in the bass. The frequent dotted eighth/sixteenth rhythm on beat one is striking. Does this rhythm sound like a downbeat or an upbeat? When the metric placement of this motivic rhythm changes, what is the effect and how does it reflect the poem? And why does the voice often sing the dotted rhythm at different times from the piano accompaniment? What bars do not incorporate this rhythm, and why is there a change of rhythm in mm. 7, 9, and 12? The slower and less obvious whole note/half note dotted rhythm in the bass also warrants attention. How often does this occur? Why is it altered in the third beat of m. 4? How does the reversal of whole and half notes in m. 12 affect the song's closure?

Other details in "Widmung's" opening section reveal nuances of Schumann's poetic depiction. Why did he repeat the A♭ up an octave in m. 7? What is emphasized by the SYNCOPATIONS in mm. 11–12, and why does the word "ewig" ("forever") have a longer note for its first syllable?[4]

While the middle B section of "Widmung" (mm. 14–25) remains in 3/2, the eighths and dotted rhythms are replaced by quarter-note triplets in the RH piano part. What is the kinetic effect of this rhythmic shift and what is the emotional or dramatic effect? What in the text might have prompted Schumann to change texture and pace here?[5]

A modified reprise of the opening A section begins in m. 30, but the four-bar bridge from section B to section A' has a complex formal design that is greatly amplified by temporal conflicts. The poetic material of the bridge completes both the verse begun in section B and the poem as a whole, but even as this occurs, the piano accompaniment begins to repeat rhythms from the song's opening for a modified reprise, section A' (mm. 30–39). This then requires that section A' repeat poetic lines already presented, and the altered reprise is a complex closing section in both poetic presentation and the song's overall formal design. In temporal terms, Schumann begins the return of section A prematurely, while the singer alone finishes section B. The abbreviated section A' that ensues repeats the opening four lines of text, omits the next two, and concludes with the final line from the text of section B. Schumann's bold alteration of the poem's structure seems prompted by two musical concerns: first, to give the song a rounded (ABA') form; and second, to conclude the song with greater enthusiasm than was possible with the triplet figuration of the middle section B. Schumann's penchant for taking liberties with the poetry he set is well known, and performers need to realize both the effect of this on the poetry and the musical rationale for these changes.

In view of the musical and poetic alterations in the bridge to section A', numerous questions arise about how Schumann expresses and articulates the flow of the shortened closing section. How does he vary rhythms of earlier material in mm. 30–39? Why did he write two equal quarter notes in both voice and piano in m. 36? Why did he write the accent on the piano E♭ under "ich" and why the accents over "du" in mm. 5 and 33, and over "Him" in mm. 7 and 35? What is emphasized through these markings, and what made less important?

One final detail about Schumann's notation and the song's tempo warrants consideration: How often does Schumann indicate a tempo? How often does he use a RITARD, both in this song and in general, and what functions do the various *ritards* serve? Further, how often does a dotted line follow the ritard, and do some ritards extend only as far as the barline? What accounts for these differences and how does this apply in the postlude (mm. 40 and 42–43)?

Schumann's "Widmung" serves as a rich example of rhythmic, metric, and formal complexities in the piano accompaniment that are illustrated clearly by the song's notation and that pose numerous interpretive challenges to both performers and the ensemble. For a contrast to Schumann's characteristic focus upon the piano accompaniment, we turn next to the notation and poetic depiction of Wolf, a composer especially concerned with the nuances of the vocal line in the service of faithful text declamation. Wolf's setting of Mörike's "Gesang Weylas" is a masterpiece of notation and temporal placement in the vocal line, and every note is a reflection of the poetic text.

While the accompaniment to this song remains a series of rolling majestic chords evoking the waves of the sea (with but one interjection of a melodic figure in mm. 12 and 13), the vocal line is a virtual study of precise text declamation. Wolf emphasizes the important words or metrically stressed syllables in four customary ways (using theoretical definitions): (1) metric placement on strong beats, especially the downbeat; (2) agogic accent, where a word or syllable is stressed through syncopation and longer duration; (3) syncopation in general, where a word or syllable is emphasized through unusual rhythmic accent; and (4) registral placement, where a word or syllable gains emphasis by being dramatically higher or lower than other words in a line.

Whereas Mörike's iambic meter (˘ /) puts stresses on "bist" ("are"), "-plid" ("Orplid"), "Land" ("land"), "fer- " ("distant"), and "leuch- " ("gleams"), Wolf initially emphasizes other crucial words of text by special devices. The word "Du" ("you") is placed *on* the beat, and the word "bist" is emphasized agogically by duration and syncopation. This begins a pattern of giving longer duration to all stressed syllables in the first line until the word "leuchtet," where Wolf places the stressed syllable higher than the unstressed one. The word "Land" occurs on a downbeat; the syllable "fer-" is given another agogic accent, where the pitch extension demonstrates the idea of distance. In phrase 2, Wolf conveys the overriding importance of the sun and mist over other elements of nature by stressing "Sonn-" from "Sonne" ("sun") and "Ne-" from "Nebel" ("mist"). He also avoids any possible singsong effect with "Götter Wange feuchtet" ("gods' cheeks bedews") by giving agogic accent to the words "Wange" and "feuchtet," each on a different position within the bar. In fact, the second phrase is notable for its preference for agogic emphasis over the traditional downbeat stress of phrase 1.

Wolf's use of agogic emphasis includes syncopation, particularly in the song's second half. The double stress of "Du bist" in phrase 1 turns into syncopated double stresses on the words "uralte" ("ancient"), "Wasser" ("water"), and "steigen" ("rise"); the meaning of this final word is also conveyed by its placement on high D♭. The metric stress on "Hüf-" from "Hüften" ("waist") is overshadowed by the agogically stressed "Kind" ("child"), which itself pales with the song's vocal climax on a metrically stressed G setting the word "Könige" ("kings").[6] Because Wolf's notation can seem to lack any logic or pattern, many singers may initially experience this and many other of Wolf's vocal lines with awkwardness and discomfort. However, with careful study, the wisdom of the vocal rhythms and their notation will emerge alongside the meaning of the poetry, and Wolf's expert text declamation will become a source of great significance and pleasure.

Our demonstration of notational nuance concludes with a brief examination of Schubert's equally meticulous poetic depiction in "Nähe des

Geliebten." Here we have a strophic setting in which each verse of poetry receives the same musical treatment, no matter what shifts in stress or scansion might occur in the poetry. Goethe's verse lends itself to this strophic setting since each six-line stanza has the same pattern of syllables per line:

4

7

4

followed by a period or semicolon, then

4

7

4

Schubert sets the two halves of each verse in two equal three-bar phrases, and while the musical design might seem overly rigid, the song abounds in small details of differentiation that negate any possible predictability or dullness.

The variations used by Schubert fall into two categories: (1) alterations in setting the poem's iambic meter ($\smile$ /) and (2) differences in setting poetic articulations (commas, semicolons, etc.) with musical ones (rests). In the first line of stanza 1 ("Ich denke dein"; "I think of you"), Schubert introduces an upbeat or ANACRUSIS in order to stress "denke." The fourth line is set more melismatically, ending with an upward leap of a fourth on a weak part of the beat.[7] The dramatic effect of this alteration is increased with the rest after the high G♭. Schubert also has to adjust the vocal line's rhythmic pattern to the poetry's systematic extra syllable in alternating lines (e.g., "Schimmer/Flimmer" of stanza 1). The result is a long–short rhythm in mm. 7 and 13 that greatly contrasts with the single syllable phrase endings in mm. 5, 9, 11, and 15.

Schubert's attention to poetic articulation is characteristically clear. Musical phrases generally incorporate rests or sustained notes wherever Goethe uses punctuation. There are, however, some inconsistencies. A rest occurs in m. 7, where punctuation is absent except for a comma after "ferne" in stanza 4. Later in the stanza, the period after "Sterne" is not given a similar musical pause. Such inconsistencies need to be acknowledged and considered in light of the text, especially in a strophic setting.[8]

Determination of Tempo

Composers's tempo indications fall into two broad categories: (1) external instructions given above the first measure (and elsewhere), including such words as *accel.*, *ritard.*, etc. and (2) internal indications, such as the lengths of phrases, the number of words within a given amount of time, the mood of the music, etc. To these basic categories we add another factor: performer ability, for example, the singer's ability to sing really slowly or terribly fast, and how this physical ability influences tempo as well. Because the composer's "indications" can only be interpreted and performer ability is variable within an ensemble, the choice of tempo is a personal and subjective matter. All we can demonstrate here is the *process* of determining a tempo, a method of testing for a pace that both reflects the composer's tempo indication and suits both performers's capabilities.

As a first step, all performers should test out the range of possibilities for pace of many of the more common *Lied* tempi: what is the range of pace for "*langsam*" or "*mässig*," for "*schnell*" or "*geschwind*"? Within these general ranges of tempo, then, each song offers a unique set of characteristics that must be taken into consideration. We demonstrate with the two Schumann songs just discussed, "Widmung" and "Die Rose, die Lilie."

Schumann tends to be less than specific in writing tempo indications than other *Lied* composers. The tempo he suggested for "Widmung" is "*Innig, lebhaft*"; what does that mean in English and what does it mean in Italian? The pianist should experiment with different paces; play the opening at 120 to the quarter note, then at 144. What feels better at which speed? Then play the opening at 72 to the half note, then at 88. Which feels better? Finally, play the beginning at 144 to the quarter, then set the metronome at 72 and play at 72 to the half. Should we think of the song in three or in six? After finding a speed that seems perfect for the beginning, set that speed on the metronome and start playing at m. 15: Does that feel too fast or too slow, and what does this reveal?

The pianist's preference for a given tempo must, of course, be agreeable to the singer, who has additional concerns around "speaking the text." For the singer, the tempo cannot be too fast to "get the words out" nor so slow that the singer must gasp for breath in the middle of a phrase meant to be sung without a break.[9] The singer can experiment similarly to the pianist's tempo trials. Speak aloud the line "daß du mich liebst, macht mich mir wert" as rapidly as you can manage. Then sing it (mm. 21–23) as rapidly as possible. What is the fastest pace you could sing this phrase smoothly and comfortably?

Now the singer must consider the punctuation: How often do commas occur in the first section of the song? In the phrase "Du bist die Ruh', du bist der Frieden" ("you are repose, you are peace," mm. 14–17), there is no rest, but there is a comma, so a singer could breathe after "Ruh'"; in mm. 18–21, however, there is no comma in the phrase "Du bist vom Himmel mir beschieden" ("you are from heaven bestowed upon me"), so any breath in the middle of the line will sound incorrect.

Once singer and accompanist agree on a tempo that is mutually comfortable, another factor must be taken into account: does the tempo remain more or less stable or does it fluctuate, with a certain amount of speeding up and slowing down of pace? Does the composer seem to prefer a steadier pace or tend to use changes of pace? Is there a motoric element at play that should keep the pace going? Or is the piece more rhapsodic or episodic in nature?

This last question of pacing is particularly important to singers, who must decide whether or not to relax the tempo when taking a breath. If there is no rest at a spot where a singer wants to breathe, the options are as follows: (1) bend the tempo by slowing up before taking the breath; (2) bend the tempo by inserting a small pause while the breath is taken; (3) steal time from the preceding syllable to take a breath; (4) come in late on the next syllable; or (5) employ a combination of all these techniques.

In the case of "Widmung," we can see that there are not many places where a tempo fluctuation for breath is necessary. Schumann seems to prefer a flexible tempo; he includes numerous *ritards*, and at one point calls for an acceleration ("*eilend*"). While this apparent freedom in tempo might help the singer breathe more comfortably, the freedom also might have been suggested for other musical reasons: to provide a general excitement, or to help shape the song's formal divisions.

Just as the tempo of "Widmung" is vague and open to interpretation, that in "Die Rose, die Lilie" is a simple but puzzling "*munter*" ("cheerfully"). Disregarding the circus act opted by some singers of dispatching the song in one breath, we need to find a pace that will match the exuberance and good cheer of the poem without being excessively fast or unmusical. In addition, there are two other issues that are particular to the singer: the need to articulate the text clearly and the need to find breathing spaces. Concerning the articulation of the text, the line "liebt' ich einst alle" ("loved I once all") demonstrates a typical problem. The poet/singer is excited, breathless, and virtuosic, and the outpouring must race forward at a headlong pace. However, saying or singing such lines must be slow enough to get the poetic *sounds* out. There are not only a number of consonants clustered together in this phrase, but three of the words start with a vowel, and may *not* be connected to the previous word by any sort of ELISION.[10]

In addition to the rapid parlando vocal style, the steady beat of the jaunty piano part tells us that this short *Lied* does not need a lot of rubato, or bending of the pace. Schumann does provide two places for a *ritard*: that leading up to a special emphasis on the word "Taube" ("dove") in mm. 11–12, and another rounding out the cadence at the end of the poem. In addition, unmarked *ritards* occur at those moments where a quick breath is needed (for example, after "Sonne" ["sun"] in m. 12); in such cases, the pianist needs to be attentive to the singer's requirements and usually only the slightest of hesitations is necessary.[11] The difference between unmarked and written in *ritards* can be described thus: performers make the audience aware of marked *ritards*, while they ease the unmarked ones by without attracting attention.

Another song that poses interesting questions about tempo is Schubert's "Der Neugierige." Let's look first in terms of the song's overall shape and form. How many sections are there and how many different tempo indications? Are there any instructions for tempo fluctuation, such as "*ritard*"? The first section is marked "*Langsam*"; are there any long phrases that might call for a faster tempo?

Look next at the vocal line. Are there any tongue-twisters in the text? How fast can you say "auch kein Gärtner"? At what speed might the duplets in mm. 17 and 19 sound too fast? Does this first section (mm. 1–22) seem to ask for a more parlando or a more legato style of singing? What clues lead you to that conclusion?

Now let's consider the different tempi for the various sections. Try the first section at various speeds from 50 to the quarter up to 90; what sounds the best? The second half of the song is marked slower: "*Sehr langsam.*" Could we measure this slower tempo by playing the sixteenth notes more slowly in m. 23 than in m. 21? How slow can this section go? Try 40 to the quarter; then try counting in six. Why might it be kept in three?

One of the necessary ingredients for a successful performance of this and many other songs is to find a tempo that will enable the singer to breathe comfortably without destroying the musical cohesion. Notice the lack of rests in the voice in mm. 47–51. This section is obviously too extended to be sung in one breath, but where can a singer breathe? An appropriate experiment would be to try mm. 47–51 in the following ways: (1) a very slow, steady tempo, with the singer sneaking time to breathe from the notes before; (2) a more rapid tempo, with the singer sneaking breaths in the same manner; (3) a moderate tempo, with the pianist slowing down to help the singer breathe at prearranged places; (4) a very slow tempo, with the same slowing down and bending of the pace. Which of these techniques do you favor? There is no one correct answer to this question, and this is one case where listening to several performances or recordings of the song can prove instructive.

Two additional points warrant our attention in this song. First, at m. 33, the flow of sixteenth notes is broken in the piano and we hear only two chords sustained beneath the vocal phrases. Could this be an example of recitative style? Try these measures in strict time, then faster and more freely; which do you prefer? Second, consider the two very long vocal phrases in mm. 35–41; how much faster do you need to take these measures in order to get everything in one breath? Remember, we are in a section marked "*Sehr langsam.*" Is it possible to sing these phrases at the pace we have chosen for m. 23? Is it advisable?

Schubert's "Der Neugierige" has exemplified those songs that neither remain in one tempo throughout, nor require a steady tempo. Because mm. 1–20 do not contain any problematic long phrases, the texture remains consistent, the style is light and probably parlando, the pace can be steady throughout. At m. 21, however, there are several ways to convey the pause in action: on the one hand, a slight *ritard* can prepare for it, or, on the other hand, a sudden interruption of sound might be more dramatic and expressive. The section marked "*Sehr langsam*" is most certainly more legato and more expressive (slower pace, slur markings, more duplets), and a bit more freedom of pacing might be permitted. Tempo changes then continue: a much quicker recitative pace is suggested in mm. 33–34, and the ensuing mm. 35–40 also might utilize a faster tempo. At m. 41, a return to the slower pace seems desirable, giving plenty of time for breathing from there to the end.

We conclude this section on tempo with a brief examination of Brahms's setting of Hölty's "Die Mainacht." The choice of tempo is influenced by two contradictory factors: first, there are several extremely long and taxing phrases that suggest taking a comfortably rapid tempo; second, however, the tempo indication is "*Sehr langsam und ausdrucksvoll,*" which, in 4/4, suggests a slower performance. Given these conflicting indications, additional information is needed to choose an appropriate tempo, and we turn to our two gauges of pacing: how the vocal line enunciates the words of the poetic text and what tempo is suggested by the characteristics of the piano accompaniment.

Looking first at the piano accompaniment, the articulations in the piano RH, mm. 1–14, help keep the feel of the song in four rather than in two. The lift after the first eighth note of each group helps accent the second eighth note, which falls either on the second or the fourth beat, and prevents rushing. Try this passage at various speeds, and see what pace best suits this articulation. The accompaniment figure in mm. 33–38 is similar; one cannot play these figures too rapidly and still be able to hold down every other note, as well as perform a *crescendo–decrescendo.*[12] At what speed does this passage sound best under your hands?

Turning next to the vocal line, we need to consider breathing and tempo changes. The vocal phrase in mm. 3–5 sounds better when taken in one breath rather than two; the same goes for the parallel phrase in mm. 6–8. Try singing these phrases in various slow tempos to see how slowly they can go without losing effectiveness. Later, in mm. 16–19, test the phrase setting "girret ein Taubenpaar sein Entzücken mir vor"; can you sing it in one breath at this speed? Should this section be taken faster? Should the whole song be taken faster? Then, in mm. 23–26, are you able to sing "suche dunklere Schatten" in one breath? Avoid slowing down; Brahms has composed a "written-in *ritard*" at this point, with each measure having longer note values than the one before.

In mm. 27–31 we come to the crucial point in our search for a performance tempo. The article "die" ("a") should not be separated from the adjective "Einsame" ("solitary"), which modifies and should not be separated from "Träne" ("tear"). Given that, the only possible places to interrupt the phrase with a breath are after "und" ("and"), where a breath would come too early to be needed, or before "rinnt" ("flows"), which unfortunately falls between subject and verb. Brahms seems, thus, to have imagined the whole phrase in one breath. If that is so, performers have these considerations:

1. Should I speed up at this point? If so, how much?
2. If not, how slowly can I sing this phrase?
3. Does the altered tempo work for the remainder of the song?

Most performers of German *Lieder* are likely to reach some sort of compromise, rushing forward slightly during the difficult phrases, taking a little extra time when breaths are needed, and generally bending the pace here and there throughout a song such as "Die Mainacht." Brahms's music usually calls for a certain amount of rubato, and the frequently used "*espressivo*" certainly suggests, even encourages, a modest degree of rhythmic freedom.

Timing between Partners

There are a few axioms about how singer and pianist stay together. A chord or note in the piano normally sounds with the vowel of the singer's syllable. This could mean that the pianist plays in time and the singer makes sure to articulate the consonants *before* the beat. Schubert's "Wanderers Nachtlied I" demonstrates this: sing and play mm. 1–4, observing the slight difference in timing of "üb-," "al-," "Gip-," and "Ruh'," the last with a rolled *R*. The timing change on "Ruh'" creates an agogic emphasis; by singing the consonant *on* the beat, the pianist's chord comes later, effectively shifting the beat. It is also axiomatic that the pianist should "follow," that is, allow the singer to "lead" with a particularly expressive, interesting, or sensitive note placement.

Several other *Lieder* offer additional case studies of ensemble coordination in timing. The vocal line of Schubert's "Die Forelle" contains several elaborate melodic figures that require ensemble adjustment. At mm. 17 and 41, the singer performs an elaborate melisma, first on the word "süßer" ("contentedly"), then on the words "nicht gebricht" ("is not broken"). In m. 17, the singer may well decide to stretch this figure to reinforce the feeling of expansive well-being that is expressed, while in m. 41 the density of the language itself may call for taking a little extra time. Indeed, this song might use a delay to introduce a desired degree of insouciance.

Schumann's "Im Rhein, im heiligen Strome" contains a figure in m. 34 similar to those cited in Schubert's "Die Forelle." The piano RH at "unsre liebe Frau" ("our dear lady") doubles the voice an octave below, the vocal tessitura being very high. Since the spirit of the text here is one of awe and devotion, not frivolity, the gesture suggests a bit of stretch that the pianist must coordinate.

While these examples suggest deference to the singer's *rubato,* other *Lieder* that build on a motoric, strongly rhythmic accompaniment suggest the opposite: that the singer must adapt to the accompaniment's tempo needs. Schubert's "Wohin?" is a case in point. After the waterlike triplets of the opening, a *ritard* in m. 78 seems inappropriate. In order that the singer not feel rushed, however, the pianist would continue more or less in time, and the singer's final "fröhlich nach" can then trail off at its own pace.

Schubert's "Gretchen am Spinnrade" is a famous example of the power of the accompanimental figuration to propel the song forward. In mm. 114–120, this changes dramatically, where the gradual slowing down of the piano's spinning wheel convey's Gretchen's exhaustion as she can only repeat what she has so often already said. In this case, the singer should follow the pianist, and might also take extra time with "ist schwer" ("is heavy") independently from the pianist's pace.

Strauss's "Ständchen" offers a final example of ensemble timing where both performers must adapt. In mm. 48–49, the words "ist wach" ("is awake") are full of consonants, and the pianist might want to give the singer a little extra time; later, on the words "sitz' nieder" ("sit [down]"), the singer cannot coordinate precisely with the pianist, whose accompaniment requires a persistent, steady pace. This timing is encouraged by the prevailing nocturnal mood and atmosphere of smoothness and calm.

Exercises

Use the repertory from Chapter Three for these exercises.

Exercise 4.1: Nuances of notation

Find examples of the stated musical effects indicated and discuss why they are used:

1. Syllables that have been lengthened for emphasis
2. Syllables placed on high notes for emphasis
3. Stressed syllables that have been placed on weak beats
4. Shifts in articulation within an accompaniment pattern that is *not* in the figure

Exercise 4.2: Tempo

Try reading five *Lieder* at three metronome settings that are approximately 20 points apart (e.g., 60, 80, 100). Note the changes in timbre and clarity.

CHAPTER FIVE

Elements of Interpretation

This chapter focuses upon those musical elements that help shape the musical expressivity of *Lieder:* the composer's use of dynamics, timbre, register, and techniques of stress and emphasis that the performer must interpret during performance preparation and convey with conviction during actual performance. In addition to the elements of musical sound mentioned already, this unit also explores the performer's need to consider the concept of persona, the understanding of whose "voice" is being expressed within a given musical line or section. In all these areas, the interpretations and decisions are based first and foremost upon understanding the poetic text and how the composer is conveying that text in musical sound.

Dynamics

While composers often give specific instructions to performers as to how loud or soft their music should be, there are almost limitless shadings of "*forte*" and "*piano*," depending on range, texture, and individual abilities. As a consequence, the broad range of variables in choosing dynamics remains in the hands and voices of the performers themselves. We examine some of these variables in several *Lieder,* beginning with Schubert's famous "Gretchen am Spinnrade."

Since dynamics reflect the ongoing temporal advance, we consider the issue of dynamics chronologically. Measures 1–5 are to be performed at an extremely low dynamic level: "*pp.*" However, *soft* does not mean *quiet* in this case. Gretchen is distraught and obsessed, so the vocal line could be sung with more sound than, say, the opening of "Wanderers Nachtlied I" or the end of "Morgen!".

Starting at m. 6, a quick crescendo begins leading not to "*p,*" "*mp,*" or even to "*mf,*" but rather to "*f*" in mm. 8. Schubert thus creates a violent contrast. In m. 13 we return to the original dynamic level, not to a medium dynamic level of "*mp,*" but to the low "*pp.*" Mm. 18–21 are marked "*mf.*" There is no crescendo leading into this, so our dynamic change must be as efficient and sudden as possible.

The phrases starting in m. 22 are marked "*crescendo,*" ending on "*f*" and beyond by the time we get to m. 26. A wise performer might start m. 22 a little more softly than mm. 18–21; this creates a proper "*crescendo*" without requiring singers to scream and pianists to pound. What is *not* left to the performers' choice, however, is the fact that the downbeat of m. 28 is the loudest moment in the section. In mm. 29–31, we again return quickly to "*pp*," and again at m. 36 we begin a quick crescendo to "*f*" on m. 37.[1]

In both mm. 42 and 51, Schubert writes "*pp*." While there is no intervening change of dynamic, he obviously wants different levels of sound. A skilled ensemble will find two timbres that create differing effects, making sure that m. 42 is just a little bit softer than m. 51. Next, Schubert calls for a long gradual *crescendo* from m. 55 to a "*f*" at m. 60. This can be accomplished in two different ways. First, each two-bar phrase can be a bit louder than the one before; this is particularly comfortable for the singer. Second, the ensemble can produce a steady growth in a straight line; this tends to be better for the pianist. Mm. 64–68 are marked even louder, "*ff*" with "*sforzandos*" on each downbeat. While the instruments of Schubert's day naturally had a sound that decayed very quickly, making it easy to give the sharp, loud accents called for here, modern pianists have to work to make an accent that is sharp, loud, and shallow at the same time.

In m. 68, a hairpin marking in the piano part just after the "*fz*" looks like a short "*decrescendo*," and similar markings also occur in mm. 8, 10, 28, 37, 39, 79, and 81. In the orthography of Schubert and his contemporaries, this is *not* a "*decrescendo*," but rather an accent. The placement in m. 68 is not very clear, but Schubert is calling for the B♭ on beat 2 to be accented, probably even louder than the downbeat.

After the spinning wheel gets started again (mm. 69–72), Schubert gives us exactly the same formula from earlier sections in mm. 73–83. However, the change over measures 82–83 only subsides to "*p*," not "*pp*." In mm. 85–91 the composer again asks for a long "*crescendo*," this time starting a little louder than the one at m. 55.

Schubert reaches the "*ff*" plateau at m. 93, where we remain until m. 112. His only variation is to add "*fz*" accents in the bass starting at m. 101. Most performers will add a few interpretive nuances to Schubert's sparse instructions; they will sing and play the phrase "an seinen Küssen vergehen sollt" ("and from his kisses I should die") more softly than the phrase "und küssen ihn so wie ich wollt" ("and kiss him as I would like"), since it is a step lower. They will also back off a bit at mm. 101, 105, and 109, so that each phrase will have its own "*crescendo*," from about "*f*" to "*ff*."

In mm. 112–113, the pianist is instructed to get all the way from "*ff*" to "*pp*." Since a further "*diminuendo*" occurs in m. 118, many pianists opt for a steadier decline in the dynamic level. However, Schubert's instructions seem clear: a quick return to the hypnotic level of the opening, and a further fade in the postlude.

This discussion shows how a composer's dynamic instructions are often augmented or even second-guessed by performers. Honest musicians will naturally try to reproduce what the composer has written, following all interpretive dynamic markings diligently. However, the goal is to project to the audience the composer's instructions, and this calls for thoughtful, intelligent interpretation by the ensemble.

Our exploration of dynamic usage in *Lieder* continues with two Schumann songs. In "Im Rhein, im heiligen Strome" the piano part is evocative of the majesty of a great Gothic cathedral, and might even assume the persona of one such place, filled with visual spaciousness and echoes of organ music. While the song's opening offers clear dynamic markings, other musical issues tend to complicate the ensemble's sense of loudness and softness. For example, at the outset, Schumann marks all parts "*f,*" but the voice starts in a very low range, where it is difficult to sing loudly and the vocal line is doubled by accented *octaves* in the bass. In this case, a pianist's "*f*" might overshadow the singer's line, and discretion is necessary. In a similar way, the dynamic decline to "*p*" in mm. 16 and 17 is undermined by the fact that the piano still doubles the voice with octaves. Once again, the pianist must gauge the level of sound with consideration of the singer's sound projection.

A different dynamic concern arises in mm. 21–23, where the bass echoes the gesture of mm. 1–3 with accented octaves. Such accents automatically raise the dynamic level, and Schumann acknowledges this in m. 27, where he repeats his "*p*" marking. Thereafter, no more dynamic indications are given whatsoever. Wise performers are likely to add their own, rising and falling with the contour of the phrases, using a "*crescendo*" somewhat to underline the rising sequence in mm. 35–39, and coloring the various words and images by making them louder or softer. The postlude is also devoid of dynamic inflection, "*mf*" from m. 44 to the end. While the normal shaping of the phrases will call for some dynamic shading, a steady dynamic level could effectively mimic the sound of the organ echoing implacably through the cathedral.

The paucity of dynamic indications in Schumann's "Mondnacht" poses a different set of interpretative challenges. Schumann calls for nothing more than "*p,*" except for the final cadence, which is marked "*pp.*" Accordingly, performers must make many dynamic shadings on their own, using other musical factors to create their nuances. How much dynamic shaping might be appropriate in the piano introduction? Should there be two swells, m. 1 into m. 2 echoed in mm. 3–4, or would one long arch be better? As a singer negotiates the extremely touchy phrases in mm. 8, 16, 30, and 38, should the dynamics be kept as level as possible, or should the line "*crescendo*" as it rises? Schumann does indicate the loudest note in each phrase; however, the downbeats of mm. 12, 20, 34, and 42 present decorated held notes with an ornamental turn.

The most problematic section of "Mondnacht" is the third strophe. Schumann notates a "*crescendo*" no less than eleven times between mm. 44 and 59, but only gives "*decrescendo*" markings at the end, in mm. 59 and 60. Performers of the song are faced with a huge decision: Should they try to make each phrase a little louder than its predecessor, or should they retreat dynamically after each phrase? Another consideration here is that while Schumann does want crescendos, "Mondnacht" must not be allowed to become too loud, lest it lose its moonlit character.

The biggest dispute about Schumann's dynamics in this song concerns the phrase "flog durch die stillen Lande" ("flew over the silent land") in mm. 53–55. Here Schumann sets the final two lines of Eichendorff's poem with the same notes he has used four times before, with the dynamic indication "*p.*" Did he leave something out here? Is this phrase in fact intended to mirror the earlier phrases, soft and floating? It does contain the word "stillen," which suggests a softness of sound. Or should mm. 53–59 be sung strongly, capping off the gradual increase in dynamics that began ten measures earlier? No matter what you decide, notice how Schumann staggers the dynamics in mm. 58–60. The voice part climaxes on the word "Haus" ("home"), but the piano part continues to grow until the IV chord a measure later and extends the tension of the final phrase until the arrival of the tonic in m. 61.

Timbre

One aspect of musical sound that usually has no specific instruction by the composer is that of TIMBRE, meaning tone quality or tone color. Occasionally a specific effect is requested; in "Die Alte," Mozart instructs the singer to sing "*Ein Bißchen durch die Nase,*" or "a little through the nose," in order to sound like an old busybody crone. Even so, one singer's concept of a nasal sound might be quite different from another's, and both might be equally effective.

The instruction "*espressivo*" also might be considered a request for tonal color; "*espressivo*" usually results in more rhythmic freedom, more emphasis, and a more intense timbre. In some places a composer may ask for "*dolce*" (in German, "*zart*" or "sweet"), which might suggest certain types of sounds to performers. However, to some performers indications such as "*espressivo*" and "*dolce*" might suggest dynamic changes rather than timbral ones.[2]

Two factors may assist performers, especially pianists, in thinking about tone color in *Lied* performance. First, the songs of Mozart, Beethoven, and Schubert were written for quite a different-sounding instrument than ours and knowledge of the timbre of the nineteenth-century pianoforte can influence how the pianist thinks about such things as use of pedal, attack and decay, and so forth. Second, pianists can gain tremendous insight about timbre from studying orchestral accompaniments in *Lied* settings of Strauss, Wolf, Wagner, Berg, and most especially Mahler, where details of tone color were clearly evident in orchestral instrumentation. The pianist might try to develop what is sometimes called an orchestral palette, imagining the sounds of various instruments and trying to imitate these timbres on the keyboard. Such a rich, "orchestral" sort of playing can be quite appropriate in the works of later *Lied* composers.

Several *Lieder* illustrate various timbral choices a singer or a pianist might make in order to remain true to both the drama and nuance of the poetry and the composer's presumed musical intentions. It is helpful to separate the issues of the vocal line from that of the accompaniment, though timbral decisions need to be a collaboration of the ensemble.

Vocal Timbre

In "Mondnacht," Schumann gives a few indications suggestive of vocal color. He uses the words "*zart*" ("sweet") and "*heimlich*" ("in secret" or "secretly," thus conjuring up associations such as whispering), and a "*p*" marking not only in m. 1, but at the beginning of the first two verses *in the vocal part*, an unusually strong reminder to "keep it quiet."

In addition to these directions, aural images suggest timbre. The opening sounds heard by the singer in the piano introduction convey the twin images of the earth and the sky through an exaggerated interval of a ninth that spans four octaves. The single low bass note is so quiet as to soon become almost a background, warm but not noticeable. It is followed by a sort of disembodied floating-down of quiet sounds, a different timbral effect altogether. This same earth/sky dichotomy is repeated in m. 5, with less extreme spacing but with similar effect: a low bass tone is followed by gentle sounds far removed from the foundation in the pianist's LH. These aural images cast a timbral hush over the song, which can "color" the vocal line even before the singer begins.

Perhaps an even more important timbral suggestion is inherent in the vocal line itself. The first phrase begins in an upper-middle register, "*p*," and ascends by step, a maneuver which must be accomplished delicately and with great care, not by intensification and "*crescendo*". Schumann explicitly rules out the latter with his "*p*" marking, and his vocal line is written such that its relation to the introduction and the mood of the poem should be obvious. In the second phrase ("die Erde still geküsst"; "the earth quietly had been kissed"), the music starts high again, but then descends an octave. This results almost automatically in a great increase in timbral richness and warmth, where the singer has to sing "still ge-" differently from the floating quality of "hätt' der Him-" ("as though the sky").

Schumann also sets up an effective timbral contrast *within* his vocal line; the actual vocal RANGE covers only a major ninth, but the range of vocal color is more expansive.[3] The images of flying, dreaming, the earth/sky opposition, and the moon are all inherent in the writing for the voice.

In Brahms's "Die Mainacht," the text also offers clues for timbre in the vocal line. This example will be most effective if the phrases in question are sung or at least heard for the timbral variations. Beginning with the first phrase (mm. 3–5), what vocal color is suggested by starting so low in the voice? What is Brahms emphasizing by using this vocal range? What might he have done if he had wanted to paint a picture of the "silvery moon?" In mm. 9–10, how does Brahms set "und die Nachtigall flötet" ("and the nightingale flutes") apart from the surrounding phrases? What sort of vocal tone quality is natural here? (Note how difficult it is to sing very loudly here in this range.)

Timbral associations are also suggested when the text speaks of the sounds of birds (mm. 9, 10, 15–19). Brahms uses the same pitches when talking of doves and the nightingale, two contrasting bird images. What does the voice sound like in mm. 25–26 on the word "Schatten" ("shadows")? What does the voice sound like in that complete phrase (mm. 23–26)?

Like Schumann's "Mondnacht," Brahms uses a very restricted vocal range: most of the song lies within an octave from Eb^1 to Eb^2, excluding the low Bbs of the opening upbeat leap and the falling leap on "Schatten," the one lower neighbor on "Wang" ("cheek") in mm. 46–47, and the high Fb's of "wende" ("turn") and "heisser" ("hotter"). Yet in his poetic depiction he exploits the natural sounds and inherent timbres throughout this limited compass with great skill. The singer's challenge is to find these nuances within the vocal line and the text being expressed.

Our third exploration into possible vocal timbres is Strauss's "Morgen!" Again the song stays essentially within the compass of an octave, spanning from G^1 to G^2. "Morgen!" has fewer notes in the higher part of this range than "Mondnacht" and fewer lower pitches than "Die Mainacht;" thus while the ranges are comparable, the TESSITURAS of the three songs are each unique.

Strauss's instructions are helpful, if not specific. He begins with "*Langsam sehr getragen,*" which is actually more colorful than the Italian counterpart, "*Lento molto cantabile.*" While "*cantabile*" means "singing," "*getragen*" connotes "drawn out" and "sustained." A performer trying to follow this particular direction would play or sing with as much sustaining of notes as possible; the singer would also try to present a long line, minimizing differences between adjacent notes, melding tones together as much as possible so that the phrase as a whole, rather than individual notes, receives our attention.

Strauss's next instruction, "*sehr ruhig*" ("*molto tranquillo*"), is written above the voice part as a special reminder to the singer. The instruction is similar to "*sehr getragen*": emphasize a long line of phrase and match the tones effortlessly. In terms of timbre, "*sehr ruhig*" suggests a tone quality that is unforced and steady, without excessive vibrato.

Strauss knew the capabilities of the human voice very well; in fact, this song is one of four composed as a wedding gift for his wife, the famous soprano Pauline DeAhna. He was therefore sensitive to another important aspect of vocal color: the relative openness and closedness of vowels. In German, vowels on accented syllables followed by only one consonant are referred to as CLOSED; sometimes these sounds are bright, as in "wieder," "Wege," "gehen," and "werde"; sometimes, they are quite dark in timbre, as in "wogen." Open vowels are less extreme and more neutral in their formation; they occur on most unstressed syllables and on stressed syllables which are followed by two consonants, for example, "Sonne," "Glück," and "stumm."

You can discover much about this particular aspect of vocal technique by making the following experiments with "Morgen!":

1. In order to start in somewhat neutral territory, try singing "Sonne" where it is written (D in the original, mm. 15 and 22); what sort of tone color does this have?

2. Now sing the following words on the same pitch D instead of the actual B where they are set: "wieder," "Wege," "gehen," and "Erde." What does this feel and sound like?

3. Sing "Glück" in a high register (in the original, E♭ and F♯); notice the effort required to do this.

4. Finally, sing on a high note "wo-", keeping the vowel as closed as possible (as in the first part of the English word "woe"); notice how very small this sound is, and how unusual. What does this contribute to the mood of the song?

The ideas touched upon in this discussion show how carefully singers must consider matters of tone color. Besides the more obvious considerations of wanting a beautiful vocal sound, performers need to seek shadings of timbre which will support their interpretations. These may reflect choices regarding *Stimmung*, character, or dramatic intent; they may also be latent in the details of the German language and of the musical setting.

Accompaniment Timbre

Three songs demonstrate how to think about timbre in the piano accompaniment, beginning with Schubert's "Wohin?"[4] Schubert instructs us to play "*pp*" throughout "Wohin?" except for a "*crescendo*" at m. 29 and a "*p*" from m. 66 to m. 74. He also slurs the first measure in the RH and expects that articulation to continue. In the LH, meanwhile, he writes many different articulations. He does not suggest how much pedal to use, nor what sort of color to create; whatever the pianist devises must be: (a) reminiscent of water; (b) joyous; (c) occasionally mysterious; and (d) quiet enough that the singer can be heard clearly.

We will experiment with various timbres one phrase at a time. First, play mm. 1–6 quietly, with plenty of pedal. Then play them again, half that loudly. Then play them again, even softer, and with your foot as high on the pedal as you can get and still have reverberation. Schubert most definitely means for us to play "*pp*."

Now play mm. 11–15 with a slight "*crescendo-decrescendo*" over the phrase. Is it possible to do this with just the LH, or must the RH come along with the swell? What sort of tone color is produced when you make this slight swell? Play mm. 22–26 with more sound in the bass; can you make the bass line sound like cellos or double basses? Is it possible, or desirable, to keep the RH "*pp*" here? Finally, play mm. 33 and 34 very quietly, then m. 35 quieter still. Now play mm. 33 and 34 as quietly as you just played m. 35, with m. 35 even more muted.

In "Wohin?" we see Schubert's ability to find all sorts of levels and colors within a very quiet range. The entire song is to be performed quietly, with the performer finding interesting timbral variations within the small compass provided. Schubert's "Gretchen am Spinnrade" also uses sixteenth-note figuration throughout. In that song, however, the pianist must: (1) sound like a wooden machine; (2) project a dynamic range from "*pp*" to "*ff*"; and (3) convey a huge range of emotions, including hysteria, longing, and numbness.

Our approach to this work is a series of different touches. Try the opening RH with no pedal. Accent the first note of the sextuplet. Try it without the accent. Try making your finger action as smooth as possible. Try lifting your fingers high. Try it softer, then softer still. Now, still without pedal, add the LH. Make it sound wooden. Make it sound inhuman and hard. Try the tenor louder than the bass. Try the bass louder than the tenor. Try the tenor very flat and monotonous, with the fourths in the bass accented and vicious (mm. 4 and 6).

Now play mm. 13–21, observing the dynamics. What timbral change occurs with the change of dynamics at m. 18? Next play mm. 42–50 with no pedal; then play mm. 51–54 more softly, with pedal. Go back and try it again, playing mm. 42–50 as softly as you can, then mm. 51–54 even softer, but with pedal. What change in tone color occurs here?

Finally, play mm. 101–112 as loud and as fast as you can, "*ff*," with accents in the bass. What do the bass notes sound like? Use pedal heavily, then sparingly. How loud is loud enough?

Our third example of accompanimental timbre is Strauss's "Allerseelen." This is a good example of an accompaniment with an orchestral tone quality. As you play or listen to it, try to imagine what sort of orchestration you might use. Most of the song would probably be quite full and luxurious in timbre. If you were to play this luxuriously, with plenty of pedal and a full piano sound, what change of tone color happens at m. 12, where Strauss indicates "*pp*"? What about m. 23? Notice how Strauss exploits the full range of the piano, from very low to quite high, and spaces his arpeggios for maximum sonority. He also doubles frequently, writing octaves and rich chords.

Although the composer never says it explicitly, everything he puts on the page implies a sense of timbre; the range of dynamics in "Allerseelen" is the same as that in "Gretchen am Spinnrade;" but the two *Lieder* cannot be played with the same sort of tone color.

Ensemble Timbre

When we look at Schumann's "Ich hab' im Traum geweinet," we notice immediately that voice and piano do not come together until late in the song. This immediately poses the question: Are voice and piano engaged in a dialogue, or are they entirely separate? This merges the issue of persona with that of timbre, a feature of this brief *Lied*. The idea that vocal line and accompaniment are somehow in opposition is reinforced by differences in articulation: the first vocal phrase is very legato and the first piano phrase very staccato.

Unlike the opening separateness, more interaction between singer and pianist occurs in mm. 7–9, where the piano punctuates the voice with more urgency and participation. As the song progresses, more interrelation occurs; for example, the dotted rhythm of the piano is reiterated in the vocal line in mm. 5 and 10.

The dramatic, unprepared shift in the piano accompaniment at m. 22 adds a new dimension to the ensemble relationship. The accompaniment suddenly takes over the vocal phrase and "sings" as sustainedly as the voice for the next twelve measures. In terms of tone color, therefore, we have the following progression of timbral changes within the ensemble:

mm. 1–2: voice—muted, but expressive, smooth, and tragic;

mm. 3–4: piano—more muffled, expressionless;

mm. 4–6: voice—quieter, devoid of hope, less legato;

mm. 6–7: piano—muffled, dead;

mm. 7–9: voice and piano—more intense, more alive, full of pain;

mm. 10–11: voice—slower, more sustained, hopeless;

m. 11: piano—muffled, dead, final.

This sequence is then repeated in mm. 12–22. At that point the singer and accompanist seem to exchange roles. The piano suddenly assumes the role of the suffering, intense singer, playing the opening phrase with warm, rich chords, and a "*crescendo-decrescendo*" swell, while the voice answers more softly in mm. 24–26, with *no* "*crescendo*." It is as if the piano has assumed the voice's struggle, while the voice has adopted the piano's hopelessness. From m. 26 through m. 33, both parts grow together, and the tone quality in both must be intense and vibrant. The silence in m. 34 is stunning, and asks the question: Which will emerge, the suffering of the voice or the bleakness of the piano? The final piano chords, surrounded by silence, must be especially pale, muffled, and pitiless.

"Ich hab' im Traum geweinet" has demonstrated how the combined forces of vocal line and piano accompaniment create a strong connection between timbre, dynamics, and persona. The duality of expression within the *Lied* ensemble is a recurring factor and remains a major consideration in any ensemble experience, whether the focus is on texture, dynamics, or timbre. Our next two *Lied* examples emphasize this duality, as two Wolf songs set poems about love conflicts, where the singer is one and the pianist is the other in a love pair.

Wolf's "Mein Liebster singt" depicts an unhappy scene of frustrated lovers caught in their yearning and disappointment. Wolf indicates the first strophe to be played and sung "*pp*," except for a swell on the word "Bette" ("bed") in m. 10. What sort of "*pp*" would be appropriate at this point? We consider first the piano sound. The accompaniment represents the lover serenading the singer outside her house. It is night; the sound must be penetrating enough to carry, and expressive enough to represent the ache felt by the persistent lover. On the other hand, we are not allowed to play loudly at the beginning: Wolf marks a "*crescendo*" to only "*mf*" in m. 12. The timbre of the piano thus needs to be soft but clear.

Next we consider the proper timbre for the singer in mm. 1–11. Again, it must be very soft. The narrator must hide her longing from her mother, and she is exhausted from weeping. The color of her voice will be pale, distraught, tired, but with inner passion.

If singer and pianist find subdued tone colors at the outset, the passionate ("*leidenschaftlich*") outburst at mm. 12–17 will be all the more effective. Here both partners can indulge in a full-bodied, intense, rich timbre, as both serenader and lover allow their feelings to erupt to the surface.

The alternation of subdued and passionate timbres lasts throughout this song. The meaning of the piano figuration throughout, like that in "Gretchen," requires special consideration about the role of timbre. Play the final four measures of "Mein Liebster singt," where the unlucky serenader evidently walks off, his song growing softer as he moves down the street. What do the chords in the left hand remind us of? Are they not the sounds of the young man's guitar? Try this passage again, playing the chords crisply, with very little pedal, in emulation of guitar chords. After you think that you have captured the proper tone color, go back to mm. 1–11 and try this sort of touch and timbre in the first part of the song.

The same sort of guitar image might be implied in Wolf's "In dem Schatten meiner Locken," from the *Spanischesliederbuch*, where the recurring accompaniment figure suggests a bolero. The rolled chords, as in mm. 4, 25, and 26, are also guitar gestures. The dynamics range from "*ppp*" to "*f*," but the accompaniment figures remain similar throughout. A bright, light guitar timbre seems to be called for. In mm. 17–19 Wolf wants the downbeat chords to be played "*sforzando*," these also could be guitar-like, as when a guitarist strums vigorously and percussively.

The tone quality of the vocal part can also cover a wide range of possibilities. The narrator vacillates between flirtatiousness and passionate complaint, and the singer should find timbres which help to convey this. Both extremes of the singer's dynamic range should have a passionate, intense color; the woman is caught in powerful ambivalence about her lover.

Vocal Accent and Stress

The German language, like English, derives much of its characteristic flavor from having a mixture of stressed and unstressed syllables. However, as suggested in the discussion of poetic meter in Chapter Two and temporality in Chapter Four, aligning musical stresses or accents with poetic ones is not always clear-cut. Composers use several devices to emphasize a word or syllable beyond its normal metric stress, for example, through agogic emphasis (syncopation or duration) or placing a note in a high or low register.[5] In the same manner, the performer may decide to underscore one word more than another by making it louder, by stretching it slightly, or by delaying its onset through the performer's sense of agogic accent. Thus the subject of accent and emphasis combines features of texture and temporality with those of performance practice, and calls for a special sensitivity on the part of the performer. For the most part, such interpretive decisions are best used when closely aligned with the composer's markings; only rarely does an unusual reading of a vocal line lend charm and personality to a performance.

As discussed in the context of Wolf's notated vocal line in "Gesang Weylas," the employment of word stress is crucial for the proper setting of a text. We have already seen a variety of approaches to text declamation; at one extreme was the equal-syllable treatment in Schubert's "Der Leiermann" that created a cold, mechanistic, stilted, or subdued effect, and at the opposite extreme was the more florid, elongated vocal treatment in Schubert's "Ave Maria" for an altogether different musical effect. The *Lied* repertory offers a variety of approaches to musical emphasis and stress, and we offer two brief examples of composers emphasizing words within complex vocal lines.

We begin with a return to Brahms's "Die Mainacht." Musical emphasis or stress is most easily identified when the rhythmic and metric norms are clear. We note the predominance of quarter notes in section 1 (mm. 1–14), and see where the quarter notes occur in vocal phrases. How many quarter notes are there in the vocal line of mm. 3–5? How many in the second phrase (mm. 6–8)? What rhythmic/metric difference is there between the two phrases? Other questions arise: What note values are used in mm. 9–13? What is the longest note value sung in the first section? Beyond that, what note value does Brahms use for his longest, most emphasized syllables?

Another issue of rhythm in the vocal line involves the rhythmic pattern of mm. 3, 6, 9, and 11. As each phrase in this section starts with the same rhythm, how does Brahms vary the measures that follow? Which words receive emphasis through this? In the accompaniment, meanwhile, the bass at the outset has chords on beats 1 and 3 of every measure. What emphasis occurs with the shift to beats 2 and 4 in mm. 9 and 10?

The song's second section (mm. 15–26) starts with the same rhythm in the voice as verse 1. After that, which words receive temporal stress? Why might the first syllable of "aber" ("but") receive an accent through syncopation (this is the theoretical sense of agogic accent)?

We have noted a number of instances of varied repetitions in "Die Mainacht." Others include an extended reiteration of mm. 27–31 in mm. 39–48. Why is the first syllable of "Träne" elongated so extraordinarily? Similarly, the phrase in mm. 33–38 is a modified version of mm. 3–8. What rhythmic variations occur? Why are there rests in mm. 34 and 35, but not in mm. 4 and 5? And finally, what is the effect of the syncopation in m. 37 where the word "find" ("find") occurs on the second beat?

Another, equally revealing way to examine musical accent in "Die Mainacht" is to compare the musical with the poetic accents. Like the German language generally, this poem is full of trochees, or words with a strong first syllable and an weaker second one (/ ˘). A fruitful analysis would be to see how many different ways Brahms notates such words in this elegant setting.

Wolf's "Auch kleine Dinge" offers another demonstration of musical accent and emphasis to reinforce the poetic text. Again we pose a series of questions. In the song's first section, mm. 5–8, what word is emphasized first? How does Wolf ensure that "Dinge" ("things") receives more stress than "entzücken" ("to delight")? How does he differentiate the second "kleine" ("small") from the first, and how does the change in rhythm go with the change in pitch? What is the difference in character of the second "Dinge" from the first? Why underline "teuer" ("precious") through the dotted rhythm?

In the second section, mm. 8–12, what does the line "Bedenkt, wie gern wir uns mit Perlen schmücken" ("Think how gladly we ourselves in pearls deck") sound like with the word "wir" ("we") falling on the downbeat rather than before it? Why does Wolf have it where it is? We could emphasize either "schwer" ("much") or "bezahlt" ("bought") if we were speaking these words in a phrase; why does Wolf make the choice he does? What character results from the interruptions in the vocal line in m. 12? Why does Wolf have the singer do that again in m. 13?

The final section, mm. 13–21, includes several alterations of musical structure. What words does Wolf underscore in this last strophe? We note that the rhythm in m. 19 is unique; what effect does it produce to have equal notes here? What might a singer strive for? Which syllables in this phrase are normally accented in speech? (Just as in English, the word "so" is very expressive in German.) Wolf accents all three words of "wie ihr wisst" ("as you know"); how? Which is probably the one receiving the most emphasis?

This brief foray into the issue of musical accent and emphasis in the vocal line encourages the singer to be sensitive to rhythms in the vocal line, both norms and exceptions, that assist in the articulation of the poetic text. These musical accents are important first and foremost because they help in text declamation; in addition, they also highlight the composer's nuances of text depiction and the subtleties of melodic design, two issues essential to the singer's command over the vocal line.

The Concept of Persona

As stated earlier, the concept of persona concerns the question, in a poem and its setting: who is speaking (called the persona) and to whom the persona speaks (called the mode of address).[6] We return to this topic here to detail how important determining persona and mode of address is to *Lied* performers: the vocal line projects a persona who is communicating to someone or something, and the piano accompaniment embodies one or more voices or personas that project outward as well.

From the start, *Lied* performers need to know the identity of the *poem's* persona, since the singer, at least, will assume that role in performing the vocal line. In many cases, the poem's (and song's) title indicates the poetic persona: "Gretchen am Spinnrade," "Schäfers Klagelied," "Der Atlas," "Der Rattenfänger," and so forth. In addition, some poems and settings include more than one character or persona, and performers need to be aware of the transition from one character's "voice" to the next as occurs, for example, in "Erlkönig," "Vergebliches Ständchen," or "Der Tod und das Mädchen."

In addition to knowing the poem's persona, performers also must consider the mode of address: to whom does the singer sing and the pianist play? This varies considerably, as for example, the several personas in "Erlkönig," "Vergebliches Ständchen," and "Der Tod und das Mädchen" speak to one another, while the personas in, say, "Gretchen am Spinnrade" and "Schäfers Klagelied" speak, for the most part, either to an unidentified listener or to themselves.

Our investigations into the personas of performers extends beyond simply identifying the poetic persona to include two additional issues: (1) understanding the attitude(s) and mood(s)—the psychology—of the persona and (2) differentiating the persona(s) of the singer from that of the accompanist. For the sake of simplicity, we separate the singer's approach to persona from the pianist's; later, however, we will see that the personas of two performers interact in a variety of important ways, including that of assuming different parts of the same persona.

Vocal Personas

The vocal line presents the words of the poet, and the singer's interpretation of the persona will affect how the role of that "character" is conveyed in musical performance. The singer first poses questions: Who is speaking in the poem and singing in the vocal line? What is the persona's psychological state? Is the persona happy or sad, calm or agitated, approving or disapproving? And does the psychological state of the persona change over the course of the poem and setting? These questions may be clear from the text or they may have to be inferred or speculated about from the poetic imagery and progression.

The identification of and psychological perception of the persona has great consequences for the singer, whose vocal line can be sung with nuances that convey many subtle emotions or sensibilities inherent within the poem. The singer's challenge here varies with whether or not the protagonist is readily identified (for example, sailor, shepherd, male, female, maiden, etc.) and whether or not the psychological situation of that character is clear and unambiguous. The singer's work is intensified when the poetic persona is not obvious from the outset or changes midway through, and when the psychological issues are complex and full of ambiguous dichotomies or ironies.

The singer also must determine the mode of address: To whom do I sing? The different choices of mode of address can affect the singer's projection significantly. When the singer sings to another poetic character, or in response to the pianist's persona, the vocal line is directed outward and toward a specific listener; when, on the other hand, the singer sings a soliloquy or in an introspective mode, the vocal line is more inwardly directed, more responsive to internal thoughts and emotions.

Four well-known *Lieder* demonstrate the singer's challenge in determining and understanding the poetic persona and mode of address. In Brahms's "Wie Melodien zieht es mir," the speaker never is clearly identified, never says "ich" ("I"), but only discusses and describes. The singer has at least two options for persona: (1) assume the persona of the text personally, singing the song completely as if it were the singer's own "voice"; or (2) present a persona that is a recreated or imagined persona consistent with the drama of the poetry and the music. The following clues in the words and their setting of "Wie Melodien" help us determine this persona: first, the speaker is contemplative: the music is quiet and not aggressive, and the text dwells on inward thoughts, self-examination, and poetry; second, the speaker is probably educated, as suggested by the literary subjects and the sophisticated introspection; third, the speaker is sensitive: there are tears and there is emphasis on fine nuances of thought and feeling; and finally, despite the tendency toward poetic sensibility, both the speaker and the musical setting are well-balanced, self-contained, and expressive of contentment.

In adopting the persona of this song's narrator, then, a sensitive singer would assume the role and "voice" of that intelligent, sensitive, and contemplative character. The mode of address, meanwhile, would be one of the introspective types: the poet/singer speaks inwardly (perhaps the poem is actually thinking, not speaking) or rhetorically, the vocal line representing a monologue within the poetic self.

For Schubert's "Die Forelle," the following questions attempt to discern the singer's persona and essential character: Who can "ich" be within the poem? Is the narrator male or female?[7] Why did you answer that? What emotions or moods are expressed in the poem? Are the fisherman and the trout symbolic figures? If so, of what? What is the relationship between the poet and the fisherman?

Within the musical setting, other questions arise: Are there musical clues for the various characters mentioned? Are there musical clues for the attitude(s) of the narrator? And finally, in what state is the persona at the beginning and the end of the poem and its setting?

While the singer's persona is more evident here than in "Wie Melodien," having a clearer understanding of the poet's true nature and the poem's actual meaning (does the poem express real or symbolic events?) will affect the singer's projection and expressivity. The mode of address likewise is different from "Wie Melodien." The poem seems more a narrative account rather than an inner musing. The vivid description of the poetic scene and the poet's response to the fisherman all are conveyed with a sense of drama to a would-be listener, all of which needs to be conveyed in performance much like a story is recounted, that is, in the form of a musical reenactment.

Strauss's "Morgen!" offers another example of a poem and setting where the persona is not entirely clear. Here, however, another character plays an important role in the poetic drama and assumes, possibly, the role of listener or mode of address. Again, we begin with the text: Who are the "wir" ("we")? Why do you reach that conclusion? Are there any indications of any differences between these characters? Or are they presented as acting in unison? Are there any indications of gender? What mood pervades the poem?

Within the musical setting: What is the pervading mood in the setting? What personal characteristics do you ascribe to the narrator, and which of these do you choose because of what you hear in the music?

Regarding the question of mode of address, does the singer sing to the other character, or is this another example of soliloquy or internal reverie? What do you think from reading the poem as opposed to what you infer as Strauss's choice of mode of address from his musical setting?

Finally, in Brahms's "Vergebliches Ständchen": How many characters speak in the poem? How are characters's attitudes illustrated in the poem? In the music, how does Brahms convey the different attitudes within the interchange? How does he convey the difference in gender? Is there any differentiation in the vocal line, or is it all in the accompaniment? Can you think of more than one attitude (or subtext) which could work for the female? Can you think of more than one for the male? Will this couple ever get together? Will they have a chance at happiness?

Accompanimental Personas

The determination of persona and mode of address by the *Lied* accompanist is even more challenging than that of the singer, for in addition to the multiple choices for mode of address, there are at least three different kinds of personas the piano accompaniment can convey, and both persona and mode of address may change within a given *Lied* as well. In the simplest case, the pianist will share the general persona and mode of address of the singer, the accompaniment functioning as embellishment to the singer's projection. A second, more complicated persona type involves the possibility that the pianist not only accompanies the singer's persona but also adds a separate dimension to that persona, singer and pianist representing two different sides of a poet's consciousness or two different aspects of a poet's conflict. In this case, the mode of address occurs in the form of a dialogue between singer and pianist, much like a vacillation between two sides of a conflict. A third type of persona presentation, which is the most complex, involves the pianist conveying not one but several different personas throughout the setting, sometimes sharing the singer's persona, other times adding one or more additional "voices." In this case, the mode of address obviously will change with the persona, which in turn will alter the pianist's musical projection.

At this point it is important to clarify that the projection of an accompanimental persona is not to be confused with those special accompanimental effects of texture, rhythm, and other elements that convey specific poetic issues that are heard but not necessarily "spoken." Well-known examples of such musical effects are the rhythms of horses' hooves (for example, Schubert's "Die Post;" Schumann's "Im Walde"); flowing water figures (for example, Schubert's "Wohin?" and "Auf dem Wasser zu singen"; Brahms's "Auf dem See"); hunting horn calls (for example, Schubert's "Die Post" and "Eifersucht und Stolz") and musical instrument sounds: harp-like chords (Schubert's "Der Harfner"; and Schumann's "Aus den hebräischen Gesängen") and guitar sounds (Schubert's "An die Laute," and Wolf's "Auf dem grünen Balcon"). Composers also employ familiar historical references to flavor a setting, for example, the use of a chorale phrase by Brahms in "Auf dem Kirchhofe," the use of old-fashioned, organ-like figures by Schumann in "Am Rhein, am heiligen Strome" and "Stirb, Lieb und Freud'," or the archaic effect of Wolf's incomplete triads in "Führ' mich, Kind." An even more elaborate example is the extensive quote by Brahms of a familiar carol in his setting of "Geistliches Wiegenlied"; here the recurring melody, played by an obbligato viola, assumes a special persona and adds a whole new dimension to the setting.

Another special musical effect is the recurring pedal point that serves as a metaphor for a particular poetic idea in *Lieder*. When used on the tonic, as in Schubert's "Wiegenlied," the pedal supports a feeling of stability and rest. When used on the dominant, as in Schumann's "Mondnacht," the pedal can create a feeling of anticipation and of postponed arrival. The tension-producing dominant pedal is by far the more common; in "Die liebe Farbe," Schubert uses a repeated V pedal through the entire song to indicate the narrator's haunting despair.

Many of these musical effects merely convey poetic elements that contribute to the poetic atmosphere, but do not represent "voices" or personas that speak to the listener. Even so, when the "text painting" just described are not considered to be actual personas, they still may have a profound effect upon the true personas and listeners within the setting. Do these sound effects represent only aspects of the scene in which the narrator speaks, or do they reflect something the poet experiences or at least is aware of within his or her world?

In contrast to those musical effects of ambient poetic elements, some instances do occur where these external musical elements have an independent presence of their own such that they in fact can be considered personas. When this occurs, the poet personifies the brook or horn call and experiences them as separate personas that "speak" to the poet; as a consequence, the poet becomes the person addressed, the listener who responds to the babbling brook or beckoning guitar. In addition, the poetic experience of such musical depictions of poetic images may include silent personas that are seen or felt rather than heard, as in the light of the moon or loneliness of the forest. Decisions about these issues have tremendous implications for the pianist, who will present musical figurations differently depending upon whether they are simply part of a general poetic scene or whether they assume the role of a separate persona within the setting.

Two Schubert songs demonstrate the possibility of a piano accompaniment containing descriptive musical gestures that might assume actual personas of their own. In Schubert's "Der Lindenbaum," both the title and the piano introduction prompt us to identify the piano figurations with the rustling of the linden leaves, even if we remain unsure about the meaning of the little two-note figure that answers the figuration. We may also label the rocking motion heard under the voice in mm. 29ff. and similar places as a gentle lulling motion of the tree, especially since the narrator mentions the tree's comforting effect. It is, in fact, the combination of the persistent piano figuration and the narrator's anthropomorphic description of the tree that suggests the pianist might consider the accompaniment as having its own persona. This enhances the shock of the piano entrance in m. 45, with the "rustling tree" motive from m. 1 now recast to depict the tree as storm-tossed and frozen in winter. The tree seems to call after the narrator, particularly with the return of the rocking figure in the last strophe, where the narrator hears the tree calling him back. This then places the poet in the role of person addressed, a common result of accompanimental figurations becoming actual personas. The elevation of the piano figuration from "text painting" to persona enables the accompanist to assume a greater voice in the poetic drama and causes the ensemble to experience a more dramatic interaction.

As already suggested, the famous piano figuration of Schubert's "Gretchen am Spinnrade" also prompts the question of accompanimental figuration as persona. While the listener assumes Schubert intended the figuration as the spinning wheel (because of the title; the spinning wheel is not mentioned in the poem), the pianist can consider the accompaniment to either represent the physical activity that symbolizes Gretchen's dreary life *or* to project a rhythmic undercurrent that represents the agitation within her as she expresses her anguish and despair. In the former interpretation, the accompaniment has symbolic meaning but does not "speak" as a persona. In the latter, the accompaniment as expression of inner turmoil "bespeaks" the agitation, despair, and paralysis that Gretchen experiences.

Notably, the spinning wheel is activated only by Gretchen. It never becomes independently possessed, never enters into a dialogue with the half-crazed girl; it gets faster and slower only in reaction to Gretchen's foot as she proceeds with her psychological drama. Unlike the departing beloved in "Mir ward gesagt" or the personified tree in "Der Lindenbaum," the spinning wheel persona is a more passive voice that articulates the girl's feelings along with her, sometimes stating them before she does, sometimes speaking with or for Gretchen. The spinning wheel is thus a separable part of Gretchen's persona, not merely an element in her environment that takes us outside her experience.

The accompanist encounters other complex issues of persona(s) and modes of address. Wolf's "Mir ward gesagt" illustrates the question of whether or not the piano shares the same persona with the vocal line. At first glance, this song seems well integrated in mood and persona. The vocal and accompanimental phrases are parallel in slur marks, dynamic patterns, and phrase structure, and the two parts grow simultaneously in increasing intensity. The emotional intensity of the speaker seems fully mirrored by the accompaniment, as the poet's anxiety and devotion seems to pervade every detail of the song.

However, two factors suggest the vocal line and piano accompaniment as being indeed separate personas. First, another presence seems to walk through this *Lied*. The constant repeated eighth notes seem to represent someone walking almost inexorably: Could this depict the departing beloved? The postlude encourages this interpretation with its powerful musical image of dispersal and a movement into the distance. Second, the piano bass line continually moves in a direction *away* from the vocal line, contrary motion that might signify a separation of personas. The steady fall of the bass line is accentuated by the series of repeated notes in the vocal line of phrases 1, 2 5, and 6, a musical image that vividly conveys the singer/poet's immobility as the lover departs.

Another contributing factor to the idea of the piano accompaniment representing a separate persona involves rhythmic placement and mode of address: at the outset, the bass moves first, thus provoking a response from the voice; this separateness and interaction could represent the duality of the lovers in conflict, as each of the pair assumes a different persona, and each serves as the other's mode of address.

The presence of two personas in "Mir ward gesagt," the poet speaking through the vocal line and the departing lover through the piano accompaniment, thus shapes the ensemble presentation. The duality of persona and mode of address helps mold the direction of phrases and the choice of pacing; in addition, it suggests ways to present certain interactions between singer and pianist, such as the voice and piano alternation in mm. 17 and 18 being heard as a conversation between the lovers. This song demonstrates that while the two personas may have many similar characteristics and may share the same level of intensity about the imminent parting, the two personas also have different characters and roles within the drama. Only the piano persona, for example, is resolute enough to keep going at the end, while the vocal persona remains immobile in tearful acceptance.

The modes of address bring another complexity to the setting. While the singer's persona may speak either inwardly or directly to the departing lover, the pianist's departing lover persona represents a persona that exists but does not speak. The pianist thus conveys the departing lover through a silent presence whose existence or actions, rather than actual "voice," prompts the singer's distress.

We conclude this examination of accompanimental persona with a return to two famous songs discussed previously, Strauss's "Morgen!" and Schubert's "Erlkönig." In "Morgen!" a second persona in the accompaniment was suggested earlier. The accompaniment of mm. 1–14 is repeated in its entirety in mm. 16–29; this repetition of a complete musical section gives the accompaniment more structural weight. In addition, both the elements of text and where they occur signify the presence of two personas. When does the poem's first word appear? What words occur when the voice doubles the piano? Does the voice double the top line of the piano at first? At what point does the doubling start? Along similar lines, what is the symbolism of the inexact, shadow doubling of the singer and pianist in mm. 24–27? Why does the motion stop in mm. 31–38?[8] Finally, what is the last punctuation of the poem? Who speaks last? Why does Strauss end on a 6/4 chord?

Schubert's "Erlkönig" has multiple personas, and changes in the accompanimental figuration help convey the dramatic progression in the poem's narrative. The song also allows us to focus on the use of accompanimental solos: introductions, interludes and postludes, as musical sections where accompanimental personas "speak" alone, either to the singer or directly to the audience.

The four characters who speak—narrator, father, son, and Erlking—have specific musical sections. What are the accompanimental differences in sections expressing the narrator, the father, and the son? Why is the Erlking given different figuration? Whose music includes the long prelude? What sort of action does this music describe? What sort of emotion is conveyed?

One feature of this *Lied* masterpiece is the appropriation by the Erlking of motives formerly associated with the father and son.[9] When the Erlking does speak over the octave triplets ("ich liebe dich, mich reizt deine schöne Gestalt"; "I love, I am excited by your beauty"), how does Schubert alter the motives formerly assigned to the other characters? Could this mean that the Erlking is getting closer to his prey? Or is he getting closer to taking the father's place? Or is he becoming more real?

The accompanimental solos are thus not just musical connections to vocal sections but have as well separate dramatic functions. Specific statements by accompanimental persona(s) affect the singer, who functions as mode of address in one or other of the four different dramatic characters. This is a vivid example of the use of accompanimental solos as personas that frame and interact with the vocal persona. The sensitive ensemble will confer about the personas in all piano solos and coordinate these personas and modes of address with all the various "voices" and "listeners" in the vocal line.

No matter what the form of accompanimental persona(s), the ensemble must take time to discuss their respective persona(s) and modes of address as they prepare their performance. In the case of the two performers assuming the same persona and mode of address, the task is agreeing on the nature of the speaker and listener so a unified presentation can be made. In the case of the two musicians assuming different personas, the ensemble must work through the differences and understand the implications of several "voices" or personas sounding simultaneously and to different listeners. This is particularly important in those moments where one persona responds to another, where, for example, the singer's phrase is in response to a piano interlude, or the pianist's postlude presents a final "statement" after the vocal line has ended.[10] When the singer responds to the pianist, the pianist obviously has spoken *to* the singer (the singer being the mode of address), while the accompanimental postlude can "speak" to any number of listeners, including, but not exclusively, the now silent singer.

Exercises

Use the Repertory list at the end of Chapter Three for these exercises.

Exercise 5.1

1. Find one example each for the German vowels *o, u, e, ü,* and *a.*
   Sing the word or syllable in low, medium, and high range; sing

it first loudly, then softly. What range and dynamic has the composer used in each instance? Discuss your findings.

2. Take five examples of a repeating accompaniment figure and play each at *pp*, *p*, *mp*, *mf*, *f*, and *ff*. What dynamic does the composer indicate? Discuss your findings.

Exercise 5.2

1. Read five poems aloud, deciding which syllables you would like to accent. Then check with the composer's setting; has he emphasized something different?

2. Sing the first verse of Schumann's "Wenn ich in deine Augen seh" three times, accenting any word except that which Schumann puts on the highest note of each phrase. Discuss your findings.

Exercise 5.3

In ten of the *Lieder,*

1. Who is the speaker?

2. Who is being addressed?

3. Does the accompaniment assume a separate persona? If so, what?

4. Is there a shift in persona or mode of address during the song?

Part III
The Language of Music

Chapters Six through Nine constitute the theoretical part of this volume. As usual, we model everything using the *Lied* repertory, returning to many songs discussed in earlier chapters. In many instances, we analyze songs in considerable detail, and we urge careful reading of these analyses as well as the sections of theoretical explanation. It is also important in these chapters that all terms in small capitals be used as quickly as possible in written assignments and when talking about music in the classroom or during rehearsal. These terms form the vocabulary for expressing your thoughts and ideas about many of the central issues of music: harmony, melody, form, etc., and your understanding of the material will be greatly strengthened when you learn to use language that is articulate and precise.

CHAPTER SIX

Harmony and Tonality

This chapter summarizes what *Lied* performers need to know about harmony and tonality to perform well some of their most important tasks: sight-reading new repertory, learning new pieces thoroughly, and participating in actual performances. You have probably learned some of the material in harmony classes, but you may find new ideas and ways of thinking in familiar territory. In addition, some of the later sections on "Directional Tonality" and "Implicit Tonality" will probably cover musical structures you have never encountered or considered in the way we suggest. Harmony is the substance of musical flow in common-practice music, and tonal structure is the basis of form and coherence. Thus this chapter explains the musical foundation of the German *Lied,* its building blocks and its architecture.

Harmonic and Tonal Norms

The common-practice tonal system includes a wealth of pitches and pitch relationships within melodies and harmonic progressions that are organized within a limited number of musical principles. These basic principles of harmony and tonality are the same whether we discuss small-scale form, that is, harmonic progression within phrases, or large-scale form, namely, tonal relations in the context of a large section or a complete work.

Preliminary Terms and Concepts

The foundation of the common-practice tonal system is what we call the TONIC/DOMINANT AXIS, the harmonic fulcrum of tonic and dominant harmonies and tonalities that form the backbone of musical structure. Norms of tonal and harmonic structure are based upon the tonic being the most stable harmony and the dominant being the primary means of articulating the tonic. This ARTICULATION[1] occurs on two levels: the harmonic level, where V creates phrases and CLOSURE[2] through half and authentic cadences; and the tonal level, where in many cases the key of the dominant is the primary tonal contrast.

We begin with small-scale function. The dominant creates musical phrases through half and authentic cadences that function as punctuation of musical SYNTAX.[3] We will review these basic cadences in the section "Small-scale Structure"; knowing basic cadence patterns in all keys is a prerequisite to be able to sight-read new repertory effectively and perform any piece with complete mastery of harmonic articulation.

On the large-scale form, the dominant has two distinct roles within a tonal design. First, tonal closure, or the use of an emphatic arrival on V to signal a work's imminent conclusion, occurs when the dominant resolves to the tonic in the most basic form of the tonic-dominant axis: the authentic cadence.[4] This large-scale closure occurs in one of two ways: either a single dominant chord is placed in a metrically stressed position or a prolonged dominant pedal (in some forms called the "retransition") heralds the return of the original tonic and the work's impending close.[5]

The metrically accented half cadence has the same formal effect in a *Lied*, no matter how many secondary keys might have been touched upon or how much chromaticism might have been used. Performers should be able to sing or play through any *Lied* and identify this important moment of tonal closure; in addition, performers need to note whether such closure coincides with the conclusion of the poetic text (and thus the end of the singer's part), or if the pianist continues with a piano postlude that reflects some special feature of both text depiction and the pianist's persona.[6]

The motion toward closure or the final tonic is one of the abiding features of tonal music, and when this directional impulse is understood and felt by a performer, it can be transmitted to an audience with interpretive nuance. This need for closure is also a perfect metaphor for many emotions present in most poetic texts: a final resolution of yearning, desire, impetus, the search for release, the search for fulfillment, and so forth.

The large-scale dominant has a second important function in most major-mode works of the common-practice period: it creates tonal tension through its function as TONAL POLARITY, where the dominant key opposes and contrasts with the opening tonic. We will discuss the importance of tonal polarity in our summary of mode and tonality later; for the moment, we stress that any major-mode *Lied*, particularly one composed earlier in the nineteenth century, will use the dominant to create final closure and, possibly as well, a primary contrasting tonal area.

Our general review of tonal and harmonic function is based on the performer's ability to make two critical kinds of distinctions: (1) distinguish between structural pitches, harmonies, and tonalities from those that are subservient or embellishing, and (2) understand the difference between musical progression and its opposite, musical prolongation.

Structural vs. Embellishing Elements

The distinction between a musical entity that is "structural" as opposed to "embellishing" reflects the fact that in music there are pitch hierarchies within melodies, harmonies, and tonalities. A STRUCTURAL pitch, chord, or tonality is heard as self-contained and unambiguously significant within the formal design of the piece, a musical space wherein the performer will feel stable and secure.[7] In contrast, then, an EMBELLISHING pitch, chord, etc. functions as an ornament to the more structural elements to which the embellishment ultimately will resolve, either immediately or eventually over time. When a performer does not completely understand what pitches need resolutions or how certain embellishing pitches do resolve, a performance will lack vitality and focus; when, on the other hand, a performer does understand the functions of structural and embellishing elements, the performance will have conviction and even panache.

In those musical contexts where the structural vs. embellishing element is unclear, the performer can be guided by metric and phrase norms of musical syntax. For example, structural harmonies usually occur in metrically stressed positions (such as downbeats, beat 3 in 4/4, and "beat 2" in 6/8)[8] and within certain norms of phrase structure, and in a similar way, structural melodic pitches are usually supported by harmonies within strong rhythmic/metric positions.[9] Embellishing harmonies and melodic pitches, on the other hand, usually occur in rhythmically and metrically weak positions: in 4/4, beats 2 and 4 and in 3/4, beat 3. When they do occur on strong beats, they create some of the most beautiful and expressive dissonances in tonal music, SUSPENSIONS and APPOGGIATURE, which resolve to structural pitches that are temporarily displaced to weaker beats.

To demonstrate the issues that arise in determining and articulating structural vs. embellishing elements, we examine the opening eight bars of Schubert's strophic setting of Hölty's "An den Mond," D. 259.[10] The poem is a poignant remembrance of lost love, where the poet speaks to the moon of happier times gone by. Schubert sets the poet's initial address to the moon in each stanza with two phrases in A major; these then are contrasted by the two a minor phrases that set the rest of the stanza and end the song. Read the poem and listen to mm. 1–8; then determine the harmonic progression and the function of melodic pitches in the piano RH. What harmonies and melodic pitches suggest themselves as phrase goals? Do all chords and melodic pitches occurring on strong beats have structural functions?

Your analysis should proceed from the large-scale design, phrases and cadences, to the small scale, chords and melodic pitches within phrases. The excerpt subdivides into two large four-bar phrases, each of which ends on a half cadence. Schubert greatly restricts his harmonic vocabulary to I, I[6], V[6], and various inversions of V[7], both phrases beginning on I[6] and ending on V. The limited harmonic vocabulary simplifies the determination of structural vs. embellishing harmonies; the tonic and dominant chords in root position are the most structural: I in root position occurs in mm. 1, 3, 5, and 7, and V in root position occurs in mm. 4 and 8. While the I[6] chords that begin the phrases in mm. 1 and 5 are structural, the use of first inversion creates a subtle metric tension that will be described later. As the Roman numerals

(RNs) on the score indicate, both the $V^{6/5}$ (mm. 2, 3, 6, and 7) and $V^{4/3}$ (mm. 2 and 6) have the embellishing neighbor (N) function to I; this demonstrates the common use of V^7 inversions as neighboring (N) or passing (P) chords that resolve to structural I or I^6 harmonies.

Melodic analysis parallels that of harmony: the RH piano line moves parallel to the bass in mm. 1–2 and 5–6, and in contrary motion to the bass in beat 2 of mm. 3 and 7. Melodic tonic pitches E and C♯ are structural, while B, D, and F♯ are embellishing: B is N to A and C♯, and D is N to C♯; D also functions as P between E and C♯ in mm. 1 and 5. Most of this doubles the vocal line, which adds a few additional embellishing pitches in m. 3 to emphasize the arrival of V in m. 4.

Two special melodic pitches warrant mention here. In m. 7, the drive to the half cadence of m. 8 is enhanced by a chromatic harmony and two special melodic pitches: the chromatic D♯ in m. 7 and the F♯ of m. 8 in both piano and vocal line. The melodic D♯ is a chord tone within the applied chord (secondary dominant) $V^{4/3}$ of V, D♯ functioning as leading tone to the melodic E of m. 8.[11] The arrival on E there is further emphasized by the F♯ embellishment on the downbeat of m. 8. The melodic A below is held over as a suspension from the applied chord of m. 7; the melodic F♯ is an appoggiatura (APP) or accented incomplete neighbor (AIN).

The seeming simplicity of harmonic vocabulary and use of structural and embellishing harmonies and pitches in "An den Mond" is a bit deceptive. The poetry is rich in images and powerful emotions, and Schubert's use of simple harmony and melody is enhanced by a subtle use of metric ambiguity. While the downbeats of mm. 1 and 5 initiate the phrases with the tonic, the use of first inversion weakens beat 1 and strengthens the root position I on beat 2. Metric confusion continues in mm. 2 and 6, where only embellishing chords ($V^{4/3}$) occur on the downbeat, and a clear structural chord on a downbeat is avoided until mm. 3 and 7. These metric subtleties balance the simplicity of harmonic and melodic means, and the distinction between structural and embellishing elements helps to illuminate this important aspect of Schubert's setting.

Understanding the distinction between structural and embellishing elements thus enables performers to make more careful decisions about shaping embellishing dissonances, especially those receiving unusual metric stress (suspensions, appoggiature, etc.) with dynamics, shading of resolution patterns, tone quality and the like. We will discuss the nuances of such phrase shaping more fully in Chapter Eight in the section "Norms of the Phrase."

Prolongation vs. Progression

Another important distinction in understanding music occurs between music that "prolongs" as opposed to that which "progresses." This difference is crucial for understanding generally how musical structure unfolds over time and, within our study of *Lieder*, how musical motion conveys poetic progression. The term PROLONGATION means one structural pitch or harmony continues to be in effect over a long period of time despite intervening, less important, embellishing pitches or harmonies. The term PROGRESSION, on the other hand, means the musical syntax actively moves from one note or chord, etc. to another. Prolongation occurs in a variety of contexts and implies a form of musical stasis, of standing still over time; this contrasts sharply with sections of musical progression, which involve a clear change in musical space. These two opposing forms of musical syntax, one static and the other mobile, depict poetry in dramatically different ways: prolongation can convey a poetic state of immobilization or suspended activity, and progression can denote the poetic processes of change and movement.

While, in its simplest form, musical prolongation occurs when pitches or harmonies are simply repeated, prolongation usually occurs in more complicated ways. In the majority of musical contexts, for example, distinguishing between structural and embellishing pitches or harmonies helps determine what is being extended or prolonged. This is demonstrated in the first fifteen bars (the piano introduction and first two vocal phrases) of Schubert's setting of Rückert's "Du bist die Ruh, " D. 776. Again, we begin with the larger view: the phrase structure. The accompaniment's opening seven-bar introduction is followed by two four-bar vocal phrases. While each phrase includes several different harmonies, it begins and ends on the tonic and all the phrases and the entire opening section are understood to simply prolong I. This simplicity of harmonic meaning along with the constant closure on the tonic, as opposed to the more tension-producing half cadence, help convey the poet's awe and reverence: both poetry and music present simple, focused self-contained statements of love and devotion.

In contrast to static prolongation, progression denotes clear melodic, harmonic, and/or tonal movement from one place to another. In the next ten bars of "Du bist die Ruh" (mm. 16–25), the initial tonic prolongation yields to harmonic motion away from the tonic and toward the dominant: V is approached twice by applied chords (vii$^{4/3}$, mm. 16 and 20) and vii^7–V^7, m. 18). The excerpt divides into two phrases, a four-bar phrase ending in a half cadence followed by a six-bar phrase ending in an authentic cadence. The general concept of progression involves beginning and ending in different places, and the fact that both phrases open with applied chords heightens the feeling of progression, especially when the applied chord of m. 16 resolves at the half cadence, m. 19. The two phrases exemplify the ANTECEDENT/CONSEQUENT period structure, the first phrase ending on V and the second ending on I, and the opening chromaticism creates a greater sense of progression than normally might be expected. This contrasts greatly with the opening tonic prolongation and reflects the text's more active expressivity: "Ich weihe dir/Voll Lust und Schmerz" ("I consecrate you/full of happiness and pain").

In harmonic terms, then, a progressive phrase begins with one tonal function, usually I or V, and ends in a different function, usually I to V or V to I. In tonal terms, progression involves motion from one tonal center or key to another, resulting in a tonicization or modulation, two terms that will be explained in precise detail in the later section "Large-scale Tonal Design." While harmonic progression is fairly straightforward, tonal progression can occur in numerous ways and demands a variety of performance decisions. For example, tonal progression might entail a clear tonal shift with pivotal harmonies and a concise establishment of the new key through an authentic cadence. Or, it might be abrupt or ambiguous, where the second key is either not expected or not entirely clear. In either case, we hear the music as "progressing" from one key to another.

We summarize the two contrasting types of musical syntax, prolongation and progression, with a return to the opening of Schubert's "An den Mond." We have already discussed how *harmonically* the I chord is embellished by inversions of V^7. We can now state that the embellishing V's prolong I for the first three bars of the two four-bar phrases. Since the goal of both phrases is V, however, the three-bar prolongation of I is an emphasis on I within a general progression from I to half cadences on V.

The *melodic* design, meanwhile, demonstrates the two concepts of prolongation and progression in a different way. The first melodic phrase, mm. 1–4, shows clear melodic progression: the first structural pitch, E, (pickup to and downbeat of m. 1) moves downward to important C♯s, on beat 2 of m. 1 and the downbeat of m. 3, which in turn lead to the melodic goal B, the second half of m. 4. This melodic progression seems to repeat itself in the second phrase, mm. 5–8, but the motion down to B is replaced by upward motion that returns to the original E for the strong half cadence of m. 8. The first vocal phrase is thus progressive, E to B, while the second is prolongational, E to E. This contrasts with the underlying accompaniment, where *both* phrases are progressive, I^6–V.[12] The rationale for the more prolongational nature of the second vocal phrase seems to be preparation for what follows in the song's concluding phrase. The prolonged E creates a vocal anchor just prior to the changes in mode and texture that mark the song's conclusion. Indeed, the final section in a minor features the vocal pitch E throughout the vocal line, including the final vocal gesture in m. 16 and the echoing piano postlude concluding in m. 18.

The ability of *Lied* performers to make clear distinctions between what is structural, embellishing, prolongational, and progressive is crucial for playing and singing a repertory that uses complex relationships and ambiguity of function to convey a vast array of poetic issues.

Small-scale Structure

Because we assume some familiarity with the concepts of phrase structure and cadence formulae, we offer but a quick review of phrase and cadence types within a larger demonstration of the formal power of the tonic/dominant axis. For this review we use Schubert's "Wiegenlied" of 1816, D. 498; after reading the text and translation in Appendix I, listen to all verses of the song. The poem is a simple lullaby of maternal love and peaceful sleep; the strophic setting is given the simplest harmonic elements: only tonic and dominant chords occur throughout, mostly in root position (exceptions being I⁶ and vii⁶ occurring in mm. 5–6).

The setting demonstrates two of the three phrase types: (1) mm. 1–2 comprise an OPENING PROGRESSION, I–V; (2) mm. 3–4, 5–6, and 7–8 present three CIRCULAR PROGRESSIONS (they begin and end with the same harmony), the first and last prolonging I and second prolonging V. The piano postlude then prolongs the tonic with a I pedal, above which V–I authentic cadences bring the song to a close. The only phrase type not employed is the CLOSING PHRASE, V–I; however, the last two phrases create a large-scale V–I, as phrase 3, which prolongs V, moves to phrase 4, which prolongs I.

The song also presents two of the four basic cadence types: half cadences (ending on V) and authentic cadences (ending on I through a V–I progression). Cadences represent different degrees of pause within time; the half cadence is analogous to the comma or semicolon in prose, and the authentic cadence is analogous to the period. To these basic cadence types, we add the PLAGAL CADENCE, IV–I, and deceptive cadence, V–vi (or ♭VI), which are not used in this song but do occur to great effect in many *Lieder*.[13]

Schubert's use of simple harmony, phrase structure, and cadence formula portrays the rocking of the lullaby and the overall serenity of "Wiegenlied." This underscores the power of the tonic–dominant axis on the level of small-scale design. In the absence of any chromaticism or key change in "Wiegenlied," the dominant is the sole element of musical tension, where the V⁷ chord must resolve to I, and where melodic pitches of V⁷ (especially the leading tone, G, and the 7th of V⁷, D♭) need to resolve to tonic pitches (A♭ and C respectively).

Large-scale Tonal Design

We turn now to examine the principles underlying large-scale tonal design, where we divide a musical work into smaller subsections and demonstrate how all the subdivisions relate to the design of the whole.[14] In general, we can anticipate certain musical events before even hearing or examining a specific piece of music. We know, for example, that all sections of music are distinguished from one another by cadences, and that some sections also are differentiated by change in key. We also know that composers often signal a new section of music through changes in texture and rhythmic elements, changes that will most easily be heard within the *Lied's* piano accompaniment. Finally, we can expect that the opening and closing sections of a piece will be in the same governing tonic and that internal sections might be in other, probably closely related, keys.

Change in Tonality: Tonicization and Modulation

Tonal shift is the most dramatic element of large-scale tonal design to convey poetic progression in *Lieder*. The two terms commonly used to denote changes in tonality are TONICIZATION and MODULATION. Both terms refer to change in key, but they should not be used interchangeably; each term has a distinctive meaning with altogether different implications for musical form, poetic portrayal, and, ultimately, musical performance. Essentially, the two terms convey different degrees of removal from the original key: tonicization denotes a brief shift and modulation creates a lengthier one. Careful use of the terms will lead to greater understanding of how tonal design conveys poetic and psychological changes and will, as well, assist the performer in understanding how these changes *feel* differently, in the throat or the fingers, within the context of a given work.[15]

In its simplest meaning, the concept of "change in key" means one key heard originally as tonic is replaced by another, new tonic. The first tonal shift in a piece signals three additional things to the performer: (1) in most cases, we eventually will return to the original tonic; (2) the second tonic usually is structurally less important than the first; and (3) since change in tonality connotes a significant shift in poetic progression, the performer moves to a different musical and dramatic place.[16] While some young performers may intuitively understand the first two points, the third cannot be overstated: both singers and pianists cannot perform *Lieder* effectively if they do not understand how tonal shift conveys changes in poetic meaning, including changes in persona and mode of address.[17]

An important aspect of a *Lied*'s use of several different keys over time is the clear tonal reprise at the song's conclusion, the fact that a work usually begins and ends in the same tonal space. Arnold Schoenberg's term for this tonal return, MONOTONALITY, also suggests that the original tonic maintains a hierarchical superiority to all other "keys," that all keys that are tonicized or to which the music modulates ultimately relate back to this superior, governing tonic.[18] As discussed earlier, this tonal reprise follows a strong dominant and creates both the onset of tonal closure and the conclusion of the tonal frame that creates tonal coherence.

The notions of tonal hierarchy and coherence have many implications for performance. When performers consider all sections of a piece to be in separate but equal keys, the performance will not convey the relative weights of different keys and the shaping force and poetic expressiveness of tonal design. Thoughtful analysis, as conveyed in part by careful use of RNs, will enable the performer to place the tonal hierarchy within a work's *large-scale* tonal design. For example, Figure 6.1 shows a tonal design that begins in C major and has contrasting sections in a minor and d minor. Rather than hearing the piece in three separate, distinct keys, we hear C as I and the internal "keys" as functioning *within* C: a minor = vi; d minor = ii.

FIGURE 6.1 Tonal relations within a governing tonic.

Form:	Section 1	Section 2	Section 3		Section 4
key:	C major	a minor	d minor		C major
analysis:	I	vi	ii	V	I

The tonal hierarchy, as demonstrated by the RNs in Figure 6.1, shows C major as the prevailing tonic, with sections in a and d minor providing temporary tonal contrasts. The V that occurs after the d minor section is not a new key (that is, V is not a tonal polarity, wherein G major would be tonicized), but rather V functions as the important large-scale V mentioned earlier: the crucial V that brings tonal closure through its eventual resolution to the final I.

As already stated, the distinction between tonicization and modulation is one of degree; the briefer tonicization usually involves either an immediate return to the original tonic or a shift to yet another "key," while the lengthier modulation is more structurally significant. Each term denotes a specific type of departure from the tonic; a tonicization might occur momentarily within a large section governed by another key, while a modulation might encompass an entire section of a song. A sensitive performer will note the tentativeness of a tonicization and how the brief shift away from a given key signals a particular type of poetic departure or distance. This is altogether different from the effect of a modulation, which is experienced as a more substantial tonal removal or distance that is responding to a more profound poetic alteration.

Performers sensitive to tonal flux know the formal effects of both departure from and returning to the original tonic. Using a variety of performance techniques, for example, those of rubato, touch, and timbre, both singer and pianist can convey the different psychological states of temporarily leaving the tonic (moving somewhere less stable for a time) and returning for closure (returning to a place of anchor and finality).

Embellished Half Cadence

In the small *Lied* forms, it can be difficult to determine whether a tonal shift is a tonicization or a modulation. For example, in Schubert's well-known "Heidenröslein," the arrival on V can be considered a tonicization, since the music returns quickly to I, while a case for modulation can also be made since the time spent *in* the dominant is six of sixteen bars. Either term will work in this case, as long as the performer can make a clear case for the choice. In addition to the difficulty of determining whether there is a tonicization or modulation in a given piece, confusion also can easily arise between a tonicization of V and the common musical structure known as "an expanded arrival on V" or an "embellished half cadence." While the enhanced arrival on the dominant occurs through use of its "applied" or "secondary dominant" chords (V of V, vii°⁷ of V), an actual change in key does not occur; V is merely embellished by its applied chords and maintains its function as dominant in the original key. It is thus crucial to be able to distinguish between use of applied V, V^7, or vii°⁷ chords as a means of emphasizing various harmonic functions within a key as opposed to using authentic cadences (V^7–I or vii°⁷–I) to create new, even if temporary, tonics.

Figures 6.2a and b offer two brief examples of expanded arrivals on nontonic harmonies, in both cases the frequently emphasized dominant, that are *not* tonicizations. Each shows poetic depiction more subtle than that usually conveyed through real change in tonality; as always, begin by reading the text and performing or listening to the songs.

In Figure 6.2a, Schubert closes the first phrase of "Nachtviolen" with an elaborate arrival on V in m. 8. After a four-bar piano introduction, the first vocal phrase begins with a two-bar prolongation of the tonic, C major, and concludes with a two-bar phrase ii to V in a sequence using applied chords ($V^{6/5}$ of ii–ii–V^6–$V^{6/5}$ of V–V) that sets the descriptive words: "dunkle Augen, seelenvolle" ("dark-eyed, soulful"). The next phrase begins again on C major as I, and this confirms that V had functioned not as a new tonic, but simply within an embellished half cadence. This opening phrase is in great contrast with that beginning in m.19, where V *is* tonicized for ten bars in setting the descriptive text: "Grüne Blätter streben freudig, /Euch zu hellen, euch zu schmücken; /Doch ihr blicket ernst und schweigend /In die laue Frühlingsluft" ("Green leaves strive joyously,/ you to brighten, you to adorn;/ but, you gaze earnest and silent,/ into the mild spring air"). In tonal contrast to the poet's own thoughts and feelings set within the tonic, both the embellished half cadence (*on* V) and the tonicization of V (*in* V) set poetic personifications that intensify poetic meaning. While in both places V similarly depicts such personifications, the musical effect of the embellished half cadence in m. 8 is altogether different from the section *in* V mm. 19–26.[19]

In "Ave Maria" (Figure 6.2b), Schubert creates an even more elaborate half cadence in mm. 7–8. The tonic, B♭, is prolonged in mm. 1–5 through both a deceptive cadence (mm. 3–4) and an authentic cadence (mm. 4–5). The ensuing phrase, beginning with the anacrusis to beat 3 of m. 5, then commences a progression away from B♭ that ultimately leads to a half cadence in m. 8. When the next bar begins on a V^7 of B♭, the strong arrival on F in m. 8 is heard as an elaborate arrival on V *as* V, not as a new tonic. The text translation for this strophic setting shows that the phrase that ends on V in m. 8 sets the final verse of the first, third, and fifth stanzas, and that the resolution back to the tonic begins the opening lines of the second, fourth and sixth stanzas. The phrases of text sung on the applied dominant to V thus set the subjunctive verb tense, and the half cadence of m. 8 conveys the tentative connotation of the verb.

FIGURE 6.2A Schubert, "Nachtviolen," mm. 1–8 and mm. 19–22. Embellished arrival on V.

Tonal Polarity

As suggested earlier, the term TONAL POLARITY relates directly to the concepts tonicization and modulation.[20] More specifically, tonal polarity connotes the tonal contrast between an original tonic and a second important key. Within the common-practice period, the tonal polarity in major is usually between I and V, and the tonal polarity in minor is most often between i and III, the relative major. The tonal polarity between the two keys maintains the work's prevailing musical tension or drama, and is resolved

FIGURE 6.2B Schubert, "Ave Maria," mm. 7–8. Elaborate arrival on V.

continued

only at the work's conclusion. The harmonic design of the sonata form most clearly demonstrates how this polarity works; it is shown in Figure 6.3.

In sonata form, the first thematic area is in the tonic and the second is in a closely related key (depending on the mode, V or III). The first large section of the piece, the Exposition, ends in the second key, at which time the polarity is at its most intense state. The ultimate harmonic function of the Development section, then, varies according to the work's mode. In major, this section returns the dominant to its original function; V ceases its function as a contrasting key and returns to its initial harmonic function of defining the original tonic. In minor, on the other hand, the development progresses from tonal focus upon III to a return to the original tonic, that return signaled by the large-scale V that prepares for the tonal reprise. The

FIGURE 6.2B *continued*

Recapitulation's harmonic function, then, is to solidify that tonal return, resolve the tonal polarity, and to prepare for the work's harmonic closure.

As the model in Figure 6.3 suggests, the mode of a work bears directly on the common-practice norms of tonal polarity, a role of mode that will be examined more fully in the next section. Within the *Lied* genre, the use of tonal polarity is directly connected to the requisites of the text: the tension of the polarity can reflect any number of different poetic problems or dialectics, and the resolution of the musical tension likewise can depict many

FIGURE 6.3 Norms of tonal polarity in sonata form.

	Exposition			Development	Recapitulation		
	Theme Group 1	Theme Group 2	Closing Material		Theme Group 1	Theme Group 2	Closing Material
major mode	I	V	V	V	I	I	I
minor mode	i	III	III	V	i	i	i

diverse types of poetic dénouement or resolution.[21] In later sections, we will see how *Lied* composers, especially in the latter half of the nineteenth century, expanded common-practice tonal norms by using more distantly related, chromatic keys as tonal polarities. This practice resulted in part from the interest in stretching the tonal language and in part from the desire to capture more poignantly the dramatic tensions within German Romantic poetry.

Tonality and Mode

The potential impact of mode upon a song's tonal design is of far greater consequence than the more commonly noted "coloristic" effects of a change in mode. As just stated, the mode of the opening tonic will strongly suggest a particular tonal polarity (for example, minor i–III), and a change in mode once a piece is underway (for example, minor i–major I or vice versa) can alter the anticipated tonal design. The effect of mode upon tonal design depends, in turn, upon which of two dramatically different types of modal pairing is employed: the parallel major/minor pair or the relative major/minor pair.[22]

Parallel Major/Minor Pair and Mixture

In a piece using the PARALLEL MODE PAIR, both major and minor modes occur but the *tonic remains the same.* Along with the mode change, the quality of most chords reverses (major to minor and vice versa) and some of the chord use changes as well. In the major mode, for example, the most commonly used harmonies would be I, ii, IV, V, and vi, with iii and vii (respectively, a minor and diminished chord) occurring only in certain contexts. In minor, on the other hand, the harmonies III and VII become major triads and occur much more readily, and the V chord has several different forms (major and/or minor) and functions. The more frequently used harmonic vocabulary in minor, thus, is i, III, iv, V♯, VI, and VII.[23]

The switching from one mode to the other of the parallel mode pair occurs in many guises and fulfills many functions. One common form of parallel mode change involves an entire contrasting section in the opposite mode. This adds variety and the coloristic change alluded to earlier; more importantly, it provides a musical depiction of a poetic shift without having to change the overall tonic.[24]

Two Schubert songs illustrate the variety of musical effects created by change within the parallel mode pair; "Der Lindenbaum" (D. 911, No. 5 from *Winterreise*) shows the common shift from the major to the minor mode and "Am Feierabend" (D. 795, No. 5 from *Die schöne Müllerin*) shows the reverse, a shift from minor to the major mode. The text in "Der Lindenbaum" describes the poet's reencounter with a tree that had offered much comfort during the poet's youth, and the essentially happy recollection of the *past* stated in stanzas 1 and 2 are presented in the key of E *major.* When in stanza 3, the poet experiences the tree within the *present,* it is "in tiefer Nacht" ("at dead of night") and the *minor* mode recasts the tree imagery into the darker side of the E tonality. Stanza 4, when the tree again acts as a comforting friend, is set back in the major mode, but the minor mode recurs to set stanza 5, where the tree assumes a persona of cold inhospitability: "Die kalten Winde . . . Ich wendete mich nicht." ("Cold winds . . . I returned not."). When the song ends in major, the stark contrast of the minor-mode sections convey the poet's conflicting relationship with the linden tree: in major, the tree is a source of comfort and hope; in minor, the tree symbolizes alienation and despair.

In "Am Feierabend," the young miller's anxiety about working hard enough to earn the maiden's approval is set in a minor. This minor-mode depiction of the youth's general stress is then contrasted with two shifts to A *major* (mm. 13–24 and again m. 66) which underscore the young man's recurring wish: "könnt ich drehen/alle Steine!/Daß die schöne Müllerin merkte meinen treuen Sinn!" ("could I turn/ every mill-stone!/ that the fair miller's daughter might mark my true worth"). The parallel mode pair thus conveys the dichotomy within the poet, his constant worrying (in minor) alongside his recurring hopefulness (in major).

The brief incursions into the major mode of "Am Feierabend" demonstrate another, more profound function of the parallel mode: its use to facilitate tonal shift. The large-scale tonal design of this song includes a middle section that moves through C major, the relative major of a minor (mm. 40–45), d minor (mm. 46–49 and later mm. 60–64) and its relative major, F major (mm. 50–59). While these keys all seem principally related to the *minor* side of parallel mode pair, the keys of d minor and its relative, F major, also are close to A *major,* where C♯-as-major-third in A major becomes leading tone in d minor.[25]

This connection of d minor/F major to A *major* is exploited in mm. 46–64, when d minor/F major sets the text: "in der stillen kühlen Feierstunde,/und der Meister spricht zu allen:/ Euer Werk hat mir gefallen;/ und as Liebe Mädchen sagt/allen eine gute Nacht" ("in the quiet coolness of closing time,/and the master says to all: Your work has pleased me; and the lovely maiden says/ to all a good night"). Just as A major had set the miller's hopes for appreciation from the maiden, so the related d minor/F major section sets the text describing fulfillment of the young man's wishes: the master's praise and the maiden's good wishes. This section might represent either a youthful fantasy or an expression of the miller's hopes for the future. Either way, the section contrasts distinctly with the song's conclusion, when Schubert rounds out the song with a repetition of the words and music of the a *minor* opening. The modal contrast of the parallel mode pair thus highlights the two emotions within the young miller and the shift in his focus: from the a minor daily stress of hard work to the A major/d minor/F major hopes for (or fantasy about) future success.

A final, equally important, function of the parallel mode pair is the use of an opposite-mode element (harmony and/or melodic pitch) within a given mode known as MODAL MIXTURE. Modal mixture usually occurs when a *minor* element is used within the *major* mode, but the reverse can happen as well. While the utilization of smaller elements of modal mixture may seem less consequential than wholesale repetition of phrases or entire sections in the parallel mode, mixture actually occurs much more frequently and often serves more significant functions than other parallel mode usages.[26] Since mixture usually involves minor mode pitches, principally ♭3̂ and ♭6̂, the chords most often altered through mixture are those having the predominant (or dominant preparation) function: in the major mode, ii, IV, and vi become ii°, iv♭, and ♭VI.[27]

Two popular *Lieder*, Schumann's "Ich grolle nicht" (from *Dichterliebe*) and Schubert's "Die liebe Farbe" (D. 795, No. 16 from *Die schöne Müllerin*) demonstrate the power of mixture in poetic depiction. Schumann's "Ich grolle nicht" uses mixture in its most common form: a minor-mode version of a chord occurs within a major-mode work. The song's major-mode setting is fittingly ironic as it sets Heine's sardonic view of love: "I'll not complain because in my dreams you suffer pitifully." The minor-mode ii°[7] that sets various uses of the word "Herz" (mm. 3, 21, 28–29) belies the poet's spoken words of indifference; the depiction of "Herz," with the mixture harmony of intense darkness and dissonance, reveals the poet's true feeling of hurt and pain.

Schubert's "Die liebe Farbe" employs a less common but perhaps even more dramatic form of mixture, the use of a *major* tonic within a *minor mode* setting. The poem uses the metaphor "green" to speak of love's dichotomous nature; it brings both joy and pain, and the young miller's fear of love's pain is conveyed by the overall setting in b *minor*. Schubert then underscores the irony of this fear of love by setting the recurring word "gern" (how much the color green is loved by the desired maiden) on a *major I*[6] chord. The unusual poignancy of the major mode connotes the frailty of the poet's yearning for love even as he feels its pain.

Relative Major/Minor Pair

In the parallel major/minor pair, the two modes shared the *same tonic* but the chord quality and use changes. In the RELATIVE MAJOR/MINOR PAIR, on the other hand, a key signature and several common chords are shared, but the two modes have *different tonics*. This presence of two different tonics creates a tonal tension or polarity not found within the parallel mode pair, and *Lied* composers use the relative mode pair for different tonal designs and for more profound poetic depiction.

The normal shift within the relative mode pair is *from* the minor i *to* the relative major, III, and within this mode change, the degree of tonal shift can vary a great deal. For example, in the simplest form of relative major usage, the change to major is no more than an emphasis on III within the minor mode, while in a more complicated usage, the relative major functions as an altogether different key or a tonal polarity. Determining the function of the relative major within the minor mode can be tricky: Is the relative major an emphasis on III or a tonicization of III? When deciding whether or not the relative major is tonicized seems difficult or even impossible, the performer is urged to recognize *both* possibilities and not worry unduly about choosing one over the other.

Two Schubert songs illustrate the various relationships between the minor tonic and relative major: "Der Tod und das Mädchen," D. 531, exemplifies a use of the relative major that might be either a tonicization of III or merely a focus upon III within the governing tonic, and "Der Wasserfluth," D. 991, No. 6, (from *Winterreise*) demonstrates the use of the relative major/minor pair where tonicization is clear. In "Der Tod und das Mädchen," the piano introduction and first vocal line (mm. 1–12) present the opening d minor tonic. Within the second vocal phrase, the applied vii^{o7} of iv (m. 13) suggests motion away from d minor as the maiden says to Death: "Ich bin noch jung,/geh' Lieber, und rühre mich nicht an" ("I am still young; go, my dear,/and do not touch me"). The setting of the second line of text (mm. 15–17) in the relative major is clear: $V^{6/3}$–I^6–$V^{4/3}$–I–V all in F major. While this might seem a tonicization of the relative major, it is brief; Schubert immediately returns with a repetition of the same text in d minor, and both phrase and section ends on a strong half cadence in d minor. The phrase in F major thus could be considered either a brief tonicization of III *or* the harmony III being prolonged and embellished by applied chords.

A similar shift into the relative major then occurs in the section setting death's response. On the text, "komme nicht zu strafen" ("come not to punish"), the applied chord to C major emphasizes that chord as V of III and the phrase ends on F major as a possible new tonic. The next phrase then moves to B♭ as it sets the text: "Sei gutes Muths!/ich bein nicht wild" ("Be of good cheer!/I am not harsh"). The phrase can be heard either as tonicizing B♭ or emphasizing IV of F with applied chords. When the phrase and song ends back in d minor, the section in F and B♭ (mm. 28–33) thus can be heard in two ways: (1) as tonicizing the relative major and emphasizing IV of F, or (2) as presenting a circle of fifths progression (C–F–B♭) *within* d minor, B♭ functioning as VI of d that resolves to V of d in m. 34.

This song thus demonstrates the potential difficulty of determining whether or not the relative major is tonicized once or even twice, *or* is heard as an embellished III (through applied chords) within the single d minor tonality. Both interpretations are feasible, but each considers the F major sections differently, closer or further away, in relation to the tonic d minor.

If the relative major is believed to be tonicized, for example, those sections in F major represent a *tonal contrast* to d minor, the distance between the two tonics creating a tonal polarity or tension. If, on the other hand, the relative major sections are heard merely as prolongations of III, the tonality remains intact and musical contrast is one of mode not key, a less powerful difference. Performers need to consider both interpretations and then choose one. As always, the text will assist them in making this kind of decision: Does the poetry set in F major seem closer or more distant from poetry set in d minor? Does the poetry offer tensions best musically depicted by modal contrast or by tonal polarity?

Schubert's "Wasserfluth" offers a more straightforward use of the relative mode pair, where tonicization of the relative major is unambiguous. The opening f♯ minor dominates the song's first half (mm. 1–14), as the minor mode connects the snow imagery of Stanza 1 with the poet's grief in stanza 3. In the song's second half, the alternate stanzas 2 and 4 describe, respectively, springtime images of melting snow and the poet's love. The music accordingly shifts to the relative major, beginning with the modulatory piano interlude in mm. 15–18 and continuing through m. 26. When the song ultimately concludes back in f♯ minor, the poet is immobilized within the winter landscape. The tonicization of the relative major, which comprises ten measures of a thirty-two-bar setting, provides a musical analog to the dramatic contrasts within the poem; the setting of the past warmth and love in the contrasting tonality of A major sets into poignant relief the present-day despair in the governing key of f♯ minor.

The tonal shift in "Wasserfluth" underscores the influence of the relative major upon the tonal design of *Lieder*. Two Schubert settings of Goethe poetry, "Erster Verlust," D. 226, and "Schäfers Klagelied," D. 121, dramatize this influence in decidedly different ways. Schubert's setting of "Erster Verlust" demonstrates how slippery the relative major/minor pair can be, as the song literally vacillates between f minor and its relative, A♭ major; "Schäfers Klagelied," on the other hand, exemplifies the potential for tonal richness, when both the parallel and relative modal pairs are explored in a more complex tonal design.

The text translation of "Erster Verlust" suggests why Schubert set the two tonalities in opposition: the poem moves between the loneliness of the present (in f minor) and the happy days of the past (in A♭ major). This dichotomy of two different times and two contrasting psychological states poses many challenges to performers, who wander between the two keys and often exist in neither one completely.[28] An adequately "*langsam*" tempo, careful phrase shaping, and attention to dynamics all will help clarify the tonal shiftiness, and performers will want to note how the voice or hands feel differently in f minor, in A♭ major, and in areas of tonal flux.

The song ends with a dramatic tonal shift in the piano postlude. While the singer concludes within the reverie of the past in A♭ major, the pianist,

representing the lonely present, continues on to recover the original f minor
tonality. The "*pp*" dynamics mute the importance of this postlude, which
offers both the closure of mode and key and the return to the present-day
context for the poet's *Sehnsucht*.

The tonal dichotomy between the singer's close in A♭ and the pianist's
cadence in f minor suggests that the vocal line could be considered essentially in A♭ and the accompaniment essentially in the relative minor. This
double tonal scheme is compelling in performance, where the singer's
close seems altogether convincing and the pianist's cadence sounds like a
distant and remote echo. In discussing the relative major/minor pair in the
first two songs of *Dichterliebe*, Charles Rosen confounds potential for the
tonal dichotomy one step further. He notes that Schumann "treats the relative minor . . . as a variant form of the tonic, using it rather for a change
of mode and not of tonality." This is achieved, Rosen says, by a tonal design
that derives its form from a "potentially infinite oscillation" of both stable
and unstable sonorities and the relative major/minor tonalities.[28]

Schubert's "Schäfers Klagelied" demonstrates the use of the relative
mode pair, and, as well, the parallel mode pair. This song thus summarizes
our general discussion of mode, as it exemplifies the richness and versatil-
ity of both basic types of modal pairing. Schubert's setting of Goethe's
lengthy portrait conveys the poetic progression as follows: stanza 1, where
the shepherd, bowed over his staff, looks down into the valley from his
world on the mountain top, is set in c minor; stanza 2, when the shepherd
turns away from his flock and ponders a return to the valley, occurs in the
relative major, E♭. The section in E♭ major thus creates a tonal polarity based
on the relative major/minor pair that underscores the existence of two
worlds: the shepherd's world atop the mountain (in c minor) and the
"other" world of the valley (in E♭ major). The modal relationship, along with
the different textures and rhythms of each mode, suggest further that the
world of the mountain is melancholy, while that in the valley is more lively.

Stanzas 3 and 4 are set in A♭ major/minor. The new tonality depicts the
poetic shift to nature imagery, and the parallel-mode duality underscores the
ambivalent forces of nature: A♭ *major* sets the benign, comforting images in
stanza 3 and a♭ *minor* sets the menacing, fearful images in stanza 4. The
song's climax, where the shepherd realizes "all is a dream" occurs in the relative major of a♭ minor, C♭ major. This key of epiphany is dramatically distant from the opening, c minor, and this tonal distance depicts the poet's
extensive "journey" from his mountain retreat to his recognition of the pain
of lost love. These images prompt the shepherd into further introspection
in stanza 5, where with a return to E♭ major he recalls his lost love. This recall
of the E♭ major of stanza 2 is significant. E♭ major once again represents the
lively world of the valley but now its meaning is clearer: that world once was
shared by him and his love. In the final stanza 6, where the shepherd retreats
to his flock on the mountaintop and to his lonely isolation, we return to

c minor, the tonality representing the loss of love in which the song began and now ends.

The use of both the relative and parallel major/minor pairs in this song dramatizes the different effects of the two modal pairs. The parallel minor functions more simply; the two stanzas remain linked musically as they are linked through the use of nature imagery. However, while the parallel pair (A♭ major/minor) underscores the duality within the valley's nature world, the relative major/minor pair (c minor/E♭ major) conveys the dramatic shift in poetic space and emotion.

The song's various tonalities and modal pairings exist within a large-scale tonal hierarchy. The relative major/minor pair, c minor and E♭ major, is the song's primary polarity, the song's ending in c minor casting E♭ major as a secondary key to the real c minor tonic. This captures the poetic conflict of worlds, as the valley remains somehow distant from the shepherd's loveless life in the mountains. The tonal tension between E♭ major and A♭ major/minor, meanwhile, is a secondary polarity, A♭ major/minor being heard as IV/iv of E♭. The hierarchy of modal pairing thus underscores the changing perspective of the poet's experience; the relative pairing dramatizes the poet's psychological conflict between two opposing worlds and the parallel pairing, in yet another key, personifies the shift from internal brooding to a more metaphoric experience of conflict through nature.

Tonal Shift and Enharmonic Puns

The diverse tonal relations in "Schäfers Klagelied" emphasize the unique impact of mode upon a song's tonal design. These tonal shifts are achieved in various traditional ways (use of pivots, and so forth), but a special device that contributes to the success of the tonal shift is called ENHARMONIC REINTERPRETATION. Enharmonic reinterpretation occurs when certain chromatic pitches have the *same sound* but *different functions;* these enharmonic pitches are called ENHARMONIC PUNS and through reinterpretation they help to interrelate or connect different keys.[29] Enharmonic reinterpretation of musical puns is a powerful resource for connecting tonalities in tonal music of all genres, and within the miniature scale of the *Lied,* both performers can emphasize these chromatic pitches and assist the listener's perception of the musical links and the poetic connections they depict.

"Schäfers Klagelied" offers a clear example of both the context for and the application of such enharmonic puns. For example, enharmonic reinterpretation is extremely important when connecting two keys that might seem remote or even unrelated. This is the case with the two minor mode keys, a♭ minor and c minor, which appear remote from one another but which actually depict similar poetic ideas: c minor depicts the poet's loveless isolation atop the mountain and a♭ minor represents the menace of the storm. While these poetic ideas might initially seem unconnected, they actually convey different aspects of a single poetic element: the poet's internal despair. The c minor isolation provokes an ongoing pain of loneliness within the shepherd, and the a♭ minor storm captures the menacing, painful feelings that arise when the poet remembers his lost love. Schubert conveys this poetic connection through the enharmonic pun, B♮/C♭, where B♮ is the leading tone in c minor and C♭ is $\hat{3}$ in a♭ minor and $\hat{1}$ in its relative, C♭ major. In this way, the enharmonic pun links two keys and two poetic ideas that might otherwise have remained separate. Enharmonic reinterpretation and pun thus can have tremendous impact on both performer and listener alike; these subtle musical associations convey significant poetic connections and thus offer a richness of meaning and a depth of detail that is a hallmark of the *Lied* genre.

Just as enharmonic puns connect remote tonalities in "Schäfer's Klagelied," so such puns also occur in simpler tonal contexts. In "Wasserfluth," for example, the pun E♯/F♮ connects the keys of the relative major/minor pair, as the E♯, leading tone of f♯ minor, is reinterpreted as F♮ (♭$\hat{6}$) within A major. Enharmonic puns are especially useful in linking tonalities a chromatic third apart in songs employing chromatic tonal relationships. This chromatic tonal relationship occurs frequently in the *Lied* repertory and will be examined in the section "Chromatic Third Relations."

We have shown how different uses of the parallel and relative mode pairs both depict diverse poetic situations and create a great variety of musical structures. The sensitive performer will note a change in mode, whether parallel or relative, as conveying either a bold or a subtle shift in poetic meaning, and the ensemble will need to make many judgments about the possibility of tonicizations or the connection of tonalities through enharmonic puns. Two resources can assist performers in interpreting these tonal relationships: first, the musician must hear the tonalities in question and perceive the tonal design aurally; second, the performer must always look to the poetry for clarification and validation of an interpretation of a tonal relationship.

Harmonic and Tonal Innovation

Building upon the harmonic and tonal foundation called common-practice tonality, nineteenth-century composers constantly expanded and developed the tonal language in a variety of ways, including increased chromaticism, more complex harmonic progressions and tonal designs, and greater exploitation of the ambiguous relationships inherent within the tonal system. These inventive and adventurous harmonic and tonal usages occurred within all musical genres but were particularly important to opera and *Lied* composers who sought harmonic and tonal innovations to create more elaborate and vivid text and drama depictions. In this unit, we examine three of the harmonic and tonal innovations most important to *Lied* performers:

(1) chromatic third relations, (2) a form of double tonality called directional tonality, and (3) an unfulfilled suggestion of a key called implicit tonality.

Chromatic Third Relations

One way in which composers attempted to stretch common-practice musical syntax was through use of more remote harmonic and tonal relationships. The most common such distant relation was the chromatic third, a use of harmonic and tonal relations by major or minor third, including a special series of chromatic third relations called "third chains." Numerous types of third relations were available within the tonal system: major thirds up or down, for example, I–III♯ (C major–E major) or I–♭VI (C major–A♭ major) or minor thirds up or down, e.g., I–♭III (C major–E♭ major) or I–VI♯ (C major–A major). Each type had a unique musical effect. Charles Rosen describes the use of mediant relationships by the "generation of composers born around 1810. They reconceived modulation not as the establishment of an opposition but as a chromatic coloration of the original tonic—and this original tonic was often loosely enough defined to contain both its own minor node and the relative minor as well."[30] Rosen continues: "Renouncing the force of tonal opposition may eventually have weakened the tonal language, but it did not weaken the music, which in fact had gained a new source of power."[31]

Several songs demonstrate third relations characteristic of the *Lied* genre. Schubert's famous "Meeres Stille," D. 216, typifies the dramatic use of chromatic third relations within *harmonic* progression. Four more complicated songs: Schubert's "Der Neugierige," D. 795, No. 6, and "Der Musensohn," D. 764, along with two songs examined earlier, Schumann's "Widmung" and Brahms's "Die Mainacht," illustrate chromatic third relations within large-scale *tonal* designs. And three remarkably different settings: Schubert's "Der Jüngling und der Tod," D. 545, Brahms's "Immer leiser," and Wolf's "Und steht Ihr früh" exemplify the most dramatic form of third relation, the third chain, each song using the third chain to convey a particular poetic idea with a unique musical effect.

We begin with Schubert's "Meeres Stille." As the text translation shows, the poem describes a sailor's anxiety at a "fearfully deathly calm" sea, as he senses that a powerful force is somehow veiled by the water's eerie stillness. The sea's calmness is depicted in C major, the tonal anchor that is presented simply in rolled chords in the middle register, and the listener is lulled into the sea's initially deceptive motionlessness. The chromatic third relation, E major, that concludes the first phrase immediately undermines the placidity of C major, and the listener senses the poetic tension in the harmonic remoteness of C major to E major.[32] While the ensuing phrases then use more familiar harmonic relations, a minor and F major, V of E major returns to end the penultimate phrase that sets the text "Todesstille fürchterlich!"

("Dread, deadly calm," m. 24) and an authentic cadence in E major occurs on the text "ungeheuern Weite" ("vast expanse," m. 28). When the song ends in C major, the tension between C and the chromatic third E major (I–III♯) remains unresolved; this aptly conveys the sailor's lingering anxiety as he continues to survey the foreboding stillness.

Within the tonal domain, we examine songs utilizing two of the most common chromatic third relations: the major third down, I–♭VI and the upward major third, I–III♯. Schubert's "Der Neugierige" and "Der Musensohn" use the same chromatic third, G major/B major, but in opposite ways; in "Der Neugierige" the tonal progression in B major is I–♭VI and in "Der Musensohn" the tonal progression in G major is I–III♯. Schumann's "Widmung" and Brahms's "Die Mainacht" also use the downward major third tonal relation (I–♭VI); despite the use of similar formal designs the two songs convey extremely different poetic texts.

Schubert's "Der Neugierige" (from *Die schöne Müllerin*) describes the young miller summoning up courage to ask his companion, the brook, whether or not his heart speaks the truth, whether or not the maiden loves him. It is a moment of great anxiety, as the youth realizes the implications of the answer, "yes" or "no," to his questions: "die beiden Wörtchen schließen/die ganzer Welt mir ein" ("these two tiny words enclose/my whole world"). In dramatic contrast to the B major tonic, Schubert dramatizes the poet's fear of a negative response by setting this text in G major (♭VI). When the final stanza of hopeful inquiry returns to B major, the distance between the two keys remains a metaphor of the ongoing tension within the young miller, who continues to wait for a response to his earnest questions.

Schubert's beloved setting of Goethe's "Der Musensohn" differs from "Der Neugierige" in that the use of the chromatic third relation B major/G major occurs in reverse form: the opening tonic is G major and the sections in B major create the chromatic major third *above* the tonic, I–III♯. The song thus presents on a *tonal* level the same chromatic third relation, I–III♯, heard as a *harmonic* relationship in "Meeres Stille." "Der Musensohn" employs this third relation within an unusual rondo-like form, so that the third relation occurs not once but twice, and creates a form of tonal vacillation. This tonal flux intensifies the effect of the third relation; the B major sections describe images of springtime and the power of love that contrast with the G major sections depicting the poet's wandering about in a state of longing for his own love: "Wann ruh ich ihr am Busen/Auch endlich wieder aus?" ("When shall I at last find rest again on your bosom?"). The tonal tension of this wavering chromatic third relation is especially dramatic as Schubert makes no attempt to connect the two tonalities through mixture or some sort of modulatory progression. The resulting musical animation creates a vivid portrait of the poet's energy and eagerness.

While Schubert's "Der Musensohn" uses the chromatic major third I–III♯ for tonal vacillation, Schumann's "Widmung" and Brahms's "Die

Mainacht" both explore the tonal chromatic third I–♭VI for contrasting middle sections within the common *Lied* ternary ABA form. In both cases, the remote keys of the flat submediant (in Schumann, F♭ major in a song in A♭ major; in Brahms, C♭ major in a song in E♭ major) depict shifts in poetic direction, the chromatic third relations dramatizing shifts in textual progression in both the poetic and the psychological realms.

In Rückert's "Widmung" the images of the poet's love shift from the earthly to the more spiritual: "Du bist die Ruh, du bist der Frieden,/ Du bist vom Himmel mir berschieden" ("You are repose, you are peace,/You are from heaven bestowed upon me"). The images of peaceful death and spiritual salvation so characteristic of German Romantic poetry are cast in F♭ major, a tonality as remote from the A♭ tonic as heaven is to earth.

In Hölty's "Die Mainacht," the poet progresses through three different states: (1) an unfocused melancholy wandering; (2) a painful response to nature's love images; and (3) a recognition of the pain of lost love within the numinous natural world where the poet feels the most deeply. In Brahms's setting, the poet wanders about a moonlit landscape in E♭ major, the diffused moonlight and vague shadows reflecting the poet's initially imprecise and meandering emotional state. While the poet's vague wandering resonates with nature's diffusion in E♭ *major,* a profound emotional response to the nightingale's lament (end of stanza 1) is underscored by a modal shift to e♭ *minor.* This then prepares for the poet's second state of increasing emotional pain in stanza 2, when the happy love song by a pair of cooing doves forces the poet to turn away and weep, all of this set in the tonality of C♭ major (♭VI). The tonal shift thus reflects the poetic progression away from nature's vague outer world and into the poet's inner world of emotional turmoil. The close tonal relationship between e♭ minor and its relative, C♭ major, is aligned with the twin nature images of nightingale lament (in e♭ minor) with cooing doves (in C♭ major); the minor mode in e♭ thus connects opposing nature images and at the same time uses mixture as a pivot to the key of C♭ major. The closeness of the e♭ minor/C♭ major relative major/minor relation is then contrasted by the return to E♭ *major,* where the poet in stanza 3 turns outward once again and addresses directly the lost love.[33]

The return to E♭ major incorporates rhythmic figuration from the C♭ major section, whereby Brahms conveys the transformative nature of the poet's experience. The return to nature, and the key of E♭ major, now includes the poet's feelings of lost love, the poet's affinity with nature intensified by the journey inward, all depicted through the chromatic third relation. The modified reprise of the opening A section thus dramatizes the chromatic third relation E♭ *major/*C♭ major; the tonal tension remains at the song's conclusion as the poet's pain continues unabated within the nocturnal landscape.

An especially unusual and effective form of third relation during this period was the use of several chromatic third relations in a series or sequence called a third chain. This use of sequential third relations replaced normal syntax with new harmonic and tonal progressions that provided *Lied* composers with a unique form of text depiction. Schubert's "Der Jüngling und Tod" models this special use of third relations in a relatively conservative way, wherein the chromatic tonal relations are mediated by modal mixture; later songs by Brahms, "Immer leiser," and Wolf, "Und steht Ihr früh," then show even more imaginative uses of the device for dramatically different effects.

Even though the poem "Der Jüngling und der Tod" involves a singular theme: the youth's longing for peaceful death and death's gentle embrace of him, the poetic progression involves a series of shifts in focus, from responding to the setting sun, to yearning for peaceful death, to appealing directly to death, to death's gentle response. Schubert captures these poetic shifts by a third chain featuring minor thirds: c♯ minor–E major–G major–B♭ major, each tonality representing a new aspect of the poetic progression. The initial image of the setting sun, which prompts the youth's yearning, is set in a c♯ minor piano introduction, the pianist adopting the persona of the sunset as the singer-as-poet silently watches nature's move toward night. As the singer begins to express the poet's yearning, c♯ minor shifts smoothly to the relative major, E, that key setting the poet's wish: "Und weit in schön're Welten ziehn!" ("and journey to fairer worlds!"). Figure 6.4 aligns the tonal with the poetic progression. In stanza 2 the youth speaks directly to death, and the tonality shifts to G major, the key in which the poet pleads: "O komm und rühre mich doch an!" ("O come, and touch me!"). The speech by death then concludes in the song's closing tonality of B♭ major, the embrace of death ending the third chain a minor third away from the opening tonality of c♯ minor.

While Schubert's use of this minor third chain is certainly unusual, he links the chromatically related keys of E major, G major, and B♭ major through two common techniques: the use of mixture mentioned earlier and the use of mediating or pivotal harmonies. As Figure 6.4 outlines, mixture connects the major mode keys in a systematic way: in m. 19, E major yields to e *minor*, which then functions as relative minor of the ensuing G major; similarly in m. 27, G major turns to g *minor*, which becomes relative minor to the concluding tonality of B♭ major. Certain pivot or mediating keys also assist in this process: the C major in m. 19 functions as VI of e minor that becomes IV of G major, and the E♭ major of m. 28 functions as VI of g minor that becomes IV of B♭ major. The third chain thus moves seamlessly through the cycle as the youth moves inexorably toward the release of peaceful death.

The artistry of Schubert's smooth progression of chromatic minor thirds is in sharp contrast to the bold tonal juxtapositions within the same

FIGURE 6.4 "Der Jungling und der Tod": Third chain and tonal imagery.

Die Sonne sinkt,   o könnt' ich mit ihr scheiden,
The Youth: The sun is sinking: O might I   too take my leave,
        C$\sharp$ min $V^{6\,5}$–I– *V/E maj*

Tonal imagery: c$\sharp$ minor = sun E major = leave

Mit ihrem letzten Strahl entfliehn! Ach diese namenlosen Qualen meiden
(and) with its dying rays *depart;*   these nameless torments *escape,*
            (V^{7}/A)   ($V^{6\,5}$/f$\sharp$ min)

Und weit in schön're Welten ziehn!
and *on to fairer worlds* journey!
    $V^{6\,5}$/*E maj*   *E maj*

Tonal imagery: E major = move on

O komme, Tod, und löse diese Bande! Ich Läche dir, o Knochenmann,
O come, death, and loose these bonds. I smile on you, spectre of death;
(A) $V^{4\,2}$/E $V^{6\,5}$/A   V/E $V^{6\,5}$–i/e min   (c major)

Tonal imagery: e minor = smile; C major = Knochenmann

Entführe mich leich in geträumte Lande!
Lead me   gently   to the land of dreams.
    V/ G maj

Tonal imagery: G major = lead away to dream world

O komm und rühre mich doch an!
O come, and let me feel your touch!
    V/ G maj

Tonal imagery: G major = touch

    Es ruht sich kühl und sanft in meinen Armen,
Death: You will rest cool and gentle in my arms.
        g min   (E$\flat$ maj)   *B$\flat$ maj*

Tonal imagery: g minor = will rest

Du rufst, ich will mich deiner Qual   erbarmen.
You call, I   will   on you in your agony have compassion.
c min $V^{6\,4}$/g min (E$\flat$ maj) V^{7}–I/*B$\flat$ maj*
Tonal imagery: B$\flat$ major = Death's compassion

minor third chain in Brahms's "Immer leiser." The poem presents, in two
stanzas, the anguished thoughts and feelings of a poet who in facing death
is consumed by torment over the lover that will live on and love another.
While the setting is essentially in c$\sharp$ minor/major, Brahms uses the third

chain (E major–G major–B♭ major–D♭ major) to convey the intensification of anguish, the third chain concluding the setting in a climax of turmoil and longing. The third chain at the end is foreshadowed at the conclusion of the song's first half with a partial chain, E major to G major, mm. 14–17. After the song's opening in c♯ minor, this third chain fragment sets the dream of the lover being outside the door (but unable to enter), a depiction made all the more anguished by use of tension-producing syncopation and chords in the unstable 6/4 position. The first section concludes back in c♯ minor and the piano interlude reconfirms that key as the governing tonic.

The setting of the second stanza, with the image of the lover kissing another, then begins in the tonic but shifts to E major once more on the text: "Eh' die Maienlüfte wehn . . ." ("Ere May breezes blow . . ."). This launches the complete third chain, which sets the rest of stanza 2, where the distracted poet shifts from bleak despair to images of spring and an urgent plea to see the lover once more. The third chain now is complete: E major–G major–B♭ major–D♭ major, the concluding D♭ tonality enabling the song to end in the same key (enharmonically respelled) as the opening, but in the parallel mode. As earlier, the frenzy of the cycle is intensified by the use of harmonic juxtaposition, rhythmic syncopation, and use of 6/4 position.

While both Schubert and Brahms use the exact same third chain, the chains differ musically in several important ways. First, Brahms's third chain juxtaposition is bolder and more dissonant than Schubert's smooth third chain presentation. Second, while Schubert's is an innovative form of *tonal* progression, Brahms's third chain replaces a *harmonic* progression. Even though the chromatic juxtaposition in the Brahms is somewhat jarring, it is balanced by the use of a fairly conventional tonal design within the tonality of C♯ minor/major and the minor relative, E major. The third chain in Schubert's "Der Jüngling," on the other hand, involves a *chain of tonalities* a chromatic third apart, a form of *tonal* dissonance made even more pronounced by the fact that the work begins and ends in different keys.[34]

In contrast to the minor third chains of the Schubert and Brahms *Lieder* the third chain in Wolf's "Und steht Ihr früh" sets the poem's first half with a twice-presented chain of *major* thirds: E major–A♭ major–C major–E major. This third chain is similar to that in "Immer leiser" in that the chain is harmonic rather than tonal and it occurs in a format of juxtaposition rather than smooth progression. Unlike the Brahms, however, the chain does use a connecting device: the reinterpretation of a V⁷ sonority as a chromatic augmented sixth chord. We will see presently that this seemingly helpful pivot actually contributes to the tension created by the third chain itself.

The poem is an Italian lyric that combines love and religious devotion in a description of the poet's beloved preparing for and attending mass, a vision that prompts a powerful response within the poet. The first of two third chains sets the poem's opening, where the beloved's rising from bed, dressing, and going to mass is portrayed with loving appreciation. With each advance of the chain, the beloved is moving further ahead toward the church and religious observance. The tension created by the chain of thirds reflects the excitement that the poet bestows upon each event, where each commonplace act by the beloved has enormous impact upon everything around him or her. The second third chain, which depicts the beloved participating in Mass, is abbreviated, and the music that follows then changes altogether, as it conveys the poet's shift in focus from admiring the beloved to reflecting upon the beloved's closeness to God.

As already suggested, the juxtaposition of harmonies within the third chain is both softened and intensified by the use of a complex pivot chord, a systematic destabilizing of the prevailing chord from I to V^7 of IV followed by reinterpretation of that V^7 as an augmented sixth. The augmented sixth, which normally resolves to V, resolves irregularly into the next harmonic link in the chain. This process repeats itself over and over throughout the third chain, creating three unresolved tensions: (1) how to understand the V^7 chord that becomes an augmented sixth; (2) how to understand the unusual resolution of the augmented sixth; and (3) how to determine whether the third chain is a harmonic or tonal progression?

The first issue becomes clear only in the song's second half, when in m. 34 the recurring unresolved V^7 of IV does in fact resolve to IV in setting the text: "Wie hold und selig hat Euch Gott begabt,/ die Ihr der Schönheit Kron' empfangen habt!/ Wie hold und selig wandelt Ihr im Leben" ("How gracious and blessed has God given you,/ The crown of beauty you have received!/ How gracious and blessed you travel through life"). The initial attempts toward IV had been thwarted by the third chain, which depicted the beloved *in the process* of coming to this state.

The second tension produced by the song's pivot, the irregular resolution of the augmented sixth to root position I rather than the customary V, can only be understood as an intensification of the irresolution of the V^7 of IV along with the juxtaposing of harmonies that is so prominent in the song. The new harmony (or key) resulting from this curious resolution thus has a sense of ambiguity about it that is somewhat but not completely alleviated by Wolf's use of pedals to help confirm the new link in the third chain.

The third factor creating tension around the third chain is a basic question of function: Does the third chain represent a harmonic or a tonal progression? While the shift from one link to another in the chain seems like a change in key, complete with pivot chord reinterpretation, the chain actually functions more like a harmonic progression than a series of key changes. This ambiguity of function becomes clear in, again, the latter part of the song, when the song's final phrase, mm. 30–38, replaces the third chain phrase with a relatively normal harmonic progression.

The complexity of Wolf's third chain is typical of the richness and innovation that characterizes his poetic settings. Within the third chain, the balance of stability and instability, harmonic prolongation and dissonant juxtaposition, and various forms of musical ambiguity all help to depict the series of actions toward poetic transformation within religious devotion. In this context, the third chain depicts both the systematic ritual of religious observance and the ever-increasing response in the heart and soul of the poet.

Directional Tonality

Two final issues remain in our review of large-scale tonality: the prevalence of a monotonal rather than a double-tonal design and the difference between implicit, or suggested, as opposed to explicit, clearly-drawn, tonality. Two major *Lied* composers, Schubert and Wolf, broke with the nineteenth-century monotonal norm and wrote numerous pieces in double-tonal schemes[35] and all *Lied* composers used the idea of suggesting but not fulfilling tonal shift to convey special poetic ideas. The poetic depictions that resulted from these tonal innovations created some of the most vivid, expressive moments within the genre.

As already mentioned, the concept of monotonality was a basic norm of tonal design throughout the common-practice period. Beginning and ending a work in the same key was the basis of tonal coherence and concluding a work back in the original key was a component of tonal closure. Nevertheless, despite the logic of closing a musical work in the key in which it began, both Schubert and Wolf created settings that began and ended within different keys using in a bold tonal design known today as DIRECTIONAL TONALITY.[36]

The issues that arise in a directional tonal design are predictable: How does a work cohere and have clear closure when it begins and ends in different places? How does the tonal shift occur over time? How does the composer reconcile or connect the two different keys that shape the song's tonal design? How do the performers reorient themselves to a change in tonal anchor? To begin answering some of these basic questions, we examine briefly two *Lieder* that explore this tonal design: Schubert's setting of von Collin's "Leiden der Trennung," D. 509, and Wolf's "Mir ward gesagt, du reisest in die Ferne."[37] In both cases, the composers's fidelity to text depiction may well have encouraged this unusual use of double tonality.

Von Collin's poem is a short lyric describing the longing of a wave to return to its source, the sea, that image functioning as a German Romantic metaphor for the poet's longing for peaceful death. After reading the poem and translation, listen to Schubert's setting. The song begins clearly in g minor, the piano prelude and the singer's first three phrases ending in half cadences in mm. 2, 4, 6, and 10. The song then concludes in the key of the relative major, B♭, the new key closing on a strong authentic cadence in mm. 22–23 followed by a four-bar piano postlude that confirms B♭ as closing tonic. This form of double tonality not only associates different keys for different psychological states (longing and torture in g minor and peaceful release in B♭ major) but the directional tonal design also dramatizes the poetic progression from one state to another.

While the literary impetus for beginning and ending a poetic setting in different keys is compelling, performers must also experience the tonal shift in musical terms that are independent from the text. The new closing key, B♭, is musically anticipated in m. 8 (the harmony B♭ there heard as III of g minor), and then B♭ takes hold as new tonic more or less from m. 14 to the song's conclusion. Both performers need to try to determine where the new key of B♭ truly becomes operative as I of B♭ and not III of g minor. While there may be different interpretations as to the exact moment of tonal shift, the *process* of changing keys is critical to vital performance. For example, both singer and pianist must be clear about three distinctly different tonal states within the song: certainly (1) when g minor ends its role of tonic and (2) when B♭ takes over as new tonic, but also (3) when in the song each performer feels tonally adrift, like the wave of the poem, unsure of what tonality is operative. Additional questions to ask are: How does the composer make the ending so unambiguous, so secure? How is closure created in the vocal line and in the piano accompaniment? And, in addition to the change in key, what else differs about where the performers begin and end the song?

Wolf's setting of "Mir ward gesagt" uses a directional tonal design to convey a dramatic poetic progression from intense anxiety to hopeful acceptance. The poem traces the emotional process of someone learning of a departing lover and struggling to come to terms with this through a series of reactions: anxious questions, to tearful resignation, to acceptance with hope that the poet will not be forgotten.[38] Along with directional tonality, the song also uses an elaborate opening tonal and metric ambiguity to depict the poet's confusion and despair. The setting thus captures the transformation of the poet's emotional and psychological state in two musical ways; the opening tonal ambiguity depicts the initial anxiety and confusion, and the closing, newly emerged D major tonality depicts the final state of tearful but hopeful acceptance.

The opening ambiguity is a feature of many of Wolf's *Lieder*, and is particularly challenging for performers here who must perform phrase after phrase without clear or sustained tonal anchor. The pianist begins on an incomplete triad, the third G–B, and the singer's opening pitch B can be either $\hat{5}$ of e minor or $\hat{3}$ of G major; however, neither key emerges as tonic and the first phrase concludes on a V⁷ of a minor. This tonal wandering continues through a vaguely defined circle of fifths: b minor (mm. 4–5) to f♯ minor (mm. 9–10) to V⁷ of c♯ minor (m. 13) before the harmonic syntax becomes clearer. Beginning in m. 14, the tonality of D major emerges with more traditional harmonies, and the song concludes with a strong, metrically clear authentic cadence in mm. 17–18. This coincides with the poet's final state of acceptance: "Mit Tränen bin ich bei dir allerwarts—/Gedenk' an mich, vergiss es nicht, mein Herz!" ("With tears I am with you every-where—/Think of me, do not forget, my heart!") The piano postlude recalls some of the earlier musical tensions, I becomes V^7 of IV and minor iv occurs as a chord of mixture in an elaborate plagal cadence. The B♭ of minor iv is an enharmonic pun with earlier A♯s and the mixture chord recalls the opening minor mode. The accompanist may consider this postlude as representing the departing lover, the contrary motion of treble and bass signifying the act of separation and the wide range of mm. 18–19 conveying the emerging distance from the poet.[39]

Implicit Tonality

The term IMPLICIT TONALITY refers to a section of music where a key is suggested (i.e., implied) but not fully (i.e., explicitly) presented. Historically the notion of implicit vs. explicit tonality arose when common-practice tonal function and syntax became so predictable that dissonant harmonies such as V^7 could function without traditional resolution patterns and keys could be suggested or alluded to without complete modulation or tonicization procedures.[40]

Implicit tonality occurs in a number of guises, for example, when dissonances, especially the tonality-defining dominant, do not resolve properly or when progressions within a key are not clarified by authentic cadences in that key. Lack of clear resolution of tonality-defining dissonances (for example, V^7, vii°⁷) takes several forms such as when a section ends on a V^7 chord that resolves deceptively or when such a dissonance remains unresolved. A well-known example of the latter is the first song of Schumann's *Dichterliebe*, "Im wunderschönen Monat Mai," where both the song's recurring unresolved V^7s throughout and ending on V^7 convey the poet's unfulfilled longing and desire. The absence of a tonic resolution within the song intensifies the irresolution of the concluding V^7; while the song's position within a cycle complicates the issue a bit, the challenge to performers is clear: Determine whether the V^7 chord at the end of Song 1 resolves somehow at the beginning of Song 2, or whether the ending of Song 1 actually remains unresolved.

To make a decision about the ending, read aloud poems 1 and 2 and listen to Song 1 without continuing on to Song 2. There are at least three ways to interpret the ending of Song 1: First, the song remains uncomfortably unresolved until the beginning of Song 2; Second, the V^7 chord resolves implicitly (tacitly) in the listener's ear; or Third, the dissonance is to remain unresolved, i.e., to implicitly linger in irresolution. No matter what each performer decides, interpretation of this wonderful moment in Schumann's cycle occurs in the space *between* the first two songs: if the V^7 is to resolve only implicitly in the listener's ear or is to remain unresolved, the pause will be lengthier; if instead the second song is to resolve the closing V^7 of the first, then the pause will be briefer and will have a completely different meaning.[41]

The notion of suggesting but not fully realizing a key afforded *Lied* composers a rich resource for conveying all sorts of poetic issues such as conflict, anticipation, recollection, or many other moments that exist outside a primary poetic space. To capture such poetic distractions or wanderings, composers played with musical expectations by setting up progressions or dissonance patterns and then deferring or even denying the anticipated resolutions.[42] Tonality by suggestion or by implication thus created a new kind of musical tension that enhanced the setting of more complex poetic ideas such as ambivalence or irony.[43]

Another Schumann example, "In der Fremde," demonstrates a clear instance of implicit tonality where a chord progression suggests but never cadences unequivocally in a given key. After the authentic cadence of m. 9 signals the close of the opening A section in f♯ minor, a new section B begins with a D♯ in the bass that takes us outside the domain of the song's tonic. Careful harmonic analysis of mm. 9–12 reveals that the D♯ functions as leading tone to E, E major being V of A major, the relative major of f♯ minor. This tonal shift to III is certainly reasonable in any minor-mode work; however, there is never a root position authentic cadence in A major, and the cadence that ensues in mm. 14–15 confirms the goal of section B as not A major, or III, but rather as b minor, or iv of f♯ minor.

However, mm. 9–12 are not *in* b minor and *sound* as if they are in the key of A major. This is implicit tonality: the key is *suggested* (V^{6}_{5} of V, mm. 9–10, ultimately to V^{6}_{4}–V^{4}_{2}, m. 11, to I^{6}, m. 12 all in A major) but is not completely realized. The absence of an authentic cadence in A major does not negate that key, but the key remains implicit, tentative, rather than explicit or actual. The implicit key of A major conveys the longing for peaceful death ("Wie bald, . . . kommt die stille Zeit, da ruhe ich auch" ("how soon, . . . comes the quiet time, there rest I also") in such as way as to amplify the fact that it *will be* in the future (i.e., is implicit) rather than already exists (i.e., is in an actual key).

Understanding the notion of implicit tonality is crucial for effective performance, and both pianists and singers need to recognize the vague, unsettled quality of such moments in *Lieder*. How do you project an implied key, conveying its tentativeness or elusiveness? Do mm. 9–16 of "In der Fremde" feel differently within A major from the ensuing section within b minor? Can you feel the difference in moving to an implied key as opposed to cadencing in an actual key? Does A major feel less real? Does it feel disorienting to slide out of A major and into b minor?

A performer has two vehicles for determining implicit tonality. First, if one feels tonally disoriented or unsettled, it might be because a key is in fact being suggested but not fulfilled. If this is the case, the disorientation and insecurity can be replaced by a sense of assurance and excitement. Second, a performer should always see if the text suggests the use if implicit tonality. If there is a poetic rationale, then the performer can feel more certain in identifying implicit tonality and the connection between the music and the poetry will, once again, embolden the performance.

Our discussion of components of large-scale tonal design has reviewed concepts of normative tonal shift and the use of mode as it relates to key change, and tonal innovations called chromatic third relations, directional tonality and implicit tonality. In each instance, we have stressed how the different tonal and modal relations convey various musical distances from a governing tonic that correspond to analogous poetic distances. In addition, we have suggested that understanding the harmonic and tonal context of a given moment within a *Lied* greatly enhances the performer's role in musically expressing the world of German Romantic poetry. The feeling of a harmonic progression or a tonality shift conveys with delicacy and power the nuances and development within the poet's world.

Exercises

Exercise 6.1: Structural vs. embellishing

Using the Schubert songs below, notate on staff paper which pitches and harmonies are structural (use noteheads and stems) and which are embellishing (use noteheads but no stems). Embellishing pitches will have one of three basic functions: N (neighboring tone), P (passing tone) and CS or arp (chordal skip, i.e., leap within a chord, or arpeggiation). Test the results by playing only the structural elements of each piece; these should sound like the bare bones of the song.

1. "Hoffnung"
2. "An den Frühling"
3. "Heidenröslein"
4. "An den Mond"
5. "Abendlied"

Exercise 6.2: Prolongational vs. progressive

Indicate whether each phrase in the Schubert songs listed below are prolongational (PL) or progressive (PG). In prolongational phrases, indicate what harmony is prolonged, in progressive ones, indicate where the progression begins and ends.

1. "Hoffnung"
2. "An den Frühling"
3. "Heidenröslein"

4. "An den Mond"

5. "Abendlied"

Exercise 6.3: Determining small-scale structure

Using Schubert's "Wiegenlied" as a model, give instances of the three phrase types (opening, closing, circular) and three cadence types (authentic, half, deceptive) in the following Schubert songs. Indicate how each of these types reflects some aspect of the poetry.

1. "Hoffnung"

2. "An den Frühling"

3. "Heidenröslein"

4. "Abendlied"

5. "Schwanengesang"

Exercise 6.4: Determining large-scale design

Using Schubert's "Wiegenlied" as a model, indicate for each Schubert song the overall tonal design, noting any tonicizations, modulations, and embellished half cadences.

1. "Der Tod und das Mädchen"

2. "Das Mädchen"

3. "Des Mädchens Klage"

4. "Schwanengesang"

5. "Erster Verlust"

Exercise 6.5: Tonicization of V vs. embellished half cadences

Using Schubert's "Nachtviolen" as a model, list all instances of either tonicizations of V or embellished half cadences; indicate by measure number and explain how these tonicizations or half cadences reflect the poetry.

1. "Hoffnung"

2. "An den Frühling"

3. "Heidenröslein"

4. "Der Tod und das Mädchen"

5. "Schwanengesang"

Exercise 6.6: Use of modal pairing

Using Schubert's "Schäfers Klagelied" as a model, indicate how mode is used (relative major/minor = RM; parallel major/minor = PM; both relative and parallel pairs = R&PM).

1. "An den Mond"
2. "Der Tod und das Mädchen"
3. "Das Mädchen"
4. "Schwanengesang"
5. "Des Mädchens Klage"

Exercise 6.7: Chromatic third relations

Find any chromatic third relations in the following songs. Note all connecting mechanisms such as enharmonic puns and mediating or pivot harmonies. Identify the poetic reason for using this bold chromatic relationship.

1. Schumann, "Die Lotosblume"
2. Brahms, "Ständchen"
3. Brahms, "Wie Melodien zieht es mir"

Exercise 6.8: Directional tonality

Using Schubert's "Leiden der Trennung" as a model, trace the use of Directional Tonality. Indicate the opening and closing keys and determine when the closing key begins to assert itself and any areas of tonal overlap or ambiguity. Also indicate connecting mechanisms such as enharmonic puns and mediating or pivot harmonies.

1. Schubert, "Klage an den Mond"
2. Schubert, "Der Wanderer," op. 4, no. 1
3. Wolf, "Lebe wohl"
4. Wolf, "Begegnung"

Exercise 6.8: Use of implicit tonality

Using Schumann's "In der Fremde" as a model, indicate by measure number any sections of these Schubert songs that use implicit tonality and state how these implied tonalities reflect the poetry.

1. "Gretchen am Spinnrade"
2. "Des Mädchens Klage"
3. "Litanei"
4. "Schwanengesang"
5. "Erster Verlust"

CHAPTER SEVEN

Melody and Motive

This chapter offers some general guidelines and analytical procedures for understanding how melody works within *Lieder*. The melodic component of a *Lied* is extremely complex, and we suggest three analytical approaches that demonstrate different aspects of melodic design: First, the *Melodic Overview* helps identify the poetic and harmonic context for the melody and determines general characteristics of melodic construction and design; second, *Linear Analysis* demonstrates important elements of the underlying melodic structure; and third, *Motivic Analysis* identifies the repetition of small melodic ideas that creates melodic coherence. While each approach will be shown separately, performers will want to combine them all when preparing a *Lied* for performance. The song we chose to demonstrate these analytical procedures is one well known for its beautiful melody: Schubert's strophic setting of "Litanei."

Melodic Overview: Context and Characteristics

The approach called Melodic Overview has three goals. The first two establish the context for the melody: How does the song's overall structure relate to the poem it sets? What is the song's tonal framework and, therefore, the melody's harmonic support? The third goal focuses more on the melody itself: What are the song's characteristic melodic elements and how are they put together to form a unique melodic design?

Comparison of Poem and Setting

As a preface to the analysis, read "Litanei" aloud and study its several stanzas; then listen to the song, hearing at least two or three stanzas so you can experience the repetition so characteristic of strophic settings.[1] You will note that the poem's essential content remains the same despite the variation in each stanza. In all stanzas, line 1 describes the different souls needing rest; a lengthier middle four-line group explains the various earthly torments suffered by those mentioned in line 1; and line 6 reiterates the prayer: "all souls rest in peace!" in a closing religious refrain.

The musical setting reflects the poem's ternary (ABA) form as follows: a one-bar piano introduction and three-bar piano postlude frame the ABA musical form; the two A sections set lines 1 and 6 in two-bar phrases; the interior B section sets lines 2–5 in a lengthier five-measure section subdivided into a 3 + 2 bar phrase structure. The repeated setting for lines 1 and 6 links the description of the various souls (line 1) with the prayer for them (line 6) and at the same time the full reprise of section A at the song's conclusion creates clear musical coherence and closure. The musical setting thus coincides completely with the form of the poem and the melodic design corresponds similarly to the lines of text.

The Tonal/Harmonic Context

The song's tonal design is relatively straightforward. The A sections prolong the tonic, E♭ major, section A material ending with authentic cadences in mm. 3 and 10. The two phrases of the B section begin in c minor (m. 4). Phrase one ends with a half cadence in c minor in m. 5; the ensuing phrases return to E♭ major, with two half cadences in E♭ in mm. 6 and 8. The motion to c minor, the relative minor of E♭ major, is unusual in that there is no modulatory progression: we just begin in c minor on the downbeat of m. 4.[2] This abrupt shift to c minor presents an unusual context for the vocal line in section B: the voice begins a new phrase in a new tonal context without any preparation.

Unique Melodic Features

Focusing our attention now on the vocal line only, we note first some general melodic characteristics. The opening and closing melody of the two section A's is serene and gentle and is confined to a small musical space or range in middle register. By contrast, the middle section's description of torment is set with a more active melody full of tension and dissonance. The melodic space is opened up with larger leaps and a wider overall range, and new expressive elements include a more varied use of rhythm and an extensive use of melodic or linear chromaticism.

We now need to amplify these broad melodic statements with a more detailed description of melodic construction. The following questions serve as a guide.

1. Is the line predominantly CONJUNCT (motion by step) or DISJUNCT (motion by leap)?

2. Is the line confined to one clear musical space or does it divide into several different spaces or registers?

3. What is the line's overall shape or contour, and where is the climax?

4. Do any pitches seem more important than others?

5. Does the line include any chromatic elements?

6. Is the line characterized by certain rhythmic figures or motives?

7. Are any pitches emphasized by such things as registral extreme, sudden shift in dynamics, unusual timbral indication, rhythm, etc.?

The vocal line of "Litanei" can now be described more concisely: the line is more disjunct than conjunct, especially with leaps by thirds; there is uniformity of dynamics (p) and musical range (the line spans a minor tenth, C^1–$E♭^2$); the vocal line moves in concert with the piano accompaniment, using a recurring dotted-rhythm motive (quarter note/eighth note and diminutions) against constant sixteenths in the piano RH; the line is focused around the pitch G, and the two accidentals that are sung are the F♯ of m. 5 and the A♮ of the downbeat of m. 8.

Upon answering these general questions, the performer quickly grasps the melody's unique character and identifies those features that give the melody its expressive power. With the above description in mind, listen to "Litanei" again, noting how your own performance might be different with these new insights about the poem, the tonal/harmonic context, and the song's unique melodic characteristics.

Once the melodic overview has set up the framework for understanding the melody of a *Lied*, two additional analytical procedures offer deeper insight. Linear Analysis traces the underlying structure of the melodic design and aligns the melodic structure more clearly with its harmonic support. Motivic Analysis divides the melodic line into melodic cells whose systematic recurrence creates a special type of continuity within the melodic fabric. These two approaches are more extensive and time consuming, and at least some of the principles underlying both linear and motivic analysis will seem intuitive to you; however, the more time you give to understanding the nuances and complexities of melodic lines, the more beautifully and effectively you will perform them.

Linear Analysis

The term LINEAR ANALYSIS describes the existence of a pitch hierarchy within melodic structure and traces how melodic pitches relate to one another and to harmony over time.[3] This analytical approach is similar to that of Heinrich Schenker (1868–1935), a celebrated German theorist whose work has been studied, especially in this country, for several decades.[4] While Schenker's sophisticated theories are beyond the scope of our work here, we do adopt a modest analytical procedure based upon two of his important concepts: the PRIMARY TONE and prolongation.[5] These two concepts show *Lied* performers how melodic activity tends to focus around one primary melodic pitch (called the primary tone) and how melodic lines unfold and develop over time (through melodic prolongation).[6] In explaining the two concepts, we will suggest several notation devices that are similar to those proposed by Schenker. However, what we label and notate as "linear analysis" in no way represents Schenkerian analysis, which is a much more complex and sophisticated system.

As already suggested, the primary tone is a structural melodic pitch of the tonic triad (usually $\hat{3}$ or $\hat{5}$, and not $\hat{1}$) that functions as the chief melodic focus. This primary tone recurs systematically throughout, receiving metric weight or emphasis, and embellishment by other, less important, melodic pitches. The primary tone is prolonged in a similar way: the pitch often begins and concludes melodic phrases and is both the point of initiation and the goal for many melodic embellishments.[7]

Once the primary tone is established, we then trace its prolongation through three kinds of embellishment: (1) the neighbor-note figure (N); (2) the linear third (3rd); and (3) the perfect fourth (P4). While N figures are stepwise, the intervals of 3rd (major or minor) and P4th (all other fourths are dissonant) can approach the primary tone either from above or below, either by step or by leap.[8]

Returning to "Litanei," we recall how the melody focuses upon G, how A♭ and F♯ are also important pitches, and how leaps by 3rd and 4th recur. Figure 7.1 sketches section A: the piano introduction and opening vocal phrase, mm. 1–3. The sketch uses specific notation: the primary tone is designated by a stemmed open note (downbeat of mm. 1, 2, and 3), all structural pitches are stemmed black notes, and all embellishing pitches are unstemmed. All structural pitches have clear harmonic support, with sup-

FIGURE 7.1 "Litanei": Linear analysis, section A, mm. 1–3.

porting bass pitches stemmed, and most such pitches are metrically stressed: they occur on the downbeat or beat 3 of each measure. Figure 7.1 thus reads as follows: G functions as the primary tone (3̂ within the tonic triad) and is supported by the tonic throughout. The slurs show how G is prolonged by the usual ornaments, Ns and 3rds. Two of the three Ns embellish G: the F of m. 2 returns to G directly in m. 3, and the A♭ of m. 3 is an incomplete N (IN).[9] The third N is also incomplete; the D of m. 3 embellishes the E♭ that concludes the phrase.

The two melodic 3rds, meanwhile, are the 3rd leap above the primary tone, G to B♭, in m. 2 and the 3rd stepwise descent G–F–E♭ at the cadence, m. 3. Where the F had been a N of G in m. 2, it now functions as a passing tone (P, circled) in m. 3 connecting G to E♭. Figure 7.1b summarizes those embellishing figures that prolong G. There is one P4, B♭ to F, m. 2, which is less important than the two other motives: B♭ is the 3rd above G and F the N to G. The P4 will recur in section B, however, in more significant guises.

In tracing how embellishing pitches ornament structural ones, two factors emerge. First, the melodic line of the voice and/or RH piano part form a contrapuntal structure with the melodic line of the bass, a more complex melodic design that will be discussed later in the section "Contrapuntal Structure of Melody and Bass." Second, certain melodic dissonances or pitches isolated by leaps remain unconnected within a phrase, an irresolution of melodic tension that corresponds to various poetic tensions. Figure 7.2 uses dotted slurs to highlight the two melodic pitches in section A that remain in some way unconnected at the end of vocal phrase 1. The B♭ of m. 2 remains isolated in the upper 3rd register and the A♭ of m. 3 remains unresolved as an IN. By maintaining some melodic irresolution in section A, the vocal line can more easily continue into section B despite the powerful closure of section A in m. 3. Also, we will see in a moment that the B♭ of m. 2 gets picked up by the C of m. 5 and the A♭ IN of m. 3 is resolved on the G downbeat of m. 4.

As already noted, section B is more complex than section A. The three half cadences that articulate this five-bar section are: V of c minor, m. 5 beat 3 followed by V of E♭, m. 6 beat 3, and m. 8 beat 3. A general summary of the

FIGURE 7.2 "Litanei": Linear analysis, section A, unconnected pitches.

melodic activity is as follows: the G is sustained for the full m. 4, the line then leaps up a P4 to C, which is followed by a stepwise rising 3rd C to E♭, which in turn is followed by a dramatic downward leap of a diminished seventh, E♭–F♯, the F♯ resolving, through the grace note F♯–G on beat 3 of m. 5. This G coincides with the half cadence in c minor, and is followed by an upper N, A♭, harmonized by V4/3 of E♭ major, which returns to G on the downbeat of m. 6, harmonized by I⁶ back in E♭. The G on the downbeat of m. 6 then begins a series of 3rds, G–E♭–C, followed by a seventh leap C up to B♭, the B♭ moving down by step to F, which is the melodic point of repose over the half cadence in E♭, beat 3.[10]

Some of the dissonant melodic intervals convey more expressiveness in part because of their greater size, but also because of their underlying harmony. The descending diminished seventh E♭–F♯ in m. 5, for example, is expressive because of the wide leap *and* because the F♯ is a chromatic or altered tone in the key of E♭ major that has an added plangency to the ear. In m. 6, then, where the singer has a minor seventh leap from C¹ to B♭¹, the B♭ is embellishing not structural; this non-chord tone adds even more pathos to the expressive melody.

The melodic material of this section is certainly more varied and complicated, and the underlying harmony offers only some assistance in our melodic analysis. Figure 7.3 outlines section B, mm. 4–8. The phrase begins

FIGURE 7.3: "Litanei": Linear analysis, section B, mm. 4–8

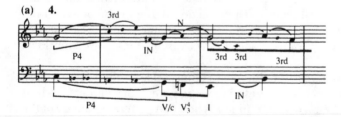

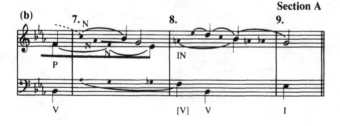

with the primary tone G, but the harmonic support is not the tonic E♭, but rather the unprepared c minor. While the singer simply reasserts the primary tone, G, the note may *feel* differently within the new tonality and the altered accompanimental figuration.

The complexity of the material in section B becomes simpler when it is considered as development of material from section A. The main melodic ideas of section A were the Ns around G and E♭ and the two 3rds above and below G. Figure 7.3a summarizes the ideas of section B, phrase 1, as they relate to material in section A. The opening G of m. 4 resolves the lingering A♭ IN from m. 3. The 3rd C–E♭ in m. 5 recalls the 3rd G–B♭ of m. 2 and provides a registral link with that isolated B♭ of section A as well.[11] The 3rds G–E♭ and E♭–C in m. 6 derive from the 3rd of mm. 2–3 and the high C–E♭ 3rd of m. 5, and the A♭ and F♯ continue to function as embellishing Ns to G.

While the P4 of section A was less important than other figures, the P4 of mm. 4–5 is more significant; the G–C rising P4 links the primary tone G to the C that is N to the B♭ of m. 2. Schubert echoes this P4, inverted, in the bass, C–G in the same bars.[12]

Figure 7.3b shows the concluding phrase of section B. The harmonic rhythm slows down (from a chord change each beat to one every two beats) allowing for the 3rds to become arpeggiations. While these arpeggiations suggest the 3rd leaps of m. 2, 3, and 6, their more important function is that of a series of N figures: C–B♭, A♭–G, F–E♭. The IN A♮ to B♭ intensifies, with an applied V^7 to V of E♭, the motion to the half cadence that concludes section B.

The complexity of section B is as dramatic as section A had been simple; even so, the two sections utilize similar material. The primary tone continues to recur (mm. 4, 5, 6, and 7) and is again embellished by Ns and INs: A♭ in mm. 5, 6, 7; F♯ in m. 5. The general N idea continues to recur in section B within the arpeggios of m. 7, and the A♭ to G N connects the end of section B, m. 8, to the repeat of section A in m. 9.

The melodic 3rd idea, first expressed as G–B♭ in m. 2, is recalled by the C–E♭ 3rd in m. 5. The minor 3rd interval is the same, and as already stated, the C of m. 5 connects *registrally* with the B♭ of m. 2. This connection then recurs in m. 7, as the C of the downbeat connects as IN to the B♭ of beat 3.

One final melodic element in section B is the use of registrally extreme pitches in the vocal line: low C and high E♭. The high E♭ of m. 8, to which the voice leaps a tritone from A♮, is the second melodic climax. It recalls the earlier high E♭ of m. 5, and the resolution of the E♭ to the D over V of E♭ recalls the IN D–E♭ of mm. 1 and 3. Meanwhile, the dotted slur in Figure 7.3a illustrates how the low C, m. 6 ultimately connects to the low D of m. 10, which in turn resolves to E♭ in that bar at the end of section B. This link between low C, m. 6, and the D to E♭, m. 10, has two important functions: first, section B connects with the return of section A, and second, the C–D–E♭ in the lowest register recalls that important 3rd (m. 5) as the melodic climax, an octave higher, within section B.

The development in section B of melodic ideas from section A, and the registral links between sections of unconnected high and low melodic pitches are common devices of melodic construction, and in *Lieder* the pianist should identify similar melodic designs within the accompaniment. Ultimately, knowledge of these melodic relationships and registral connections strengthens the melodic expression of poetry, and enables both singer and pianist to perform melodies with greater clarity and conviction.

The Contrapuntal Structure of Melody and Bass

The contrapuntal structure of melody and supporting bass is a crucial framework for all tonal music. Determining this contrapuntal structure in *Lieder* is extremely useful to the ensemble preparation, as the singer's line is directly connected to the accompaniment, most often the bass line. "Litanei" again exemplifies. Within the harmonically simple section A, the bass anchors all melodic activity to the tonic, the dominant creating the half cadence of m. 1 and the authentic cadence of m. 3. The bass of the V⁶, m. 2, is heard as an N figure that embellishes the tonic. Figure 7.4 shows how the singer's line often creates tenths with the bass: G over E♭, several times F over D, D over B♭.[13] The less stable sixth created in m. 2 by melodic B♭ against bass D intensifies the isolation of B♭ that lingers at the close of section A.

Figure 7.5 shows how the more complex section B offers a more varied bass for the developing melodic line. The resulting contrapuntal structure is as follows: the stark P5 between primary tone G and the new tonic c minor yields to sixths as the bass begins its destabilizing chromatic descent. The counterpoint becomes more stable as the bass arrives on the half cadence in c minor, the bass forming octaves with the voice; that P8 helps to emphasize the half cadence that clarifies the unprepared key of c minor. This brief cadence in c minor then gives way to tenths once again as we shift back into E♭, the tenths in mm. 5 and 6 returning us to the consonant, rel-

FIGURE 7.4: "Litanei": Contrapuntal structure, section A.

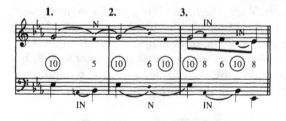

FIGURE 7.5 "Litanei": Contrapuntal structure, section B.

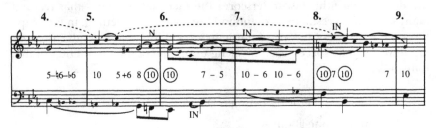

atively stable tenths so characteristic of the E♭ tonality and of section A. The bass then underscores the half cadence in E♭, m. 6, with a P5 below the voice, a stability that concludes the first phrase of section B. This P5 stability then contrasts with the great tension of the half cadence in m. 8, where the voice descends from an IN to a tenth to a seventh above the bass B♭. This cadence marks the conclusion of section B; the tension prepares for the resolution that occurs with the return of section A and the now familiar tenth of melodic G over bass E♭, m. 9.

The two moments in the song where both the melody and the harmony are the most complex and unstable are mm. 5 and 7. As Figure 7.5 shows, despite the chromaticism, the voice sings for the most part in consonant tenths against the descending bass; these relatively stable tenths and the even more stable octaves and fifths can help the singer to align with the ever-shifting bass, especially over the dissonances (augmented sixth, notated "+6," and sevenths).

In general, performers can gain much control over pitch and ensemble difficulties by rehearsing *Lied* with careful attention to the contrapuntal structure. The singer must always be aware of how the vocal line combines with the accompaniment, and the pianist must take equal care to articulate the underlying harmonic structure with clarity and consistency.

Compound Line

Another important element of melodic design occurs when a melodic line seems to have at least *two* parts, one in an upper and the other in a lower register of the *single* line. This division of a melodic line into several different melodic strands, each in a different musical plane or register, is called COMPOUND LINE, and the resulting melodic design is both complex and extremely expressive.[14]

This particular aspect of melodic design is exemplified with another famous Schubert song, his elegant setting of "An die Musik." The poem by Schober is a lyric that thanks the art of music for its comfort and transcendent power. Read the poem aloud and perform or listen to the song. The

Lied is well known for its expressive leaps, the rising P4 and more importantly the descending 6th; this underscores the fact that melodies that feature many leaps often result in a compound line. Schubert's setting, in fact, captures the richness of the art of music in a vocal line that extends into *three* different melodic spaces, each focusing upon one of the three notes of the tonic triad:

1. A low strand moving between D and the F♯ a 3rd above

2. A middle one about A

3. An upper one a P4 above, focused upon high D

We analyze compound line as we do any melody, within its tonal and harmonic context. As Figure 7.6 shows, the song remains in D major throughout, with applied chords focusing on V (through G♯) and vi (through A♯). This relatively simple harmonic and tonal design contrasts with the melodic complexities that flourish above. In fact, the recurrence of a small number of harmonies throughout the song enables the listener to focus more closely upon the many leaps and increasing development of the melodic line.

Looking now at the vocal line, the song's melody subdivides into four four-bar phrases. During the first two phrases, the song's vocal line moves freely from one space to another. Then, within the third phrase, the different registers get somewhat connected through an arpeggiation, and during the final phrase, the upper two registers are completely merged through a new use of stepwise motion.

Figure 7.6 traces the three separate strands. In order to highlight the line's triple focus, we give all three tonic triad pitches the open-note notation usually reserved for the single primary tone, using slurs to connect pitches within each strand. The dotted slur now has special importance: it traces the reconnection of individual strands over the course of the song. The opening phrase introduces the three strands: the line begins on A (5̂) in the middle space; this is followed immediately by a leap to the second, uppermost space around high D (1̂). The final strand then begins with the leap down to F♯ (3̂) in m. 4, and F♯ opens up the lowest strand that spans the descending 3rd, F♯–low D (1̂).

Tracing each strand in turn, the dotted slur indicates that the high D of m. 3 is temporarily suspended by the leap down to F♯ in m. 4. The upper register then returns in m. 11, as the D moves to its upper N, E, a motion that recurs again in m. 13.[15] The middle register, meanwhile, begins on A in m. 3 and continues with its N, B, in m. 4. The dotted slur shows how this register is then neglected until m. 7, where the A–B figure recurs only to be abandoned once more until m. 12.

The lowest strand, then, is the most developed at the outset of the song. The F♯ of m. 4 connects to low D by 3rds (mm. 5–6), first by leap and

FIGURE 7.6 "An die Musik": Compound line.

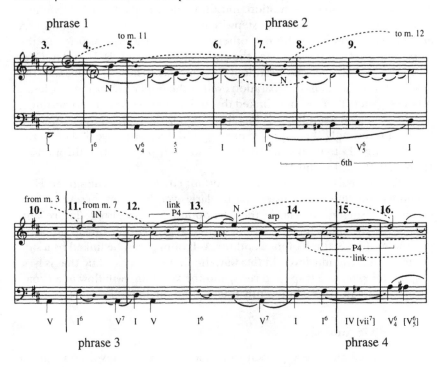

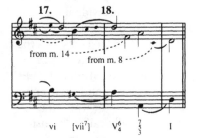

then by step. This register then yields to the A–B figure of the middle strand in m. 7, but returns for two bars in mm. 8–9. The melodic development then shifts from the lower to the middle and upper strands, and after the F♯ of mm. 11–12 and 13–14 the lowest register is neglected until the F♯ and low D of the final cadence in m. 18.

As suggested earlier, phrase 3 begins a process of bringing together the heretofore separate strands. The V⁷ arpeggio of m. 13, E–C♯–A–G, fills in the 6th descent E to G and connects by 3rds the upper and middle strands. The final phrase 4 completes the process, as characteristic leaps of 6ths and 4ths give way to more stepwise motion, most notably the filled in P4, A (middle strand)–D (upper strand). The stepwise connection between the middle A and upper D combines the two otherwise isolated lines just prior to the close. Schubert then brings back the expressive 6th leaps, D–F♯ and A–C♯ to recall the initially separate strands at the song's conclusion; in this way, the lowest strand maintains its separation even as the upper two strands coalesce. All the registers then become linked through the expressive piano postlude, which creates a descending RH line from high D through middle A down to low D. Interestingly, the only note missing in the scalar octave descent is the middle range F♯ that, as primary tone, had such prominence throughout (mm. 4, 6, 9, 12, 14, and 18).

This analysis underscores an important challenge for the singer: How to connect the different registers, particularly over the course of several measures? The singer can clarify the compound line by using timbre and nuances of dynamics to connect the various registers over time. For example, the A of m. 3, the B of m. 4 and the A–B of m. 7 can be linked by a similar tone and dynamic level. In this way, the singer creates a line that is lyric despite the extensive leaps and rests, and the vocal line will flow in a broad sweep despite the line's inherently fragmented quality.

Motivic Analysis

Our final analytic approach to melody in the *Lied* involves a shift in emphasis. In previous analytical approaches, we focused upon the integrity of the melodic line; in this last one, however, we detach individual melodic elements from the line and trace how they are reiterated over the course of the song. These separate melodic units or cells are called MOTIVES and the process of tracing the recurrence of such units is called MOTIVIC ANALYSIS.

By definition, a motive is a small (as small as two notes) melodic element that is readily identifiable as a repeated musical idea and that recurs systematically throughout a work. A motive can occur with or without a distinctive rhythmic identity;[16] it recurs in what are generally called "transformations," altered forms that include transposition, use of sequence, inversion, retrograde, and other varied states.[17]

We already identified the most frequently used melodic motives in the context of linear analysis; the neighbor-note figure (N or IN),[18] the disjunct or linear 3rd, and the disjunct or linear P4 are all melodic figures that readily occur in tonal music and can easily recur throughout a given *Lied*. In fact, motivic analysis will seem very similar to linear analysis. The difference in the two approaches is that linear analysis focuses on deeper levels of structure and the contrapuntal structure of melody and bass, while motivic analysis explores both deeper-level and more surface-level melodic elements. While innumerable instances of these common melodic figures occur in any song, our focus will be those repetitions that involve *structural* pitches, separating structural Ns, 3rds, and 4ths from those that are merely part of the tonal fabric.

Melodic or linear motives recur within two different categories: (1) untransposed vs. transposed, and (2) diatonic vs. chromatic. Reiterated motives using the same exact pitches are called "untransposed"; those that recur with different pitches are called "transposed." Both types recur often in tonal music. Diatonic motives exist within the governing tonality and thus recur more easily, while chromatic ones are outside the key and recur in a more complicated context, for example, during a tonicization or modulation. Generally speaking, diatonic and transposed motives are repeated more often, but untransposed and chromatic motives recur in more significant places.

"Litanei" has already demonstrated some motivic repetition, and will amply illustrate the process of motivic analysis. Piano introductions usually introduce important motives in *Lieder*, and the opening bar of "Litanei" functions at least as a partial guide to the motivic design of the whole song. Figure 7.7 traces how various N motives in the piano introduction recur throughout Sections A and B. The G–F–G N in the topmost voice of the RH part, m. 1, reappears in the vocal line in mm. 2–3. The middle voice of the RH, meanwhile, presents the N E♭–D–E♭, with D as IN heard later in m. 3.

FIGURE 7.7 "Litanei": Motivic analysis.

The RH lowest voice N, B♭–C–B♭, is echoed in the topmost part of the vocal line, where the B♭ of m. 2 connects with C of m. 5; the motive then recurs in mm. 7 and 12.

At this point we realize that each pitch of the E♭ tonic triad is embellished by at least one N and in the case of the primary tone, G, and scale degree $\hat{5}$, B♭, both upper and lower Ns recur. This is common in tonal music, and the extensiveness of melodic embellishment through N and IN figures cannot be overstated. After the G–F–G figure in mm. 1–2, the A♭ N constantly embellishes the primary tone G. The pitch B♭ is then embellished by the upper N, C, and in m. 8, by the lower IN A♮, where the chromatic embellishment enhances the song's climax.[19] Finally, while the tonic note E♭ ($\hat{1}$) is only embellished by the lower N, D, the leading tone N is powerful (see the RH piano, m. 1), and the N figure creates the two vocal climaxes on E♭, first Eb alone in m. 5 and then E♭ resolving to D in m. 8.

The use of both upper and lower Ns as pitch embellishments leads to the possibility of a double N figure, where convergence upon a pitch from both directions creates unequivocal emphasis. Figure 7.8 shows how the double-N, which closes the vocal line at the end of section A (mm. 3 and 10), is featured in the piano postlude. In addition, the structural notes embellished by double Ns reassert the two main melodic figures of the song, the N A♭–G (circled) and another motive mentioned earlier that warrants further examination, the 3rd E♭–F–G. The piano postlude thus uses the small-scale double Ns to summarize and emphasize the large-scale, more structural motives that have just been heard.

Figure 7.9 traces the 3rd motives featured in "Litanei." Two 3rds are prominent in section A: the disjunct G–B♭ (called X) appearing in m. 2 and the 3rd G–F–E♭ (called Y) occurring in m. 3. Of the two, the E♭–G 3rd is the more structurally significant; the motive closes both section As, as well as both the vocal line and the piano postlude. This 3rd also recurs in the bass line of mm. 5–6 where the 3rd takes us from c minor back to E♭ major, the E♭ bass supporting I⁶ of E♭.

FIGURE 7.8 "Litanei": Double N figures in piano postlude.

FIGURE 7.9 "Litanei": Third motives.

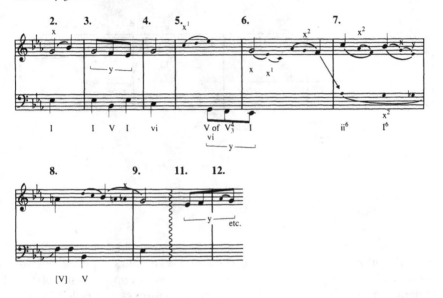

Transposed Motives

So far, we have focused upon important N and 3rd diatonic, untransposed motives, those most commonly found in *Lieder*.[20] We now examine two other motivic types: several different *transposed* 3rd motives, and several *chromatic* untransposed motives. The disjunct 3rd G to B♭ (X) in the voice, m. 2, puts the idea of a linear minor 3rd in the ear. This motivic interval then recurs in transposed forms. The climactic C to E♭ 3rd (X^1) of m. 5 was mentioned earlier, as were the arpeggiations of m. 7. Another minor 3rd, A♭ to F (X^2), closes the first phrase of section B, m. 6, leading to V of E♭.[21] Meanwhile, the double N figures in the piano postlude all utilize minor 3rds of different spellings (mm. 11–12). What is heard in this form of motivic repetition is a recurring *interval size*, not specific pitches, an interval that reappears at important moments (phrase openings, closings, the line's climax) in the overall melodic design.

Untransposed Chromatic Motives as Mediators and Enharmonic Puns

Untransposed chromatic motives tend to facilitate tonal shift, for example, tonicization or modulation. Figure 7.10 indicates several recurring

FIGURE 7.10 "Litanei": Chromatic motives.

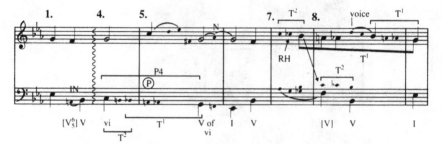

untransposed chromatic motives: the A♮–B♭ IN mentioned earlier, and the F♯–G IN within the c minor section. These motives emphasize pitches or harmonies (A♮ being part of V of V of E♭) and often appear at important cadences. Expanded forms of such chromatic motives can be called "mediators" when they facilitate the change from one key to another. For example, the bass A♮ in m. 5 moves not as a N to B♭, but rather as a connecting *passing* note (P) from B♭ (B♭–A♮–A♭–G), G supporting V of c minor. We label this motive T¹ (for "tonicization") because it mediates the tonicization of c minor within section B; it recurs twice in the ensuing return to E♭ major: first in the piano RH mm. 7–8 and then in the voice m. 8.

A similar chromatic motive, C–B♮–B♭ (labeled T²), is also introduced with the unprepared tonicization of c minor, m. 4. The bass begins this chromatic descent en route to G, V of c minor, incorporating the pitches of motive T¹ to complete the P4 from C to G. The entire chromatic descent uses pitches that emphasize the two keys involved: B♮ is the leading tone in c minor and A♮ is the leading tone to the dominant of E♭. The motive then recurs twice in section B: the upper part of the piano RH chromatically fills in the C–B♭ IN in m. 7 followed by the lower RH part N, B♭–C– C♭–B♭, in m. 8.[22]

These motives are more elaborate forms of the enharmonic pun discussed in Chapter Six, which also facilitates tonal shift.[23] The use of such enharmonic puns was already demonstrated in "Schäfers Klagelied" in Chapter Six; in "Litanei," the chromatic pun F♯/G♭ facilitates the tonicization of c minor and the subsequent return to Eb major. The F♯ is first heard within c minor, F♯ functioning as leading tone to V of c, m. 5. The function of the pun then changes; G♭ is now heard as a chromatic P that fills in the space from G (V of c minor) to F, V of the dominant of E♭, mm. 7–8. Thus, one version of the pun, F♯, reinforces the arrival on V of c minor, and the reinterpreted function, G♭, reinforces the return to E♭ through emphasis on V of V of E♭.

The use of chromatic motives and enharmonic puns in moments of tonal shift is common in *Lieder*, and performers will want to highlight these motivic recurrences wherever they occur. For example, this can be particularly effective when in "Litanei" the voice and accompaniment emphasize the imitation of motive T^2 in mm. 7–8, or when the pianist projects clearly the longer recurring chromatic lines formed of T^2 (C–B♮–B♭) +T^1 (B♭–A♮–A♭–G), in the bass mm. 4–5 which is then a bit veiled in the uppermost voice of the RH, mm. 7–8. The enharmonic puns also should be articulated carefully: the F♯–G and G♭–F resolutions in both "Litanei" and "Schäfers Klagelied" need slight emphasis, as do the other puns in "Schäfers Klagelied."

Motivic Parallelism

One final type of motive warrants our attention here, namely, MOTIVIC PARALLELISM, the term designating that a motive originally heard as a linear element recurs on a deeper level of structure, often as part of a harmonic progression. Motivic parallelism is another concept derived from Schenker that is particularly useful to performers.[24] Motivic parallelism involves the transformation of a simple melodic gesture into a more complex, lengthier melodic line or a bass line conveying a harmonic progression. This creates a profound change in structural value: the initial melodic idea becomes a melodic or harmonic structure that has deeper structural weight, with greater consequences for melodic and/or harmonic design.

Once again "Litanei" provides a simple example. We noted earlier that the piano introduction presented a N figure in the RH around the tonic note: E♭–D–E♭. This linear motive, in the middle voice, is then put into the harmonic domain, LH, in mm. 2–3, as the bass plays the figure in octaves in a I–V$^{6/5}$–I progression. The added structural weight of this parallelism is illustrated by the fact that a linear motive that had taken three beats now takes five and spans over a bar in length. In addition, the progression derived from the figure provides harmonic support for the opening vocal gesture. The accompanist of "Litanei" must take care to bring out this parallelism, emphasizing the E♭–D–E♭ of the RH, mm. 1–2, and its imitation in the LH, mm. 2–3.

We close our study of motivic analysis with a look at another famous Schubert song, "Erlkönig," which demonstrates remarkable manipulation of motivic elements, including motivic parallelism.[25] Understanding how the drama unfolds in the poetry is critical to appreciating the setting's motivic development; read the text in Appendix I, preferably aloud so that the voices of the personas can be heard clearly.

As is well known, Goethe's text presents a drama wherein a father struggles against death, the Erlking, for possession of his son. The story is told by a narrator who introduces the characters and later brings the story to a close, and the struggle includes speeches from all three characters: the father, the son, and the Erlking. Schubert uses motivic repetition to depict the unfolding struggle in what must be considered a motivic *tour de force* within the *Lied* genre.

Figure 7.11 shows the motives introduced within the piano introduction and the narrator's opening section. The well-known opening LH piano gesture includes a N, D–E♭–D which is followed by other vocal Ns and a P4 motive, D–G. As these motives recur in both transposed and untransposed forms, Schubert's motivic design proves ingenious. He associates certain motives, keys, and modes with specific characters in the narrative, and the recurrence of these motives, keys, and modes in transformed contexts traces the changes in the unfolding drama.

Figure 7.12 shows how the motivic associations with the son are the N, D–E♭–D, and the diminished vii°⁷ chord; those of the father are the P4 and the plagal areas of tonic g minor, especially the subdominant, c minor. The Erlking does not have a motivic associate at the outset but is represented musically by the major mode, beginning with the relative major, B♭. The lack of motives for the Erlking is symbolic; over the course of the song, the Erlking will take over or appropriate the motives of both the father and his son.

While a quick overview of motivic design in "Erlkönig" barely does justice to Schubert's masterpiece, we trace four forms of motivic reiteration. First, the Erlking gradually encroaches upon father and son by systematically taking away their motives; second, the son's "Mein Vater" refrain is transposed in a particular way so as to create a climax of increasing terror and symbolism; third, a motivic parallelism with the N figure D–E♭–D brings the song to its climax; and fourth, the song's climax merges the motives of father and son and thereby dramatizes their tragic defeat.

The Erlking's gradual appropriation of the father's motivic associations symbolizes his taking away the father's child. The Erlking first takes the father's P4 motive on the symbolic words "meine Mutter" ("my mother") in mm. 68–69 and he then adopts the father's key, c minor, but transforms it into the Erlking's major mode, in mm. 86–95. Eventually the Erlking takes away the tonic itself: g minor-as-key-of-struggle-*against*-death (key of father and son) becomes g-minor-as-key-of-death's-triumph (key of Erlking).

The boy's own struggle against the Erlking is depicted in his frenzied "Mein Vater" refrain beginning on the D–E♭–D N, mm. 71–72. The transposed reiteration of this N motive, up semitones over time through m. 126, depicts not only the boy's increasing terror but also his gradual defeat in the struggle against death. This ascending motivic sequence leads to the song's climax, mm. 127–129, where all the important motives merge on the words "Erlkönig hat mir ein Leids gethan!" ("The Erlking has hurt me!").

The motivic synthesis of the climax occurs as follows: first, the boy's recurring N motive becomes a P figure, F–F♯–G, that accelerates his final

FIGURE 7.11 "Erlkönig": Motives in piano introduction and narrator's opening speech.

FIGURE 7.12 "Erlkönig": Motivic associations.

shriek. This climactic arrival upon G also concludes the boy's rising line that began on D in mm. 72ff. The boy's G at m. 128 thus completes a P4 chromatic ascent, D to G, the motive associated with the father. The boy's presentation of the father's D–G fourth is ironic and tragic: the father's P4 is completed by the son at the very moment the boy is taken from his father.

In addition to these various forms of motivic transformation, Schubert's D–Eb–D motivic parallelism also dramatizes the final encroachment of the Erlking upon the boy. Figure 7.13 shows first the opening piano LH figure introducing the D–Eb–D N, and then the boy's first "Mein Vater"

FIGURE 7.13 "Erlkönig": The D–E♭–D motivic parallelism.

continued

refrain on those pitches. In m. 111 this melodic N recurs in the harmonic domain, as each note becomes tonicized in a 12–bar section leading to the song's climax in mm. 122ff. The piano interlude in mm. 111–115 tonicizes d minor; then the Erlking's final luring of the boy begins in E♭ major (♭VI) and retonicizes d minor, mm. 116–122. The harmonic progression that leads to the boys final scream, then, is a motivic parallelism of the boy's initial N motive: the Erlking's section progressing D–E♭–D thus claims the boy's motive as the boy himself is seized.

This brief foray into "Erlkönig"'s motivic design has demonstrated the effectiveness of several forms of motivic transformation and parallelism in a song of remarkable motivic development. While most performers can readily identify such recurring ideas as the "Mein Vater" N motive, many other recurring motives create a dazzling network of motivic exchanges and transformations that elegantly mirror the poem's powerful story. Even though the physical and interpretive demands upon performers of this song are sizable in and of themselves, motivic analysis can help bring nuances of meaning and expressivity to a performance that will enhance the experience of the performers and their audience.

Motivic Mislabeling

Our study of motive in the *Lied* must include a caution about a different use of the term "motive" (spelled "motif") in several well-known and

FIGURE 7.13 *continued*

valuable *Lied* studies by two British musicologists, Richard Capell and Eric Sams.[26] Both use the term *motif* to denote musical figures, often in the accompaniment, that convey poetic images through musical analogs (rhythms, melodic gestures, harmonies, and even progressions) to specific words or more general poetic ideas. Some of these are similar to the melodic motives we have discussed here; however, the term motif as used by these writers is different in several significant ways.

The concern of both Capell and Sams is less in the tracing of motivic development in the way just outlined and more in identifying recurring "motifs" in a composer's *oeuvre*, and assigning a particular *poetic* meaning to these repeated musical ideas. For example, Sams notes that a falling semitone, especially the falling melodic gesture ♭$\hat{6}$–$\hat{5}$ in major, conveys acute grief, and any song using that gesture is depicting some sort of anguish inherent in the poem being set. While this general association of a melodic gesture with a specific emotional or psychological idea can be helpful to those just beginning to study how music depicts poetry, the linking of musical ideas with specific poetic notions is problematic. First, this detailed categorization runs the risk of overgeneralizing correspondences between music and poetry and thus can easily mask both more subtle and more complex poetic depictions in a given song. Second, these categorizations and generalizations reflect the interpretations of each author, and offer only one scholar's notion of how the music reflects the poetry. Students must resist the temptation to adopt these interpretations too quickly and in so doing fail to take the necessary time to develop their own understanding of the many ways music depicts poetry.[27]

In addition, the discussions of motif by Capell, Sams, and others contradict two important issues under discussion in this chapter: the richness of correspondence between music and poetry and the systematic study of motive as part of performance preparation. While many of the interpretations of poetic meaning behind musical motifs are useful to a degree, the concern about the poetry tends to be general and at times even vague. In contrast, we stress the nuance of both poetic meaning and musical depiction, and warn against assigning any musical-poetic correspondences that are too glib and superficial.

Finally, the characterization of poetic meanings behind musical gesture is but a first step in understanding motivic design. The motive should not just be noted, but rather, its repetition should be traced throughout a song, both as a recurring musical element and as an ongoing means of conveying poetic progression and transformation.

Melody in the Accompaniment

In this last section, we return to study of the melodic line as a more complete musical entity. Until this point, we have focused primarily upon melody in the vocal line, and we now turn to consider melody within the accompaniment. To be sure, the accompanist also plays melodies, especially in the RH, and the analytical procedures detailed for the vocal line are wholly applicable to the piano part as well, especially when the piano RH doubles the vocal line. Two other uses of melody within the accompaniment are also powerful tools for text depiction: the use of a countermelody in the piano RH and the more unusual use of melody in the LH.

As alluded to in previous chapters, the use of melodies that accompany or even supersede the vocal line derives from the depiction of special poetic elements including particular personas.[28] For example, the recurring melodic figures in the RH of Schubert's "Im Frühling" and "Auf dem Wasser zu singen" recur throughout as countermelodies to the vocal line or as melodies within piano solos. In "Im Frühling," the accompaniment's melody can represent the memory of the poet, recalling past scenes of happiness, while in "Auf dem Wasser zu singen," the melody can depict poetic images of shimmering waves and gleaming wood that symbolize the poet's wings of escape through death. These melodies present a musical space within which a singer enunciates the poet's words; they are equal elements with the singer's melody and should be neither over- nor underplayed.

The melodic elements in piano solos are as important as the vocal line and deserve as much analytical attention.[29] In addition to the analytical approaches suggested above, the pianist and singer will want to explore the personas of these piano melodies, especially interludes that are framed by vocal lines. For example, the interludes in "Im Frühling," especially with the melodic variation that occurs, help convey the poetic progression; the piano accompaniment anticipates the singer's next words, simulating the way an emotion is felt before it is articulated. In this sense, performers must determine who responds to whom, whether singer prompts the accompaniment or vice versa.[30]

Melodies in the bass have an even greater effect because their prominence is so unexpected. In Schubert's "Du bist die Ruh," for example, the main melodic line of the accompaniment is in the tenor range, while the RH accompaniment doubles the voice and the "bass voice" enters only for cadences during the song's first half and to underscore tonicizations in the song's second half. This gentle tenor melody captures the spiritual "Du" of the poem to whom the singer speaks. Wolf's "Auch kleine Dinge" also uses a high bass melody, where it depicts the theme of preciousness in "little things" that underlies the Italian lyric. The descending scale sails quietly downward amid the RH shimmer in an appropriately simple melodic line, and the high register of this lowest line emphasizes the sweetness of the small musical space.[31]

The sensitive accompanist will take time to understand the poetic meaning of any accompanimental melody that differs from the vocal melody. Both performers will want to discuss the roles of various melodies throughout a song, noting how the entrance of a new melody connotes a new poetic image or persona and being aware of the converging of poetic issues when two different melodic lines are performed together.

Exercises

Exercise 7.1: Linear analysis

Showing the compound structure of treble and bass, choose the primary tone and sketch structural and embellishing pitches. Slur embellishing to structural pitches and indicate underlying bass notes to all structural pitches.

1. Schubert, "Auf dem Wasser zu singen," mm. 1–16
2. Schubert, "An den Frühling," mm. 1–10
3. Schumann, "Du bist wie eine Blume"
4. Schubert, "Nachtviolen," mm. 1–14
5. Schubert, "Wiegenlied"

Exercise 7.2: Motivic analysis

Identify recurring motives and trace their repetition in both vocal line and piano accompaniment.

1. Schubert, "Auf dem Wasser zu singen," mm. 1–16
2. Schumann, "Die Lotosblume," mm. 1–17
3. Schumann, "Mondnacht," mm. 1–13
4. Schubert, "Nachtviolen," mm. 1–14
5. Schubert, "Widmung," 1–13

Exercise 7.3: Compound line

Locate and sketch (with dotted slurs) two or more melodic strands in the following vocal lines; be sure you understand the underlying harmonic progression.

1. Schubert, "Auf dem Wasser zu singen," mm. 1–16
2. Schumann, "Die Lotosblume," mm. 1–19
3. Schumann, "Du bist wie eine Blume"
4. Schumann, "Mondnacht," mm. 1–13
5. Schumann, "Widmung," mm. 1–13

Exercise 7.4: Chromatic mediating motives

Identify a recurring chromatic motive and show how it facilitates tonal shift.

1. Schubert, "Ave Maria"
2. Schubert, "Des Mädchens Klage"
3. Schumann, "Die Lotosblume"

4. Schubert, "Du bist die Ruh"

5. Schumann, "Du bist wie eine Blume"

Exercise 7.5: Enharmonic puns

Identify the enharmonic pitch that mediates between several different tonalities. Indicate the two functions of the puns and the two keys involved. (Note: the different tonalities include implied keys and/or secondary or applied functions.)

1. Schubert, "Das Mädchen"

2. Schumann, "Die Lotosblume"

3. Schubert, "Im Frühling"

4. Schumann, "Widmung"

Exercise 7.6: Melody within the accompaniment

Indicate the poetic image or persona in all the melodies within the piano accompaniment.

1. Schubert, "An die Musik"

2. Schubert, "Nachtviolen"

3. Schumann, "Mondnacht"

4. Schumann, "Schöne Fremde"

5. Schumann, "Widmung"

CHAPTER EIGHT

Rhythm and Meter

To study rhythm is to study all of music. Rhythm both organizes, and is itself organized by, all the elements which create and shape musical processes.

Thus begins one of the first important twentieth-century books devoted solely to issues of rhythm and meter: *The Rhythmic Structure of Music* by Grosvenor W. Cooper and Leonard B. Meyer.[1] This chapter can in no way be as thorough as that or the many other significant books on rhythm that have appeared in the past two decades; rather, we offer here some basic definitions of terms and concepts along with general guidelines for considering rhythm and meter in their manifold functions within *Lieder*. This chapter has two parts. In the first, we review the norms of rhythmic, metric, and phrase structure and organization, and in the second, we illustrate some deviations from those norms, namely, how *Lieder* vary these norms to create special musical effects that convey issues within the poetic text.

Rhythmic, Metric, and Phrase Norms

Rhythmic and Metric Norms and Organization

Our review of basic terms and concepts rests upon two essential tenets of rhythmic structure. First, music is a temporal art and all basic issues related to rhythmic flow and organization deal with how music is organized and perceived *in time*.[2] Every aspect of rhythm relates to how a musical element—whether a small rhythmic gesture or an entire symphony movement—is perceived within a given time span. The notions of time and rhythm are, in fact, interdependent: a time span is only perceptible as a discrete unit when some aspect of rhythmic organization makes it so.

The second principle of rhythm states that rhythmic structure and organization are, like pitch, HIERARCHICAL, occurring on several different levels of activity. Small rhythmic motives combine to create larger musical phrases, which in turn combine to create entire musical sections, and so forth. Meanwhile, in a more sophisticated sense, the metric pattern of beats within a measure is enlarged to encompass whole units that project a strong/weak metric pattern on the next deeper level of structure, units called "hypermeasures." This is beyond the scope of our review here, but it is worth noting that the surface rhythms of notes and phrases are only part of a larger framework of rhythm that includes deeper-level structure and organization.[3]

The term "rhythm" thus has both a specific meaning and a more general one that combines many aspects of the way in which music organizes time. Performers intuitively understand many of the most common aspects of rhythm. They can sense that cadences interrupt the musical flow to enable musicians to "breathe"; they can sense that some beats or measures are more accented than others, and so forth. This chapter goes beyond intuition and offers *Lied* performers a more systematic way to examine both the basics and the nuances of music's time and rhythms. We begin with basic elements: pulse or beat, meter, and accent. We then turn to more complex aspects of duration, grouping, and harmonic rhythm.[4] We also recall two aspects of rhythm mentioned in earlier chapters: tempo and stress. The important decisions these require of the performer are assisted by a systematic study of temporal flow and rhythmic complexity.

In its simplest definition, the term BEAT or PULSE refers to the recurring, "bottom-line" durational unit that is heard and felt (both physically and psychologically) throughout an individual piece. All units are equal, like a metronome tick, and the perception of the beat, even during moments of silence, sets the framework for all rhythmic and metric elements that occur.[5] This common definition must be distinguished from a more sophisticated one where the terms beat and pulse are separated. While the pulse remains the metronome tick mentioned earlier, the beat assumes a more structural function, time being organized through beats that are either strong or weak at various rhythmic levels. Perception of the beat greatly influences tempo decisions, as discussed earlier in Chapter Four.

The term METER refers to the grouping of beats into recognizable, reiterated patterns that provide systematic emphasis through organizing strong/accented and weak/unaccented beats.[6] In the tonal repertory, beats are usually grouped into three different metric patterns: DUPLE, TRIPLE, or COMPOUND. These meters, indicated by time signatures, form the basic vehicle for systematic rhythmic accent. In all meters, the strongest beat is beat 1 (coinciding with the bar line at the beginning of the measure); this is also called the DOWNBEAT. Most meters also have secondary accented beats, for example, beat 3 in 4/4, beat 2 in 3/4, and "beat 2" in 6/8 (the fourth eighth-note).

Most meters involve at least two levels of activity, the level of the beat (in 4/4, the four beats) and the level of organization within the measure (in 4/4, the two groupings of beats into [1 + 2] and [3 + 4]).[7] This grouping of beats results from beat 3 receiving a secondary accent that is less than that of beat 1 but greater than the unaccented, weak beats 2 and 4.

As already suggested, the different levels of metric structure create a hierarchy of meter; the beat is subsumed within the measure which is incorporated into larger units having metric accents similar to those within the bar.

Duple and triple are the simple meters. As already suggested, some meters are more complex than the common 2/4, 3/4, or 3/8 because of the two levels of activity: a level of the *beat* and a level of *beat groupings* within the bar. We've just described this in 4/4: four beats and two groupings of two beats. A more complex example of this is compound meter, where the beats group into multiples of three and the units organize into either duples or triples. Figure 8.1 shows two common types of such compound meter. In 6/8, the eighths are grouped into threes (1-2-3 and 4-5-6), while the number of three-groupings is two ([1-2-3] + [4-5-6]). Both performer and listener are aware that the duple and triple units coexist. The meter 9/8 signifies that the eighths are grouped in threes, with three such groups per bar. In this case, the meter has two different *types* of triple units: three within the beat and three beat groupings per bar.

The potential complexity of rhythmic groupings within compound meter enabled *Lied* composers to depict poetry with much nuance in rhythmic organization and stress. For example, by setting "Schäfers Klagelied" in 6/8, Schubert could readily alter the ever-changing accompanimental textures and vocal gestures as the text progressed.[8] The opening and closing

FIGURE 8.1 Compound meter (two different groupings per bar).

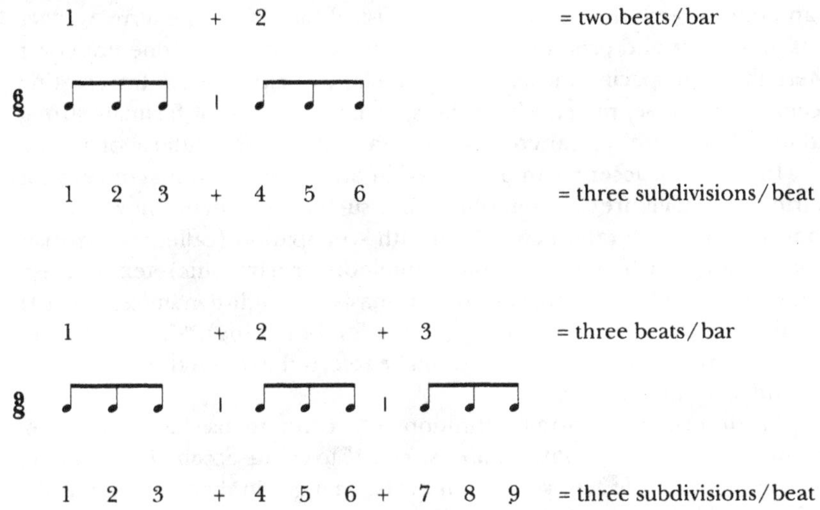

| 1 | + 2 | = two beats/bar |

| 1 2 3 + 4 5 6 | = three subdivisions/beat |

| 1 + 2 + 3 | = three beats/bar |

| 1 2 3 + 4 5 6 + 7 8 9 | = three subdivisions/beat |

C minor sections depict the lonely shepherd in the song's characteristic 6/8 rhythm:

♩ ♪ in the piano and ♩ ♪♩. ♫ in the voice

The juxtaposed E♭ music of the animated valley uses a different, livelier 6/8 figure in the accompaniment:

♫♪ ♫♪

But the middle A♭ major/minor sections adopt first more active and then more agitated rhythms inherent within 6/8 meter:

𝄾 ♫♫♪ 𝄾 ♫♫♪ and 𝄾 ♫♫♩ ♫♫♩

to convey the nature imagery so important in the poem's middle stanzas. The music's initial increase and eventual decrease in rhythmic complexity thus traces the poem's progression with a wealth of rhythmic variation readily available within compound meter.

The notions of "accent" and "stress" inherent within the concept of meter require special attention. The two terms are difficult to define precisely, and there is disagreement among theorists about how they are used. For our purposes, we will adopt a formal definition for "accent" but use "stress" only as an noun or verb that helps describe musical "accent."[9] The term ACCENT in its most basic and profound sense denotes an emphasis of one note over others through specific musical devices. The principal device for creating accent is, of course, meter, where the systematic pattern of formally strong and weak beats within a bar creates a natural ordering, or pattern, of accent.

In addition, accents can be created in other ways, without concern for metric context. Figure 8.2 exemplifies four such ways from two now-familiar songs: (1) longer duration combined with syncopation (called by theorists AGOGIC ACCENT; (2) changes in pitch (melodic or harmonic), texture, register, or contour; (3) changes in or emphasis through dynamics; and (4) articulations (bowings, tonguings, pauses for breathing).[10] These devices create important musical effects and will be referred to often throughout the remainder of this chapter.

In contrast to this formal definition of "accent," we use "stress" in a simpler, more generic sense. Pitches are "stressed" to create accent, for example, meters use accents to "stress" certain beats; changes in dynamics and articulation markings create "stresses" irrespective of their metric context, and so forth.

FIGURE 8.2 Musical devices for rhythmic accent.

Brahms, "Die Mainacht"

3. dynamics and duration

Schumann, "Seitich ihn gesehen"

4. articulations, agogic accent, and leap

Two other basic concepts of rhythm and meter are duration and grouping, both of which are illustrated by "Schäfers Klagelied." DURATION indicates the amount of time a musical event is sustained ("how long it lasts"), as measured in beats or fractions of beats. Many pitches of longer duration reinforce the inherent metric accent by beginning on strong, accented beats (including secondary accents). Note, for example, that in the vocal line of "Schäfers Klagelied," the longest pitches most often begin on the downbeat or on beat 4 (that is, the second strongest of the eighths within 6/8). These notes are the most structural both in the melodic contour and, as we will see presently, in the phrase structure. In contrast to this pattern of longer duration on strong beats, lengthier pitches can occur as rhythmic stresses that alter prevailing metric groupings at particularly significant moments of a setting. Two such instances in "Schäfers Klagelied" signal that something important is either occurring or imminent: the dotted quarter note B♭ in m. 16 slows down the vocal line in preparation for the tonal shift and the sustained E♭ on beat 1 of m. 27 emphasizes both the cadence and the minor mode in m. 28.

The term GROUPING is often used somewhat vaguely, but it essentially designates how rhythmic patterns combine pitches together into specific gestures which, like the metric groupings just described, occur on various levels of rhythmic structure.[11] In "Schäfers Klagelied," for example, both the song's vocal line and its accompaniment offer at least five different surface-level rhythmic groupings that reflect different moments within the poetic text, and each change in grouping reflects a specific shift in poetic and psychological orientation for both performers. These surface groupings can be analyzed on deeper levels of rhythmic activity as well, using the more complex analytical procedures that involve the concept of structural levels. This form of analysis is outside our scope here; however, readers are urged to peruse the numerous studies on the topic. The concept of structural levels of rhythm has an immense impact on the perception of rhythmic flow over time, and the implications for performers are profound.[12]

The issue of TEMPO was discussed in some detail in Chapter Four. The tempo of a work is its pace, how fast or slow the rhythmic/metric organization flows through real or clock-time.[13] This has important implications for the listener, who often perceives complex rhythmic and metric elements more easily in a slower tempo, where there is more clock-time to absorb the complexities. *Lied* composers suggest tempo both overtly (by tempo indications above the score) and more subtly (by metric choices and other notations); however, there is much room for interpretation by the performer, who will want to consider all the issues of this chapter as well as Chapter Four before making a final tempo choice.

Our final definition is the term HARMONIC RHYTHM, which refers either to the rate or to the pattern of harmonic change within a given work.[14]

The notion of harmonic rhythm is based on the idea that the rhythmic pattern of harmonic changes creates a certain pace (or tempo) of harmonic flow. This has important implications for determining tempo in general. Indeed, the issues of harmonic rhythm and tempo are intertwined. Where harmony changes constantly, for example, on every beat, a piece is perceived to be faster-moving than one where, given the same meter and tempo, harmony changes less frequently, for example, every three beats.

Two other norms of harmonic rhythm help to articulate musical form. First, musical closure often involves an acceleration of harmonic rhythm at the approach to the cadence, where the increase in harmonic activity emphasizes the close of a phrase or of an entire piece.[15] Second, a large tonic reprise or final tonic cadence in a piece is sometimes prepared by a dominant pedal, a slowing down of harmonic rhythm that emphasizes the imminent resolution of V to I that will follow.[16]

Schubert's "Der Neugierige" demonstrates how harmonic rhythm can influence the flow of music through time. The song's first section, in 2/4, changes harmony in various patterns. The first vocal phrase (mm. 5–8) begins with a slow harmonic rhythm, one chord per bar. The harmonic rhythm then increases slightly within the tonicization of the dominant (mm. 9–10), and a flourish of harmonic changes at almost every eighth note accelerates to the cadence in the dominant (m. 11). The next section (mm. 13–21) resumes the slower harmonic rhythm, one chord per bar, but again increases for cadential emphasis (mm. 19 and 21). In the 3/4 section that follows, the change in meter is accompanied by dramatic changes in harmonic rhythm, both of which reflect the poetic text. Where the miller questions the brook about love (mm. 23–32), the harmonic rhythm slows drastically. The tonic harmony is sustained for several bars at the beginning of each phrase. And when the miller considers the hopeful answer "yes" (mm. 33–34), the accompaniment becomes completely immobile. This immobility is then unraveled when the miller considers the painful answer "no" (mm. 35–40): the quick eighths emphasize faster harmonic changes, sometimes two per bar, other times more. The increased harmonic rhythm conveys the youth's agitation until he resumes his questioning (mm. 43ff.). At this point the harmonic rhythm returns to the slower one that began the 3/4 section. This slowing of harmonic rhythm signals a change in the poetic progression, as the miller queries the brook one last time. The song concludes not in the initial 2/4, where the miller pondered the difficulty of finding his answer, but rather in 3/4, where the young lad beseeched the brook for the answer. The harmonic rhythm of mm. 43 to the end thus recalls that of mm. 23–33. In this way, the two sections frame the internal struggle (mm. 34–42) between "yes" or "no" responses, with the accelerated harmonic rhythm expressing the emotional turmoil of not knowing.[17]

Norms of the Phrase: Length, Development, and Combination

The concept of PHRASE STRUCTURE is often discussed in the context of musical form, that is, how phrases are organized into larger units or musical sections.[18] However, a phrase is first and foremost a rhythmic structure: a unit of duration that combines in a rhythmic pattern with other similar durational units.

While performers intuitively understand what a phrase is, a precise and comprehensive definition is almost impossible. In a general sense, a musical phrase is analogous to a sentence of prose or a line of poetry: all are more or less complete ideas that come to some sort of pause or closure. In literature, such pauses are indicated by punctuations, for example, commas, colons, semicolons, or periods; in music, such pauses are created by cadences, for example, half cadences, authentic cadences, or, less frequently, deceptive cadences. While we have already discussed some of the elements of phrase content, such as harmonic progression and cadence types, melodic shape, rhythmic and metric structure, elements of texture, timbre and register, we emphasize here that a phrase is most importantly a self-contained harmonic/tonal *motion*. A phrase does not just end on a cadence; rather, it comprises a tonal motion that concludes with a cadence. William Rothstein underscores the point: "a phrase should be understood as, among other things, a directed motion in time from one tonal entity to another; these entities may be harmonies, melodic tones (in any voice or voices), or some combination of the two. *If there is no tonal motion, there is no phrase.*"[19]

Given this basic definition of the term "phrase," we now consider three essential characteristics of phrase structure: (1) norms of phrase length; (2) phrase development (through expansions and contractions); and (3) phrase combination (phrases joined together to form larger units or musical sections).[20]

Various authors differ in their basic definitions of phrase structure and in their use of terminology, and we offer here a way of thinking about phrase structure that is especially pertinent to *Lied* performers. For example, even though many theorists consider the eight-bar phrase to be normative,[21] we suggest the four-bar phrase (or in a slow work, a two-bar phrase) as the phrase norm for *Lieder*.[22] The four-bar unit is long enough to set a line of poetry that usually can be sung in one breath, and its even number of measures creates a sense of symmetry and balance. Schubert's setting of "Meeres Stille" shows such a systematic use of the four-bar phrase. Here, the normative pattern contributes to the eerie calm of which the poet/sailor speaks. The harmony and melody flow in a predictable stream of rolled chords, in an unbroken one-bar harmonic rhythm grouped into four-bar phrases. This regularity of temporal flow exemplifies the sea's calm, while the rigid phrase structure, each four-bar phrase being essentially a self-contained unit, projects a disquietude corresponding to the poet's anxiety and dread.[23]

A second norm of phrase structure in both *Lieder* and tonal music generally is the pairing of two 4- or 8-bar phrases into a "question/answer" unit called the ANTECEDENT/CONSEQUENT PHRASE or PERIOD structure.[24] The antecedent/consequent phrase pair generally provides a twofold tonal motion, the first phrase moving to V (half cadence) and the second resolving that V to I at the end of the second phrase (authentic cadence). This structure is exemplified by mm. 5–8 of Schubert's "Der Neugierige." The four-bar phrase comprises a period of two 2-bar phrases: mm. 5–6 move I to V and mm. 7–8 resolve V to I.

The two-phrase antecedent/consequent structure can easily carry a modulation. In such cases, the half cadence of the first phrase, in one key, is followed by a second phrase that concludes in a new key. A clear example of this is Schubert's setting of von Leitner's "Der Kreuzzug," D. 932. The poem describes a monk, isolated in his cell, watching the knights embark upon their holy crusade. The monk's initial regret at remaining behind is eventually transformed into identification with the pilgrimage, which, he comes to understand, can be made as readily "at home" within himself. Schubert's setting captures the duality of the monk versus the knights through vacillation between D major and b minor. The very first vocal period, mm. 5–12, demonstrates the shift from the monk's key of D major (m. 8 ending on V of D) to the crusaders' key of b minor (m. 12 ending on I of b).

The final norm of phrase structure in most tonal music is the use of a balanced or even number of measures: two-, four-, or eight-bar phrases. In *Lieder*, this is reinforced by various norms of the usual poetic texts, for example, the rhymed couplet. All the norms of phrase length, pairing, and evenness contribute to a predictable musical flow that conveys a remarkable variety of poetic moods and progressions in *Lieder*.

Predictably, *Lied* composers readily disrupt these phrase norms in the interest of text depiction. Indeed they utilize two devices of phrase development, phrase extension and phrase contraction, to convey particular moments of poetic tension and ambiguity. Four-bar phrases can be extended, either to an odd-numbered five-bar phrase for a more jarring effect or to the longer even-numbered six-bar phrase for a less disruptive expansion. Or phrases can be contracted, either a four-bar phrase to a three-bar unit or, an eight-bar phrase to a five-, six-, or seven-bar phrase. These truncated phrases all have similar disquieting effects; the ear expects the music to continue a bit longer and the premature phrase ending is abrupt and unfulfilled.

Of the two types of phrase development, phrase extension or expansion is the more common. PHRASE EXPANSION (OR EXTENSION) can occur at three points of the phrase: (1) within a phrase beginning, (2) as an INTERPOLATION within the interior of the phrase, and (3) as an extension at the phrase ending.[25] The third type, phrase extension, is the most common, but opening and interpolation extensions do occur to great effect. Two well-known *Lieder* illustrate the relationship between such phrase expansions and text setting; Schumann's "In der Fremde" shows both a phrase expansion through an introductory measure (mm. 1–5), and a phrase extension at its end (mm. 10–15). Schubert's "Im Frühling" exemplifies the less common phrase interpolation (mm. 7–10).

In general, introductory phrase expansion in *Lieder* usually occurs within a piano introduction. Most typically, an opening piano solo projects a complete phrase in itself, setting the stage for the song by establishing the phrase norm, as well as other significant features such as the harmonic design and melodic structure. Occasionally, however, a one-bar piano introduction does not in itself constitute a separate phrase. Schumann's "In der Fremde" shows the effect of such an opening. The first bar presents the expressive rolling sixteenth-note accompaniment in a low register and the vocal line begins with an upbeat to a four-bar phrase, mm. 2–5. This phrase is followed by another four-bar phrase and the performers are likely to exclude the first bar from their analysis of the phrase structure, which otherwise appears to conform to the four-bar norm.[26] We will return to ponder the "meaning" of this introductory measure in a moment.

After the apparent four-bar norm of the opening section, the middle section tends to have less distinct, lengthier phrases. The four-bar phrase in mm. 10–13, is followed by a two-bar phrase extension (mm. 14–15). This six-bar phrase extension (4 + 2) is then repeated by another: the ensuing four-bar phrase (mm. 16–19) is also extended by two bars (mm. 20–21). Both six-bar phrases trace the poetic progression through tonal excursions. In the first, the poet's four-bar *Sehnsucht* in the implied A major is extended into the key of b minor; in the second, the poet's four-bar experience of the loneliness of the woods within b minor concludes back in f♯ minor. The concluding section, mm. 22–25, also breaks the four-bar norm, here dividing the four bars into two two-bar phrases. This phrase shortening, along with the tonic pedal, helps create closure after the expansiveness of the middle section, and the song concludes with a four-bar piano postlude.

While the phrase extensions seem clearly aligned to the poetry and tonal design, we have yet to understand the function of the opening bar of introduction. Three interpretations are possible. First, in light of the poetic imagery, the opening bar could be "counted" as part of a five-bar opening phrase, an opening tension of uneven phrase length that conveys the poem's ominous clouds and lightning. This uneven opening phrase then is replaced by more normal phrase lengths as the poet's alienation and loneliness is clarified.

A second interpretation is that the one-bar piano introduction can be considered in conjunction with the four-bar piano postlude, mm. 25–28. When combined, the two solos comprise five bars, the uneven length conveying, once again, the alienated, "foreign" mood of the poem. This interpretation helps the performers understand the opening introduction as "setting the scene" within which the poet/singer expresses the poetic progression.[27] The piano postlude then returns us to the opening "scene" as the poet/singer ceases to "speak" but is still surrounded by the landscape that had prompted the poetic musing.

The combining of the opening piano introduction with the piano postlude does not eliminate the "extra bar" of the song's accompanimental frame. Rather, the breaking up of the five-bar solo material (1 + 4) creates a tension of phrase structure at the song's opening which remains at the song's conclusion. This subtle tension expresses two important elements in the poetic setting: (1) the opening poetic imagery of foreboding (clouds, lightning) that is a metaphor for the poet's internal distress, and (2) the initial tension of the melancholy poet before the poetic transformation from alienated loneliness to yearning for peaceful death.

A third interpretation is that the "extra bar" is combined neither with the four-bar vocal phrase that follows nor with the piano postlude, whose four-bar phrase confirms the phrase norm at the song's conclusion. Instead, the opening piano measure is a bar of upbeat that is not counted as part of any phrase at all. This interpretation brings with it subtle tensions between the performers. The pianist's opening gesture, which sounds like a downbeat phrase opening, will be contradicted by the singer's opening gesture, which accents the downbeat of m. 2, as if that is the beginning of the phrase. In this interpretation, the ensemble tension is part of the poetic depiction and should be savored, not minimized; even though the opening tension will remain throughout the song, the performers will be anchored by the cadences throughout.

The use of phrase interpolation—extending the phrase from within— is demonstrated in the first vocal phrase of Schubert's "Im Frühling." The norm of a four-bar phrase length is established by the piano introduction, and the first vocal phrase initially seems to be a varied repetition of that opening piano solo. However, while one expects an authentic cadence in m. 8 analogous to that in m. 4, the phrase expands the pre-dominant function and arrives at V in beat 4 of m. 9 and at I on the downbeat of m. 10. The interpolation in mm. 8–9 results in a six-bar phrase; the performers and listeners will hear the phrase as somehow enlarged from within and will realize that the cadence has been delayed. One consequence of this delay is that the tonic occurs not on beat 4 as it had in m. 4, but rather on the downbeat in m. 10. This creates a stronger cadence and, therefore, a more definitive phrase ending. The interpolation emphasizes the text "Wo ich beim ersten Frühlingsstrahl/einst, ach, so glücklich war." ("where I in spring's first gleam,/once, ah, was so happy."); these poetic lines, and the phrase interpolation that sets them, express the poet's underlying pain when remembering a former springtime of happiness and love.

The two-bar phrase extension of the four-bar norm is the most common phrase expansion. The six-bar phrase creates surprise and/or tension;

in "In der Fremde," it accompanies two tonal shifts that require correction
of both tonal design and phrase structure. The tension of the six-bar phrase
also occurs in Schubert's "Du bist die Ruh," where a general tension of
uneven phrases of varied lengths intensifies the poet's expression of love and
devotion. The piano introduction is an unusual seven-bar length and leaves
the question of phrase norm to be established by the vocal line. The singer's
first three phrases do establish the four-bar phrase norm by m. 19, but the
next phrase is expanded to six bars on the text "zur Wohnung hier/mein
Aug' und Herz," ("as a dwelling here/my eye and heart"). The additional
two bars allow Schubert to repeat the text "mein Aug' und Herz." The music
and phrase pattern is repeated in the section that follows (mm. 43–48) with
the text "Voll sei dies Herz/von deiner Lust" ("full is this heart/of your joy");
again a six-bar phrase is used to repeat a line of text, now "von deiner Lust."
These extensions from four- to six-bar phrases then lead to further extensions during the remainder of the song, where the four-bar norm is
expanded by five- and seven-bar phrases. All of the phrase expansions reflect
the poetic progression, where the poet's opening thoughts of repose and
quietude evolve into more ecstatic expressions of joy and pain.

One additional comment about the six-bar phrase is necessary here.
The phrase extension of 6 = 4 + 2 is not to be confused with a balanced six-
bar phrase that combines two three-bar phrases (6 = 3 + 3), which is analogous to the eight-bar period combining two four-bar phrases. The effect of
such balanced six-bar phrases (6 = 3 + 3) is to turn odd-numbered phrases
into a smoother even-numbered phrase pair. This will be explored in the section "Rhythmic, Metric, and Phrase Deviations," where three-bar phrases in
Brahms' "Die Mainacht" are combined into six-bar periods.

A final issue of basic phrase construction is how phrases are connected
to one another.[28] There are two basic ways that phrases combine. First, discrete separate phrases may simply be juxtaposed, one phrase concluding
and the next phrase beginning immediately thereafter. Second, phrases may
overlap, the ending of one coinciding with the beginning of the next. This
construction is called PHRASE OVERLAP OR ELISION. Each type of phrase combination creates a different musical effect and, as a result, a different poetic
depiction. Phrases that are clearly distinct, separate units generally set lines
or stanzas of poetry more clearly, and emphasize certain lines of text through
emphatic cadential repose. The musical structure is more concise and
cadences are clearer, with stronger pauses on V or I. In contrast, phrases connected through overlap create a more seamless musical flow with a tendency
toward acceleration. A moment that functions simultaneously as an ending
and as a new beginning creates momentum by not allowing the usual
"breath" associated with the end-of-phrase; this can readily depict such
poetic issues as increased excitement or anxiety.

Phrases that are distinct, with clear separation, tend to group themselves through the antecedent/consequent phrase structure mentioned

above. The separate four-bar phrases are thus combined into a clearly cohesive eight-bar phrase group, which enhances the musical flow and creates a longer musical unit. In contrast, when phrases do not combine into balanced, fluid phrase pairings, the result is a more fragmented musical syntax. Schubert's "Meeres Stille" illustrated this earlier; the pervasive use of discrete four-bar phrases challenges performers to create and maintain musical flow in a musical syntax that is characterized by fragmentation.

Simple phrase concatenation, including the antecedent/consequent phrase pair, is by far the most common type of phrase combination in *Lieder*, where phrase overlap or elision is the exception. Both types are illustrated by Schubert songs. "Die liebe Farbe," like many songs from *Die schöne Müllerin*, employs a seemingly simple phrase design that mirrors the simplicity of the poetic text. Each musical phrase ends clearly on either V or I (mm. 5, 9, 13, 18, 22), the four vocal phrases creating a pair of antecedent/consequent periods or phrase pairs. Despite the harmonic simplicity and phrase clarity, however, the song captures the poem's poignancy through its uneven phrase lengths: the opening piano introduction is five bars, which is immediately contradicted by the 4 + 4 period structure of the first two vocal phrases that ensue. The next vocal period, mm. 14–22, is nine bars in length (5 + 4), the uneven five-bar phrase recreating the tension of the opening five-bar phrase.[29]

An elision in this song occurs at the conclusion of the vocal line, m. 22, where the voice closes on the tonic just as the piano introduction recurs as a five-bar piano interlude/postlude. Even though the five-bar piano solos clearly frame the vocal stanzas with the same material, the separation of the piano introduction from the vocal entrance in m. 5 contrasts dramatically with the phrase overlap of the voice and piano interlude/postlude in m. 22. While the piano solo serves as a refrain between stanzas as well as the final piano solo, its recurrence through phrase elision creates a tension and acceleration that effectively leads to either the next verse or, ultimately, the song's conclusion.

Schubert's "Nachtviolen" also presents initially distinct phrases followed by elision for expressive purposes. The four-bar piano introduction concludes with an authentic cadence and sets the norm of both four-bar phrases and distinct phrase separation. Separate phrases occur during the first 37 measures, even when the four-bar norm is extended to six-bar phrases in mm. 13–14 and 27–28. Elisions then occur within the song's modified reprise that begins in m. 29. Here the phrase overlap (mm. 38 and 43) adds more tension to the ongoing use of six-bar phrases. The elision in m. 38 underscores the connection of poet and nature that will not be severed.[30] In m. 43, then, the vocal line concludes at the same time the piano repeats the opening music as a postlude.

Interestingly, both songs elide the concluding vocal line and the ensuing piano postlude. In both, the elisions merge the otherwise distinct personas of singer and accompanist and thereby dramatize their interaction as the poetic progression comes to a close. The difference in effect, however, is dramatic, as each elision reflects the different personas assumed by the accompaniment.[31] In "Die liebe Farbe," the insistent piano pedal and simple harmonic and melodic patterns represent the miller's pain and anguish as he contemplates death at the loss of his love. In "Nachtviolen," by contrast, the lilting piano solo represents the muted, melancholy gaze of the violets with which the poet identifies and creates a transformative bond.

Rhythm as Motive

One final elementary rhythmic device warrants attention, namely, the motivic projection of a recurring rhythmic figure. As suggested in our discussion of linear motives in Chapter Seven, a rhythmic motive is a rhythmic group that recurs at least on the surface and possibly also on deeper levels of rhythmic structure.[32] William Rothstein calls such small rhythmic figures "subphrases" that are embodied within larger phrases, several subphrases often occurring within a single phrase.[33] Two well-known examples of such rhythmic motives are Gretchen's "Meine Ruh ist hin" ("My peace is gone") refrain from "Gretchen am Spinnrade" and the son's "Mein Vater" ("My father") cries from "Erlkönig." Composers generally use such rhythmic figures or motives to create continuity and coherence in a work, and *Lied* composers also use such figures to depict various poetic ideas. This was discussed to some extent in Chapter Seven, in the section "Motivic Analysis," where the often superficial use of rhythmic motives was contrasted with the more substantive linear motives (such as neighbors, 3rds, 4ths, etc.) that involve pitch. But *Lied* performers need to be mindful that both reiterated rhythms and linear motives occur in obvious and in more subtle guises, and that the two types of motives serve the twin functions of creating continuity and expressing the poetic text.

While we discuss motivic rhythms only briefly here, we stress the need to interpret recurring rhythmic figures in ways that go beyond mere "text painting." Three examples from Schubert's Goethe settings illustrate. Schubert's "Erlkönig" is famous for the rhythmic motive of the triplet RH eighths that begin in the piano introduction and recur throughout the song. These triplets are generally interpreted as the galloping hooves of the horse which carries the frantic father and son homeward. That is a likely meaning in terms of text painting. Another interpretation serves the setting on an even deeper level. Since the only times the figure does not occur is when the Erlking speaks, one can expand upon the meaning of the galloping horse to include the symbolic embodiment of the father and son struggling against the Erlking. In this way, the pianist is not just conveying the horse's gallop but is depicting as well the ongoing battle of father and son against the menace of death.[34]

Another famous rhythmic motive used for both the musical continuity and text depiction is the sixteenth-note figure in "Gretchen am Spinnrade," where the recurring RH rhythmic pattern, along with the reiterated vocal refrain, creates coherence throughout the song. While many consider this rhythmic figure to represent the motion of the spinning wheel, with its various symbolic meanings, an even more important connotation for the sixteenths is their depiction of Gretchen's emotions: her unremitting anxiety and turmoil. Each interpretation of the sixteenths has a different effect on the performers. If the sixteenths are considered to be the spinning wheel, then the pianist metaphorically adopts the persona of Gretchen's imprisonment, a persona separate from the conflicts within her mind and soul. If, on the other hand, the sixteenths are considered to reflect Gretchen's emotional state, then both pianist and singer represent two sides of Gretchen's distraught and anguished mind and soul. These two different interpretations obviously have dramatically different implications for both the pianist and the ensemble.

Our final example of a rhythmic motive having different levels of interpretation is the more subtle dotted rhythms in "Wanderers Nachtlied I." The dotted rhythm does not appear in the piano introduction, but occurs at least once in each bar of the vocal line, mm. 3–8. At first glance, these rhythms might not be considered motivic; they occur in both quarter–eighth and eighth–sixteenth figures, at different points in the bar, and within different rhythmic contexts. In addition, while most of the dotted rhythms occur on strong beats (1 and 3), the repetitions setting "allen" ("all"), "Wip(feln)" ("Treetop"), "spürest ("feel"), "schweigen" ("hushed"), "Walde" ("woods") and "warte" ("wait") all occur in metrically ambiguous contexts, where beat 3 sounds like a downbeat. We will return to this metric ambiguity in the upcoming section "Rhythmic Tension and Ambiguity."

The lack of systematic usage might easily cause a performer to not consider the dotted rhythm a motive, and this in turn will make the more systematic and pronounced use of the rhythm in mm. 9–12 seem disconnected from the song's opening. However, further scrutiny shows that Schubert uses the dotted rhythm not to convey a single idea or emotion, but rather to convey the progression within the poetic text. The motive initially is used within subtle, almost undetected occurrences, muted within the poet's experience of nature's peaceful setting. The change to the more overt, focused usage then occurs when the poet shifts from observing nature to experiencing the internal longing for peaceful death.

This interpretation has great import for performers. The dotted rhythms have been confined to the vocal line through m. 8 and the singer must recognize the motivic repetition within the varying rhythmic contexts without any assistance from the accompaniment. The pianist, meanwhile, has not played a dotted rhythm before m. 9, and the new accompanimental rhythm creates an analogously new interaction between accompanist and singer. The role of the pianist shifts from the initial persona of the landscape (mm. 1–8) to a part of the poet/singer's yearning, perhaps the persona of the peaceful death the singer eagerly awaits.[35] In addition, the integration of vocal line and accompaniment achieved through the recurring dotted rhythm in these measures underscores the moment of poetic climax, where the wanderer's attention turns inward and the performers combine to convey the quintessential *Sehnsucht* of Goethe's masterpiece.

Metric, Rhythmic, and Phrase Deviations

Having established norms of rhythm, meter, and phrase structure, we now turn to the deviations from those norms that characterize much of the expressivity and beauty within *Lieder*. Metric deviation can occur as a shift in normative metric accent, where normally weak beats are stressed, and as metric ambiguity, where downbeats are unclear and thus meter is uncertain. The more subtle rhythmic deviation also occurs in two forms: (1) normative accents can change within a given metric context, so that the accent of a rhythmic figure contradicts the prevailing meter; and (2) unusual rhythmic accents can arise from complex rhythmic configurations, where particular beats are stressed for expressive purposes without regard either to the prevailing meter or to other norms of rhythmic usage. All metric and rhythmic complexities contribute both subtly and powerfully to text setting.

Metric Tension and Ambiguity

The systematic rhythmic accent created by meter can be altered in three ways. SYNCOPATION stresses a usually weak beat. SUSPENSION is a form of syncopation where the shift of stress from strong beat to weak beat occurs through a rhythmic displacement of one voice.[36] HEMIOLA is a brief but systematic shift in meter from duple to triple or vice versa. Syncopation and suspension tend to reinforce the meter through unusual stresses on normally weak beats; hemiola, in contrast, tends to create metric tension.[37] Many of these altered accents occur in the *Lieder* of Brahms, who was a master at manipulating rhythm and meter. We show syncopation in his song "Die Mainacht" and hemiola in "Heimweh II." Schumann's "Seit ich ihn gesehen" illustrates the suspension.

While the 4/4 meter of "Die Mainacht" suggests regular metric accents on beats 1 and 3, Brahms creates metric tension by stressing strong downbeats only in mm. 4 and 7 and secondarily strong third beats only in mm. 5 and 8. This metric fuzziness of the opening two phrases reflects the shadows of the moonlight and the wandering of the poet, and while duple meter is firmly established by the half cadence in m. 8, the confusion of the bar line (where the downbeat occurs) remains unresolved. In the ensuing phrase, mm. 9–11, Brahms accompanies the shift toward G♭ major (♭III) with two bars of syncopation (mm. 9–10), where two-beat agogic accents in the bass stress beats 2 and 4, the latter causing notes to be held over the barline to a weakened beat 1.[38] The syncopation thus intensifies the already murky metric scheme, with unexpected accents on normally weak beats. These stress reversals combine with the chromatic harmony ♭III to depict the nightingale's lament and the pain it resonates in the poet's heart; the specific poetic image and its emotional connotations take the poet outside the nocturnal landscape of E♭ major to a remote harmony and a diffused meter. Only when the poet begins to sadly wander about does the more normative 4/4 pattern return with relative clarity, along with the original key of E♭ recast in the minor mode.

While syncopation thus contradicts the normative accents of a prevailing meter, it also reinforces that meter; the listener hearing the metric ambiguity tries to feel the normative metric pattern to compensate. Hemiola, on the other hand, temporarily alters the prevailing meter in a systematic way. For example, in 3/4, two bars of 3/4 become three bars of 2/4; in 2/4, three bars of 2/4 become two bars of 3/4 occur. Figure 8.3 illustrates. Brahms's "Heimweh II" ("O wüßt ich doch den Weg zurück") demonstrates the hemiola; the song is in 6/4 meter, the duple of the compound meter being emphasized by dotted half notes in the bass. A hemiola passage occurs twice in the first eight bars, first in the piano introduction, m. 3, then within

FIGURE 8.3 Hemiola.

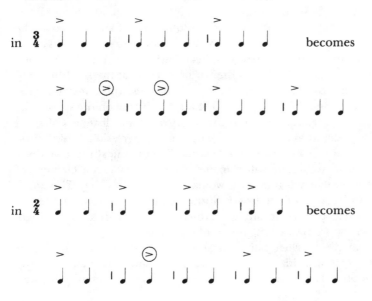

the first vocal phrase, m. 7. In these measures, the duple grouping of the 6/4 is briefly transformed into 3/2, where two dotted bass half notes are replaced by three half notes. The effect is expansion and intensification, as the harmony changes more quickly in anticipation of the arrival on V in mm. 4 and 8. This underscores the most common use of hemiola: to approach a cadence with increased rhythmic and harmonic activity.

Suspensions are aptly used in Schumann's "Seit ich ihn gesehen" to emphasize, in both the vocal line and piano RH, the two phrases of text "Taucht aus tiefstem Dunkel" ("rising out of darkest depths," mm. 11–13) and "Seit ich ihn gesehen," ("Since seeing him," mm. 27–29). These are intensified by dramatic leaps in the voice and the low register of the accompaniment RH, all of which depict the strong reaction in the young woman to "having seen him." These measures show the typical three-part design of suspensions: (1) the pitch to be suspended is prepared as a consonance on a weak beat; (2) it is suspended as a dissonance (or other nonchord tone) on a strong beat; (3) it is resolved stepwise (usually downward) on the next weak beat. The dissonance at the moment of suspensions thus marks (and stresses) an already accented strong beat.

In addition to these devices of metric deviation, many *Lieder* also depict certain poetic issues through more subtle forms of metric ambiguity.[39] Such metric ambiguity often occurs at the opening of a setting, where it conveys an initial poetic confusion or anxiety, or where nature images are shadowy or blurred. Several now-familiar *Lieder* exemplify such use of metric ambiguity to depict poetic issues. Our example for the suspension, "Seit ich ihn gesehen," uses metric confusion to initiate a song cycle devoted to the powerful confusions and passions of a young woman growing to maturity through various experiences of love and fulfillment. The opening metric confusion suggests the tentativeness and disquietude of young love — the poet's fears and anxieties — as she is "blinded" by her first love. This ambiguity results from a systematic stress on beat 2, which suggests that the preceding B♭ chord is an upbeat, that the bar line occurs at the E♭ chord, and that the following B♭ chord occurs on beat 2. Because this contradicts the normative placement of B♭: I–IV–V in 3/4 (as it is written on the score), the accent on beat 2 creates confusion for performers and listeners alike. If the B♭ chord is heard as an upbeat, the opening progression could sound like V–I in E♭ major. And even when B♭ is clarified as tonic, by its own dominant, the metric ambiguity still remains, projecting a vague element of uncertainty or hesitancy as the young woman begins her journey. The song's opening phrase recurs both at the conclusion of the first song and at the end of the entire cycle; the metric ambiguity thus can be interpreted as an ongoing symbol of this woman's struggles in life and love.

Our example of syncopation, Brahms's "Die Mainacht," also opens with metric ambiguity, this time depicting the moonlit night surrounding the troubled poet. The metric ambiguity occurs in connection with the harmonic ambiguity mentioned earlier, the persistent 6/4 within the dominant pedal that resolves to V in root position, but does not resolve properly after the final 6/4 chord which in turn never resolves to the tonic. The ambiguous effect is further enhanced when the 6/4 occurs, at times, on weak beats. The repeated cadential 6/4 occurs over the bar in mm. 2–3, and the thwarted cadence of mm. 2–4 is intensified in mm. 4–5, where the cadential 6/4 does not resolve to root position V. These opening 4½ bars thereby suggest a 3/2 meter, as one tries to "hear" the 6/4 chord on downbeats. The harmony begins to progress more straightforwardly after the I⁶ downbeat of m. 5; our earlier harmonic confusion resolves at the same time, as the meter is clarified as 4/4.

The ambiguous meter in the accompaniment of mm. 1–4 is not clarified by the vocal line there. When the voice enters, its B♭–E♭ can be heard to be a pickup to F, following the precedent of the piano RH melody in mm. 1–2. The vocal F (m. 3), and the subsequent long E♭ (m. 5), suggest that the barline is on written beat 3, rather than beat 1. This opening metric ambiguity aptly depicts the poetic imagery of diffused moonlight shining through the foliage; we will return to this example a bit later to examine in greater detail how the opening confusion continues and develops.

Some *Lieder* contain a sustained metric ambiguity that persists past the opening, intensifying over all or at least a large part of the song. The opening passage in Wolf's "Mir ward gesagt" illustrates this sustained ambiguity, as it depicts the ongoing confusion and anxiety of a woman whose lover is departing unexpectedly. The opening accompanimental gesture creates immediate ambiguity as the three 8th-note pickups do not suggest a duple 4/4 meter. The metric ambiguity continues in the ensuing two phrases. The downbeat of the LH F♯ (m. 1) suggests that the opening three 8th notes were pickups. Then the agogic accent on beat 4 of that bar suggests that it is a downbeat, putting the meter into 3/4. The sense of 3/4 is carried on by the agogic accent in the voice, on the C of m. 2 (three quarters after the earlier agogic accent on "rei-"). But the harmonic rhythm of m. 2 suggests the written 4/4. And the agogic accent of the LH, on the low E♮ of the same measure, suggests some other meter incompatible with both harmonic rhythm and vocal line.

The next measures repeat the first phrase in sequence, but without the emphasis on beat 4 in m. 3. At this point, we might feel we are indeed in 4/4, but Wolf confuses the meter further, through a hemiola in mm. 5–7; here the meter shifts into 3/4 through a sequential progression (most clearly heard in the LH "bass" line). The opening and increasing metric ambiguity of this song's first half is a vivid portrayal of the poet's ongoing distress, and only at the song's conclusion, when the poet is resigned to the lover's departure, is metric clarity created and maintained.⁴⁰

A final example of sustained metric ambiguity occurs in Brahms's "Immer leiser wird mein Schlummer," which depicts the slumbering haze of emotions and dreams within a dying poet who begs to see her lover one more time. The opening ambiguity arises again from an unsettlingpickup, this time a prolonged 6/4 chord that, along with the vocal line, misplaces the barline from beat 1 to beat 3 as it resolves and prepares a cadence in m. 3. This confusion over the true downbeat continues and is aggravated by subtle stresses on weak beats such as the syncopation and agogic accent on beat 2, m. 8 and the metrically ambiguous vocal entrance in m. 10. The next section in the relative major, mm. 14–21, undermines the 4/4 with a chronic syncopation in the accompaniment RH and stresses on beat 2 in the vocal line. As this agitated section comes to a close, the importance of the return to the minor tonic is underscored by a written-out two-bar shift to 3/2, which lengthens both the approach to V and the strong arrival on I.

The song's second half is a varied repetition of the first half. The final cadence is given emphasis not by metric clarification, but rather by more syncopation in mm. 48–50, and the song concludes in the same state of metric tension with which it began. This song eloquently exemplifies how metric ambiguity is used to convey *Sehnsucht:* the poet longs for what is unattainable, and performer and listener wait for a resolution of metric ambiguity that never comes.

Rhythmic Tension and Ambiguity

Rhythmic tensions and ambiguities involve the concept of accent as it occurs outside the patterns of stress within meter. These were described first in Chapter Five and reviewed in the preceding section "Rhythmic and Metric Norms." To illustrate some of these unusual rhythmic accents, we return to Schubert's "Wanderers Nachtlied I" and Brahms's "Die Mainacht," both of which show rhythmic complexities and ambiguities in rich detail.

"Wanderers Nachtlied I" illustrates how certain melodic and harmonic accents change the grouping normally arising from the given 4/4 meter. From the outset, unusual musical accents cloud the song's actual meter; the piano's opening two bars establish a duple meter and two-bar phrase norm, but the recurring emphasis on beat 3 creates more of a slow 2/4 than the written 4/4. This is most clearly evident in the vocal line; in mm. 3–5, the downbeat is continuously undermined by accented pitches on beat 3: the C upper neighbor of m. 3, the high E♭ of m. 4, and the C at the beginning of a new phrase, m. 5. These vocal accents are reinforced by the changes in accompanimental groupings: the vocal leap of m. 4 is accompanied by leaps in the piano LH, and the emphasis on C of m. 5 is underscored by a dramatic change in accompanimental figuration.

The systematic emphasis on beat 3 instead of beat 1 continues into m. 6, where changes in metric accent and phrase structure set the phrases "Ruh, in allen Wipfeln/spürest du kaum einen Hauch." The setting of "Ruh, in allen Wipfeln" ("peace, in every tree-top") occurs over six beats and thus forms a measure of 3/2 while the ensuing phrase "spürest du kaum einen Hauch" ("you feel scarce a breath") creates a one-bar approach to the arrival of V on beat 3 of m. 6, which sounds like a downbeat, not beat 3. All of these metric confusions are created by special accents: in addition to the accent on beat 3 caused by the vocal leap of a fourth, B♭ to E♭ in m. 4, the downbeat of m. 5 sounds weak, like beat 3 of a 3/2 bar. Beat 3 of m. 5, then, sounds like another downbeat, with the change in texture, the vocal leap, and the arrival on V. These special accents all create a rhythmic/metric tension analogous to the text, which speaks of the poet feeling "scarcely a breath." In addition, these accents faithfully follow Goethe's poetic meter, as was described earlier in Chapter Two, in the section "Model Analysis: Goethe's 'Wanderers Nachtlied I'."

Several irregularities of Brahms's "Die Mainacht" have been mentioned already, including syncopation, opening metric ambiguity, and three-bar phrase lengths. To these, we add unusual rhythmic accents that undermine the prevailing meter as the song progresses. Beginning in m. 15, the accents occur generally in two forms: leaping RH gestures that accent written third beats and syncopated agogic accents that occur in the vocal line. The leaps occur in the RH gestures of the middle section, mm. 15–26, where, in depiction of the cooing love birds, beat 3 is accented through ascending sixth leaps. The second form of accent, syncopated agogic emphasis, highlights key words of struggle and pain: m. 21 ("aber;" "but"); m. 23 ("suche [dunklere Schatten]"; "seek [deeper shadow]"); and m. 37 (the query "find [ich . . . dich]"; "find [I . . . you]"). A similar syncopation then occurs in mm. 47–48 on A♭ from beat 4 to beat 1; this underscores the physical arena of pain, "Wang" ("cheek") where the tear falls.

Rhythmic ambiguity in "Die Mainacht" also occurs in the domain of phrase structure. The three-bar phrases were mentioned earlier as, possibly, a six-bar phrase norm, but closer inspection reveals a more complex relation between vocal phrases and accompanimental solos. For example, the six-bar opening vocal phrase, mm. 3–8, discounts the two-bar piano introduction, while the next six-bar vocal phrase, mm. 9–16, has to include the piano interlude, mm. 13–14. Do we count mm. 13–14 but ignore the piano introduction? The pattern of accompanimental interludes completing phrase lengths continues in mm. 15–20, where the piano interlude of mm. 19–20 completes a six-bar phrase; however, the final phrase of this section, mm. 21–26, comprises a six-bar phrase (3 + 3) using the vocal line throughout.

While six-bar phrases (some including piano interludes, others not) continue throughout the song, the song concludes with other phrase irregularities. The phrase beginning in m. 39 is extended to a ten-bar final vocal phrase eliding into a four-bar piano postlude. One can consider the four-bar piano postlude to combine with the two-bar piano introduction, thereby creating a six-bar accompanimental frame for the vocal part; the 2 + 4 subdivision of that frame, however, deviates from the 3 + 3 norm and thereby creates an opening phrase tension that remains unresolved at the song's conclusion. The four-bar extension, mm. 45–48 also contradicts the three- and six-bar norms; this tension is a powerful depiction of the ever-increasing pain of the poet.

A final and unusual rhythmic/metric device in "Die Mainacht" is a clear 4/4 meter in the phrases setting the text "und die einsame Träne rinnt" ("and a solitary tear flows," mm. 27–31) and its enlarged variant "Träne bebt" ("tear trembles," mm. 39–48). In direct contrast to the surrounding rhythmic and metric tensions and ambiguities that set nature's shadowy landscape, these phrases of relative rhythmic and metric clarity set the important metaphor of the poet's inner pain (the solitary tear that flows and then trembles down the poet's cheek) with clarity unique to human capacity. The resulting contrast of rhythmic/metric clarity versus rhythmic/metric ambiguity underscores through temporal means the central dichotomy of the poem: the struggle through nature's murky, elusive world enables the poet to experience clearly the emotions held within.

While the examples on rhythmic, metric, and phrase deviations have been brief, they do offer ways to think about rhythmic, metric, and phrase alteration and ambiguity within the *Lied* repertory. To some readers, these deviations may seem difficult to identify or understand; nonetheless, comprehending these aspects of rhythm, meter, and phrase structure is critical to achieving confident and persuasive performance. We thus close this chapter with a few guidelines to help performers work through the complexities of music's temporal domain. First, performers can use their own intuitive experience to help locate moments of rhythmic, metric, or phrase deviance and ambiguity. For example, when a particular moment or section or a complete work (particularly a song composed later in the century) feels awkward, out of sync, or insecure, that might well indicate a place of deviation in one or several areas. In such cases, performers then must look for the norms that might be operative and see how these norms are broken. What is the indicated meter and what meter does the piece feel in the hands and throat? What is the phrase norm? Are there any unusual rhythmic accents?

Another clue is the text. If the poet speaks of confusion, anxiety, ambivalence, or any number of uncomfortable, unsteady feelings, the setting might well use rhythmic, metric, or phrase deviation to capture the poetic difficulty. In such cases, one again finds the norms and deviations, and then traces them in direct correspondence to the flow of text. This is one of the most compelling reasons why understanding the text is so crucial to understanding the musical setting.

No matter what approach you take in identifying rhythmic, metric, and phrase irregularities, your work will be well rewarded. Such areas of complexity in the temporal domain occur in some of the most exquisite moments within the *Lied* genre, and performers with a full grasp of the temporal complexities will convey more convincingly to their audience the richness of nuance and complexity so characteristic of the German *Lied*.

Exercises

Exercise 8.1: Harmonic rhythm

Indicate how change in harmonic rhythm depicts poetic elements in the following songs:

1. Schubert, "Am Feierabend"
2. Schumann, "Mondnacht"
3. Schumann, "Widmung"
4. Schubert, "Der Jüngling und der Tod"
5. Schubert, "Der Lindenbaum"

Exercise 8.2: Phrase structure

Determine the phrase structure of the following songs, noting norms, extensions or contractions, and use of elision:

1. Schubert, "Wasserfluth"
2. Schubert, "Der Lindenbaum"
3. Schumann, "Widmung"
4. Schumann, "Seit ich ihn gesehen"
5. Schubert, "Der Neugierige"
6. Schubert, "Auf dem Wasser zu singen"
7. Schubert, "Im Frühling"
8. Brahms, "Immer leiser wird mein Schlummer"
9. Brahms, "Sappische Ode"
10. Wolf, "Auch kleine Dinge"

Exercise 8.3: Rhythmic and metric deviations

Demonstrate the use of rhythmic and metric deviation and ambiguity, including syncopation, suspension, hemiola, agogic accent, and unusual rhythmic accents; in addition, cite poetic issues these deviations depict:

1. Brahms, "O wüßt ich doch den Weg zurück"
2. Schubert, "Der Jüngling und der Tod"

3. Schubert, "Wasserfluth"
4. Schubert, "Lied eines Schiffers"
5. Schumann, "Seit ich ihn gesehen"
6. Schumann, "Widmung"
7. Strauss, "Morgen!"
8. Wolf, "In dem Schatten meiner Locken"
9. Wolf, "Mein Liebster singt am Haus"
10. Wolf, "Und steht Ihr früh am Morgen"

CHAPTER NINE

Form in the German Lied

The term "form" in music can be confusing; it can have several different meanings, particularly since music can be analyzed on several levels, from the smallest unit to the most vast compositional whole. Small-scale formal organization, which deals with the shape and interplay of phrases, was discussed in Chapter Eight; here we will examine other issues of formal organization that shape and mold music's temporal flow.

Form in *Lieder* differs from that in many other genres in two significant ways. First, the miniature scale of the *Lied* often precludes the lengthy developmental sections found in larger forms, and second, the *Lied* cycle is similar only in part to the large, multimovement form found in instrumental sonatas, symphonies, or the vocal opera genre. While cycles such as *Die schöne Müllerin, Winterreise,* and *Dichterliebe* are large in overall scope, the interrelation between songs in these and other "cycles" varies greatly, with no common set of formal relationships. We begin our study of form by examining more general issues, such as use of repetition and contrast, and the reinterpretation of musical elements.

Introduction

Principles of Form

Just as poems are often arranged in verses or strophes ranging in length from two to eight or more lines, almost all songs consist of short units consisting of anywhere from two to twenty phrases. These units, or sections, can be combined by being either repeated or contrasted with one another, and sections become effective building blocks in the construction of a whole composition by creating unity and cohesiveness along with contrast and diversity. We analyze form first by identifying sections that are self-contained units, each unit articulated by a clear cadence. Each unified section is designated by a letter label; thus, section A is the first unit in a composition, section B the second, and so on. Many factors contribute to this subdivision into sections. The cohesiveness and unity can be tonal: section A may be entirely in one key, and section B in a different key. Or a change of texture can divide a work into contrasting sections, for example, the accompanying figures in section B may be moving four times as fast as those in section A. Or the melody in section A can be significantly different from that in section B. These distinguishing characteristics of different musical sections are almost always immediately recognizable by ear. As a result, the return of any section creates a sense of recognition in the listener. If this return involves some sort of variation or modification, including a shortening of the material, we use a prime sign after the letter, for example, section A' or ABCA'.

The central issue of form in the temporal art of music is the use of departure and return. Formal "departure" creates contrast and digression while formal "return" (in other genres also called REPRISE and RECAPITU-LATION) creates repetition, cohesion, and, at the work's end, closure.[1] A setting can use repetitive or contrasting elements at the small, note-to-note, level and at the large-scale level, using entire blocks or musical sections. For example, a poem made up of five quatrains can repeat the same music five times or introduce new material with each succeeding strophe. The first option would be labeled AAAAA and the second ABCDE. Other solutions are also obvious: ABABA or ABACA. Most of these schemes involve at least one element of departure or contrast labeled B and many conclude with a return of A for the song's closure.

Lied *Form and Historical Precedents*

The small number of formal designs developed by the great nine-teenth-century *Lied* composers arose from earlier forms called "historical precedents." The recurring "AAAAA" model was prevalent in German culture in the church chorale and sacred song, where numerous verses were set in a simple, homophonic style to enable a congregation to easily follow along. The systematic repetition of one section of material over and over for each new poetic stanza is called STROPHIC FORM. A piano prelude and/or a postlude can be added, but the form is easily recognized through the use of repeat marks on the printed page.

Another popular form used extensively in vocal music, especially by late Baroque composers such as J. S. Bach, Handel, and Alessandro Scarlatti, is called the DA CAPO aria. We diagram this form simply as ABA: a more or less self-contained A section is followed by a B section of contrasting material, that is, one marked by contrasts in key, melody, rhythm, and/or texture. At the conclusion of this B section, the A section then returns, either in part or in full. Eighteenth-century composers often did not bother to write out this return, but simply marked the instruction "da capo" ("from the top") thus giving us the form's popular name. This ABA or TERNARY form satisfies the pervasive desire in Western art for a secure return to some familiar base as part of a work's closure, and was used by most *Lied* composers, especially Brahms.

A more elaborate variation on the scheme of departure and return is the RONDO, a form often associated with eighteenth-century instrumental music, but which also can be found in the operatic arias of seventeenth-century French and Italian composers. The principle of rondo form involves returning to the A theme or section after each digression: popular eighteenth- and nineteenth-century versions of this can be diagrammed ABACABA and ABABA. The rondo form is thus closely akin to the ternary ABA form.

Another vocal form prevalent throughout the Baroque period was the "monodic recitative." Here the vocal line imitated speech over a simple accompaniment, not bothering to repeat itself in any significant musical fashion; the music began at point A and concluded elsewhere, for example, at point B or E. Music organized in this manner is called THROUGH COMPOSED (from the German *durchkomponiert*), and *Lied* composers using this form compensated for a lack of substantial formal repetition by creating unity or coherence through rhythmic, motivic, and harmonic or tonal closure.

Analysis of Form in *Lieder*

We can see that only a few forms are typically used in *Lieder*. Each will be examined in turn; some songs offer clear examples of the basic forms and others expand upon the formal designs to create new, unique structures. No matter which form we illustrate, however, basic principles of form affect both the composer and the performer in specific ways. The following questions relate to all *Lied* forms and need to be kept in mind.

Questions for the composer:

1. How is repetition in a text treated musically?
2. How is repetition used to unify a text that essentially proceeds in a straight line, telling a story?
3. How is poetic contrast and development musically depicted?

Questions for the performer:

1. What implications for performance does repetition have?
2. What implications does contrast have?
3. What choices do performers have conveying the effect of a return or reprise?
4. Does the return of previously heard material require a reinterpretation by either the performer or the listener?

Strophic Form

As already mentioned, the formal principle inherent in strophic *Lieder* is that of whole-scale repetition: one musical setting is repeated for each stanza of the poem. While this may be considered the simplest formal design for setting a multiverse poem, it challenges the composer, who must find a single musical design to convey a variety of poetic verses.[2] Our examination of this form must therefore take into account how composers created sufficient interest and musical tension in their strophic settings, including subdividing the musical strophe into an ABA or ABA' design or using piano solos as both interlude between verses and postlude at the song's conclusion.

Simple Strophic Form

Two Schubert *Lieder* studied in earlier chapters, "Wiegenlied" and "Litanei," offer an interesting comparison of strophic settings.[3] "Wiegenlied" represents the simplest strophic form; the repeat signs encompass the entire song, including the interlude and postlude. Indeed, mm. 9–10 serve the dual purpose mentioned above; they form an interlude or bridge between verses and then function as a postlude after the third and final verse. The success of this whole-scale repetition results from the parallel construction of the poetic stanzas: Each of the three stanzas has the same number of syllables, so the exact same melody can be used for all.

"Litanei" follows the same plan, but adds an introduction before verse 1. Again, each verse of the poem has the same number of syllables, so the musical repetition is exact in each detail. Here, however, the harmonic and melodic language is more complex than that of "Wiegenlied," and the setting can be divided into a clear ABA form, the A sections, mm. 2–3 and 9–10, stating and restating the prayer and the contrasting B section, with its tonal instability and chromaticism, conveying various descriptions of the suffering souls. The contrast between the ritualistic A sections and tension-filled B sections creates a rich form that invites repeated hearings. Indeed, this ABA design uses the strophic form to underline both the formulaic nature of the prayer, and the dramatic tensions of the poem's interior descriptions. This vividly contrasts with the musical language of "Wiegenlied," where the three repetitions have the soothing effect of familiarity appropriate for a lullaby.

Schubert's "Morgengruß" (D. 798, no. 8 from *Die schöne Müllerin*) demonstrates an even more complex ABA' strophic setting. As commonly occurs, repeat signs surround the four verses, and a prelude introduces the opening verse. But the fourfold repetition is not tedious, for like the B Section of "Litanei," various ambiguities in the B and A' sections of "Morgengruß" enable and encourage repeated listening.[4] The C major song has a harmonically unstable B section, where a sequence using modal mixture includes a half cadence leading to but not resolving to D (major or minor). In addition, a metric ambiguity involving the A' section creates unresolved metric tension that prompts the need for repeated hearings. The vocal line develops the opening vocal gesture of the A section and this two-bar phrase is imitated in the piano RH. Within a two-bar phrase, then, the vocal downbeat E in m. 16 is contradicted by the downbeat piano RH pitch E in m. 17. Which is the correct downbeat for the two-bar phrases? This metric and phrase ambiguity continues to the end. The vocal line comprises four 2-bar phrases (16–17, 18–19, etc.), but the RH piano part disputes each with three 2-bar phrases beginning one bar later (17–18, 19–20, etc.). When the piano postlude is taken into account, both the vocal line and piano accompaniment end on a weak beat. As each verse concludes, the listener welcomes repeated hearings in order to make sense of the tonal ambiguities of the B section and the metric confusions of the A' section.

In setting "Morgengruß," Schubert also was challenged by metric variations in the poetry. The poem has varying numbers of syllables in the four verses, and this requires the addition or subtraction of notes and rhythms in order to maintain the overall musical repetition. An interesting exercise is to speak the poem aloud and see if you agree with Schubert's solutions to the various scansion problems presented by the text.

Other songs in *Die schöne Müllerin* with strophic settings include "Das Wandern," "Ungeduld," and "Des Müllers Blumen." While "Tränenregen" also uses a strophic form to set its seven verses, the concluding verse changes dramatically, using the minor mode and differences in both vocal line and accompaniment to depict the final poetic statement.

While it is easy to recognize strophic form when a *Lied* is printed with clear repeat signs, there are instances where composers and/or publishers print a strophic song with written-out repetitions. "Der Schmied" by Brahms is always printed in such a way that the first two verses are written together, while the third verse, which is identical, is written separately. This suggests that the third verse is to be performed with different emphasis and interpretation from the first two. Other examples of written-out strophic *Lieder* can be found among the works of Schumann: "Im wunderschönen Monat Mai" and "Erstes Grün," both of which contain identical verses.

In determining strophic form, then, printed scores may veil a strophic setting. Once the form is ascertained, formal analysis must consider the use of an internal subdivision, such as the commonplace ABA, and the function of piano solos. Finally, the relationship of the poetry and the musical form must be compared: What in the poetry prompts the choice of strophic form, and what poetic elements suggest use of melodic, harmonic, and/or metric ambiguities or tensions that create interest in a repeated musical strophe.

Modified Strophic Form

The MODIFIED STROPHIC form involves using some kind of variation within an otherwise simple strophic setting. This occurs when a composer preserves the large-scale strophic repetition but adds changes between verses that go substantially beyond adjustment of vocal line to fit poetic syllables. Schubert's "Gute Nacht," the first song in *Winterreise*, D. 911, offers a good example. Verses 1 and 2 are printed within repeat signs, and verse 3 is identical except for dynamics and the direction of the vocal line in mm. 42 and 46. In verse 4, however, Schubert creates a dramatic change, as the song concludes in the parallel mode, D major. Despite this vivid change, it is easy for the listener to follow this scheme, even at the first hearing; the four verses are self-contained and almost entirely parallel, and the major-mode verse is obviously only a variant of the first three. "Gute Nacht" thus modifies an essentially strophic pattern in order to convey a poetic shift, but not so much as to disrupt the formal pattern of whole-scale repetition.

A more elaborate modification occurs in Brahms's "Vergebliches Ständchen." Here alternate verses are sung by a boy (B) and a girl (G), thus: BGBG. Brahms uses almost the exact melodic and harmonic material for each verse, with one large exception: Verse 3 is set mostly in the parallel minor mode, and the piano accompaniment has various changes in texture, as in mm. 63ff. Nonetheless, the listener can immediately grasp the song's strophic form on first hearing.

A more subtle example of strophic modification can be found in Wolf's "Auch kleine Dinge." The poem presents four quatrains, the last three parallel verses praising in turn the charms of pearls, olives, and roses. Wolf sets the poem in four distinguishable strophes, each rhythmically self-contained, and each ending with either an authentic cadence (mm. 8, 12, and 21) or half cadence (m. 16). The first four poetic syllables of each verse are set with an easily recognizable descending motive traversing either a semitone, C♯–C♮ in verse 1 and A–G♯ in verse 3 or whole step, C♯–B in verses 2 and 4. Despite the changes in pitch and interval, the vocal similarity amongst verses is obvious to the ear. The similarity of sections and initial vocal gestures, then, creates a strophic setting for this song. And the changes in the third verse (the vocal gesture beginning on A instead of C♯ and the accompaniment ascending rather than descending) creates only a modification of the strophe. As a modified strophic song, "Auch kleine Dinge" illustrates the balance of parallel repetitive structure with variety and modification. The song also shows the variability of formal designs and labels. While a case for modified strophic form is clear, another valid interpretation of form could be AABA, where the B label suggests a greater difference from A than the modified strophic form denotes. The choice of form for "Auch kleine Dinge" thus reflects how much difference one hears in the third verse. If the difference is perceived to be only slight, then the form is modified strophic; if the difference is heard as more substantial, then AABA better conveys the form.

An even subtler use of exact repetition occurs in Strauss's "Morgen!". The opening piano (or orchestral) solo in mm. 1–14 is repeated exactly when the voice enters in mm. 16–29. As far as the pianist is concerned, therefore, the song is a two-verse strophic song with postlude. However, for the singer, the issue is more complicated. The text is sung only over the second "verse," at first independently from the piano melody, and then joining it in m. 21. The unusual vocal line thus represents the "modification" of the accompaniment's strophic setting. Symbolically, the modified strophic form of "Morgen!" suggests that the thoughts and feelings expressed in words in verse 2 had been in the mind and soul of the singer, and were conveyed in the piano solo, long before they were uttered.[5] The opening piano solo can then be interpreted in several ways. The accompaniment's persona could be the emerging feelings that are then articulated in the vocal line, or the accompaniment has a completely different role in a drama between two lovers: perhaps the image of the lover in the mind of the singer, or perhaps the lover who is addressed directly.

Performance Implications

When singing or playing a strophic *Lied*, musicians obviously must decide how much variation could and should be introduced into a performance. An underlying criterion for these decisions remains how to communicate the meaning of the text, but performers also must maintain the interest of the audience. If a listener hears no progression, and feels that the performance is not "going anywhere," then boredom sets in, and the performance is considered empty and unmusical.

Even in the most repetitious of *Lieder*, therefore, it is incumbent on the performers to be attentive to the meanings and colors of individual words. Taking Schubert's "Wiegenlied" as an example, the repeated first two words, "Schlafe, schlafe" ("sleep, sleep"), could be inflected differently, the second being perhaps more gentle than the first. In mm. 5 and 6, verse 1 gives us the shift from "sanfte" ("gentle, smooth") to "milde" ("mild, soft"), two similar words that can convey varying degrees of gentleness through their coloration. By contrast, verse 2 presents the same word, "alle" ("all"), on the "sanfte" and "milde" notes, so a singer might want to present the second "alle" more intensely than the first, or the singer could shift the emphasis from the first half of the measure to the second half, stressing "Wünsche" ("wishes") and "habe" ("have") rather than the two "alles." Similar personal choices can be made in "Litanei"; the performers can decide which descriptions are the most intense and which of the two prayers, the beginning or ending one, is the more peaceful.

Performers are also free to make arbitrary or artificial distinctions in order to vary their reading of a strophic Lied. For example, the three verses of "Wiegenlied" could be performed with a continuous decrease in the dynamic level, depicting the gradual approach of sleep. Or "Litanei" could be performed so that the second verse is louder than the first and the third verse softer. This could express the fact that the old and young souls of verse 2 deserve the most intense prayers of intercession.

Beyond these different performance decisions is a basic premise of artistic interpretation: Is the protagonist in the same place dramatically, emotionally, and/or physically at the end of the piece as at the beginning? The possibility of an "emotional or psychological journey" is a crucial element of many works of art, and in *Lieder,* performers convey two basic types of poetic experience. On the one hand, the text and music can indeed indicate a progression or redefinition that moves from one point to another. And on the other hand, text and music might depict a more circular focused expression, where emotional intensification occurs instead of ongoing progression. This could be a departure followed by a return, or a series of contrasting but essentially static repetitions. Songs conveying an emotional journey such as "Vergebliches Ständchen" or "Morgengruß" convey a "plot" that assists performers in determining how to vary elements such as dynamics, tempo, etc. in order to tell the story. In contrast, songs such as "Litanei" or "Das Wandern" do not tell an overarching story but rather convey a singular state of being, and performers must rely more on subtle differences inherent in the poetry and setting to add color and variation to their interpretation.

ABA Ternary Form

The ABA form mentioned in the context of the strophic settings of "Litanei" and "Morgengruß" can be a song's overall design itself, without the overriding strophic repetition. This form uses repetition of an opening A section (A or A') to follow a large-scale contrasting B section, the return of A representing both an element of reprise and a means of balancing the large-scale form. The ABA form can also be called ternary, meaning three-part subdivision that includes a return of A, or in the case of a varied reprise, A'.

A simple ABA song is Schubert's "Mein!" of *Die schöne Müllerin.* In section A, the miller is convinced of the girl's love. In section B, he decides that all the voices of nature are not sufficient to express his love, and that he must sing of it himself. It is therefore utterly logical that he return to the A section and sing it through again, adding only a last emphatic repetition of the final line. The contrasting B section does not change the miller's feeling, but rather reinforces it with nature imagery and a shift to rhetorical questions, which in turn lead up to his determination that he alone can express his joy. The return to A restates the initial poetry, but presumably with more conviction and exuberance.

Schubert's "Der Müller und der Bach," the penultimate song in *Die schöne Müllerin*, offers a more complex example of this form. The three sections of the poem are clearly separated from each other, and the speakers are noted in the text: first the miller, then the brook, and then the miller again. The song's setting conveys the different speakers with immediately recognizable melodic phrases and parallel mode changes; the miller's first and third statements have distinctive melodic features and are set in minor, and the brook's response in verse 2 has a different melodic outline both in pitch and in rhythm and is clearly in major. The first two verses are also varied in terms of piano accompaniment: the flowing accompanimental figure (representing the flowing water) to the brook's speech in verse 2 contrasts nicely with the halting chords that had accompanied the miller's lament in verse 1. The setting of verse 3, however, is not a simple repetition of the first, but rather provides several differences in both melody, harmony, and, most strikingly, a continuation of the flowing accompaniment from verse 2, all in the minor mode.

The continuation of the accompanimental figure through verse 3 and the song's conclusion represents a significant formal variation that conveys the shift in poetic progression. Verse 3 conveys the miller's response to his companion's message of death, and continuing the brook's figuration is a way of acknowledging the miller's assent. This underscores the dramatic shift in the miller's journey; by the end of verse 3, the miller's desire for suicide is clear.

While Schumann is often associated with the three-part ABA form, it occurs less frequently in his *Lieder* than one might think.[6] A good example, however, is the famous "Widmung," which demonstrates Schumann's complex use of the ternary form as well as his penchant for changing the poetry to suit musical needs. As already discussed in Chapter 6, the song alters the poem drastically to accommodate Schumann's musical conception. The first verse is set in a clearly defined section A, with distinctive vocal line and accompaniment in A♭ major. The rather abrupt contrasting section B in F♭ major (♭VI of A♭ major, spelled E major) is easily identified because of its completely different texture and meter. This beautiful contrast seems inspired by the introduction of the words "Ruh" and "Frieden" ("rest" and "peace") in the poem's second and final verse. Thus far, the song's form, while faithful to the text, creates a problematic AB design, with no sense of reprise. Schumann solved this formal problem by repeating the opening verse, with modifications, and the resulting ABA' design necessitated a complete reformulation of Rückert's poem.[7] The remarkable bridge from B to A' was described in some detail in Chapter Six, in the section "Chromatic Third Relations." Schumann introduces the accompaniment figure from A and a modulation back to A♭ major *before* the end of the B section. In so doing, the recapitulation of A can occur as soon as the text to section B has been sung. The return of the music and the text of section A begins in m. 30, but is altered both musically (m. 35) and texturally (m. 37ff., where the final text of verse 1 is replaced by the final lines of verse 2). The resulting musical form and poetic alteration creates a dramatic poetic setting: the B section has elements of the A section (the accompaniment figure in mm. 26–29), while the A' section includes elements of the B section (the final two lines of the poem). The song thus concludes with the final lines of Rückert's poem, a fidelity to the poetic closure that was initially undermined by the return to verse 1. Schumann has thus cleverly solved the formal problem of reconciling return with novelty, mixing the old and the new in a revision of Rückert's poem in the service of creating a ternary musical form.

A popular modification of this three-part form involves repeating the A section before proceeding to the B section: AABA or AABA'.[8] A classic example of the latter, AABA', is Schubert's "Die Forelle." The poem is made up of six quatrains. Schubert sets the first two, which describe the joy of watching the trout play in its stream, as section A. The next two quatrains, where the narrator remains confident that the fisherman will not catch the fish, are then set to exactly the same music. When, however, the fisherman resorts to trickery and catches the trout, Schubert creates a contrasting B section, with a new melody, new harmonies, and a new texture. The tragedy of the story continues into the last quatrain and the B section lasts for six lines (one and a half quatrains) of the poem. The A material then returns with the final two lines of poetry and the final two phrases of the original A section. Schubert's setting mirrors the emotional journey of the text, returning to the familiar texture, harmony, and melody of section A only when the struggle ends and the narrator regretfully concludes with the moral of the story.

Another way to modify a ternary ABA form is to enlarge upon the contrasting B section. This is the case in Wolf's famous *Lied* "Verborgenheit." Mörike's poem is comprised of three quatrains, each with the rhyme scheme ABBA. Wolf decided to cast his entire *Lied* in the same form, making the large-scale musical structure the same as the small-scale poetic structure. In order to do this, however, a fourth section of music had to be included, even though the poem has only three verses. Wolf solves this puzzle by repeating in modified form the B section, using different music to the new text, and repeating verbatim the A section, using the same words and music. The resulting form is ABB'A; the return of A creates the sense of reprise, while the altered B' section conveys the poet's emotional journey to escape the stress of life and to return inward for peace.

Two-part (A/B) Forms

Another effective arrangement of the common two formal elements A/B is the binary form ABAB. This format allows for a vacillation between two repeated sections and does not rely on a total return of A for closure.[9] Schumann's "Waldesgespräch" exemplifies this, as he alternates radically differing music to depict the man (in E major) and the witch (initially in C major), who alternate without the mediation of a narrator. While the vocal lines present a clear ABAB pattern, Schumann does round out the song with a return to the initial tonic, E major, during the final B section and with a piano postlude in E major that recalls the opening piano introduction. This brings up another issue of interpretation: whether to determine form by melodic elements or tonal ones. While it is easy to hear the melodic form of this song as ABAB, it is altogether feasible to interpret the form as ABA', thus reflecting the tonal design. Yet another way to understand the form is a different concept of ABA', where the A' combines the melodic material from B with the tonal context of A. In this case, A' is a hybrid of both A and B, a formal design that reflects the poetic progression from dialog between the man and Lorelei to the entrapment of the man by Lorelei. Lorelei sings her final statement, but in the man's key: she has appropriated E major as a symbol of seducing the man himself.

The less frequent formal design AAB (often called bar form) effectively demonstrates how closure can occur without a return to the original section A. Schubert's "Klage an den Mond" illustrates this in a setting of three stanzas that begins in F major and ends in d minor. The song uses directional tonality, as described in Chapter Six in the section "Directional Tonality"; the first two verses, where the youth speaks to the moon of his torment, are set in F major, with clear cadences in that key at the end of both A sections. The third verse, then, where the youth speaks not of torment but of release through death, is set altogether differently, with clear changes of melody, tonality, and texture. While the poetic progression and tonal design deny the possibility of a reprise in mood or tonality, the strong final cadence in d minor creates the necessary closure for the song to come to an end.

Rondo and Refrain

A variation of the use of two (or more) elements which is strongly identified with instrumental music is the rondo, a form in which the A section returns significantly after more than one contrasting section, for example, ABACA. Schubert's "Der Musensohn" offers a fine, and simple, example of this form, where the five sections of Goethe's poem are set by two alternating sections that differ in melodic lines and tonalities and follow the scheme ABABA.[10] Schubert uses these differences in section B to reflect a poetic shift from the youth's general experiences out in the world (verses 1, 3, and 5) to more specific images (garden and tree in verse 2 and linden tree and young couple in verse 4).

Schumann's op. 24 song "Schöne Wiege meiner Leiden" became a rondo through another text alteration: the first four lines of Heine's poem set as section A (mm. 1–20) are repeated, slightly abridged, as a final section A' (mm. 94–108). Within these two statements, a second section A (mm. 20–39) is followed by first an accelerated section B in the parallel minor, and then another section A (mm. 53–70). This second section A is altered to create an elision into the abrupt and passionate outbursts of section C (mm.

70–93). The graphic depiction of anguish and despair is then balanced by the closing section A' that quotes the first verse and returns to a more peaceful setting. It is almost as if the protagonist is exhausted and can only repeat what has already been stated.

The essence of the rondo form is a recurring repetition of a clearly identifiable section A that opens and closes a work despite one or more digressions. The recurring music usually sets different verses, so the repetition is musical with changing text. A repetition of music that repeats the poetic text adds a deeper dimension of reiteration. Such a recurring section of both text and music is called a REFRAIN. This device is often used by poets to unify a longer work by the reiteration of a tag, sometimes ironic, of two or more lines, usually after each verse.[11] Musical settings that utilize such a refrain include Wolf's "Wenn du zu den Blumen gehst" from the *Spanischesliederbuch*, where the first quatrain becomes a recurring refrain throughout, and another Spanish song, "Mögen alle bösen Zungen," where each new section inevitably returns to a quote of the *Lied*'s first two phrases. The witty and ironic nature of the text is matched by the liveliness of the musical setting, and the various repetitions in the *Lied* could make a sort of refrain-rondo form.

Two of Schubert's most celebrated *Lieder* also utilize the refrain device, "Gretchen am Spinnrade" and "Erlkönig." Goethe's "Gretchen" consists of seven quatrains with no repetitions of text. However, Schubert shows sensitivity and daring beyond his seventeen years by portraying Gretchen's compulsive fascination with Faust through a repeat of the first quatrain, both music and text, at mm. 31ff. and 70ff. This motive then returns in abridged form at the end (the first two lines of the poem only) in a way that recaptures Gretchen's obsessiveness. We sense that she has returned to her starting place, and is condemned to repeat the same thoughts and experience the same feelings over and over. The form of "Gretchen am Spinnrade" is diagrammed thus (r = refrain): ArBArCArDr.[12]

Both the poem and the setting of "Erlkönig" present aspects of refrain and rondo. The Rondo form occurs from the alternating dialogue between the father and son and the Erlking; the refrain elements occur as either repeated rhythmic motives or vocal repetitions of key words. The opening piano bass motive in m. 2 recurs like a refrain at mm. 33, 113, and 132 and brings with it something akin in feeling to a recurring section A. The neighbor-note motive on the word "mein Vater," meanwhile, is sung in conjunction with each return of section A as well. These modified A' sections contrast with the B, C, and D sections sung by the Erlking, whose music differs in mode, tonality, piano texture, and melodic outline. We have seen in Chapter Seven that the melodic and tonal elements of "Erlkönig" progress and transform themselves throughout the *Lied*. In counterbalance to this progression, however, Schubert constructed continuity in the form of a refrain/rondo, with rhythmic and textural elements emphasizing motivic repetitions.

Our final example shows use of refrain within a large-scale ternary form in Brahms's "Die Mainacht." Section A extends from m. 1 through m. 14, with a feeling of completeness despite the virtual lack of root-position tonic. Section B begins in the tonality of ♭VI, and reaches a half cadence back in E♭ major at m. 26; the ensuing phrase, "Und die einsame Träne rinnt," extends the dominant until we arrive at a return to section A in the tonic in m. 33. This lasts for only one quatrain, however, or one half of the original section A material; at this point (m. 39), a modified refrain of "Und die einsame" occurs, with the text and setting extended, but nonetheless audible as a refrain. The musical refrain was clearly suggested in the text, as the poetic refrain concludes verses 2 and 3. Brahms thus creates a musical analog to the poetic refrain and places it within an otherwise ABA' setting, giving "Die Mainacht" the form A-Br-A'r'.

Through composed Form

This chapter has emphasized the necessity of formal repetition in order to establish unity and to create closure in *Lieder*. Sometimes, however, we find compositions that display very little in the way of repetition. These songs seem to describe an emotional journey so direct and complete that no turning back is possible or necessary; indeed, in these works conveying the poetic progression takes precedence over creating a particular cyclic musical form. While such songs are called through composed (*durchkomponiert*), the term must not be taken too literally. Musical works that do not use large-scale repetition do find ways to create musical coherence and continuity, and such formal devices are as important as the identification of large A sections or contrasting B sections.

Schubert's "Wanderers Nachtlied I" provides an excellent example of a through composed song that nevertheless coheres because of small motivic elements. We have already described recurring rhythmic motives in Chapter Eight; in addition, several other unifying elements are clearly audible: mm. 2, 13, and 14 are the same, even though they are too brief to count as a sectional return. Similarly, mm. 1 and 3–4 sound alike, but again do not comprise whole sections. Even so, while we cannot label large-scale "A" repetitions, we can show melodic and motivic repetitions that recur systematically at the beginning and again at the song's conclusion. The melodic motive of m. 2 (piano RH) recurs in the vocal line in mm. 10 and 13 and in the accompaniment, m. 13–14. The sixteenth-note figuration in the accompaniment from m. 5 to m. 8 sounds like a contrasting section and indeed creates contrast with the opening and is not heard again. Thus, if mm. 1–4½ are section A, then mm. 4½-8 comprise section B. The ensuing material creates the most formal difficulty. It is not a return to the opening material, and it differs from both section A and section B. However, there are numerous repetitions: the slow-moving cadences in half notes recall a similar cadence in section A (m. 2); the dotted eighth-sixteenth rhythm that characterizes mm. 9–12 derives from mm. 5, 7, and 8; and the thirds of the vocal line and accompaniment originate in m. 2, the tenor descent F to D. Thus while the form of "Wanderers Nachtlied I" might be labeled ABC, the *Lied* uses a variety of unifying elements: rhythms, melodic gestures, tonality, *Stimmung*, and range in place of large-scale formal repetition. And it is one of the many wonders of this song that these devices create coherence and closure as convincingly as formal reprise of a section A would have accomplished.

Schubert's settings of Goethe's metaphysical poems "Ganymed," "Prometheus," and "Grenzen der Menschheit" also proceed from beginning to end without sectional returns but utilize instead small-scale repetitions. The musical form parallels the poetic construction, where the poems are written in blank verse (without rhyme scheme); however, such poems include their own literary devices of coherence. The setting of "Ganymed" starts with a self-contained and recognizable A section in A♭ major that uses a repeating accompaniment figure throughout. The vocal line consists of three phrases that are obviously related: falling sixth, rising half-step and third. At m. 19, a contrasting dominant-centered area occurs (section B), with new melodic contours and accompaniment figures, both emphasizing rising figures. At this point, we expect a return to A material, but the arrival at m. 31 is in the key of C♭ major, with seemingly different melody and accompaniment figures. Schubert does employ unifying devices here: the RH piano figuration is made up of descending sixths and ascending seconds and thirds and the vocal line contains these motives as well. These subtle motivic repetitions may not be perceived by the listener, however, and the newness of the section tends to overshadow any unifying effects.

When we arrive at m. 46, another new section, D, occurs in E major. Again, melodic contours in mm. 52–55 of the vocal line reflect the mirror image of the opening phrases, as do the piano lines in mm. 56–59. As section E moves into F major/d minor, we continue to be swept ahead tonally to the song's conclusion in F major, a chromatic third away from the opening tonality of A♭ major. The song has been composed of a series of ever-different sections without a single sectional reprise of any sort, and we recognize that the setting emphasizes constant forward motion in order to parallel the protagonist's journey from earth up into heaven. Even while Schubert's lack of sectional repetition prevails, however, the music continues to cohere through motivic repetition in both vocal line and piano accompaniment. Whether the listener perceives these reiterations is unclear; however, the performers can certainly make every effort to project these repetitions as they occur, balancing the forward momentum with the constant reiteration of elements of coherence.

Another *Lied* that sounds through composed but actually includes many unifying elements is Schumann's "In der Fremde." As described in Chapter Seven, the opening A section includes two phrases, mm. 1–5 and mm. 5–9, having the same melodic shape with only slight variation in harmony. The ensuing B section, mm. 10–15, presents clearly new material in tonality, vocal line and accompaniment, which then leads to section C, mm. 15–21. While this section moves into the key of b minor, it brings back the accompanimental figuration, vocal line character, and eventually the opening tonality of section A. Section C thus functions both to continue the tonal flux begun in section B and at the same time to return, by mm. 20–21, to section A material.[13]

The tonal progression in b minor precludes calling this material section A', but much of the original section A material does in fact return. The closing material, mm. 22–end, also continues the accompanimental figuration and reiterates with slight modification the vocal line of section A. However, here the material is heard as a coda, despite the presentation of the final line of poetry, and the song's form is essential concluded. Despite all the melodic and accompanimental similarities, "In der Fremde" is usually considered through composed. However, performers can identify the ways section A material has been brought back after the contrasting B section, and they can thus experience, and convey, the rounded nature of this form: ABCD; CD = quasi A'.

"Ich hab' in Penna," the last song in Wolf's *Italienischesliederbuch*, is another work that unfolds so naturally that its series of phrases seem to require neither feeling of return nor contrast. The song divides naturally into two halves; the first section has text, while the second half consists of a piano "postlude." The first two F major vocal phrases (imitated by the piano RH) are somewhat sequential in nature and the next two phrases lead with more disjunct material to a cadence in D. The material that follows is clearly a contrasting section B, and when the vocal line concludes in m. 23, we have returned to the original tonic, but with altogether different music, except for a brief recall of the opening piano accompaniment in m. 17.

The piano solo that follows is purely cadential, and again no recall of earlier material seems evident. However, closer inspection reveals much repetition of melodic figures and motives throughout this song: the descending lines of mm. 2–3 (voice, then RH) are extended in the voice and RH in mm. 17–18; the major second down followed by perfect fourth up throughout the postlude derive from mm. 5, 6 (twice in retrograde), and 22; and, indeed, the melodic material of the postlude echoes the final vocal gesture over and over. Specific intervals also recur as motivic links between disparate sections: the perfect fourth alone recurs at significant places: in mm. 12, 14, and 15–16; and its inversion, the perfect fifth recurs as well, in mm. 3, 5, and 11. Finally, within the postlude, the figuration in the RH not only echoes the final vocal gesture but also reiterates earlier vocal material: the arpeggiations recall mm. 4 and 8; the linear thirds recall mm. 2–3 (voice, then RH), 4–5 (inverted voice, then RH), and 9; and the leaps of sixths and sevenths echo such leaps in mm. 4–5, 7, 13, and 18.

The Song Cycle

The term *song cycle* is often misused to denote any combination of songs placed together within a single group. Some nineteenth-century publishers grouped songs together for convenience in publication, but the grouping of songs by opus number or by a singular volume title does not necessarily mean the songs are either meant to be performed as a unit or are perceived in any way as interconnected. Schubert's *Schwanengesang* is a perfect example of this, as are all the *Lieder* volumes by Wolf. In each case, the songs were published together for expedience in publication and there is no inherent reason to consider Schubert's last "group" of songs as a cohesive unit or Wolf's *Italianischesliederbuch* or *Goethelieder* as anything but a group of songs that set texts by the same or similar poets.

There are only two musical reasons to perform *Schwanengesang* as a cycle or the Wolf volumes as a unit. First, Schubert's *Schwanengesang* represents his final *Lieder*, and even though the cycle is not inherently unified, the group has a meaningful historical interconnection. Second, the Wolf volumes have similar historical significance: most were written within a single time frame (the *Italienischesliederbuch* was written within two time periods) and each volume has a characteristic style that is unique to the nature of the poetry. A recital of the Italian songs has a stylistic unity, therefore, as do the Eichendorff, Goethe, or Mörike songs. Only Wolf's *Michaelangelolieder* were actually conceived as a cycle of three songs; they set poems that have religious connections and there is some tonal connection: song 1 begins in g minor and ends in G major; songs 2 and 3 begin in e minor and end in E major. A modal mixture thus connects the three songs and smoothes the overall tonal scheme from g minor to E major. [11]

A more precise and meaningful definition of the "song cycle" is a group of songs that are in fact united in specific ways. Schubert's *Die Schöne Müllerin* and *Winterreise* set a group of poems by a single poet, Wilhelm Müller, that tell a specific story; Schumann's *Dichterliebe* and *Frauenliebe und-Leben* sets a series of poems by Heine and Chamisso, respectively, that treat the subject of love within a unified group. In addition to unity of poet and poetic theme or story, these song cycles are musically related through well-documented tonal and motivic interconnections. [15] Schubert's *Winterreise* is united through a particular motive associated with grief, and Schumann's *Frauenliebe* is framed by a distinctive rhythm in the brief piano introduction and lengthy piano postlude set in the same opening and closing key. [16] Schumann's beloved *Liederkreis*, op. 39, which is not as coherent and organized as the cycles mentioned above, is unified by its overall tonal design. [17]

Performers should be wary of creating cycles out of song collections and need to think carefully about how real cycles are unified. The audience must hear more than a group of songs sung in order; rather, they need to hear the relationships between and among songs, the recurring motives, gestures, textures, etc. In addition, performers need to consider the timing between songs in a cycle: how much time to pause, when to move quickly ahead, when to wait a bit longer.

Conclusion

Musical form is the organization of sound over time and we have just examined several typical designs that *Lied* composers used to create musical shape in their poetic settings. Just as tonal schemes were used to bind together long expanses of music, and small melodic units or motives were used and reused to glue together musical passages, so mid-sized units or sections were manipulated to shape a song into various formats of repetition and contrast. Large-scale musical repetition creates a sense of familiarity and, when appropriate, closure, and can also be used to reinterpret material for a specific poetic depiction. Large-scale contrast promotes a sense of action and progression, and adds the variety necessary for aesthetic pleasure. Enlightened performers can help project the obvious and subtle aspects of musical form, and with their assistance, sensitive listeners can understand and enjoy more deeply the various forms of the German *Lied*.

Exercises

Exercise 9.1: Strophic form

Examine the texts of the strophic *Lieder* that follow and decide:

1. Why the composer chose the strict strophic form?
2. What words are operative in determining the differences among the verses?
3. What shifts in emphasis, color, dynamic, or attitude might be conveyed in a performance?
4. How does the composer set varying numbers of syllables?
5. Is there ambiguous material in the music that deserves repeated hearings in order to be fully grasped?

Schubert	"Liebhaber in allen Gestalten"
	"Nähe des Geliebten"
Schumann	"Im wunderschönen Monat Mai"
	"Seit ich ihn gesehen"
Brahms	"Der Schmied"

Exercise 9.2: Strophic form differences

Discover differences among the stanzas of the following strophic *Lieder:*

1. Variations in mode or tonality
2. Variations in texture
3. Variations in melodic direction or contour
4. Variations in harmonic direction

> Schubert   "Im Frühling" (This *Lied* can be called a theme
>   with variations.)
>
>   "Das Fischermädchen"
>
> Schumann   "Ich hab' im Traum geweinet"
>
>   "Zwielicht"
>
> Brahms   "Immer leiser"
>
>   "Wie Melodien"
>
> Wolf   "Auch kleine Dinge"
>
> Strauss   "Allerseelen"

Exercise 9.3: ABA ternary form

In the *Lieder* that follow, answer these questions about ABA (ternary) form:

1. Is the A section repeated before the B section is introduced?
2. Does the A section return in its entirety after the B section?
3. What modifications of texture, tonality, and melody are utilized in the return of a section?
4. What aspects of the composition make a section's return recognizable to the ear?
5. What emotional journey is involved in the story?
6. Why has the composer decided to introduce the contrasting material (B) at the point where it appears?

> Schubert   "Schäfers Klagelied"
>
>   "Der Lindenbaum"
>
>   "Nachtviolen"

Schumann   "Süsser Freund"

"Aus meinen Tränen spriessen"

"Mondnacht"

Brahms   "Wie froh und frisch"

Wolf   "Das verlassene Mägdlein"

Exercise 9.4: Determining form I

Using the designations A (mm. xx–xx), B (mm. xx–xx), etc., diagram the form of the *Lieder* that follow and answer the following questions:

1. How much modification of elements A and B is involved?
2. How does the form chosen by the composer match the form of the poem?
3. How does the form chosen illuminate the emotional journey?

Schubert   "Nachtviolen"

"Du bist die Ruh"

Wolf   "Nachtzauber"

Strauss   "Ständchen"

Mahler   "Nun seh' ich wohl"

Exercise 9.5: Determining form II

Diagram the following *Lieder*, using the format for Exercise 9.4. If you consider the changes in a repeat significant, use a prime (for example, A').

Schubert   "Der Wanderer"

"Erlkönig" (Exactly what is the A section? Is it the piano introduction? Is it the first four lines of poetry?)

Schumann   "Schöne Wiege meiner Leiden"

"Waldesgespräch" (What does the piano postlude mean?)

Brahms   "Wenn ich mit Menschen"

Wolf   "Auf dem grünen Balkon"

"Mögen alle bösen Zungen"

Exercise 9.6: Determining through composed

Decide whether the following songs are through composed or of a different formal design with repeating and/or contrasting sections. What elements help you decide — harmony, melody, rhythm, color?

Schubert	"Der Wanderer"
	"Meeres Stille"
	"Auflösung"
Schumann	"Der Sänger"
Wolf	"Lebe wohl"
	"Zitronenfalter im April"
Strauss	"Breit' über mein Haupt"

CHAPTER TEN

Different Settings of a Single Text: Comparison of Compositional Style

One way to understand the different styles of the great *Lied* composers is to compare different settings of the same poetry.[1] What are the differences between two or more settings of the same text? Do the composers use the same form? Do they choose the same or similar tonal schemes? Do they stress the same words, or set the words in the same rhythms? Since each composer has a unique style, differences in treatment of all aspects of music are inevitable. Nonetheless, the great masters of song-writing share common concerns about text setting, and there may well be some similarities among diverse settings. We will examine several such cases here, searching for similarities and differences, and speculating about the composers' rationales for the decisions they made.

Settings of "Harper I": Schubert, Schumann, and Wolf

A group of verses that exerted a strong fascination for nineteenth-century *Lied* composers was that in Goethe's novel *Wilhelm Meisters Wanderjahre* (*Wilhelm Meister's Years of Wandering*).[2] Goethe puts some of the most beautiful poetry of the German language into the mouths of the gypsy orphan, Mignon, and the wandering harp player, Lothario. Schubert, Schumann, and Wolf each set four of the Mignon poems and four of the "Harfnerlieder."[3] We will compare their settings of the harp-player song, "Wer sich der Einsamkeit ergibt," using Schubert's setting, D. 478 from 1816, Schumann's op. 98a, no. 6 from 1841 and Wolf's setting from October 27, 1888 entitled "Harfenspieler I."

The Poem

Figure 10.1 presents the text of the poem with its translation. We can see that Goethe utilizes a very tight rhyme scheme; each eight-line stanza is rhymed ababccbb, with the b-rhyme ("-ein") and the c-rhyme ("-al") the same in both verses. He also uses a strong ending on each of the sixteen

FIGURE 10.1 "Wer sich der Einsamkeit ergibt": text and translation.

1. Wer sich der Einsamkeit ergibt,	a He who to loneliness surrenders,
2. Ach, der ist bald allein;	b Ah, he is soon alone;
3. Ein jeder lebt, ein jeder liebt,	a One person lives, another loves,
4. Und läßt ihn seiner Pein.	b And leaves him his pain.
5. Ja, laßt mich meiner Qual!	c Yes, let me have my torture!
6. Und kann ich nur einmal	c And if I can just finally
7. Recht einsam sein,	b Really be alone,
8. Dann bin ich nicht allein.	b Then I will not be alone.
9. Es schleicht ein Liebender, lauschend sacht	c Sneaks a lover, listening quietly
10. Ob seine Freundin allein?	b If his beloved (is) alone?
11. So überschleicht bei Tag und Nacht	c So steals over day and night
12. Mich einsamen die Pein,	b Me lonely one the pain,
13. Mich einsamen die Qual.	c Me lonely one the torture.
14. Ach werd' ich erst einmal	c Ah will I first once
15. Einsam im Grabe sein,	b Lonely in the grave be,
16. Da läßt sie mich allein.	b There let they (leave) me alone.

lines, choosing to accent the word "einmal" on the second syllable. The line length is also compact: 4-3-4-3-3-3-3-3; the scansion usually yields iambic feet, with significant substitutions occurring with the words "Recht," "Liebender," "Freundin," and the "Einsam" of line 15.

Despite the inherent repetition of Goethe's poem, two of the three composers chose to write through composed settings, using small-scale repetitive devices in more subtle ways, and Wolf chose an ABA' form with a recurring refrain. All settings thus underscore the anguish and the wandering, tortured spirit of the harp player; his search for the release of death is treated not as a result of cyclical activity, but rather as an ongoing, arduous journey.

Schubert's Setting

Schubert's overall form can be labeled ABCD. We will examine each section in turn, emphasizing those cohesive elements that compensate for the lack of a return of A material. Figure 10.2 diagrams section A. The opening section A establishes the key of a minor and offers a vocal line of predominantly stepwise motion, including grace-note neighbor figures. The vocal line also includes triplets that are incorporated into the accompani-

FIGURE 10.2 Schubert's "Wer sich der Einsamkeit": section A.

mm.	Poem lines	Texture	Tonality	Special features
1–5	None	Piano introduction; rolled chords	a minor	French augmented sixth
5–8	1-2	Homophonic	a minor	♭II; florid vocal figure
9–12	3-4	Homophonic	C major/ a minor	Vocal figure
13–14	none	Piano interlude	a minor	Echoes vocal line

ment in the sections that follow. The brief section in C major is a good example of implicit tonality; C major is the relative major, but there are no transitions into or out of that suggested key.[4] The vocal line of mm. 11 (plus pickup)–12 and the imitative piano interlude of mm. 13–14 span a descending minor sixth, F–A, which extends two shorter descents in the opening: (1) the falling perfect fourth F–C in the RH piano introduction (mm. 1–4); and (2) the vocal perfect fifth descent, E–A in mm. 6–7. These recurring melodic descents give the section coherence, and the closing piano solo rounds out the section with a recall of both the material and the register of the opening.

Figure 10.3 shows section B. Schubert starts with a strong I–vii°⁷–I progression in F major (VI of a minor), followed by a brief progression toward f♯ minor (vi in A *major*). Arrival on a tonic f♯ minor chord is thwarted, however, by a deceptive cadence in m. 19 (VI in f♯ minor becomes IV in A major), which returns to A major/minor. The modal ambiguity continues to the end of this section; while the vocal line ends with a solid cadence in A major, a minor returns quickly in the accompaniment halfway through m. 21. The triplets from the vocal line of section A continue through section

FIGURE 10.3 Schubert's "Wer sich der Einsamkeit": section B.

mm.	Poem lines	Texture	Tonality	Special features
15–21	5–8	Melody with accompanying figure in triplets	F major (VI)– a minor (i)	Disjunct melody

FIGURE 10.4 Schubert, "Wer sich der Einsamkeit ergibt": section C.

mm.	Poem lines	Texture	Tonality	Special features
22–31	9–13	Triplet figuration	a minor– F major– a minor	Harmonic ambiguity; contrapuntal lines; deceptive cadence

B, lending a rhythmic coherence in a contrasting section marked by tonal and modal instability.

Goethe's second verse poses a formal problem: whether to stay true to the poem's punctuation (period after line 13) or the rhyme-scheme ("Qual" with "einmal"). As Figure 10.4 shows, Schubert chooses to preserve the punctuation in what is now section C. In m. 22, we hear a half-diminished seventh chord on F♯ that seems outside the tonic and leads to a cadence in F major in mm. 24–25. This leads to a sequential repetition on a half-diminished seventh chord on B, which functions as ii^{ø7} in a minor and leads to a strong cadence back in the governing key.

The return to a minor also is prepared in the vocal line, which repeats the triplet figure of section A in mm. 24 and 30. The return to a minor is also facilitated by several elements of coherence with earlier sections: (1) the deceptive cadence recalls the same cadence in sections A (m. 6) and B (m. 19); and (2) the descending F to A vocal gesture, mm. 30 (plus pickup)–31, recalls the same vocal descent that concluded section A.

Only three lines of poem remain to be set, and these end with the same words: "einmal," "sein," and "allein," that occurred in section B. But rather than utilize a simple reprise here, Schubert fashions a section D that incorporates elements from all three earlier sections. The new material created follows the evolving poetic progression but at the same time the need for completion and closure is satisfied through a subtler form of repetition and coherence. Figure 10.5 show section D along with those sections where earlier material had been heard. Schubert ties this to earlier sections through two rhythmic elements: (1) the flowing triplet accompaniment of all previous sections; and (2) a recurring dotted quarter–eighth–quarter–quarter rhythm heard in the opening vocal phrase, section A and in section C. The melodic descent F–A also recurs, over the span of mm. 36–39. Schubert then does something relatively rare: he repeats the last three lines of the poem. This poetic repetition (mm. 39–46) is somewhat disguised, as the vocal line's recurring rhythms create new gestures and use new dynamics (the singer's fortissimo scream of pain in mm. 35–37, is but murmured, *ppp*, in the reprise). To close the setting, Schubert's postlude recalls both the dramatic descending bass of section

FIGURE 10.5 Schubert, "Wer sich der Einsamkeit ergibt": section D.

mm.	Poem lines	Texture	Tonality	Special features
31–39	14–16	Triplets (A–C);	a minor (B);	Wide leaps,
		melody with accompaniment (B);		chromatic lines (B)
39–47		Same	a minor	Same
47–52	None	Triplets; piano postlude	a minor	chromatic lines

D and the song's opening piano introduction. While the postlude's range is wider than that of the opening, the song's final chord is exactly the same as that in m. 4, thus linking the opening and closing musical spaces.

In summary, Schubert divides the poem into four sections marked by strong contrasts in vocal line and in accompanimental texture, and uses rhythmic, melodic, and harmonic motives to create coherence in a through composed setting. All moves away from a minor are brief or merely implied, which gives the song a tonal cohesiveness as well.

Schumann's Setting

While Schumann's setting initially seems quite different, closer inspection reveals many similarities with Schubert's.[5] On first hearing, two aspects of the form are immediately apparent: (1) unlike Schubert, the tonality is vague, with cadences that may or may not resolve in several keys; and (2) like Schubert, there is no large-scale repetition in a through composed setting. While Schumann's tonal ambiguity indeed distinguishes his setting from Schubert's, the two composers share two tonal devices: First, both use implicit tonality within the relative major/minor pair (in the Schumann, constant references to the relative f minor in a song in A♭ major); and second, both emphasize VI at key moments of the setting. In general, however, the differences outweigh the similarities. In addition to its harmonic and tonal ambiguity, Schumann's *Lied* is also notable for eliding various sectional divisions, as shown in Figure 10.6.

While Schumann's poetic groupings are similar to Schubert's, the sectional changes are usually blurred; for example, the material in mm. 16–17, 26–27, and 38–39 all continues from one section to another without pausing or articulating closure in any way. This seamlessness begins at the outset, as a characteristic Schumann opening begins not on I but on ii⁶, which

FIGURE 10.6 Schumann, "Wer sich der Einsamkeit ergibt."

Section A

mm.	Poem lines	Texture	Tonality	Special features
1–8	1, 2	arpeggios, some triplets; rolled chords; duplets and triplets	ii⁶–V–I in A♭ Shift to c minor	deemphasis on I; rhythmic complexity

Section B

mm.	Poem lines	Texture	Tonality	Special features
9–25	3–8	arpeggios; triplets	b♭ minor to V of f minor	Tonal ambiguity; avoidance of tonic

Section C

mm.	Poem lines	Texture	Tonality	Special features
26–38	9–13	Chordal triplets eighths to sixteenths	A♭–D♭ Major minor	Most intense tonal instability; augmented sixth chord

Section D

mm.	Poem lines	Texture	Tonality	Special features
39–53	14–16	Chordal in quarters; sixteenths at end	D♭–f minor/ A♭ flux	Rolled chords; tonal instability; plagal cadence

moves eventually to V of A♭ by m. 5 and the A♭ tonic in m. 6, beat 2.[6] This is the first of several ambiguous progressions that result in weak, vague tonic arrivals in various keys. The enlarged ii⁶–V progression sets the first line of text, and the arrival on I sets "Ach!"; the use of the major mode here seems ironic, as in "Ich grolle nicht".[7] The rest of line 2 is set by a cadence in c minor, which immediately is displaced by a V–VI deceptive cadence in b♭ minor, mm. 10–11, followed by weak cadences in b♭ minor (m. 13) and A♭ major (m. 14) and an ultimate arrival on V of f minor, mm. 18–25. This entire section sets lines 3–4 of stanza 1 and all of stanza 2. The tonal instability and lack of clear distinction between sections are dramatic differences from Schubert's *Lied*, which set the same two verses in clearly identifiable sections A and B.

While the half cadence in f minor is prolonged, it never resolves to the tonic and a return to b♭ minor as ii of A♭ moves to V of A♭ mm. 27–31. The prolonged V⁷ of A♭ begins the setting of stanza 3, where Schumann's extended triplets are similar to Schubert's use of that rhythm in setting "Es schleicht ein Liebender" ("Steals a lover"). Once again, Schumann musically blurs the distinction between poetic stanzas, and once again a clear resolution of a strong dominant to the expected tonic, here the song's tonic A♭ major, does not occur. The remainder of stanza 3 is set in increasingly unstable, chromatic progressions, including use of the mode mixture in mm. 33–34 (d♭ minor).

This section is characterized by a strong pull toward D♭, IV of A♭, and VI of f minor. The pivotal D♭ harmony moves in between the two main keys with allusions to f minor in mm. 40, 44–45, 46–47, and 48–49 and authentic cadences in A♭ in mm. 42–43 and 46 along with plagal cadences in A♭ in mm. 49–51. This sets the final three lines of text, which Schumann emphasizes with significant piano solos that offer varied imitations of the final vocal line setting: "ach! werd ich erst einmal einsam im Grabe sein" ("Ah, when shall I at last be lonely in my grave"). The final line of the poem, then, is set in mm. 46–48, where the vacillation between f minor and A♭ is most pronounced for the song's conclusion.

The two settings have several similarities. Schumann divides the text into the same four sections as Schubert: two lines, six lines, five lines, and three lines, even though the seamlessness of Schumann's setting does not clarify these divisions as Schubert's does.[8] Both settings include the rolled chords typifying the harp playing, and the already mentioned triplet figure under the words "Es schleicht . . ." There are also several differences in the two settings. In general, Schumann uses fewer leaps in his melody than Schubert, and rather than Schubert's depiction of the singer's anguish through descending scales, Schumann has several passages with neighbor tone figures, such as mm. 8–11 and 23–25.

Schumann's through composed setting is unified through a variety of recurring elements, most obviously several textural devices. He employs the almost obligatory rolled chord harplike music in mm. 6–7 and 38–44, and he accompanies the *Lied's* entire first half with simple legato bass octaves under an ascending arpeggiated figure mixing duplets with triplets. This pianistic writing is typical of Schumann's accompaniments, and is developed at the song's dynamic climax in mm. 35–38, where the RH cascades in sixteenth notes.

Schumann also employs many recurring rhythms, motives, and even a specific harmony to create inner cohesion within his through composed design. In addition to the recurring triplets, there is another rhythmic motive: the eighth rest followed by three eighth notes recurs throughout mm. 1–22 (the sole exception being m. 19). The only recurring melody is the postlude's reinterpretation of the vocal line in mm. 39–42, but reiterated neighbor figures recur in both vocal line and accompaniment: the vocal line features a recurring C–D♭ and other neighbors such as B♭–A♮ and C–B♮; these are reiterated in the bass throughout, along with G♭–F, F–E♮, etc. In addition to these rhythmic and melodic elements, the ubiquitous b♭ minor chord, which functions variously as ii of A♭ and iv of f minor, is virtually motivic in its recurrence. The importance of the chord is underscored by the many applied or secondary dominants to b♭ minor in mm. 10–12, 21–22, 26, 28–29, 39, 41, and 47.

Wolf's Setting

Hugo Wolf was keenly aware of the songs of his predecessors and reset only those poems he felt had not yet been fully captured by others. We can thus assume he wanted to expand upon the settings of Schubert and Schumann, and we find both similarities and differences with the earlier songs. Like Schubert, Wolf starts the *Harfenspieler* songs with "Wer sich der Einsamkeit ergibt," emphasizing the tragedy of the lyrics more akin to Schubert's setting than that of Schumann. In addition, Wolf adapts the rolled chords and the use of triplets to set line 9 ("Es schleicht . . .") of both his predecessors. Beyond these overt similarities, however, Wolf's setting is different in several respects. First and foremost, the form of Wolf's setting is characteristically complex, as shown in Figure 10.7.

Unlike the through-composition of earlier settings, Wolf creates a hybrid form, combining a ternary ABA' form with a refrain (motive X). The refrain always begins with the same progression: i–♭II⁶–V in g minor, but then

FIGURE 10.7 Wolf, "Wer sich der Einsamkeit ergibt."

mm. 1–5	piano introduction: Motive X: progression i–♭II⁶–V in g minor
Section A	
mm. 6–12	Motive X, progresses through c minor, E♭ major to A♭♭⁷
m. 13	Piano interlude: half cadence back in g minor
mm. 14–17	Motive X, progresses to V of V
Section B	
mm. 18–29	Triplet figuration with syncopated pedals prolongs V: sequences through g minor and B♭ major (III); ends with resolution to g minor in section A'
Section A'	
mm. 30–35:	Motive X, progresses through c minor (like mm. 7–8); vocal line ends with strong authentic cadence in g minor
	m. 38: Piano postlude on motive X elides with vocal cadence; sequential treatment concludes setting on D major (V or new I?)

moves to various other harmonic areas, emphasizing predominant chords, ♭II, iv, VI and the relative major, III. While the close harmonic relations might seem conservative for Wolf, they are prolonged by two characteristic features of his tonal language: (1) applied chords creating chromatic voice leading, and (2) exploitation of functional ambiguity. For example, is the A♭ seventh chord setting "Pein" in m. 12 a V of D♭ that never resolves, an augmented sixth of c minor that never resolves, or an altered ♭II of g minor that ultimately moves to V but never includes resolution of the unstable G♭?

As this suggests, the Wagnerian Wolf uses more and different chromaticism than either Schubert or Schumann, and thus creates a setting that balances areas of harmonic ambiguity with areas of harmonic repetition. The setting is full of applied chords that do not resolve and the final D major chord can be interpreted as either a V of g minor that never resolves or a major tonic in its own right. The key of D major was suggested earlier by its unresolved V⁷ chord in m. 2, the strong V⁷ of mm. 16–17 (that initially suggests D as a contrasting *key*), and by the V⁷ chords of mm. 36–37.

Wolf's setting includes many contradictory elements: he uses close harmonic relations, but more chromaticism; he uses a clearer more rounded form (ABA') but employs as well a modified refrain throughout. He does begin more conservatively (on the tonic) than either of the earlier settings, but his *Lied* concludes ambiguously on V or a new tonic. These contradictory elements help convey the anguish and progression of the text. The refrain is not merely an element of cohesion, but rather could be interpreted as a way to convey the poet's brooding obsession. In addition, the constant pulls toward close harmonies or keys tend always to be thwarted or evaded; this harmonic tension and ambiguity intensifies the agony of the poet as he ponders the pain and loneliness of lost love.

Comparison of All Three Settings

Several similarities present themselves when we compare all three settings. Schubert and Wolf use descending scalar passages; Schumann and Wolf prefer stepwise motion to Schubert's leaps. All three composers use half steps and chromatic progressions to underline the pain of the speaker, and all set the lines "Es schleicht. . ." with triplets and an unresolved chord progression depicting the lover's anxiety and insecurity.

Dramatic differences among the settings tend to be in the area of formal design. Schubert's setting shares characteristics of much of his instrumental writing; it is the longest of the three settings and sounds the most repetitious. Also characteristically, Schumann's setting has the least well defined form and Wolf's formal structure is the tightest. While Wolf and Schumann reach a climax in dynamics and pitch in line 12, Schubert saves his climax for the first statement of the last line of the poem ("Then they will leave me alone") at mm. 35–37.

The settings are both similar and different in terms of musical space. All three composers convey the lyric's anguish through many phrases in a high tessitura; both Schumann and Wolf set the song for bass (baritone in modern terminology), while Schubert's setting is for tenor. The songs differ in their use of range: the range is most limited in the Schumann setting, which goes no lower than an E♮ and has one high F (above middle C); Wolf's ranges from a low B to high F; and Schubert's has the widest range: low C to high F♯.

Despite the span of years between these compositions, all three *Lieder* are similar in certain uses of the tonal language. All are filled with chromatic progressions and unresolved harmonic tensions. All exploit modal ambiguity: Schubert uses parallel and relative mode pairs; Schumann's major mode tonic is constantly undermined by the relative minor; and Wolf's ending suggests the possibility of a major ending in a different key. Finally, while the song forms are different the three settings all use motivic repetition to create inner coherence and continuity, including both rhythmic and melodic motives. Indeed while each setting displays certain characteristic features of the composer's style, the commonalty of language creates similarities that underscore the shared artistic heritage of these three great *Lied* composers.

Implications for Performers

All three settings can be powerful and beautiful in the hands of committed interpreters. To assist performers in learning these settings, responses to the following questions and suggestions will offer ways to think about and compare the settings:

Harmony

Find examples in all three settings of these important chromatic harmonies and their resolutions:

1. Diminished seventh chords

2. Augmented sixth chords

3. ♭II (Neapolitan) chords

4. Applied chords (secondary dominants)

Cadences

Find examples of

1. Deceptive cadences

2. Unresolved cadences.

Melody

1. Identify the primary tone and other structural pitches: Do these set the same words in the different settings?

2. Find embellishing pitches in the vocal line: What words do they set?

3. Find instances of melodic or motivic transformation similar to the piano's echo of the vocal phrase in mm. 39–42 of the Schumann: What element of the poem do these transformations convey?

Rhythm

1. Which lines of poetic meter do the three composers set with exactly the same musical rhythm?

2. Find instances of rhythmic or metric tension in the vocal line, the accompaniment, and in the interaction of the two parts.

Poetry

1. How are the following words set: "einsam," "allein," "Pein," "Qual"?

2. How do the composers set rhyming words?

Performance Concerns

1. Do you have a favorite among the three settings? If so, what attracts you? If not, why not?

2. Would you find a different solution for a given section if you were the composer?

3. Identify the most difficult parts of each setting for performers: Can you explain exactly what is difficult and why? Determine how to work through the difficulty, both separately and as an ensemble.

Comparisons with Brahms *Lieder*

Brahms composed songs to several poems already set by other composers, and two comparisons involve songs we have examined a good deal in this book: Eichendorff's "In der Fremde" (comparing Brahms's song with the now familiar Schumann setting) and Hölty's "Die Mainacht" (comparing the often-discussed Brahms song with Schubert's early, relatively unknown setting). Brahms set "In der Fremde" as op. 3, no. 5 in 1852–1853, some twelve years after Schumann included his version in *Liederkreis*, op. 39.

Nonetheless, the early Brahms setting is so similar to the Schumann in tonal, harmonic, and melodic elements that it seems possible that the Brahms version might have been modeled on the earlier song.

From the outset, Schumann's *Lied* seems more nuanced and refined in contrast to Brahms's more energized, *"poco agitato"* rhythmic drive punctuated by syncopations and agogic accents. However, the settings have a great deal in common. Both settings use a constant pulse throughout, Schumann in sixteenths, and Brahms in eighths, to convey the poet's yearning. In addition, Brahms's large-scale design has several similarities with that of Schumann. Both songs begin a move toward III that is ultimately thwarted: in the Brahms, a cadence in III is followed by an immediate return to the f# minor tonic; in the Schumann, III is only implied, followed by a cadence in b minor. Both tonicize a plagal relation, VI in Brahms and iv in Schumann, that also is fleeting and followed by a direct return to the tonic. Finally, Schumann's curious setting of the final line of poetry as a coda or tag occurs similarly in the Brahms song, along with the shift to major tonic and the use of V of iv that had characterized the Schumann. Indeed, in side-by-side performances of these two settings, the tremendous similarities help to highlight the unique stylistic differences between the mature Schumann and the young Brahms.

Our second Brahms comparison contrasts a more mature Brahms with an early Schubert setting of "Die Mainacht." Brahms's remarkable 1864 setting of Hölty's poem has been discussed in almost every chapter of this book and we recall its opening ambiguity of meter and tonal function (V or I?), its large-scale chromatic third relation Eb major/Cb major, and its ternary/refrain form (r = refrain): ABrA'r.

When compared to Brahms's complex form and ambiguous tonality, Schubert's 1815 strophic version comes as a surprise. Indeed, the two settings are different in almost every respect. To begin with, Brahms's setting is predominantly in the major mode, while Schubert's begins and ends in minor. In addition, the two songs have completely different presentations of the tonic: Brahms's opening is characterized by tonal ambiguity resulting from a use of unresolved 6/4 position and an avoidance of the root-position tonic, while Schubert, from the very first sound, drives home the tonic with a bass pedal, both in the initial d minor and in the section in the relative major. This difference in tonal focus conveys contrasting interpretations of Hölty's protagonist. Schubert's poet is portrayed as altogether desperate from inescapable loss, as the music (*"Ziemlich geschwind"*) depicts death with the long–short–short rhythm (as in "Der Tod und das Mädchen") within a relentless bass. On the other hand, Brahms's poet is cast in initial quietness (*"Sehr langsam und ausdrucksvoll"*) that leads to passionate revelation of deep feelings of pain rather than a frenzy of desperation.

Even though Schubert's choice of a strophic setting is an important difference from Brahms's formal design, both utilize a form of ternary, ABA':

Brahms with the refrain and Schubert within the repeated strophe. Given the poetic progression of Hölty's verse, Schubert's strophic setting may at first seem curious. As mentioned in Chapter 9, strophic songs have one setting for multiple verses and the use of the same music to depict different poetic elements can challenge performers in special ways. Indeed, Schubert's strophic setting of "Die Mainacht" contains two problematic areas of text depiction, one involving the major mode (mm. 11–16) and the other a particularly expressive melodic figure (m. 13).

The modal problem arises in the shift to the relative major for the contrasting B section. After a clear opening in d minor, Schubert moves to the relative, F major, for line 5 of each verse, and returns to d minor for the conclusion. The relative major first occurs with the mention of the nightingale's song and then for the text in verse 2 (not set by Brahms): "ihrem singenden Gatten. . ." ("to her singing husband"), where the brighter color seems appropriate. However, the corresponding text in the ensuing verses are: "suche dunklere Schatten" ("seek darker shadows") and "Und die einsame Thräne" ("and the solitary tear"), where the relative major is less convincing than the shift to minor in the Brahms version. Here the performers have to determine how to alter the brightness of F major and convey something of the shadowy darkness and the falling tear. In addition, use of the major mode for the last two verses can be interpreted as poignant or ironic. Setting the poet's pain in the domain of the cooing love birds emphasizes the strong contrast between happy lovebirds and the tearful wandering of the bereaved poet.

The problematic melodic figure occurs in m. 13, where Schubert extends the first syllable of "flötet" ("flutes" or "sings") with the little four-note melisma introduced in mm. 2, 4, 5, and 8 (inverted). Where initially this turn is splendid in depicting the nightingale's song and the singing husband, it later depicts the darker images of "Schatten" ("shadow") and "Thräne" ("tear"). Performers must determine how to convey these conflicting meanings, perhaps through changes in timbre and pitch emphasis. In addition, the ensemble must try to find a tempo that might accommodate these varying poetic ideas.

This brings up the extreme difference in tempo between the two settings. Both composers use a steady stream of eighth notes for the accompaniment, creating a constant pulse throughout. However, Schubert's setting asks for "*alla breve*," while Brahms's needs to be felt in a slow two for the sake of the long phrases. The different paces create diverse interpretive problems for the performers. Schubert's rather fast tempo is reinforced by rolling arpeggiations in the RH in addition to the long–short–short rhythmic pattern in the bass, and requires singer and pianist to decide on a quick tempo that depicts anguish and unrest without seeming frivolous or frantic. In contrast, the Brahms *Lied* requires a slow tempo that is capable of conveying the increasing passion as the song moves toward its climactic conclusion.

FIGURE 10.8 Missing stanza in Brahms's "Die Mainacht" setting.

Selig preis' ich dich dann,	Highly praise I you then,
Flötende Nachtigall,	Fluting nightingale,
Weil dein Weibchen mit dir	Because your little wife with you
Wohnet in einem Nest,	Resides in a nest,
Ihrem singenden Gatten	Her singing husband
Tausend trauliche Küsse giebt.	A thousand intimate kisses gives.

Comparison of the two settings also reveals that Brahms left out an entire six-line stanza in his setting. The missing verse was the second stanza and is translated in Figure 10.8.[9] While we can only guess at the reason behind Brahms's decision to eliminate the happy portrait of Hölty's lovebirds, it seems likely that he wanted to emphasize the dark despair of the poem and maintain a singular *Stimmung*.[10]

Other issues of poetic depiction also reveal differences. First, as mentioned in Chapter 8, in the section "Rhythmic Tension and Ambiguity," Brahms alters the poem's pattern of syllable number and rhythm from verse to verse. This contrasts with Schubert's more precise enunciation of the poetic rhythms, which are consistent throughout the poem. Second, Schubert's strophic form limits the capacity to express other elements of the poetry. While both composers start with a similar parallel sequence of lines 1–2 and 3–4, Schubert cannot convey the dramatic poetic shifts as well as Brahms. Both composers do underscore the poetic change at "Und die Nachtigall flötet": Brahms changes the texture and both shift to the major mode. However, Brahms then creates numerous other dramatic changes as the poem progresses: in section B for "Überhüllet vom Laub" ("concealed by foliage"); "Aber ich wende mich," ("ah but I turn away"); and "suche dunklere Schatten" ("seek darker shadows"); and in the refrain, "Und die einsame Träne rinnt" ("and a solitary tear falls"). In all these cases, Schubert is constrained by the music that set the opening verse.

While Brahms took full advantage of a more varied form to depict the many changes in the poetic progression, Schubert's strophic constraints create special opportunities for performers to make subtle interpretive changes as they play and sing the same music for different verses. This underscores a central point about strophic settings: even though large-scale repetition is the basis of the form, nuances in performance can convey the poetry in rich and varied detail. This is dramatized in the setting of the final verse, where both composers return to their section A material. Brahms reuses the refrain from section B to reinterpret both poetry and music, and the song concludes with a synthesis of material from both sections A and B. In contrast, Schubert's final and simpler return to the opening section A emphasizes aspects

FIGURE 10.9 Correspondence of harmonies and poetic progression in Schubert's "Die Mainacht."

The tonic sets:	vii⁷ sets:
"Mond" ("moon")	"Licht" ("light")
"[selig dich] dann"	"[mit] dir wohnet"
("[blessed you] then")	("with you dwells")
"Laub" ("foliage")	"[entzücken mir] vor"
	("delight [me]")
"lächelndes Bild" ("smiling image")	"[Seele mir] strahlt"
	("shines [through
	my soul]")

of the poetic progression through use of the same harmonies for progressive images. For example, Figure 10.9 shows how the same harmonies set key words of the text. The alignment of words and the tonic traces the poetic progression from the moonlight to the ecstasy of love birds to the muting of light by foliage (the symbol of the protective shadows) to the acknowledgment of a lost loved one, to the feeling of lost love finally experienced by the poet. The progression of images captured by the vii⁷ traces another poetic progression: the image of light is followed by contrasting love images, first the cooing doves, then the opposite: the image of the poet devastated by lost love.

While it may seem unfair to compare a relatively sophisticated Brahms song with a youthful Schubert setting, the comparison illuminates several things about the two *Lied* composers. Though seemingly limited by the strophic setting, Schubert's greater fidelity to the text conveys more careful articulation of the poetic rhythms. In addition, his use of the relative major created a variety of poetic depictions, and the stanzaic reinterpretation inherent in the form challenges performers in ways not equaled in the Brahms setting.

The more complex Brahms *Lied*, on the other hand, shows his willingness to change the poetry to suit his purposes and to be more concerned about musical design than precise poetic depiction. This underscores a general stylistic tendency of Brahms, and Schumann, to take poetic license in the interest of musical form and of Schubert, and Wolf, to protect the rhythms and integrity of the verse before bowing to musical concerns. This distinction has tremendous import for performers of these four giants of *Lied* composition. It helps explain why the accompanist's role in Schumann is far more "pianistic" than that in the others and why the different Wolf volumes have such distinctly different characters, as each volume represents a unique poetic voice that prompted an individual musical style. In a similar way, the singer will recognize the need to be especially mindful of how the vocal rhythms reflect the poetic meter in Schubert and Wolf songs, and how the vocal lines of Schumann and Brahms can include awkward word rhythms in order to create a particularly beautiful and expressive melodic line.

Settings of "Liebst Du um Schönheit": Clara Schumann and Gustav Mahler

Our final comparison takes us outside the "Big Four" and into the musical languages of two other important *Lied* composers: Clara Schumann, one of several women composers who only recently have become recognized for their excellent settings;[11] and Gustav Mahler, one of several composers whose reputation for large-scale orchestral (or operatic) works tends to overshadow their significant *Lied oeuvre*.[12] The comparison involves their respective settings of Rückert's "Liebst du um Schönheit" ("If you love for Beauty"). Clara Schumann set the text as op. 12, no. 4 in 1840;[13] Mahler's setting was written in 1905. The text translation is given in Figure 10.10.

The numerous repetitions in Rückert's text almost demand a strophic setting; nevertheless, both composers wrote out each stanza with often subtle but significant variations. Both do set the repeated poetic refrain

FIGURE 10.10 Rückert, "Liebst du um Schönheit": text and translation.

Liebst du um Schönheit	If you love for beauty,
O nicht mich liebe!	Oh, don't love me!
Liebe die Sonne,	Love the sun,
Sie trägt ein gold'nes Haar!	It wears golden hair.
Liebst du um Jugend,	If you love for youth,
O nicht mich liebe!	Oh, don't love me!
Liebe den Frühling,	Love the spring,
Der jung is jedes Jahr!	Which is young each year!
Liebst du um Schätze,	If you love for treasures,
O nicht mich liebe!	Oh, don't love me!
Liebe die Meerfrau,	Love the mermaid,
Sie hat viel Perlen klar.	She has many clear pearls.
Liebst du um Liebe,	If you love for love,
O ja mich liebe!	Oh yes, love me!
Liebe mich immer,	Love me always,
Dich liebe ich immerdar!	I love you forever and always!

("Liebst du. . .") with recurring linear and rhythmic motives: Clara Schumann employs a recurring perfect fourth vocal gesture A♭–D♭–A♭ for all occurrences of such lines in either a half note followed by four quarter notes (verses 1 and 3) or all quarter notes (verses 2 and 4). Mahler also uses a repeated gesture whose rhythm is similar to Clara Schumann's opening verse, as both composers following the rhythm of the poetry: / ˇ ˇ / /. Mahler varies the pitches slightly: verse 2 is set in the minor mode and verse 4 transposes the gesture down a major second to reflect the change from the sardonic negative statements to the unfettered positive expression: "Liebst du um Liebe."

The recurring musical refrain is but one instance of constant repetition, exact or varied, in both settings of the sequential text. Verses 1 and 3 of the Clara Schumann version are essentially the same both vocally and accompanimentally, with but slight changes in rhythm. The second half of both verses include a downward sequence by thirds and an unresolved half cadence on V of b♭ minor, a key that is suggested but never fully realized.[14] In the second half of verses 2 and 4, on the other hand, both the vocal line and accompaniment are varied. In verse 2 the vocal phrase is altered and the accompaniment plays an ascending fifth sequence. In verse 4, Clara Schumann alters both vocal line and accompaniment to signal the change in poetic meaning and create a strong closing cadence in mm. 34–36, which is followed by a piano postlude. Despite the variations of verses 2 and 4, all verses are similar enough to call this setting modified strophic. All verses use the same opening gesture, all use mixture to set line 2, and all use a sequential accompaniment to set the second half of each verse.

Mahler's setting also uses a great deal of repetition. The vocal line is the same in each verse except for the use of minor in verse 2 and the constant changes in meter that alter the accents on the same pitches from verse to verse. More subtle changes occur in the piano accompaniment, where each verse is harmonized slightly differently with a corresponding change in texture and figuration. Like Clara Schumann, Mahler alters the second half of verse 4, both to indicate the poetic change and to bring the song to a strong conclusion. The vocal line is expanded and applied chords intensify the setting: V⁷ of A♭ in m. 24 is left unresolved, and a circle of fifths using a chain of secondary dominants gives the close an expansiveness befitting the expression of joyful love. Mahler also closes with a piano postlude.

Both composers remain within a narrow vocal compass; Clara Schumann's melody never exceeds a seventh (F1 up to E♭²), and reaches the high point only once, in m. 17. Mahler utilizes a slightly wider range, from G♭¹ to the A♭² above; unlike Schumann, he keeps returning to the same high pitch in each verse (A♭²) in mm. 6, 12, 20, 25, and 29–30.

Each song has specific features that reveal elements of the composer's style. Mahler's setting demonstrates his use of shifting meter, a technique not found as frequently in Clara Schumann's time. This creates a typical

Mahlerian metric tension that keeps momentum building despite the extensive repetition. The setting also exemplifies Mahler's tendency to express an idea simply and then expand upon it in subsequent repetitions. Here the harmonic progression intensifies in each successive verse, with the introduction of minor for verse 2, the reharmonization and expanded texture of verse 3, and the use of applied chords in verse 4. Mahler also displays his characteristic exploitation of tonal ambiguity. All tonic E♭ major chords occur with suspensions (mm. 4, 6, 10, 18, 20 and 34) and there is a tendency to hear the piece moving to or being in A♭ major, especially after E♭ major becomes V⁷ of A♭ in m. 24.[15]

Clara Schumann's style is not as well known at this point, but her setting demonstrates several characteristics found in other works. Probably because she was an accomplished pianist, her accompaniment tends toward more pianistic writing (compare her accompaniment, for example, with the homophonic orchestral texture of Mahler's); her harmonic vocabulary, while modest here, can be rich with applied chords and other chromatic harmonies (for example, the ♭II⁶ in m. 33) and she often employs modal mixture and sequences.

One final aspect of this comparison is the fact that both composers are part of a special composer group whose *Lieder* is either neglected or experienced differently. In the case of Mahler, most of his songs are set with orchestral accompaniment, which places the singer in an altogether different environment. Mahler's exquisite use of the orchestra, like that of Wagner and Strauss, creates a wide spectrum of musical sound within which the singer performs, and the relationship of vocal line and "accompaniment" is much richer and more complex. Singers who are ready to attempt these masterpieces need to be able to secure their pitches more independently and to be more a part of an ensemble, where solo instruments (often woodwinds and brass) also have prominent melodic lines. An excellent comparison of settings with piano as compared to orchestra is Strauss's "Morgen!" (which also uses a solo violin) and Wagner's *Wesendonklieder*. In addition to other Strauss *Lieder* set with orchestral accompaniment, additional fine examples of this wonderful repertory are the well-known cycles: Brahms's *Vier ernste Gesänge*, Mahler's *Rückertlieder* and *Kindertotenlieder*, and Strauss's *Vier letze Lieder*.

The Clara Schumann setting also brings up the issue of the long-neglected repertory by women *Lied* composers.[16] While it its beyond the scope of this book to compare the two Rückert settings in terms of GENDER STUDIES, a great deal of research is underway to try to uncover compositional approaches or attitudes by women composers that might in fact be different from men. This area of study does not use gender differences in order to determine relative worth; rather, there is curiosity as to whether women composers might approach composing from a different perspective, might react to a text differently, and thus might compose music with unique, different qualities. This new world of gender study is complex; it offers the opportunity to explore whole new repertories of music previously unknown or ignored but at the same time it brings the danger of oversimplifying and overgeneralizing gender differences, especially the danger of using gender as a rationale for demeaning a woman composer's inherent worth. So we urge caution in thinking about "women's *Lieder*" as a special group while at the same time we urge *Lied* performers to embrace the sizeable repertory by such women composers as Clara Schumann, Fanny Mendelssohn Hensel, and Alma Mahler, to name but a few.

General questions about women's *Lieder* might be as follows: Does her setting reveal a different poetic interpretation than a setting that has been done or might be done by a man? Does she use the main components of the tonal language similarly to her male counterparts, for example, similar uses of harmony, melody, rhythm and meter, form, texture, register? Does she bring any unique characteristics to her settings? The issue of gender also applies to performers, where interpretation of poem and setting might differ between male and female musicians. A good example of this is Schumann's "Süßer Freund" from *Frauenliebe und -Leben*. The singer will obviously be a woman but the accompanist can be either male or female. One interpretation of the accompanist's persona in this song is that it represents the husband, who interacts continuously with his wife who is portrayed by the singer. This will feel very differently to a woman pianist than a man; both can portray this persona, but a woman might interpret the husband's responses differently from a male pianist. It is also possible that the accompanist does not assume the persona of the husband, but rather captures feelings within the woman as she sings about her life. This poses a fascinating challenge to a male pianist.

Conclusion

There are numerous examples of the great *Lieder* composers choosing the same great (and not-so-great) poems to put to music or, again, a composer setting a text more than once. When comparing two or more settings, we often make an immediate judgment that one composer "got it right," while another missed the essence of the poem in some important way. For example, after knowing Schubert's "Über allen Gipfeln ist Ruh," Schumann's version (op. 96, no. 1) seems pale and awkward, or since Wolf's setting of "Das verlassene Mägdlein" seems to many so superb, Schumann's earlier setting (op. 64, no. 2) might be considered altogether undistinguished, even odd. Conversely, discovery of a new and unknown setting of a familiar poem can illuminate interesting new aspects of the text that had not been considered, as, for example, Tschaikovsky's setting of Goethe's Mignon poem, "Nur wer die Sehnsucht kennt" (in Russian) or Charles Ives's settings of "Über allen Gipfeln," "Du bist wie eine Blume," and Feldeinsamkeit."[17]

We thus conclude this chapter with a caution about comparing different settings of the same text. The very enterprise of song comparison involves a fascinating examination of different composers reacting to the same literary impetus that can shed light on the two composers in a unique way. Comparisons need not attempt to determine the "better" setting; instead, they should give us more insight into the composers who set the same poem and about the poem set by several composers. While we might be tempted to choose Schubert's final version of "Nur wer die Sehnsucht kennt" as the best, given that it was his last setting, it is also possible to consider earlier settings as attempting to convey different aspects of the poem in different ways, experiments that were not necessarily cast aside, but that are part of multiple settings that each convey different things. Indeed, comparison of multiple settings is an enormously rewarding experience and can result in fascinating performances that set the different versions side by side for the fascination and delight of a willing audience.

Exercises

Exercise 10.1: The "Die Mainacht" comparison

A. Schubert's setting of "Die Mainacht" is admittedly simpler than that of Brahms. What form, other than simple strophic, might Schubert have chosen instead?

B. If Schubert had used a through composed form, where might he have introduced new sections and new material?

C. If Schubert had indulged his penchant for repetition, which lines of poetry might he typically have repeated?

D. Schubert's harmonic scheme is quite simple, compared even to his setting of "Wer sich der Einsamkeit ergibt." Try to find a spot where one or two chromatically altered chords could be introduced. What are the words at this spot? Could the text be enhanced by this alteration?

Exercise 10.2: Other multiple settings of the same texts

The listing below is only a sampling of various settings by composers of the same text. Using the analytical tools of this book and the comparisons above as models, compare some of the songs that set the greatest poets of the period.

Goethe Poems

1. "Kennst du das Land": Beethoven, op. 75, no. 1 (1809);
   Schubert, D. 321 (1815); Schumann, op. 79, no. 29 (1849);
   Wolf, *Goethelieder*, (1888); Zelter, 1795

2. "Nur wer der Sehnsucht kennt": Beethoven, 1807–1808;
   Schubert, D. 310 (1815); D. 359 (1816); D 481 (1816); D. 877,
   no. 4 (1826); and D. 877, no. 1 (1826); Schumann, op. 98a, no.
   3 (1841); Tschaikovsky, op. 6 (1869); Wolf, *Goethelieder*, 1888;
   Zelter, 1811[18]

3. "Der Sänger": Schubert, op. 117, D. 149 (1815); Schumann,
   op. 98a, no. 2 (1841); Wolf, *Goethelieder*, 1888[19]

4. "Der Rattenfänger": Schubert, D. 255, 1815; Wolf, *Goethelieder*,
   1888

5. "Ganymed": Schubert, op. 19, no. 3, D. 544 (1817); Wolf,
   Goethelieder, 1889

6. "Prometheus": Reichardt, 1809; Schubert, D. 674 (1819); Wolf,
   Goethelieder, 1889

7. "Gretchen am Spinnrade": Loewe, op. 9, no. 2 (1822) ;
   Schubert, op. 2, D. 118 (1814); Spohr, op. 25, no. 3 (1809)

8. "Erlkönig": Loewe, op. 1, no. 3 (1818); Schubert, op. 1, D. 328
   (1815)

9. "Die Liebende schreibt": Brahms, op. 47, no. 5 (1868);
   Mendelssohn, op. 86, no. 3; Schubert, op. 165, no. 1, D. 673
   (1819)

Mörike Settings

1. "An eine Aeolsharfe": Brahms, op. 19, no. 5; Wolf, *Mörikelieder*,
   1888

2. "Er ist's": Schumann, op. 79, no. 24; Wolf, *Mörikelieder*, 1888

3. Der Gärtner": Schumann, op. 107, no. 3; Wolf, *Mörikelieder*,
   1888

4. "Das verlassene Mägdlein": Schumann, op. 64, no. 2; Wolf,
   Mörikelieder, 1888

Spanish Verse

1. "In dem Schatten meiner Locken": Brahms, op. 6, no. 1, 1852;
   Wolf, *Spanischesliederbuch*, 1889

2. "Alle gingen, Herz, zur Ruh": Schumann, op. 74, 1849; Wolf, *Spanischesliederbuch*, 1889

Eichendorff Settings

1. "Mondnacht," from *Liederkreis:* Brahms, 1854; Schumann, op. 39, no. 5
2. "Die Stille," from *Liederkreis:* Mendelssohn, op. 99, no. 6; Schumann, op. 39, no. 4

Heine Settings

1. "Morgens steh' ich auf und frage:" from *Liederkreis:* Franz, op. 25, no. 3; Liszt, 1844; Schumann, op. 24
2. "Ihr Bild": Schubert, *Schwanengesang*, D. 957, no. 9 (1827–1828); Wolf, 1878
3. *Dichterliebe:* various poems set also by Franz, Liszt, Fanny Mendelssohn Hensel, Felix Mendelssohn, and Hugo Wolf
4. "Du bist wie eine Blume": Liszt, 1840; Schumann, op. 25, no. 24; Wolf, 1876

Postlude

This book has offered various tools for analyzing and understanding a body of literature within certain specific boundaries: German *Lieder* of the nineteenth century. As we have shown, while the compositions within this category often share certain characteristics, each *Lied* is unique, and is comprised of a constellation of features found only in that one composition. The shared characteristics of a body of music are sometimes referred to as a "style," as in "Schumann's style" or "German Romantic style." A style may include certain typical harmonic or textural signposts, such as the appearance of a diminished seventh chord to indicate tension, or the doubling of the vocal line in the "soprano" of the accompaniment. And at the outset of the nineteenth century, certain standards of tonal behavior were ubiquitous: major and minor modes were omnipresent and represented poles of "happy" and "sad"; modulation created tonal tension and development by creating distance from a tonic to which a return was usually inevitable; embellishing tones resolved in certain prescribed ways, and so forth. However, the great *Lied* composers sought ways to express more dramatically and faithfully the texts they set, and manipulated their inherited language in new and more complex ways. Thus Schumann's musical language sounds something like that of Schubert and Brahms, but also is individual in many ways; Wolf sounds like both Schumann and Brahms in some particulars, but has many unique features, among them the influence of Wagner's innovative language; and Strauss and Mahler share some characteristics with Brahms or Wolf, but have their individual qualities that derive from their own increased expansion of the tonal system.

More important than stylistic differences, however, are those individual strokes of genius that make a particular song distinctive and unforgettable. A masterpiece such as Schubert's "Über allen Gipfeln" or Wolf's "Lebe wohl" deserves close inspection not because it is average, but because it stands at the peak of its creator's achievement.

We hope that the questions we have raised and the tools we have provided will enable students, performers, and listeners to grow in understanding and appreciation of the German Romantic *Lied*. This is a body of literature that is an inexhaustable source of inspiration and pleasure, where words and music are combined in the formation of heightened expression. Indeed, these songs represent something of a human miracle: they are both miraculous and, as well, very human.

Notes

Introduction

1. The concept of persona in music was introduced by Edward T. Cone in *The Composer's Voice* (Berkeley and Los Angeles: University of California Press, 1974) and developed further in *Music: A View from Delft*, ed. Robert P. Morgan (Chicago: University of Chicago Press, 1989). This concept will be explored in Chapters Two and Five.

2. Appendix I provides a bibliography of reliable translations of poetry.

3. In his biography *Hugo Wolf* (London: Methuen, 1907), Ernest Newman reports that "Wolf, at his recitals, first read and expounded the poem to his auditors before he allowed a note of the music to be heard" (185).

4. The authenticity of any score can be checked by consulting the complete works editions that are available in most music libraries. There are several editions of Schubert's works: *Franz Schubert Neue Ausgabe Sämtlicher Werke.* Herausgegeben von der Internationalen Schubert-Gesellschaft. Kassel and New York: Bärenreiter-Verlag, 1964– and *Urtext der Neuen Schubert-Ausgabe (Franz Schubert Lieder)*, Walther Dürr, ed., 17 vols. (Munich: Bärenreiter-Verlag, 1980), as well as complete-works editions of Schumann, Brahms, and Wolf. A complete-works edition of Strauss is in process: Richard Strauss *Sämtliche Werke in Wiedergabe der Originaldrucke.* Herausgegeben von Ernst Hilmar. (Tutzing, Wien: Hans Schneider, 1987–).

Chapter One

1. This is the final stanza from Eichendorff's "Mondnacht," set by Schumann in 1840 as part of his *Liederkreis*, op. 39. All translations are by the authors; translation is literal in order to establish, as much as possible, the exact meaning of each German word.

2. One of the most important recent books to examine these issues in music is Carl Dahlhaus, *Nineteenth-Century Music*, trans. J. Bradford Robinson (Berkeley and Los Angeles: University of California Press, 1989). Both Chapters 1, "Introduction," and 2, "*Lied* Traditions," have selected bibliographies. An important earlier study of the issues is Friedrich Blume, *Classic and Romantic Music, A Comprehensive Survey*, trans. M. D. Herter Norton (London: Faber and Faber, 1972).

3. All terms notated with small capitals denote important terms. These should be adopted and used as quickly as possible. All such terms are redefined in the Glossary, Appendix II.

4. According to Joseph Kerman in *Listen*, 3d ed. (New York: Worth Publishers, 1980), the Storm and Stress movement was typified in literature by Goethe's *Die*

Leiden des jungen Werthers and in drama by revolutionary plays. Also in this period, according to Kerman, the mature Haydn (1732–1809) composed more dramatic and passionate works that were to influence the young Mozart (1756–1791), who wrote *Don Giovanni* in 1786 and *Symphony No. 40 in g minor* in 1788; and Beethoven (1770–1827), whose *Symphony No. 5 in c minor* was composed in 1807–1808.

5. During the period, many publications promoted the tenets of German Romanticism and offered the opportunity for published collaboration, for example, the journal *Athenaeum* that appeared in Berlin during the years 1798–1800.

6. Of the many biographies of Goethe, the most recent is by Nicholas Boyle, *Goethe: The Poet and the Age* (New York: Oxford University Press, 1991).

7. Goethe's harsh criticism of his contemporaries existed side by side with equally fervid attacks against some of his own writings, along with that of his classicist friend and colleague, Friedrich Schiller (1759–1805). Excellent discussions of Goethe's ambiguous and contentious position within German Romanticism can be found in Arnold Hauser, *The Social History of Art*, 4 vols. (New York: Vintage Books, 1951), Vol. 3, Chapter 6, and Walter Kaufmann, From *Shakespeare to Existentialism* (Freeport, N.Y.: Books for Libraries Press, 1971), Chapter 6.

8. For purposes of this discussion, the word DICHOTOMY signifies the division of something into two parts that are opposites, for example, something both real and unreal.

9. The word PARADOX is similar to dichotomy in that it connotes something contradictory, for example, Romantics sought certain kinds of clarity in night's darkness.

10. Siegbert S. Prawer, ed., *The Romantic Period in Germany: Essays by Members of the London University Institute of Germanic Studies* (London: Weidenfeld & Nicholson, 1970), 4.

11. The term *persona* as it relates to poetry and music will be defined in Chapter Two. Here the word denotes identification with a subject, real or historic, such as a shepherd or a Greek warrior.

12. Defined in *Webster's New Universal Unabridged Dictionary*, 2d ed. The use of irony as a poetic device is examined in detail in Chapter Two.

13. The poet Novalis captured this *romantische Sehnsucht* through the famous image of the blue flower in "The Dream of the Blue Flower," trans. Ralph R. Read in *The German Mind of the Nineteenth Century: A Literary & Historical Anthology*, ed. Hermann Glaser (New York: Continuum Press, 1981), 32–35. This image was combined with that of the night, the arena of intensified mystery and introspection that enabled the poet to feel and yearn the most deeply. Novalis's *Hymns to the Night* will be examined presently. Within the domain of music, Charles Rosen talks about paradox and irony in Romantic music, in particular, within the use of sound: "It is an essentially Romantic paradox that the primacy of sound in Romantic Music should be accompanied, and even announced, by a sonority that is not only unrealizable but unimaginable." *The Romantic Generation* (Cambridge: Harvard University Press, 1995), 11. Throughout Chapter 1, Rosen continues to discuss "Romantic innovations, especially Schumann's, in texture, tone color, and resonance [use of piano pedal]" (13). Change in pedal use from the Classical to the Romantic, "springs from a new sense of the role of sonority in music . . . [where] the musical idea *is* the pedal effect" (25).

14. The verse is from Eichendorff's "Nachtzauber" ("Night Magic"); it was set by Hugo Wolf in 1888.

15. Examples are Hölty's "Die Schale der Vergessenheit" ("Cup of Oblivion;" set by Brahms in 1864 as op. 46, no. 3) and von Collin's "Nacht und Träume" ("Night and Dreams;" set by Schubert in 1822(?) as op. 43, no. 2, D. 827).

16. The most well-known example of this image is Heinrich Heine's "Der Doppelgänger" set by Schubert in his cycle *Schwanengesang*, D. 957. In this remarkable poem, the poet confronts his double in a vision of the past, the double existing within the temporal dichotomy of past and present.

17. Müller's *Winter Journey* was published in 1824 and the collection was set by Schubert in 1827 as op. 89, D. 911. "Wanderers Nachtlied I" ("Über allen Gipfeln") was set by Carl Friedrich Zelter in 1814; Schubert in 1822, D. 768; Franz Liszt in c. 1840; and Schumann in 1850 (op. 96, no. 1). "Wanderers Nachtlied II" ("Der du von dem Himmel bist") was set by Zelter in 1807; Schubert in 1815 (op. 4, no. 3, D. 224); Liszt in 1843; and Wolf in 1883. The numbering of the two poems is inconsistent, and thus the poems are usually identified by their first lines. In this book, we refer to "Über allen gipfeln" as "Wanderers Nachtlied I."

18. This poem was set by Schubert in 1819(?) as D. 649.

19. This poem was set by Zelter in 1812 and by Schubert in two versions: D. 259 in 1815 and D. 296 in 1819(?).

20. Along with numerous examples of poetry about night, poems celebrating particular moments within seasons include Adolph Friedrich Graf von Schack's "Herbstgefühl" ("Autumn Feeling," set by Brahms in 1867 as op. 48, no. 7); Heine's "Sommerabend" ("Summer Evening," set by Brahms in 1879 as op. 85, no. 1); and Müller's *Winterreise*. Poems about spring, the season of renewed love, abound.

21. Well-known examples include Mörike's "In der Frühe" ("At Dawn," set by Wolf in 1888) and "Ein Stündlein wohl vor Tag" ("An Hour Before Day," set by Robert Franz as op. 28, no. 2 and by Wolf in 1888), and Eichendorff's "Zwielicht" ("Twilight;" set by Schumann in 1840 in his *Liederkreis*, op. 39).

22. Examples are Eichendorff's "Die Einsame" ("The Solitary Woman"); "Kurze Fahrt" ("Short Journey"); and "Nachtzauber" ("Night Magic"). "Nachtzauber" was set by Wolf in 1888.

23. *The Romantic Generation*, 205.

24. *The Romantic Generation*, 148.

25. *The Romantic Generation*, 159.

26. *The Romantic Generation*, 123.

27. *The Romantic Generation*, 174–175.

28. Schubert set this poem in 1819 as op. 36, no. 2, D. 672. Despite the religious themes within Eichendorff's poetry, it is the world of nature, not the church, that gives the poet blessing and a peaceful place to die.

29. The nightingale (*Die Nachtigall*) is an important and recurring symbol of the melancholy of lost love, of love that is distant or absent. The nightingale's song, often contrasted with songs of happy lovebirds, reverberates with a longing within the poet's heart.

30. For example, Heine's "Am Meer" ("By the Sea," set by Schubert in 1828, D. 957, no. 12) and Goethe's "Meeres Stille" ("Sea Calm," set by Johann Friedrich Reichardt in 1809 and by Schubert twice in 1815: first version, D. 215A and second version, D. 216.

31. The poem was set by Schubert in 1816, D. 509. Both poem and setting are discussed in Chapter Six, the "Directional Tonality" section.

32. The image of night as the domain of the mysterious recurs in numerous guises, for example, Eichendorff's "Nachts" ("At Night"); Goethe's "Nachtgesang" ("Night Song," set by Zelter in 1804 and Schubert in 1814 as op. 47, D. 314); Heine's "Mondenschein" ("Moonlight," set by Brahms in 1879 as op. 85, no. 2); and Mörike's "Um Mitternacht" ("At Midnight," set by Franz as op. 28, no. 6 and Wolf in 1888).

33. Trans. Charles E. Passage in *The German Mind of the Nineteenth Century*, 18–20; this poem was first published in *Athenaeum* in 1800.

34. According to Greek legend, eating the fruit from the lotus plant induced a dreamy languor; and thus the image of the lotus flower connotes an indolent intoxication. The poem was set by Franz as op. 25, no. 1 and Schumann as op. 25, no. 7 (1840).

35. Schubert set this poem in 1817 (op. 7, no. 3) and later adapted the setting for a variations movement in the D minor string quartet, D. 810 completed in 1824. Christoph Wolff compared the two works in "Schubert's 'Der Tod und das Mädchen': Analytical and Explanatory Notes on the Song D. 531 and the Quartet D. 810," in *Schubert Studies: Problems of Style and Chronology*, eds. Eva Badura-Skoda and Peter Branscombe, 143–72 (Cambridge: Cambridge University Press, 1982).

36. Schubert set the poem's several stanzas in 1816, D. 343.

37. Goethe's "Prometheus" was set by Reichardt in 1809, Schubert in 1819 (D. 674), and Wolf in 1889, and his "Ganymed" was set by Schubert in 1817 (op. 19, no. 3, D. 544) and Wolf in 1889; Jacobi's "Lied des Orpheus" was set by Schubert in 1816 (D. 474); and Mayrhofer's "Memnon" was set by Schubert in 1817 (D. 541).

38. This reflection of ancient times was set by Brahms in 1858 (op. 19, no. 5) and Wolf in 1888.

39. For example, Friedrich Hölderlin's "Hyperions Schicksalslied" ("Hyperion's Song of Fate," set by Brahms as op. 54); Mayrhofer's "Fahrt zum Hades"("Journey to Hades," set by Schubert in 1817, D. 526) and "Fragment aus dem Aischylos" ("Fragment from Aeschylus," set by Schubert in 1816, D. 450).

40. For example, Hölderlin's "Geh unter, schöne Sonne" ("Set, Fair Sun") and Mörike's "Gesang Weylas" ("Weylas's Song," set by Wolf in 1888).

41. Schumann set the complete poem as part of his *Liederkreis*, op. 39 in 1840.

42. Although James MacPherson's "translations" of Ossian's poetry were determined to be inauthentic, their ambiance of mists and mystery and their stories of unhappy love appealed to the Romantics, beginning with Goethe's character, Werther. Poems translated from Shakespeare include "An Silvia" ("To Silvia," from *Two Gentlemen of Verona*; set by Schubert in 1826 as op. 106, no. 4, D. 891); and the poem "Edward," a Scottish ballad from *Percy's "Reliques,"* translated by Johann Gottfried Herder, was set by Carl Loewe in 1818 as op. 1, no. 1); by Schubert as "Eine altschottische Ballade" ("An Old Scottish Ballad," D. 923) in 1827; by Brahms as a duet in op. 75, no. 1; and by Tchaikovsky as a duet in 1880 (op. 46). The poem set in Schubert's famous *Lied* "Ave Maria" (D. 839) is from Sir Walter Scott's *The Lady of the Lake*, and several poems of Robert Burns, including "Jemand" ("Someone") and "Niemand" ("No One") were set by Schumann in op. 25.

43. Wolf set this poem in 1889.

44. The poem was set by Wolf in 1888; other examples of nationalistic poems are Mörike's "Heimweh" ("Longing for Home," set by Wolf in 1888) and "Rheinlegendchen" ("Rhine Legend," from *Des Knaben Wunderhorn*, set by Mahler in 1888–1889).

45. *Frauenliebe* was set by Loewe in 1836 and by Schumann in 1840 (op. 42).

46. Mahler's well-known settings of *Des Knaben Wunderhorn* were preceded by earlier settings of folk poetry by, among others, Beethoven and Schumann.

47. In this German legend, a female seductress entices a man to a dangerous place and ultimately his death. Most often the figure is a siren singing on a rock in the Rhine that lures sailors to shipwreck; in Eichendorff's "Waldesgespräch" ("Wood Dialogue"), the setting is a forest. The Eichendorff poem was set by Schumann in 1840 within his *Liederkreis*, op. 39 and Heine's "Die Lorelei" ("The Lorelei") was set by Liszt in 1841.

48. Set by Schubert in 1817 as D. 545.

49. Set by Wolf in 1888.

50. This is the second of two stanzas; the entire poem was set by Schumann in 1849 (op. 79, no. 24) and Wolf in 1888.

51. This is the first of three stanzas set by Schubert in 1817 (D. 573). In Greek mythology, Iphigenia, a daughter of Agamemnon, was offered as a sacrifice to Artemis, goddess of the moon. Artemis saved her and made her a priestess.

52. Set by Reichardt in 1809 and Schubert, twice, in 1815; Schubert's first version is D. 215A and second is D. 216.

53. This is the first of two stanzas set by Wolf in 1888.

54. This is the first two of three stanzas set in Schumann's *Liederkreis*, op. 39 in 1840.

55. This is the opening of a lengthier poem set by Schubert in 1813 (D. 59).

56. This is the first of four stanzas set in Schumann's *Liederkreis*, op. 39 in 1840.

Chapter Two

1. For the more advanced poetry student, the material may seem elementary; Appendix III offers some additional references that discuss poetry in more depth and detail.

2. As stated in Chapter One, all important terms are printed in small capitals; each term is defined in Appendix II.

3. Those poets who broke the rules in the nineteenth century, such as American Walt Whitman, Frenchman Arthur Rimbaud, among others, will not be discussed here.

4. *Webster's New Universal Unabridged Dictionary*, 2d ed.

5. The latter image is from Goethe's "Schäfers Klagelied," set by Zelter in 1802, Reichardt in 1809, and Schubert in 1814 (op. 3, no. 1, D. 121). The tonal design of Schubert's setting of this poem is discussed in Chapter Six, in the section "Tonality and Mode" and the use of rhythm in Chapter Eight, in the section "Rhythm and Metric Norms."

6. Mahler set the poem in 1905 for voice and small chamber orchestra as well as voice and piano.

7. In addition to Schumann's famous setting of Heine's *Dichterliebe*, this fourth poem also was set by Franz as op. 44, no. 5 and Wolf in 1876, post.

8. Set by Franz as op. 25, no. 3 and Schumann as op. 48, no. 13.

9. The term *Stimmung* derives from the eighteenth-century meaning of "tuning" musical instruments. The term later was adopted by scholars of German culture in connection with poetic mood and expression, for example, Paul Roubiczek, "Some

Aspects of German Philosophy in the Romantic Period," in *The Romantic Period in Germany*, 317. Jurgen Thym adapted this useful concept within American music scholarship in "The Solo Song Settings of Eichendorff's Poems by Schumann and Wolf" (Ph.D. diss., Case Western Reserve, 1974) and *100 Years of Eichendorff Songs* in Recent Researches in the Music of the Nineteenth and Early Twentieth Centuries, vol. 5 (Madison: A-R Editions, 1983).

10. "Abends" was set by Franz as op. 16, no. 4; "Kurze Fahrt" was not set by any of the great *Lied* composers.

11. Cone has explored these concerns in both literature (poetry, novels, and plays) and musical settings of literary works (art songs and opera). See *The Composer's Voice* and *Music: A View from Delft*. In addition, a symposium on Cone's concept of persona is presented in *College Music Symposium* 29 (1989), with articles by Fred Everett Maus, "Introduction: *The Composer's Voice* as Music Theory," 1–7, and "Agency in Instrumental Music and Song," 31–43; Marion A. Guck, "Beethoven as Dramatist," 8–18; Charles Fisk, "Questions about the Persona of Schubert's 'Wanderer' Fantasy," 19–30; James Webster, "Cone's 'Personae' and the Analysis of Opera," 44–65; Alicyn Warren, "The Camera's Voice," 66–74; and Cone, "Responses," 75–80. Another study is Jurgen Thym and Ann Fehn, "Who Is Speaking? Edward T. Cone's Concept of Persona and Wolfgang von Schweinitz's Settings of Poems by Sarah Kirsch," *Journal of Musicological Research* 11 (1991): 1–31.

12. Determining which mode of address is operative has direct consequences for musical performance. If, for example, the poet is musing or brooding inwardly, the musician's personas will be more introspective and intimate; if, on the other hand, the poet speaks to someone else, the singer and accompanist will be more outwardly directed, projecting their voices to an altogether different place.

13. Cone's works were cited in note 11.

14. These special musical structures, including the personas they convey will be discussed in greater detail in Chapter Three.

15. Cone uses this song to demonstrate the issues of persona and mode of address in *The Composer's Voice*, 5–36; our brief discussion of the poem and setting here will be followed by lengthier explorations in Chapter Five, in the section "The Concept of Persona"; Chapter Seven, in the section "Motivic Analysis"; Chapter Eight, in the section "Rhythm as Motive"; and Chapter Nine, in the section "Rondo and Refrain."

16. A translation of the poem can be found in Appendix I.

17. Wolf set this poem in 1888.

18. The term DÉNOUEMENT in music derives from the French word usually applied to drama. The term denotes a period of gradual resolution toward the work's ultimate conclusion following a point of extreme intensity or climax.

19. The term TESSITURA denotes a particular pitch space at which a musical line remains for a period of time.

20. The performer has to decide what the new tonality of the piano postlude signifies: Does the instrumental persona accept what the vocal personna cannot? Is the instrumental persona part of a conflicted vocal persona—the poet/singer's subconscious—or perhaps just part of a conscious struggle between the poet/singer's brooding anger and an emerging sense of resignation?

21. A remarkably readable book about basic formal principles in poetry is John Hollander, *Rhyme's Reason: A Guide to English Verse* (New Haven: Yale University Press, 1981).

22. Rhyming sets of two lines that form completed thoughts, and therefore could be arranged as separate two-line stanzas are called *heroic couplets*; while this technique can easily become trite and monotonous, poets such as Alexander Pope used it both extensively and successfully.

23. Musical phrase structure, including phrase extension, is examined in Chapter Eight, in the section "Norms of the Phrase."

24. The tendency for older texts and scholarly books on both poetry and music to use the terms *masculine* for strong and *feminine* for weak endings is unfortunate. Such terms are now considered sexist and should be avoided altogether.

25. Verse that has no rhyme scheme, but that adheres to rhythmic and spatial rules is called "blank verse"; while this is not encountered much in German Romantic poetry, it is the format for much of the writing in Shakespeare's plays.

26. The *abba* is called the "In Memoriam" rhyme after Alfred Lord Tennyson's poem and the *aaba* is referred to as the *Rubaiyat* quatrain after the verses of Omar Khayyam. The latter was featured in Robert Frost's "Stopping by Woods on a Snowy Evening."

27. Schubert set this poem in 1822 (op. 92, no. 1, D. 764).

28. From Goethe's *Wilhelm Meister*, this was set by Schubert (op. 117, D. 149); Schumann, (op. 98a, no. 2); and Wolf (1888).

29. Alliteration was an important feature of Middle German, Middle English and Norse poetry; Wagner used it extensively in *Der Ring des Nibelungen* because of its archaic effect.

30. The three Minstrel Songs from *Wilhelm Meister* were set by Zelter (1795, 1816, 1818), Schubert (op. 12, nos. 1–3), Schumann (op. 98a, nos. 6, 3, 8), and Wolf (1888). Schubert's two versions of the first Harper song excerpted here are D. 325 and D. 478.

31. Set by Zelter (1803); Reichardt (1809); Schubert (1814, D. 120); and Brahms (op. 48, no. 5, 1858).

32. Because of our concern for precise understanding of the German language, Appendix I of this text uses *literal* translations and suggests only those translation volumes that preserve the original German as much as possible. Our translations in Chapters One and Two, however, do alter word order a bit; this gives a more refined translation where the alignment of German word and vocal line are not at issue.

33. Another metrical foot that resists simple categorization but occurs often in poetry of this period is the amphibrach, a stressed syllable between two unstressed syllables: ˘ / ˘ .

34. While much English poetry is in pentameter, German verses set by the great *Lied* composers tend to use shorter lines.

35. Just as in singing, the word "declamation" refers to clear and correct enunciation of the poetic text, so the adjective "declamatory" signifies a style of vocal line wherein the words of the text are clearly enunciated and easily understood.

36. "In der Fremde" was set by Schumann in 1840 (op. 39, no. 1) and Brahms in 1852–1853 (op. 3, no. 5). The setting is discussed in Chapter Three, in the section "Accompanimental Styles"; Chapter Six, in the section "Implicit Tonality"; Chapter Eight, in the section "Norms of the Phrase"; and Chapter Nine, in the section "Through Composed Form."

37. One scansion problem left unresolved is the possibility of beginning line 1 with an anapest: "Aus der Hei-" being scanned ˘ ˘ / instead of trochee / ˘ /. While

this is a feasible reading of the word stresses, it does not coincide with the prevailing meters just determined; at best, then, the anapest would be considered a substitution, which is described presently.

38. This line of "In der Fremde" exemplifies Schumann's tendency to change both words and word order in poems he set. He changed the poem's final line to be: "Und keiner kennt mich mehr hier," a shorter poetic line that was then repeated in the closing vocal phrase. Philip L. Miller's book of text translations, *Ring of Words* (New York: Norton, 1973), and the Elaine Brody and Robert A. Fowkes reference, *The German Lied and Its Poetry* (New York: New York University Press, 1971), both detail such text changes.

39. "Die Mainacht" was set by Schubert in 1815, D. 194 and Brahms in 1864 (op. 43, no. 2). The poem's metric pattern results from Hölty's use of the Asclepiadean Greek ode form, derived from Asclepiades of Samos (ca. 290 B.C.). This ode form prescribed a specific pattern of poetic meter to be followed throughout. As already discussed in Chapter One, the adoption of elements from antiquity such as ancient poetic meters is a common feature of German Romantic poetry.

40. In line 2 of stanza 2, the spondee emphasizes the caesura (notated ";").

41. In addition to Schubert, this famous poem was set by Zelter (1814); Liszt (ca. 1840); and Schumann (op. 96, no. 1, 1850).

42. This compact eight-line verse of quiet resignation and peaceful anticipation of death meant much to the poet; when thirty-three years later he returned to the scene of its composition, he wept when he saw how he had hastily captured it for the first time.

43. Other aspects of Schubert's setting are examined in Chapter Eight, in the sections "Rhythm as Motive" and "Rhythmic Tension and Ambiguity" and Chapter Nine, in the section "Through Composed Form."

44. "Goethe's Poetry," *German Life and Letters*, Vol. 2, Part VII (1949), 316–329. The first citation is from pp. 317–318 and the second from pp. 320–321. I am indebted to Professor Barbara Reutlinger of the Humanities Department and musician Roy Sansom of the New England Conservatory for suggesting this essay, which is an excellent introduction for study of German Romantic poetry.

45. The enjambment from line 4 to line 5 poses a special challenge to the composer, who might conservatively follow the line and stanzaic form (line 4 ending one stanza and line 5 beginning another) or might instead honor the enjambment and sentence structure (the two stanzas connected). Schubert chose the latter interpretation.

46. Set by Wolf (1888).

47. Set by Reichardt (1809), Zelter (1810), and Wolf (1888).

48. Set by Brahms (op. 96, no. 2, 1884).

49. Set by Reger (op. 75, no. 18, 1903).

50. Set by Schumann (op. 79, no. 24, 1849) and Wolf (1888).

51. Set by Mendelssohn (op. 19a, no. 5, 1830–1834).

52. Set by Reichardt (c. 1809) and Schubert (op. 3, no. 2, D. 216, 1815).

53. Set by Brahms (op. 85, no. 2, 1879).

54. Set by Wolf (1888).

55. Set by Wolf (1888).

56. This poem was set numerous times: Zelter (1807); Reichardt (1809); Schubert (op. 4, no. 3, D. 768, 1815); Liszt (1843); and Wolf (1883).

57. Set by Brahms (op. 49, no. 4, 1868).

Chapter Three

1. This is also conveyed in the accompaniment, where the piano supports the voice solidly throughout with a homophonic texture, sounding first churchlike, then like waves, but always aligning with the singer. The word *Dioscuri* refers to the twin sons of Zeus in Greek mythology, Castor and Pollux, who became the constellation Gemini after their death. We will discuss accompanimental textures in the section "Accompanimental Styles."

2. Some examples of more recitative-style passages in *Lieder* are mm. 73–87 in Schubert's "Pause," from *Die schöne Müllerin*, D. 795, no. 12, and the final two phrases of Strauss's "Morgen," op. 27, no. 4 (1893–1894).

3. A MORDENT is a lower-neighbor figure from Renaissance and Baroque performance practice; originally indicated by a specific notational device, it came to be written out explicitly in the late eighteenth and nineteenth centuries.

4. As suggested in Chapter Two, the section on "Persona and Modes of Address," the piano part in "Wohin?" assumes a persona of its own, representing the brook to whom the narrator is speaking. The concept of persona in *Lieder*, introduced in Chapter Two, will be amplified in Chapter Five.

5. *The Romantic Generation*, 61.

6. The change in the accompaniment, followed by a similar one in the voice, reflects the poet's experience of hearing the nature sounds (accompaniment, m. 5) and then responding to those sounds (vocal line, m. 7).

7. Schumann seems to indicate here that the chords should not be broken off crisply, but should be allowed to ring. However, they should not extend into the next chord, but should be stopped to allow some space between chords.

8. A MELISMA is an expressive melodic figure that sets one syllable of text with several notes, that is, in the florid vocal style. The term originates from Gregorian chant, where the melismatic style contrasts with syllabic style.

9. General stylistic differences among the great *Lied* composers are discussed more fully in Chapter Ten.

Chapter Four

1. In his book, *Musical Structure and Performance* (New Haven: Yale University Press, 1989), Wallace T. Berry considers the importance of tempo and tempo adjustments through acceleration and deceleration, as well as rubato, to be one of the two major issues confronting performers. His second concern is musical articulation, which he details along with his views on tempo in his first two chapters. We discuss musical articulation throughout the present study, especially in Chapter Five.

2. All issues of rhythm and meter are defined and demonstrated in Chapter Eight, in the sections "Rhythmic, Metric, and Phrase Norms," "Norms of the Phrase," and "Rhythmic Tensions and Ambiguity." The different uses of the terminology just explained are not contradictory. Rather, theoretical and analytical use of the terms focuses upon rhythmic and metric pattern and structure, while performance usage applies the terms to local instances of pitch emphasis through touch by voice or hand. Careful employment of the different meanings of these important terms will help sensitize the performer to theoretical understanding of musical structure and the theorist to concerns of articulation and expressivity in the performer.

3. A shift in texture is also evident in mm. 17 and 18; the low D is held through, providing the most sustained sound yet. In the two measures that follow, Schumann continues to hold the low D and alternates it with an A a fifth higher, thickening the sound in the bass even further.

4. The term SYNCOPATION, which means emphasizing a normally weak beat, is defined more fully in Chapter Eight, in the section "Metric Tension and Ambiguity." Schumann uses the same rhythm in the voice in mm. 11 and 12. The longer note on "Kum-" ("Kummer"; "grief") enables the singer to accent that important syllable, even though the unaccented syllable ("mer") is on a higher pitch.

5. The use of two against three and four against three was quite well established by 1840, when this song was written. While in earlier periods, performers would have forced the duplets into alignment with the triplets, here the complexity of the rhythmic notation results in a rich rhythmic counterpoint that enables the various lines to move horizontally in a smooth and beautiful fashion.

6. In the final phrase, the rise to the song's climax conveys the poetic progression, using ever-increasing stresses on "deiner" ("your"),"Göttheit" ("divinity"), and finally, "beugen" (to bow"), where the bowing gesture has the greatest importance of all.

7. This change is most interesting in setting Stanza 1, where Goethe repeats line 1 in line 4, a poetic repetition he does not continue in subsequent stanzas.

8. The strophic form is examined in detail in Chapter Nine.

9. A singer can choose to breathe where there is a comma, but may not need to do so.

10. The word ELISION as it is typically used to describe phrase overlap is described in Chapter Eight, in the section "Norms of the Phrase." Here the word denotes the linking of one word to the next through a consonant.

11. Such small hesitations are there not only for the comfort of the singer, but also to assist the audience as well.

12. It is probable that Brahms wanted this elaborate articulation to continue for six measures, after notating it for a measure and a half.

Chapter Five

1. There is no need to alter dynamic indications to avoid a repeated dynamic pattern in Schubert, where exact repetition occurs in various ways.

2. More specific instructions regarding tone quality occur in opera. Verdi might ask for "*un fil di voce*," or "a thread of voice," or write "*senza espressione*" ("without expression") or "*cupo*" ("covered"), a technical vocal instruction. Strauss likewise asks for such timbres as "*wie ein Schrei*" ("like a scream") in one place and "*tonlos*" ("without tone") in another.

3. The term VOCAL RANGE encompasses all the pitches used, as distinct from TESSITURA, which denotes the pitch space at which a song remains most of the time.

4. It will help to play the passages yourself, so that you can try out different effects.

5. Other devices were listed in Chapter Four, in the section "Nuances of Notation." As mentioned there, the words "accent" and "stress" are used differently by theorists and performers. In a theoretical context, "accent" means emphasis, usually within the context of meter, while "stress" has a more generic, less precise meaning;

in the performers's language, on the other hand, "accent" denotes a sharper and "stress" denotes a softer attack.

6. The issue of persona was introduced in Chapter Two, in the section "Persona and Mode of Address."

7. Because most of the poets of this period were men, most narrators and poetic voices, unless specifically indicated to be female, are presumed to be male. The voices in the cycle *Frauenliebe und -Leben* and songs like "Das verlassene Mägdlein" are obvious exceptions. There is, however, no need for a female singer to necessarily adopt a male persona in singing many *Lieder*, as has been shown by numerous female *Lied* singers over the years. The issue of gender is addressed in Chapter Ten, in the context of a comparison of settings of the same poem by Clara Schumann and Gustav Mahler. In addition, the Bibliography in Appendix III lists several works about women and music and the study of gender.

8. In the orchestral version, the RH melody is played by a violin; does that instrumental color help you imagine the appropriate persona better than the piano version?

9. Motivic relationships in this song have been studied for several years. Particularly pertinent to the discussion here is Deborah Stein, "Schubert's *Erlkönig:* Motivic Parallelism and Motivic Transformation," *19th Century Music* 18 (1989): 145–58. Some aspects of this study are discussed in Chapter Seven, in the section "Motivic Analysis."

10. The possibility of presenting differing points of view simultaneously is particularly noticeable on the stage, in opera, and in other dramatic forms. While opera has the obvious advantage of visual cues, it still remains a staggering achievement by such great operatic composers as Mozart, Verdi, and Wagner that their operatic characters often sing at the same time, but with clearly different personas and different musical statements.

Chapter Six

1. We use the term ARTICULATION to denote how musical phrases are shaped by such means as rhythmic gesture, metric placement, melodic contour, and harmonic cadence. Chapter Eight discusses the rhythmic and metric factors.

2. The term CLOSURE generally connotes the ending of a musical flow, which, because of music's temporal nature, occurs gradually. Closure can refer to the end of a phrase, a section, or an entire work.

3. The term SYNTAX is useful when talking about music as a temporal language. In general, "syntax" refers to the word structure, or ordering, in a phrase, clause, or sentence of prose; in the present context, "syntax" denotes the ordering of musical elements (pitch, chord, rhythm) in a phrase or section of music.

4. The perfect authentic cadence, or PAC, is the most decisive closure because both the bass and the "soprano" voices conclude on the tonic pitch.

5. This use of dominant pedal and "retransition" occurs in larger forms than the miniature *Lieder*, for example, in sonata or rondo forms.

6. As discussed in Chapter Five, the piano postlude, with its unique persona, adds a special dimension to the song's conclusion. Several piano postludes are discussed often in this volume: Schubert's "Wanderers Nachtlied I"; Schumann's "In der Fremde"; Brahms's "Die Mainacht"; and Wolf's "Auch kleine Dinge."

7. The word AMBIGUOUS is useful in discussing both poetry and musical depiction of poetic ambiguity; Webster's *New Universal Unabridged Dictionary*, 2d ed. defines *ambiguous* as: "having two or more possible meanings; being of uncertain signification; susceptible of different interpretations; hence, obscure, not clear, not definite; uncertain or vague." The musical depiction of poetic ambiguity will be a common theme throughout the rest of this volume.

8. "Beat 2" means, of course, the fourth 8th note; compound meter such as 6/8 is discussed in Chapter Eight, in the section "Rhythmic, Metric, and Phrase Norms."

9. Experienced *Lied* performers know that the expressive power of the genre often arises from the composer's avoidance or denial of the "norms" of musical structure described here. This will be addressed later in this chapter and in Chapter Eight.

10. Schubert set two poems of Hölty entitled "An den Mond." This one is D. 468, composed in 1816.

11. The use of applied chords is discussed in the section "Large-scale Tonal Design: Modulation and Tonicization." If this term is not familiar, see any of the harmony texts cited in Appendix III, Bibliography.

12. We will examine the melodic component of *Lieder* in Chapter Seven.

13. Because the plagal cadence does not use the tonality-defining V, it is not as strong a closing gesture and often occurs *after* a strong authentic cadence, as part of an extended cadential phrase. The deceptive cadence resolves V to vi rather than to I, where vi acts as a substitute for I; the deceptive cadence is thus a deferral of real closure and usually is followed by an authentic cadence, V–I. The plagal cadence is used to convey particular poetic sentiments, for example, the religious "Amen" ending, while the deceptive cadence creates a unique form of harmonic tension that involves delayed resolution.

14. Students usually determine musical form in one of two ways: (1) by noting the occurrence of themes or (2) by noting changes in tonality. While ideally, musical form is understood as a *combination* of both thematic structure and tonal design, we deliberately limit our attention to tonal factors here in order to focus on issues of tonal progression. Thematic recurrence is not as much a formal factor in *Lied* as in other genres and will not be part of the present study. In Chapter Seven, melodic material will be discussed in terms of linear structure and motivic relationships. At that time, the melodic component of *Lieder* will be explored *in conjunction with* harmonic and tonal design.

15. As an example, note how different both singer and pianist *feel* when performing those sections of Schubert's "Erlkönig" in B♭ major, C major, or E♭ major. While part of the difference is in the rhythm and texture of these sections, the change in key and mode takes both performers and audience into the different musical world of the Erlking, and the change is palpable.

16. We will discuss those *Lieder* that do not begin and end in the same key in the section "Directional Tonality."

17. Recall from Chapter Two that the concepts of persona and mode of address refer in poetry to who (persona) is speaking to whom (mode of address), and that in poetic settings these "voices" often are projected differently by the vocal line and accompaniment.

18. Arnold Schoenberg coined the term "monotonality" in *Structural Functions of Harmony* (New York: Norton, 1954), 19.

19. Personification was defined in Chapter Two, in the section "Poetic Representation." Essentially, it denotes the endowment of something inanimate, for example, a tree or brook, with human qualities.

20. Charles Rosen captured this term for general usage in *The Classical Style: Haydn, Mozart, Beethoven* (New York: Norton, 1971).

21. Dénouement was defined in Chapter Two as the gradual resolution of a work of art from the point of its greatest intensity or climax to the work's ultimate conclusion.

22. We dramatize the importance of distinguishing between major and minor throughout this text by use of uppercase roman numerals for major and lowercase for minor.

23. The possibility of both a minor v and major V within the minor mode results in odd-looking RNs. For the sake of clarity, notate minor v as lowercase with a ♭ to indicate a lowered third: v♭ and major V in the minor mode with uppercase RN and ♯ to indicate a raised third or leading tone: V♯. Both ♭ and ♯ are redundant, but they underscore the need to clarify the variable use of the dominant in minor.

24. In *The Romantic Generation*, Rosen comments several times about the import of the parallel mode pair in Schubert. With regard to *Die Schöne Müllerin's* "Pause," Rosen asserts that a "shift in mode represents the dimension of time, an uncertain irruption of both past and future into the present" (190), and in the case of a pivotal song in *Winterreise*, he notes [an] unreconciled opposition of tonic major and minor in "Thränenregen . . . [where] the stability of tonality makes the instability of mode all the more telling. It is also the first time in [the cycle] that the ambiguity of mode is not merely an interior detail but actually determines the large form" (181).

25. The relative major/minor pair mentioned here (a minor/C major and d minor/F major) will be examined in detail in the subsequent section, "Relative Major/Minor Pair."

26. In addition to the nuances of text depiction examined here, modal mixture chords often function as pivot chords that connect remotely related keys expressing dramatic textual changes; this topic will be examined more fully in "Harmonic and Tonal Innovation."

27. The altered mode of the tonic also occurs through mixture, as heard often with the Picardy third major endings of many Baroque and some Classical works in the minor mode. This form of mixture is not as compelling as that involving chords altered by scale degree ♭$\hat{6}$. Most harmony textbooks discuss this principle, including Chapter 22 of Edward Aldwell and Carl Schachter, *Harmony and Voice Leading*, 2d ed. (New York: Harcourt Brace Jovanovich, 1979); Chapter 21 of Stefan Kostka and Dorothy Payne, *Tonal Harmony* (New York: McGraw-Hill, 1989); and Chapter 4 of Walter Piston and Mark DeVoto, *Harmony*, 5th ed. (New York: Norton, 1987).

28. *The Romantic Generation*, 47.

29. These musical puns are similar to the poetic puns discussed in Chapter Two. The motivic use of such enharmonic links will be discussed in Chapter Seven, in the section "Motivic Analysis."

30. *The Romantic Generation*, 249. Recall Schubert's C♭ major with E♭ major.

31. *The Romantic Generation*, 257.

32. The shift to E major may be considered a tonicization by some; however, the quick shift away from E major suggests the sonority as a chromatic harmony, III♯

within C major, rather than a new tonic. The emphasis throughout the song upon E major by its dominant exemplifies use of applied chords.

33. The use of the parallel mode to facilitate modulation was mentioned in the section "Tonality and Mode." Here the remote third relation of E♭ major and C♭ major is mediated by e♭ minor, parallel minor to E♭ major and relative minor to C♭ major.

34. Interestingly, Schubert's second setting of this poem begins in c♯ minor but ends in F major. Four important discussions of tonal third chains are Robert Bailey, "Analytical Study," in *Wagner: Prelude and Transfiguration from "Tristan and Isolde"* (New York: W. W. Norton & Co., 1985), 120–121; Howard Cinnamon, "Tonic Arpeggiation and Successive Equal Third Relations as Elements of Tonal Evolution in the Music of Franz Liszt," *Music Theory Spectrum* 8 (1986): 1–24; Gregory Proctor, "Technical Bases of Nineteenth-Century Chromatic Tonality: A Study in Chromaticism," (Ph.D. diss., Princeton University, 1978); and Deborah Stein, *Hugo Wolf's Lieder and Extensions of Tonality* (Ann Arbor: UMI Research Press, 1985), Chapter 3. A discussion of double tonal designs where pieces begin and end in different keys follows in the section "Directional Tonality."

35. The number of songs in both composers' *oeuvre* is impressive and demonstrates both the daring of these nineteenth-century *Lied* composers and the resilience of the ever-developing tonal system.

36. The use of this form of double tonality was noted as early as 1947 by Schoenberg pupil and scholar Dika Newlin, who called it "progressive tonality," in *Bruckner, Mahler, Schoenberg* (New York: Norton, 1947). The concept and term was later treated by Jim Samson, *Music in Transition: A Study of Tonal Expansion and Atonality, 1900–1920* (London: Dent, 1977). Robert Bailey conceptualized more precisely and renamed the concept "directional tonality" in his "Analytical Study" of *Prelude and Transfiguration from "Tristan and Isolde."* The Bibliography in Appendix III cites numerous studies on this topic.

37. Schubert's setting was in 1816 (D. 509) and Wolf's setting was 1890. The extensive water imagery of von Collins's poem was described in Chapter Two, and issues of texture in Wolf's setting were discussed in Chapter Three.

38. This song's texture was discussed in Chapter 3, in the section "Accompanimental Styles," and persona interpretation was discussed in Chapter Five, in the section "The Concept of Persona."

39. A more detailed study of this song appears in Deborah Stein, *Hugo Wolf's Lieder and Extensions of Tonality*, Chapter 4.

40. In his "Analytical Study," Robert Bailey called this notion "indirect exposition." Bailey quotes Schoenberg's *Theory of Harmony*: "A minor, [the key and tonic chord of Tristan's *Prelude*] although it is to be inferred from every passage, is scarcely ever sounded in the whole piece. It the [key] . . . always expressed in circuitous ways; it [the chord] is constantly avoided by means of deceptive cadences" (126).

41. Charles Rosen offers penetrating insight into the tonal ambiguity between "Im wunderschönen Monat Mai" and song No. 2 in *The Romantic Generation*. He suggests that the opening song of *Dichterliebe* "begins in the middle, and ends as it began—an emblem of unsatisfied desire, of longing [*Sehnsucht*] eternally renewed" (41). Rosen further notes an "ambiguous relationship between vocal line and accompaniment: . . . The extraordinary craft of the song lies in the relation between voice and piano, the sense of the different musical spaces occupied by each, and the way resolution finally arrives only outside the space in which the tension was principally defined" (44–46).

42. The notion of resolving song 1 with the opening of Song 2 is complicated, since the first song ends on V^7/f♯ minor and the second song is in A major. Because the opening sonority of Song 2 is an incomplete triad, A–C♯, that third can resolve the V^7 of Song 1; nevertheless, the opening tonality of Song 2 begins ambiguously.

43. The notion that musical language sets up syntactical expectations that may or may not be fulfilled was first explored in the now classic studies by Leonard B. Meyer, *Emotion and Meaning in Music* (Chicago: University of Chicago Press, 1956) and Susanne K. Langer, *Feeling and Form* (New York: Scribner's, 1953). In recent years, interest in musical expressivity and perception of such things as fulfillment and frustruation has led to studying music in the context of philosophy, psychology, semiotics, and literary criticism. Bibliographies of works in these areas can be found in several relatively new works: in the area of semiotics, V. Kofi Agawu, *Playing with Signs: A Semiotic Interpretation of Classic Music* (Princeton: Princeton University Press, 1991); in the area of cognition, *Music and the Cognitive Sciences*, ed. Stephen McAdams and Irene Deliége (London: Harwood Academic Publishers, 1989); in the application of the notion of narrative in literary criticism, numerous articles by Fred Maus, including "Music as Drama," *Music Theory Spectrum* 10 (1988): 56–73, and "Music as Narrative," *Indiana Theory Review* 12/1–2 (1991): 1–24; and in the area of philosophy, Lawrence Ferrara, *Philosophy and the Analysis of Music* (New York: Greenwood Press, 1991). Finally, a book of essays entitled *Music and Text: Critical Inquiries*, ed. Steven Paul Scher (Cambridge: Cambridge University Press, 1992) offers a breadth of analytical approaches, all concerned with the relationship between music and text. A recent *Lied* study exemplifying musical analogs for poetic themes is Deborah Stein, "Schubert's 'Die Liebe hat gelogen': The Deception of Mode and Mixture," *Journal of Musicological Research* 9/4 (1989): 109–131.

44. A definition of irony was given in Chapter Two, and can be found in Appendix II.

Chapter Seven

1. The translations for this strophic song vary. The most thorough translation is in Miller, *The Ring of Words*, which offers nine stanzas. In comparison, Fischer-Dieskau presents only two stanzas and Wigmore, only three. Miller further points out that the first (posthumous) edition published stanzas 1, 3, and 6.

2. While it is common to move *to* the relative major from an opening minor tonic, the reverse, moving from a major tonic to the relative minor, is unusual.

3. Over the years, the term *linear analysis* has been used to designate several different kinds of melodic analysis within a variety of analytical approaches. As we explain next, our use of the term corresponds most closely to that used by theorist Heinrich Schenker and his followers.

4. Over the past three decades, Schenker's students have published a wealth of translations of and interpretive studies about his important theories. In addition, several harmony textbooks are based upon his theoretical framework as well. Appendix III presents a selected bibliography.

5. The term *prolongation* was defined in Chapter Six, in the section "Preliminary Terms and Concepts." The static nature of prolongation contrasts with the forward motion of progression.

6. The German word for primary tone is *Kopfton*, meaning head tone.

7. Melodic prolongation was mentioned in the analysis of Schubert's "An den Mond" in Chapter Six, in the section "Preliminary Terms and Concepts."

8. This concept of embellishment differs from that often associated with melodic ornamentation, the Baroque elaboration of a melodic line through diminutions and ornamental figures. Study of this latter type of melodic embellishment can be found in any number of Baroque treatises, for example, C. P. E. Bach, *Essay on the True Art of Playing Keyboard Instruments*, trans. and ed. William J. Mitchell (New York: Norton, 1949). Several harmony texts survey figuration and ornamentation within common-practice music; see Aldwell and Schachter, *Harmony and Voice Leading* and Piston and DeVoto, *Harmony*, Chapter 7.

9. The N and IN figures in the melody are supported by similar N and IN figures in the bass. This will be studied more fully in the section "Contrapuntal Structure of Melody and Bass."

10. While this series of 3rds may appear to create an arpeggiation, the G and E♭ are supported by the tonic but the C is part of the ii⁶ chord.

11. Even as the C of m. 5 connects with the isolated B♭ of m. 2, the high E♭ of m. 5 becomes unresolved in that register, its resolution being delayed for several measures.

12. The function of C (m. 5) as N to B♭ (m. 2) occurs through registral connection. Both the Bb and the C are approached by leap.

13. This tenth was prefigured in the piano introduction, where the treble G formed a tenth above the tonic bass E♭.

14. A compound line is also called "polyphonic melody;" brief discussions of this form of melodic line occur in Aldwell and Schachter, *Harmony and Voice Leading*, 311–12 and Piston and DeVoto, *Harmony*, 103–7.

15. The E is itself embellished by its own IN, F♯.

16. In order to be clear, we call motives that are without rhythmic distinction "linear" and motives that are rhythmic without a clear melodic profile "rhythmic." Our concern here is with linear motives; rhythmic motives are discussed in Chapter Eight, in the section "Rhythm as Motive."

17. Textbooks on form discuss motivic development in great detail, for example, Douglass M. Green, *Form in Tonal Music* (New York: Holt, Rinehart & Winston, 1979), Chapter 3. Harmony texts that discuss motive are Joel Lester, *Harmony in Tonal Music*, Chapter 11; and Piston and DeVoto, *Harmony*, Chapter 7.

18. Another term for the simple neighbor note is *auxiliary tone*; the escape tone, or échappée, is a form of IN. This is discussed in Piston and DeVoto, *Harmony*, 128–29.

19. As already noted, this chromatic pitch was anticipated in the piano introduction (LH), m. 1.

20. Along with the somewhat less recurring P4.

21. Two points need clarification. First, the vocal B♭ 7th leap from low C casts B♭ as a N to A♭, which then descends its third to F. Second, this 3rd, A♭–F, is immediately echoed in the bass of mm. 7–8. Both are labeled X² in Figure 7.9.

22. Notice that this motive is recalled in the piano postlude by the bass N figure B♭–C♭–B♭, the C♭ being an enharmonic reinterpretation of B♮.

23. Definitions of "pun" were given in both Chapter Two, in the section "Poetic Representation" and in Chapter Six, in the section "Tonality and Mode."

24. Many scholars have studied motivic parallelism; those treating *Lieder* include Charles Burkhart, "Schenker's 'Motivic Parallelism'," *Journal of Music Theory* 22

(1978): 145–75; Steven Laitz, "Pitch-class Motive in the Songs of Franz Schubert: The Submediant Complex." (Ph.D. diss., University of Rochester, 1992). Carl Schachter, "Motive and Text in Four Schubert Songs," in *Aspects of Schenkerian Theory*, ed. David Beach (New Haven, Conn. and London: Yale University Press, 1983) 61–76; and Deborah Stein, "Schubert's *'Erlkönig'*: Motivic Parallelism and Motivic Transformation."

25. This study of "Erlkönig" is based on the articles by Burkhart and Stein cited in note 24 and two others: Anne K. McNamee, "The Introduction in Schubert's *Lieder*," *Music Analysis* 4 (1985): 95–106 and Harald Krebs, "Some Addenda to McNamee's Remarks on 'Erlkönig'," *Music Analysis* 7 (1988): 53–57.

26. Richard Capell, *Schubert's Songs*, 3d ed. (Old Woking, Surrey: Gresham Press, 1973), and Eric Sams, *The Songs of Hugo Wolf* (London: Methuen, 1961); *Brahms Songs* (Seattle: University of Washington Press, 1972); and *The Songs of Robert Schumann*, 2d ed. (London: Eulenburg, 1975).

27. For decades, the most notable studies on nuances of poetic depiction in German Lieder have been by Jack Stein, *Poem and Music in the German Lied from Gluck to Hugo Wolf* (Cambridge: Harvard University Press, 1971); "Poem and Music in Hugo Wolf's Mörike Songs," *Musical Quarterly* 53 (1967): 22–38; "Schubert's Heine Songs," *Journal of Aesthetics and Art Criticism* 24 (1966). More recent research, especially by Ann Fehn and Jurgen Thym, and Susan Youens, is listed in Appendix III.

28. Persona was defined in Chapter Two, in the section "Persona and Modes of Address," and was examined within the piano accompaniment in Chapter Five, in the section "The Concept of Persona."

29. Piano solos were examined in Chapter Five, in the section "The Concept of Persona."

30. A striking example of a piano melody depicting a specific persona is Brahms's setting of "Wie Melodien zieht es mir," cited in Chapter Five, in the section "The Concept of Persona." In this case the piano interlude presents the melody mentioned in the poem that "steals softly through" the poet's mind.

31. The descending tenor line imitates in stretto the highest notes of the RH figuration.

Chapter Eight

1. (Chicago and London: University of Chicago Press, 1960), p. 1. Of all the studies of rhythm and meter, this book has been a basic resource for music students for decades. More recently, however, studies by Joel Lester, *The Rhythms of Tonal Music* (Carbondale, Ill.: Southern Illinois University Press, 1986) and William Rothstein, *Phrase Structure in Tonal Music* (New York: Schirmer, 1989) provide a clearer overview of basic issues (Chapters 1–5 in Lester and 1–4 in Rothstein) as well as a summary of the other historical and current sources on the topic. Both the Lester and Rothstein volumes include substantial bibliographies. These works were influenced by earlier work of Carl Schachter: "Aspects of Meter, Rhythm and Linear Analysis: A Preliminary Study," *The Music Forum* 4 (1976): 281–334; "Rhythm and Linear Analysis: Durational Reduction," *The Music Forum* 5 (1980): 197–232; and "Rhythm and Linear Analysis: Aspects of Meter," *The Music Forum* 6 (1978): 1–59. Other more general books that include insightful commentary on issues of rhythm, meter, and phrase structure in tonal music include Wallace T. Berry, *Structural Functions in Music* (Englewood Cliffs, N.J.: Prentice-Hall, 1976), Chapter 3; Fred Lehrdahl and Ray Jackendoff,

A Generative Theory of Tonal Music (Cambridge: MIT Press, 1983); and Charles Rosen, *The Classical Style: Haydn, Mozart, Beethoven* and *Sonata Forms* (New York: Norton, 1980). Two books about analysis and performance that treat issues of rhythm and meter in profound ways are the classic study by Edward T. Cone, *Musical Form and Musical Performance* (New York: Norton, 1968) and the relatively recent contribution by Wallace T. Berry, *Musical Structure and Performance.*

2. Two recent studies of music's temporal aspect are Jonathan Kramer, *The Time of Music* (New York: Schirmer, 1988) and Barbara Barry, *Musical Time: The Sense of Order* (Stuyvesant, N.Y.: Pendragon Press, 1990). Both books have exhaustive bibliographies and Kramer updates his earlier reference, "Studies of Time and Music: A Bibliography," *Music Theory Spectrum*, 7 (1985): 72–106.

3. Rothstein defines *hypermeter* as "the combination of measures on a metrical basis . . . including both the recurrence of equal-sized measure groups and a definite pattern of alternation between strong and weak measures" (*Phrase Structure*, pp. 12–13).

4. The basic terms and concepts reviewed here are also discussed in several well-known texts; see Aldwell and Schachter, *Harmony and Voice Leading*, Chapter 3; Kostka and Payne, *Tonal Harmony*, Chapter 2; and Lester, *Harmony in Tonal Music*, Vol. 1, Chapter 5. In addition to the Cooper and Meyer, Lehrdahl and Jackendoff, Lester, and Rothstein books cited earlier, other sophisticated discussions of rhythm and meter can be found in Arthur Komar, *Theory of Suspensions* (Princeton: Princeton University Press, 1971); Peter Westergaard, *An Introduction to Tonal Theory* (New York: Norton, 1975); Maury Yeston, *The Stratification of Musical Rhythm* (New Haven: Yale University Press, 1976); and Victor Zuckerkandl, *The Sense of Music* (Princeton: Princeton University Press, 1959). The Rothstein volume includes theoretical views of several important eighteenth- and nineteenth-century theorists such as Moritz Hauptmann, Johann Philipp Kirnberger, Heinrich Christoph Koch, Johann Mattheson, Anton Reicha, Joseph Riepel, Hugo Riemann, and Gottfried Weber.

5. There are, of course, pieces of music for which it is problematic to assert such a persistent pulse. Most of our *Lied* repertory, however, do incorporate the pulse we describe.

6. In addition to the general resources on rhythm and meter already noted, more sophisticated examinations of meter include William Benjamin, "A Theory of Musical Meter," *Music Perception* 1 (1984): 355–413; Wallace T. Berry, "Metric and Rhythmic Articulation in Music," *Music Theory Spectrum* 7 (1985): 7–33; Harald Krebs, "Some Extensions of the Concepts of Metrical Consonance and Dissonance," *Journal of Music Theory* 31 (1987): 99–120; and "Dramatic Functions of Metrical Consonances and Dissonances in *Das Rheingold*," *In Theory Only* 10/5 (1988): 5–20; and Lehrdahl and Jackendoff, "On the Theory of Grouping and Meter," *Musical Quarterly* 67 (1981): 479–506.

7. Lester discusses this in *The Rhythms of Tonal Music*, Chapter 3.

8. A review of the poetic and tonal progression of this song appears in Chapter Six, in the section "Tonality and Mode"; a translation of the text can be found in Appendix I.

9. This use of "accent" and "stress" contrasts with much discussion of rhythm and meter in the literature. Cooper and Meyer (*The Rhythmic Structure of Music*) give "stress" great importance, while Lester (*The Rhythms of Tonal Music*) and Lehrdahl and Jackendoff (*A Generative Theory*) emphasize the concept of accent and use

stress in a limited way. Discussions by Berry (*Structural Functions*) and Schachter (*Music Forum* articles) tend to define accent without a corresponding definition of stress. In addition, we use the two terms in this chapter differently from their meanings in Part II, Chapters Four and Five. Discussion of the performers's use of accent and stress in the context of attack are given in Chapter Four, in the section "Nuances of Notation," and in note 3, and Chapter Five, in the section "Vocal Accent and Stress," and in note 5. Here the performer's use of stress and accent is related to the type of attack given to a pitch or group of pitches.

10. As just cited, agogic accent was defined, along with the terms *accent* and *stress* in Chapters Four and Five. In theoretical terms, agogic accent denotes a rhythmic emphasis created by a long duration or a syncopation, or, most often, a combination of the two. To performers, the term *agogic accent* means emphasizing a pitch by using a slight delay in attack.

11. Insightful discussions of grouping in the context of meter can be found in the cited works of Lehrdahl and Jackendoff and Zuckerkandl.

12. Other studies besides those of Cooper and Meyer, Komar, Lehrdahl and Jackendoff, Lester, Rothstein, Westergaard, Yeston, and Zuckerkandl cited previously include Richard Cohn, "Dramatization of Hypermetric Conflicts in the Scherzo of Beethoven's Ninth Symphony," *19th Century Music* 15 (1992): 22–40; Lehrdahl and Jackendoff, "Toward a Formal Theory of Tonal Music," *Journal of Music Theory* 21 (1977): 111–71; Robert P. Morgan, "The Theory and Analysis of Tonal Rhythm," *Musical Quarterly* 64 (1978): 435–73; and William Rothstein, "Rhythm and the Theory of Structural Levels," (Ph.D. diss., Yale University, 1981).

13. Related studies are David Epstein, "Tempo Relations," *Music Theory Spectrum* 7 (1985): 34–71 and Erich Leinsdorf, *The Composer's Advocate: A Radical Orthodoxy for Musicians* (New Haven: Yale University Press, 1981), Chapters 5 and 6.

14. Of all the texts available, Piston and DeVoto present the best discussion of harmonic rhythm in Chapter 12. Other valuable discussions occur in Lester, *The Rhythms of Tonal Music;* Edward Lowinsky, "On Mozart's Rhythm," *Musical Quarterly* 42 (1956): 162–86 (reprinted in Paul Henry Lang, ed., *The Creative World of Mozart* [New York: Norton, 1963] 31–55); and Rothstein, *Phrase Structure.*

15. Rothstein, *Phrase Structure,* 22–23, states it thus: "a change in the harmonic rhythm . . . helps to signal the coming cadence . . . [and] provides a climax of rhythmic activity just before the cadential relaxation."

16. As discussed in Chapter Six, in the section "Large-scale Tonal Design," this phenomenon of "retransition" tends to occur in larger instrumental forms, for example, sonata form, rather than within the miniature forms of the *Lied* genre.

17. In addition to changes in harmonic rhythm, the poetic progression is underscored by a tonal change as well. The song's opening and the addresses to the Brook are in B major, while the interior struggle around the possible responses occurs in G major, a chromatic third relation to the prevailing tonic. Chromatic third relations are discussed in Chapter Six, in the section "Chromatic Third Relations."

18. Examples of this are Wallace T. Berry, *Form in Music* (Englewood Cliffs, N.J.: Prentice-Hall, 1966), Chapter 1; and Douglass Green, *Form in Tonal Music,* Chapters 1–5. Leonard Ratner, *Classic Music: Expression, Form, and Style* (New York: Schirmer, 1980) also is a well-known resource. Harmony texts that discuss phrase structure in conjunction with issues of harmony and melody are Lester, *Harmony,* Vol. 1, Chapter

5; and Piston and DeVoto, *Harmony*, Chapters 7, 11, 12, and 13. Arnold Schoenberg also treats the topic in *Fundamentals of Musical Composition* (London, Faber & Faber, 1967), Chapters 2 and 5–8; and *Style and Idea*, ed. Leonard Stein (Berkeley and Los Angeles: University of California Press, 1975). Rothstein's *Phrase Structure* discusses musical form in relation to phrase structure and hypermeter in Chapter 4, and Cone's *Musical Form* remains a seminal study of the topic in the context of musical performance.

19. *Phrase Structure*, 5. The italics are Rothstein's.

20. Rothstein's *Phrase Structure* is by far the most thorough and insightful study of phrase structure to date. Even though his work focuses on the more complex issue of hypermeter, the early Chapters 2–4 provide excellent definitions and clarifications of many points mentioned in our brief summary here. Other helpful discussions are Alfred Brendel, *Musical Thoughts and Afterthoughts* (Princeton: Princeton University Press, 1976); Lehrdahl and Jackendoff, *A Generative Theory*; Lowinsky, "On Mozart's Rhythm"; and Westergaard, *An Introduction to Tonal Theory*.

21. Rothstein offers phrase definitions in *Phrase Structure*, Chapter 2.

22. In *The Romantic Generation*, Charles Rosen applies the four-bar norm to most Romantic music and describes the challenge of this new shorter norm thus: "When the phrase lengths are uniform, the sense of monotony may be countered by varying the accent of the bar, and avoiding the relentless alternation of strong and weak bars. The interplay between phrase length and accent allows the composer to organize his structure with freedom" (263).

23. The poet's fears also are conveyed through the chromatic third relation C major/E major discussed in Chapter Six, in the section "Chromatic Third Relations."

24. Rothstein cites the antecedent-consequent phrase pair as only one of several different kinds of period phrase structures on 16–18.

25. In *Phrase Structure*, Chapter 3, Rothstein uses slightly different terms: "phrase expansion" for phrase extension, "internal" expansion for interpolation and "external" expansion ("prefixes" and "suffixes") for extensions occurring at phrase beginnings or endings.

26. In counting measures to determine phrase lengths, always ignore the measure of upbeat or anacrusis. In the Schumann work, therefore, the vocal pickup F♯–G♯ is not counted in the phrase length and m. 1 is, it seems, outside the first phrase.

27. Schumann uses this same introductory device often for a variety of poetic sensibilities, for example, "Widmung" and "Seit ich ihn gesehen."

28. The books on form by Wallace T. Berry, *Form in Music* and *Structural Functions*, and Douglass M. Green, *Form in Tonal Music*, discuss this issue in some detail.

29. The song thus demonstrates the characteristic effect of uneven phrase lengths: the lack of symmetry or balance creates tension and, in this case, poignancy reflective of the text.

30. The poetry of "Nachtviolen" was discussed in Chapter Six, in the section "Large-scale Tonal Design."

31. The issue of persona has been discussed throughout this book, beginning in Chapter Two.

32. See Chapter Seven, sections on "Linear Analysis" and "Motivic Analysis." Schoenberg discusses motive in *Fundamentals of Musical Composition*, Chapters 3, 4, and 9.

33. Rothstein, *Phrase Structure*, 30–31.

34. Indeed, the difficult fast-repeated octaves played incessantly by the pianist create an analogously exhausting physical struggle that symbolizes kinesthetically the experience of father and son.

35. Part of the pianist's dotted rhythms includes the P5 horn call which symbolizes departure, often, as here, the journey toward death. The horn call sets the text "warte nur, balde" ("wait, soon"). Similar horn or "Waldhorn" calls occur in Schubert's "Der Jüngling und der Tod," "Der Lindenbaum," and "Des Baches Wiegenlied," among others.

36. An important study of the suspension is Komar, *Theory of Suspensions.*

37. The terms syncopation and suspension are often considered rhythmic rather than metric in nature. In *The Rhythmic Structure of Music,* Cooper and Meyer offer a detailed discussion of the difficulties in defining both terms, but do state: "the difference between . . . a suspension and a syncopation lies in their placement in relation to metric pulses" (99). Lester also treats the topic in *Harmony,* Vol. I, 48, 56, 78–79, 91.

38. Interestingly, the syncopation occurs only in the bass, with the RH piano part continuing its eighth-note pattern and the vocal line presenting a normative 4/4 melodic gesture that emphasizes the downbeats in mm. 9–10.

39. In addition to Stein's study of musical ambiguity in *Hugo Wolf's Lieder,* other works cited earlier that explore rhythmic ambiguity include Berry, *Structural Functions* and *Musical Structure and Performance;* Komar, *Theory of Suspensions;* Lester, *The Rhythms of Tonal Music;* Rothstein, *Phrase Structure;* and Schoenberg, *Style and Idea* ("Brahms the Progressive," 398–441). Additional works that focus on general ambiguity in tonal music include Jonathan Dunsby, *Structural Ambiguity in Brahms* (Ann Arbor: UMI Research Press, 1981); David Epstein, *Beyond Orpheus: Studies in Musical Structure* (Cambridge: MIT Press, 1979), Chapters 4, 5, and 8; Andrew Imbrie, "'Extra Measures' and Metrical Ambiguity in Beethoven," *Beethoven Studies,* ed. Alan Tyson (New York: Norton, 1973) 44–66; and James Webster, *Haydn's "Farewell" Symphony and the Idea of Classical Style* (Cambridge: Cambridge University Press, 1991).

40. Deborah Stein, *Hugo Wolf's Lieder,* 156–68, presents a more detailed analysis of the ambiguities in this song.

Chapter Nine

1. The terms *closure* and *reprise* are defined in Chapter Six, in the section "Preliminary Terms and Concepts" and in Appendix II.

2. Strophic form was one of the earliest designs for *Lieder* and was used extensively by many of Schubert's predecessors. One of the most interesting cases involves two strophic settings of "Erlkönig": the well-known one by Loewe, which seems to some overly simplistic in comparison to Schubert's dramatic through-composed design, and a setting by his lesser-known predecessor Corona Schröter (1751–1802), who set the entire poem to one repeated eight-bar strophe, and who sang in the 1782 performance of Goethe's play, *Die Fischerin.* Goethe reportedly was pleased by these strophic settings, where the music was subservient to the text.

3. "Wiegenlied" was discussed in Chapter Six, in the section "Small-scale Structure," and "Litanei" was examined in detail in Chapter Seven.

4. In an unpublished study, David Lewin discusses, in remarkable detail, the song's various ambiguities, especially those in the realm of meter. Some of this analysis is indebted to his many insights.

5. Indeed, the first word of the text is "und" ("and").

6. Brahms also favors this form. The preference for the rounded ternary design in *Lieder*, with contrasting section (B) and reprise (A or A'), suggests that these composers chose their *Lied* form more on musical than on poetic grounds. We have already noted Schumann's penchant for altering poetry for musical reasons, and while Brahms did not take as much liberty as Schumann, his settings are focused less on poetic detail and more on formal design. As a result, both Schubert and Wolf are considered to be the two *Lied* composers who were the most faithful to the poetry they set.

7. This, of course, changes the poem's progression and overall meaning and Schumann has been criticized for his tendency toward poetic alterations in Jack Stein, *Poem and Music*, and Elaine Brody and Robert A. Fowkes, *The German Lied and Its Poetry*.

8. This scheme is used in the overwhelming majority of popular songs of the twentieth century, for example, those by George Gershwin, Cole Porter, Richard Rodgers, etc.

9. Brahms could have chosen this form for his "Vergebliches Ständchen," rather than the modified strophic form.

10. Some German editions even print this *Lied* with repeat signs: :AB:A.

11. Gustav Mahler uses the refrain in some of his *Lieder*, for example, "Oft denk' ich, sie sind nur ausgegangen!" from *Kindertotenlieder*.

12. Goethe did not approve of musicians rearranging his text, and would presumably have preferred a musical setting that would describe a continual building up of emotion, an effect one gets from reading the poem by itself. As already mentioned, he preferred the earlier, simpler settings by Zelter and Loewe to those of Schubert.

13. The contour of the vocal line recalls that of the opening: the words "und über mir rauscht die . . ." ("and over me will rustle the . . .") and the descending scalar figures for "schöne Waldeinsamkeit" ("beautiful loneliness of the woods") are exactly the same as vocal material from Section A.

14. The songs are united through motivic and harmonic connections as well.

15. Among many discussions of unity in song cycles, several are particularly notable. Studies of Schubert song cycles include Walter Everett, "Grief in Winterreise: A Schenkerian Perspective," *Music Analysis* 9 (1990): 157–75; Arnold Feil, *Franz Schubert: Die schöne Müllerin, Winterreise*, trans. Ann C. Sherwin (Portland, Ore.: Amadeus Press, 1988); Paul Robinson, *Opera and Ideas: From Mozart to Strauss* (New York: Harper & Row, 1985), 58–102; Susan Youens, "Poetic Rhythm and Musical Metre in Schubert's *Winterreise*," *Music and Letters* 65 (1984): 28–40; *Retracing a Winter's Journey: Schubert's Winterreise* (Ithaca, N.Y.: Cornell University Press, 1991); "Retracing a Winter Journey: Reflections on Schubert's *Winterreise*," *19th Century Music* 9 (1985): 128–35; "*Wegweiser* in *Winterreise*," *Journal of Musicology* 5 (1987): 357–79; "*Winterreise*: In the Right Order," *Soundings* 13 (1985): 41–50. Examinations of Schumann's cycles include V. Kofi Agawu, "Structural 'Highpoints' in Schumann's *Dichterliebe*," *Music Analysis* 3 (1984): 159–84; Arthur Komar, "The Music of *Dichterliebe*: The Whole and Its Parts," in *Schumann: "Dichterliebe"*, ed. Arthur Komar, (New York: Norton, 1971)

63–66; Patrick McCreless. "Song Order in the Song Cycle: Schumann's *Liederkreis*, Op. 39," *Music Analysis* 5 (1986): 8–11; David Neumeyer, "Organic Structure and the Song Cycle: Another Look at Schumann's *Dichterliebe*," *Music Theory Spectrum* 4 (1982): 92–105; and Barbara Turchin, "Robert Schumann's Song Cycles in the Context of the Nineteenth-Century 'Liederkreis'," (Ph.D. diss., Columbia University, 1981). Two other excellent studies are Christopher Lewis, "Text, Time, and the Tonic: Aspects of Patterning in the Romantic Cycle," *Integral* 2 (1988): 37–74, which treats song cycles of both Schubert and Schumann, and Gerald Moore, *Poet's Love: The Songs and Cycles of Schumann* (New York: Taplinger, 1981), which is a more descriptive than analytical resource for the performer.

16. These motive interconnections are discussed in Walter Everett, "Grief in *Winterreise*: A Schenkerian Perspective" mentioned in note 15.

17. This point is detailed in Patrick McCreless, "Song Order in the Song Cycle." In *The Romantic Generation*, Charles Rosen offers several insights into the song cycle. He distinguishes between a cycle and a circle of songs as follows: "where a *Liederkreis* is a set of related songs, often with a literary and musical structure that holds them together, a cycle is a monodrama, in which there is a single speaker and at least the skeletal suggestion of a narrative" (207–208). He further states: "The song cycle is the most original musical form created in the first half of the nineteenth century. It most clearly embodies the Romantic conception of experience as a gradual unfolding and illumination of reality in place of the Classical insistence on an initial clarity . . . Schubert's [*Die schöne Müllerin*] is not based on any symmetrical organization, and above all, it does not require any sense of a return. It is cumulative" (187).

Chapter Ten

1. Several translation books have information about multiple settings of a given poem, including *The Ring of Words*, Philip L. Miller, trans., and *The Fischer-Dieskau Book of Lieder*, George Bird and Richard Stokes, trans. This information includes multiple settings of a given poem by the *same* composer, Schubert having set seven poems numerous times over. An excellent source for information about texts set by Schubert is *Franz Schubert: Die Texte seiner einstimmig komponierten Lieder und ihre Dichter* (Hildesheim and New York: Georg Olms Verlag, 1974). Even though the text is in German, the changes in poetry are fairly clear to those with some knowledge of the German language.

2. The novel was written in 1795–1796.

3. With characteristic energy and determination, Schubert set each poem more than once; the two Harper I songs are D. 325 (1815) and D. 478 (1816). Zelter, Goethe's favorite composer, also set the poem in 1795.

4. An important pun here is the G♯ of A minor becoming A♭ of C major (♭$\hat{6}$ through mixture).

5. Schumann's *Lieder* alters Goethe's poem ordering by mixing the harp player's songs with those of Mignon and Philine, starting with the extravagant showpiece "Der Sänger" and ending with Mignon's vision of a peaceful heaven, "So laßt mich scheinen."

6. Schumann often begins songs on harmonies other than I. Examples include songs 1, 5, 9, and 12 from *Dichterliebe*, op. 48; "Der Nussbaum," "Lied der Braut II,"

"Hochländers Abschied," and "Aus den hebräischen Gesängen," from *Myrthen,* op. 25; "Mondnacht," "Auf einer Burg," and "Schöne Fremde," from *Liederkreis,* op. 39; "Süsser Freund" and "An meinem Herzen" from *Frauenliebe und -Leben.*

7. Irony was defined in Chapter Two, in the section "Poetic Representation," and "Ich grolle nicht" was discussed in Chapter Six, in the section "Tonality and Mode."

8. In most editions, the text of line 13 is incorrect; Schumann repeats "Mich ein-samen die Pein" rather than changing the last word to "Qual."

9. Both Schubert and Brahms changed the first word from "Wenn" to "Wann," the last word of the first line from "blickt" to "blinkt" and the last word in line 2 from "geusst" to "streut." Schubert included the missing verse. One of the many others who set this poem is Fanny Mendelssohn Hensel.

10. *Stimmung* is defined in the Chapter Two section "Poetic Progression and *Stimmung*"; the term refers to a prevailing mood or atmosphere.

11. Other women *Lied* composers of this period include Louise Reichardt (1779–1826), Josephine Lang (1815–1880), Fanny Mendelssohn Hensel (1805–1847), Pauline Viardot-Garcia (1821–1910) and, a bit later in the century, Alma Mahler (1879–1964). Nancy B. Reich has researched women composers in *Clara Schumann: The Artist and the Woman* (Ithaca, N.Y.: Cornell University Press, 1985) and "Louise Reichardt," in *Ars Musica, Musica Scientia: Festschrift Heinrich Hüschen,* ed. Detlef Altenburg (Cologne: Gitarre und Laute Verlagsgesellschaft, 1980). Examples of *Lieder* by these composers are offered in the *Historical Anthology of Music by Women,* ed. James R. Briscoe (Bloomington: Indiana University Press, 1989), which comes with cassette recordings and includes biographical, bibliographical, and discography information. Other recent studies include *Women and Music: A History,* ed. Karin Pendle (Bloomington and Indianapolis: Indiana University Press, 1991); Susan M. Filler, "A Composer's Wife as Composer: The Songs of Alma Mahler," *Journal of Musicological Research* 4 (1983): 427–41; and Edward Kravitt, "The *Lieder* of Alma Maria Schindler-Mahler," *Music Review* 49 (1988): 190–204.

12. Others in this category include Beethoven, Felix Mendelssohn, Liszt, and Wagner.

13. Reich reports that Clara's op. 12 is part of a collaboration with Robert, who uses op. 37 for the same group of Rückert settings, the complete identification being op. 37/12. Research has determined that songs 2, 4, and 11 were composed by Clara (see Reich in *Historical Anthology* and *Women and Music*). We use the "high voice" version of the Mahler to make the comparison with the "high voice" setting of Clara Schumann more cogent.

14. This is an example of implicit tonality which was explained in Chapter Six, in the section "Implicit Tonality."

15. This reflects a nineteenth-century exploitation of the technique that turned a tonic into V of IV and used that tonal tension to replace the more conventional polarities of the earlier part of the century. This has been explored by Deborah Stein in *Hugo Wolf's Lieder* and "The Expansion of the Subdominant in the Late Nineteenth Century," *Journal of Music Theory* 27/2 (1983): 153–180.

16. As suggested in notes 9 and 11, much recent research has been done to bring attention to the music of women composers, including anthologies and biographies about women. In addition, feminist studies about women and music include Catherine Clément, *Opera, or the Undoing of Women,* Betsy Wing, trans. (Minneapolis: University of Minnesota Press, 1988) and Susan McClary, *Feminine Endings* (Min-

neapolis: University of Minesota Press, 1991), both of which have extensive notes and bibliographic information. Readers unfamiliar with feminism might begin with the provocative and controversial Carol Gilligan, *In a Different Voice: Psychological Theory and Women's Development* (Cambridge: Harvard University Press, 1982) and any of the numerous collections of essays such as the relatively early *The New Feminist Criticism: Essays on Women, Literature and Theory*, ed. Elaine Showalter, (New York: Pantheon Books, 1985) and the more recent *The Feminist Reader: Essays in Gender and the Politics of Literary Criticism*, eds. Catherine Belsey and Jane Moore (Oxford: Blackwell Publishers, 1989). Both of these books have lengthy bibliographies.

17. In the realm of French *mélodie*, the poems of Verlaine received successful treatment from Fauré, Debussy, and Hahn, in turn; in English song, the poems of Shakespeare have attracted the attention of numerous composers, all trying to express in unique musical vocabularies their understanding of the bard's verse.

18. Other Mignon songs set by several composers include: "So laß mich scheinen" and "Heiß mich nicht reden."

19. The other "*Harfenspieler*" songs also set by Beethoven, Schubert (several times), Schumann, and Wolf were "An die Türen will ich schleichen" and "Wer nie sein Brot mit Tränen aß."

Text Translations

Study of German *Lieder* is predicated upon a clear understanding of the poetic text. Performers need to be careful in choosing a text translation and must be wary of text translation underlays on musical scores. These are more likely to be poems in English that parallel the *general* meaning of the German text rather than to serve as faithful translations. Three books of translations that are extremely reliable are:

> Philip L. Miller, *The Ring of Words: An Anthology of Song Texts* (New York: W. W. Norton & Co., 1973)
>
> George Bird and Richard Stokes, *The Fischer-Dieskau Book of Lieder: The Original Texts of Over 750 Songs* (New York: Limelight Editions, 1984)
>
> Richard Wigmore, *Schubert: The Complete Song Texts* (New York: Schirmer Books, 1988)

This appendix offers translations for all songs discussed in the text; most translations are derived from the above sources and modified by the authors to be most suitable for our needs. The translations are *literal*, that is, they maintain the syntax of the German. This is to assist performers in knowing the precise meaning of each German word, rather than just understanding the gist of the poetic phrase.

Literal translations create awkward English. The German language often reverses word order from that in English and uses many words, especially verbs, that are separable. An example of word order reversal occurs in the German phrase "Betend Daß Gott dich behalte"; a feasible English translation is: "Praying that God preserve you," while the literal is: "Praying that God you preserve." Because the singer needs to know that "behalte" means "preserve" and not "you," we use the literal translation. We are a bit less precise with separable verbs, where only one part is translated or the two parts are translated in one place. Two examples demonstrate. First, the German for "contain" is "einschießen", which can occur in two separate parts: "Die beiden Wörtchen schließen/Die ganze Welt mir ein." Second, we translate a separable verb such as "anfangen" in the phrase as "fange wieder an" with one English verb: "begin," rather than repeating it after the adverb "weider": "begin again begin." Occasionally, the syntax of German poetry places the object of a verb before the verb, then the verb, and then the subject. Thus, "Jeden Nachklang fühlt mein Herz" is translated word for word: "Every echo feels my heart," where the actual meaning is: "My heart feels every echo."

Despite all the twisted syntax created by literal translations, readers unfamiliar with or having only slight knowledge of German can easily understand the actual word meanings as they appear in the German verse, a more important goal than creating more fluid and poetic translations readily available in the previously cited books.

We also remind readers to seek in these translations other elements of German verse. As Chapters One and Two have shown, the German Romantic poetry set by the great *Lied* composers incorporated myriad themes, images, symbols, and metaphors in their verse and included special devices in poetic meter, rhyming, and word color to create pictures, feelings, sensations, and moods *(Stimmung)*. Understanding the meaning of these verses requires careful study of both the form and the content of the poetry, a study the composers did before they made their remarkable settings. Attention must be paid not only to the actual words and images, but also to the uses of irony, dichotomy, and ambiguity to convey the poet's deepest, most complex feelings. Finally, each poem presents a poetic progression, and each projects the voice of one or more personas spoken to one or more listener(s), either rhetorical or real.

List of Text Translations

"Abends" (Eichendorff)
"Ablösung im Sommer" *(Des Knaben Wunderhorn)*
"Allerseelen" (von Gilm)
"Alte Laute" (Kerner)
"An den Mond" (Goethe)
"An den Schlaf" (Mörike)
"An die Musik" (Schober)
"An eine Äolsharfe" (Mörike)
"Auf dem Wasser zu singen" (Stolberg)
"Auf ein altes Bild" (Mörike)
"Aus meinen großen Schmerzen" (Heine)
"Ave Maria" (Walter Scott; "Ellen's Gesang III")
"Beherzigung" (Goethe)
"Blumengruß" (Goethe)
"Das verlassene Mägdlein" (Mörike)
"Der Jüngling und der Tod" (von Spaun)
"Der König bei der Krönung" (Mörike)
"Der Kreuzzug" (von Leitner)
"Der Musensohn" (Goethe)

"Der Sänger" (Goethe)
"Der Tod, das ist die kühle Nacht" (Heine)
"Der Tod und das Mädchen" (Claudius)
"Der Wanderer" (F. Schlegel)
Dichterliebe (Heine)
    "Im wunderschönen Monat Mai"
    "Aus meinem Tränen sprießen"
    "Die Rose, die Lilie"
    "Wenn ich in deine Augen seh'"
    "Im Rhein, im heiligen Strome"
    "Ich grolle nicht"
    "Ich hab' im Traum geweinet"
"Die Forelle" (Schubart)
"Die Lotosblume" (Heine)
"Die Mainacht" (Hölty)
Die schöne Müllerin (Müller)
    "Wohin?"
    "Am Feierabend"
    "Der Neugierige"
    "Morgengruß"
    "Mein"
    "Die Liebe Farbe"
    "Der Müller und der Bach"
Die Winterreise (Müller)
    "Gute Nacht"
    "Der Lindenbaum"
    "Wasserflut"
    "Auf dem Flusse"
    "Der Leiermann"
"Du bist die Ruh" (Rückert)
"Du bist wie eine Blume" (Heine)
"Einsamkeit" (Goethe)
"Er ist's" (Mörike)
"Erlkönig" (Goethe)
"Erster Verlust" (Goethe)
Frauenliebe und -Leben (von Chamisso)
    "Seit ich ihn gesehen"
"Ganymed" (Goethe)
"Gesang Weylas"(Mörike)
Gesänge des Harfners (Goethe)
    "Wer sich der Einsamkeit ergibt"
"Gretchen am Spinnrade" (Goethe)
"Heimweh" (Eichendorff)

"Ich atmet' einen linden Duft" (Rückert)
"Im Frühling" (Schulze)
"Immer leiser wird mein Schlummer" (Lingg)
"Iphigenia" (Mayrhofer)
Italienischesliederbuch (Paul Heyse, after Leopardi, Giusti, Carducci and
              Ada Negri)
   "Auch kleine Dinge"
   "Mir ward gesagt"
   "Wir haben beide"
   "Mein Liebster singt"
   "Und steht Ihr früh"
   "Ich hab' in Penna"
"Klage an den Mond" (Hölty)
"Kurze Fahrt" (Eichendorff)
"Lebe wohl" (Mörike)
"Leiden der Trennung" (von Collin)
"Leise zieht durch mein Gemüt" (Heine)
"Liebst du um Schönheit" (Rückert)
"Lied eines Schiffers" (Mayrhofer)
Liederkreis, Op. 39 (Eichendorff)
   "In der Fremde"
   "Waldesgespräch"
   "Mondnacht"
   "Schöne Fremde"
   "Auf einer Burg"
Liederkreis, Op. 24 (Heine)
   "Schöne Wiege meiner Leiden"
"Litanei" (Jacobi)
"Meeres Stille" (Goethe)
"Mondenschein" (Heine)
"Morgen!" (Mackay)
"Nachtstück" (Mayrhofer)
"Nachtviolen" (Mayrhofer)
"Nachtzauber" (Eichendorff)
"Nähe des Geliebten" (Goethe)
"O wüßt ich doch den Weg zurück" (Groth)
"Schäfers Klagelied" (Goethe)
Spanischesliederbuch (Spanish folk songs, translated by Emanuel Geibel
              and Paul Heyse)
   Weltlich Leider No. 2
      "In dem Schatten meiner Locken"
"Ständchen" (Kugler)
"Ständchen" (von Schack)
"Trost in Tränen" (Goethe)

"Verborgenheit" (Mörike)
"Vergebliches Ständchen" (Lower Rhine Folksong)
"Verklärung" (Pope)
"Verschwiegene Liebe" (Eichendorff)
"Wanderers Nachtlied I" (Goethe)
"Wanderers Nachtlied II" (Goethe)
"Widmung" (Rückert)
"Wie Melodien zieht es mir" (Groth)
"Wiegenlied" (Claudius ?)
"Wiegenlied" (Dehmel)
"Wiegenlied" *(Des Knaben Wunderhorn)*

"Abends" (Eichendorff)

Abendlich schon rauscht der
    Wald
Aus den tiefsten Gründen,
Droben wird der Herr nun bald,
Bald die Stern' anzünden;
Wie so stille in den Gründen
Abendlich nur rauscht der
    Wald.

Alles geht zu seiner Ruh,
Wald und Welt versausen,
Schauernd hört der Wandrer zu,
Sehnt sich wohl nach Hause,
Hier in Waldes grüner Klause,
Herz, geh endlich auch zur Ruh.

"At Eventide"[1]

At eventide, already murmurs the
    forest
From the deepest valleys;
On high will God now soon
Soon the stars kindle;
How softly in the valleys
At eventide only murmurs the
    forest.

All goes to its rest,
Forest and world cease to stir;
In awe, listens the wanderer,
Yearns for home,
Here, in the forest's green cell,
Heart, go finally also to rest.

"Ablösung im Sommer"
(Des Knaben Wunderhorn)

Kuckuck hat sich zu Tod
    gefallen
An einer hohlen Weiden,
Wer soll uns diesen Sommer lang
Die Zeit und Weil vertreiben?
Ei, das soll tun Frau Nachtigall,
Die sitzt auf grunem Zweige;
Sie singt und springt, is allzeit
    froh,
Wenn andre Vögel schweigen.

"Summer Relief"[2]

Cuckoo has himself to death
    fallen
At a hollow willow tree,
Who shall for us this summer long
The time and (time) to pass?
Oh, that shall do lady nightingale,
Who sits on a green bough;
She sings and springs, is ever
    happy,
When other birds are silent.

"Allerseelen" (von Gilm)

Stell auf den Tisch die duftenden
    Reseden
Die letzten roten Astern trag
    herbei.
Und laß uns wieder von der Liebe
    reden,
Wie einst im Mai.

Gib mir die Hand, daß ich
    sie heimlich drücke
Und wenn man's sieht,
    mir ist es einerlei,
Gib mir nur einen deiner
    süßen Blicke,
Wie einst im Mai.

Es blüht und duftet heut'
    auf jedem Grabe,
Ein Tag im Jahr ist ja
    den Toten frei,
Komm' an mein Herz, daß ich
    dich wieder habe,
Wie einst im Mai.

"Alte Laute" (Kerner)

Hörst du den Vogel singen?
Siehst du den Blütenbaum?
Herz! kann dich das nicht bringen
Aus deinem bangen Traum?

Was hör' ich? Alte Laute
Wehmüt'ger Jünglingsbrust,
Der Zeit, als ich vertraute
Der Welt und ihrer Lust.

Die Tage sind vergangen,
Mich heilt kein Kraut der Flur;
Und aus dem Traum,
    dem bangen,
Weckt mich ein Engel nur.

"An den Mond" (Goethe)
(Five of nine stanzas)

Füllest wieder Busch und Tal

"All Souls"[3]

Place on the table the fragrant
    mignonettes,
The last red asters carry
    here.
And let us again of love
    talk,
As once in May.

Give me your hand, so that I
    it may secretly press
And if someone it sees,
    to me it is all the same,
Give me just one of your
    sweet glances,
As once in May.

Blooms and perfumes today
    upon each grave,
One day in the year is even for
    the dead free,
Come to my heart, so that I you
    can again have,
As once in May.

"Old Sounds"[4]

Hear you the bird singing?
See you the blossoming tree?
Heart! can you that not bring
Out of your fearful dream?

What hear I? Old sounds
Of a melancholy youth's breast,
Of the time when I trusted
The world and its delight.

The days are past,
Me heals no herb of the meadow;
And out of the dream,
    the fearful one,
Wakes me an angel alone.

"To the Moon"[5]

You fill again wood and vale

Still mit Nebelglanz,
Lösest endlich auch einmal
Meine Seele ganz;

Breitest über mein Gefild
Lindernd deinen Blick,
Wie des Freundes Auge mild
Über mein Geschick.

Jeden Nachklang fühlt mein
 Herz,
Froh' und trüber Zeit,
Wandle zwischen Freud und
 Schmerz
In der Einsamkeit.

Fließe, fließe, lieber Fluß!
Nimmer werd' ich froh;
So verrauschte Scherz und Kuß,
Und die Treue so.

Selig, wer sich vor der
 Welt
Ohne Haß verschließt,
Einen Freund am Busen hält
Und mit dem genießt,

Was von Menschen nicht gewußt
Oder nicht gedacht,
Durch das Labyrinth der
 Brust
Wandelt in der Nacht.

"An den Schlaf" (Mörike)

Schlaf! süßer Schlaf
 obwohl dem Tod wie du nichts
 gleicht,
Auf diesem Lager doch
 willkommen heiß ich dich!
Denn ohne Leben so,
 wie lieblich lebt es sich!
So weit vom Sterben, ach,
 wie stirbt es sich so leicht!

Silently with gleam of mist,
Set free at last
My soul entirely;

You spread over my domain
Soothingly your gaze,
As a friend's eye gently
Upon my fate.

Every echo feels my
 heart,
Of happy and sad time(s),
(I) alternate between joy and
 pain
In the solitude.

Flow, flow, dear stream!
Never will I be happy;
So flowed away joke and kiss,
And faithfulness so.

Happy he who (himself) from the
 world
Without hate cuts off,
A friend to his breast holds
And with him enjoys,

What by men is not known
Or not thought of,
Through the labryinth of the
 heart
Wanders in the night.

"To Sleep"[6]

Sleep, sweet sleep,
 though to death like you
 nothing compares,
Upon this couch still
 declare welcome I you!
For without life thus,
 how sweet living it (is)!
So far from dying, oh,
 how dying is so easy!

"An die Musik" (Schober)

Du holde Kunst, in wieviel
    grauen Stunden,
Wo mich des Lebens wilder Kreis
    umstrickt
Hast du mein Herz zu warmer
    Lieb entzunden,
Hast mich in eine beß're Welt
    entrückt!

Oft hat ein Seufzer, deiner Harf
    entflossen,
Ein süßer, heiliger Akkord von
    dir
Den Himmel beß'rer Zeiten mir
    erschlossen,
Du holde Kunst, ich danke dir
    dafür!

"An eine Äolsharfe" (Mörike)
(First stanza only)

Angelehnt an die Efeuwand
Dieser alten Terrasse,
Du, einer luftgebornen Muse
Geheimnisvolles Saitenspiel,
Fang' an,
Fange wieder an
Deine melodische Klage!

"Auf dem Wasser zu singen"
(Stolberg)

Mitten im Schimmer der
    spiegelnden Wellen
Gleitet, wie Schwäne, der
    wankende Kahn;
Ach, auf der Freude sanft-
    schimmernden Wellen
Gleitet die Seele dahin wie der
    Kahn;
Denn von dem Himmel herab auf
    die Wellen
Tanzet das Abendrot rund
    um den Kahn.

"To Music"[7]

You lovely Art, in how many
    grey hours,
When I by life's unruly round am
    caught,
Have you my heart with ardent
    love fired,
Have me to a better world
    borne!

Often has a sigh, from your harp
    escaped,
A sweeter, holier chord from
    you
A heaven of better times to me
    opened,
You kindly Art, I thank you for
    for that!

"To an Aeolian Harp"[8]

Reclining against the ivy wall
Of this ancient terrace,
You, a zephyr-born muse
Mysterious string music,
Begin,
Begin again
Your melodious plaint!

"To be Sung on the Water"[9]

Amid the shimmer of the
    mirroring waves
Glides, like swans, the
    rocking boat;
Ah, upon (of the) joy gently
    shimmering waves
Glides the soul on as the
    boat;
For from the heaven onto
    the waves
Dances the setting sun
    around the boat.

Über den Wipfeln des westlichen
Haines
Winket uns freundlich der rötliche
Schein;
Unter den Zweigen des östlichen
Haines
Säuselt der Kalmus im rötlichen
Schein;
Freude des Himmels und Ruhe
des Haines
Atmet die Seele im
errötenden Schein.

Ach, es entschwindet mit tauigem
Flügel
Mir auf den wiegenden Wellen
die Zeit.
Morgen entschwindet mit
schimmerndem Flügel
Wieder wie gestern und heute die
Zeit,
Bis ich auf höherem, strahlendem
Flügel
Selber entschwinde der
wechselnden Zeit.

"Auf ein altes Bild" (Mörike)

In grüner Landschaft
Sommerflor,
Bei kühlem wasser, Schilf und
Rohr,
Schau, wie das Knäblein sündelos
Frei spielet auf der Jungfrau
Schoß!
Und dort in Walde wonnesam,
Ach, grünet schon des Kreuzes
Stamm!

"Aus meinen großen Schmerzen"
(Heine)

Aus meinen großen Schmerzen
Mach' ich die kleinen Lieder;

Over the treetops of the western
grove
Beckons us kindly the red
glow;
Under the branches of the eastern
grove
Rustles the sweet grass in the red
glow;
Joy of heaven and peace of
the grove
Breathes the soul in the
reddening glow.

Ah, vanishes with dewy
wing
From me on the cradling waves
the time.
Tomorrow may vanish with
shiny wings
Again as yesterday and today the
time,
Until I on loftier, radiant
wings
Myself escape the
changing time.

"Inspired by an Old Picture"[10]

In a green landscape's
summer flowers,
By cool water, reeds and
rushes,
See, how the little Boy innocent
Freely plays on the Maiden's
lap!
And there in the wood blissfully,
Ah, turns green already the cross's
timber!

"From my great Sorrows"[11]

From my great sorrows
Make I the small songs;

Die heben ihr klingend Gefieder	They raise their resonant plumage
Und flattern nach ihrem Herzen.	And flutter to her heart.

Sie fanden den Weg zur Trauten,	They found the way to my beloved.
Doch kommen sie wieder und klagen,	Yet come they again and complain,
Und klagen, und wollen nicht sagen,	And complain, and will not say,
Was sie im Herzen schauten.	What they in her heart have seen.

"Ave Maria"
("Ellen's Gesang III"; Walter Scott)

"Ave Maria"
("Ellen's Song No. 3")[12]

Ave Maria! Jungfrau mild,	Ave Maria! Maiden mild,
Erhöre einer Jungfrau Flehen,	Listen to a maiden's plea;
Aus diesem Felsen starr und wild	From this rock unyielding and wild
Soll mein Gebet zu dir hin wehen.	Shall my prayer to you there rise.

Wir schlafen sicher bis zum Morgen,	We sleep safe until morning,
Ob Menschen noch so grausam sind.	However men still so cruel are.
O Jungfrau, sieh der Jungfrau Sorgen,	O Maiden, behold a maiden's cares,
O Mutter, hör ein bittend Kind!	O Mother, hear a pleading child!

Ave Maria unbefleckt!	Ave Maria undefiled!
Wenn wir auf diesen Fels hinsinken	When we upon this rock sink down
Zum Schlaf, und uns dein Schutz bedeckt,	To sleep, and us your care covers,
Wird weich der harte Fels uns dünken.	Shall soft the hard rock to us seem.

Du lächelst, Rosendüfte wehen	You smile, rosy fragrance wafts
In dieser dumpfen Felsenkluft.	Through this dark cave.
O Mutter, höre Kindes Flehen,	O Mother, hear a child's entreaty,
O Jungfrau, eine Jungfrau ruft!	O Maiden, a maiden cries!

Ave Maria! Reine Magd!	Ave Maria! pure maiden!
Der Erde und der Luft Dämonen,	Of the earth and the air devils,
Von deines Auges Huld verjagt,	By your eye's grace banished,
Sie können hier nicht bei uns wohnen.	They cannot here with us dwell.

Wir woll'n uns still dem Schicksal
   beugen,
Da uns dein heil'ger Trost anweht;
Der Jungfrau wolle hold dich
   neigen,
Dem Kind, das für den Vater
   fleht!
Ave Maria!

We will quietly to fate
   submit,
Since on us your holy comfort wafts;
To the virgin will graciously you
   incline,
To the child, who for its father
   prays!
Ave Maria!

"Beherzigung" (Goethe)

"Encouragement"[13]

Feiger Gedanken
Bängliches Schwanken,
Weibisches Zagen,
Ängstliches Klagen
Wendet kein Elend,
Macht dich nicht frei.

Cowardly thoughts'
Fearful wavering,
Womanish hesitancy
Anxious complaining
Turns away no misery,
Makes you not free.

Allen Gewalten
Zum Trutz sich erhalten;
Nimmer sich beugen,
Kräftig sich zeigen,
Rufet die Arme
Der Gotter herbei.

(Against) all forces
To defiance maintain,
Never yielding,
Strong one's self to show,
(This) calls the arms
Of the gods to one's side.

"Blumengruß" (Goethe)

"Flower Greeting"[14]

Der Strauß, den ich gepflücket,
Grüße dich
   vieltausendmal!
Ich habe mich oft gebücket,
Ach, wohl eintausendmal,
Und ihn ans Herz gedrücket
Wie hunderttausendmal!

(May) the bouquet I have plucked,
Greet you
   many thousands of times!
I have often bent,
Ah, at least a thousand times,
And it to my heart pressed
Like a hundred thousand times!

"Das verlassene Mägdlein"
(Mörike)

"The Forsaken Maiden"[15]

Früh, wann die Hähne krähn,
Eh die Sternlein schwinden,
Muß ich am Herde stehn,
Muß Feuer zünden.

Early, when the cocks are crowing,
Before the stars disappear,
Must I at the hearth stand,
Must the fire kindle.

Schön ist der Flammen Schein,
Es springen die Funken;

Beautiful is the fire's glow,
Fly the sparks;

Ich schaue so drein,
In Leid versunken.

Plötzlich, da kommt es mir,
Treuloser Knabe,
Daß ich die Nacht von dir
Geträumet habe.

Träne auf Träne dann
Stürzet hernieder;
So kommt der Tag heran—
O ging er wieder!

I look thus into,
In sorrow sunk.

Suddenly, then comes it to me,
Faithless boy,
That I all night of you
Dreamt.

Tear after tear then
Flows down;
So starts the day—
Oh, would it go away again!

"Der Jüngling und der Tod"
(Spaun)

"The Young Man and Death"[16]

Der Jüngling:
Die Sonne sinkt, o könnt ich mit
    ihr scheiden,
Mit ihrem letzten Strahl
    entfliehen!
Ach diese namenlosen Qualen
    meiden
Und weit in schön're Welten
    ziehn!

O komme, Tod, und löse diese
    Bande!
Ich lächle dir, o Knochenmann,
Entführe mich leicht in geträumte
    Lande!
O komm und rühre mich doch an!
Der Tod:
Es ruht sich kühl und sanft in
    meinen Armen,
Du rufst, ich will mich deiner Qual
    erbarmen.

The Youth:
The sun sinks, ah, might I with
    it depart,
With its last ray
    to flee!
Ah these nameless torments
    to avoid
And far to finer worlds
    travel!

O come, death, and loose these
    bonds!
I smile upon you, o skeleton,
Lead me gently to dream-filled
    lands!
O come and touch me!
Death:
One rests cool and gentle in
    my arms;
You call, I will on your suffering
    take pity.

"Der König bei der Krönung"
(Mörike)

"The King at His Coronation"[17]

Dir angetrauet am Altare,
O Vaterland, wie bin ich dein!
Laß für das Rechte mich und
    Wahre
Nun Priester oder Opfer sein!

To you wedded at the altar,
O Fatherland, how am I yours!
Let for the right myself and
    truth
Now priest or offering be!

Geuß auf mein Haupt, Herr!
  deine Schale,
Ein köstlich Öl des Friedens, aus,
Daß ich wie eine Sonne strahle
Dem Vaterland und meinem Haus!

Pour upon my head, o Lord!
  your cup,
A precious oil of peace, (out,)
(So) that I like a sun may shine
On the Fatherland and my home!

"Der Kreuzzug" (von Leitner)

"The Crusade"[18]

Ein Münich steht in seiner Zell
Am Fenstergitter grau,
Viel Rittersleut in Waffen hell
Die reiten durch die Au.

A monk stands in his cell
At they grey window grating,
Many knights in armour shining
Come riding through the pasture.

Sie singen Lieder frommer Art
In schönem ernstem Chor,
Inmitten fliegt, von Seide
  zart,
Die Kreuzesfahn empor.

They sing songs of holiness
In fine solemn chorus,
In their midst flies, of silk
  delicate,
The banner of the Cross aloft.

Sie steigen an dem Seegestad
Das hohe Schiff hinan,
Es läuft hinweg auf grünem Pfad,
Ist bald nur wie ein Schwan.

They climb at the shore
The tall ship aboard,
It sails away over the green path,
Is soon but as a swan.

Der Münich steht am Fenster noch,
Schaut ihnen nach hinaus:
"Ich bin, wie ihr, ein Pilger doch,
Und bleib ich gleich zu Haus.

The monk stands at the window still,
Gazing out after them:
"I am, like you, a pilgrim after all,
And remain I even so at home.

"Des Lebens Fahrt durch
  Wellentrug
Und heissen Wüstensand,
Es ist ja auch ein Kreuzeszug
In das gelobte Land."

"Of life's journey through
  treacherous waves
And burning desert sands,
It is indeed also a crusade
Into the Promised Land."

"Der Musensohn" (Goethe)

"Son of the Muses"[19]

Durch Feld und Wald zu schweifen,
Mein Liedchen weg zu pfeifen,
So geht's von Ort zu Ort!
Und nach dem Takte reget
Und nach dem Maß beweget
Sich alles an mir fort.

Through field and forest to roam
My little song to whistle,
So goes it from place to place!
And in time stirs,
And in rhythm moves
(Itself) all with me.

Ich kann sie kaum erwarten,
Die erste Blum' im
  Garten,

I can for it hardly wait,
The first bloom in the
  garden,

Die erste Blüt' am Baum.
Sie grüßen meine Leider,
Und kommt der Winter wieder,
Sing' ich noch jenen Traum.

The first flower on the tree.
They greet my songs,
And comes winter again,
Sing I still that dream.

Ich sing ihn in der Weite,
Auf Eises Läng' und Breite,
Da blüht der Winter
    schön!
Auch diese Blüte schwindet,
Und neue Freude findet
Sich auf bebauten Höh'n.

I sing it in the distance,
On ice's length and breadth,
Then blooms the winter
    beautifully!
Also this bloom vanishes,
And new joy finds
Itself on wooded hills.

Denn wie ich bei der Linde
Das junge Völkchen finde,
Sogleich erreg' ich sie.
Der stumpfe Bursche bläht sich,
Das steife Mädchen dreht sich
Nach meiner Melodie.

Then, as I by the lindentree
The young people find,
Immediately excite I them.
The dull boy swells up,
The stiff girl turns
To my melody.

Ihr gebt den Sohlen Flügel
Und treibt durch Tal und Hügel
Den Liebling weit vom Haus.
Ihr lieben, holden Musen,
Wann fuh' ich ihr am Busen
Auch endlich wieder aus?

You give to my feet wings
And drive through valley and hill
The beloved far from home.
You dear, great Muses,
When rest I upon your bosom
Also finally again?

"Der Sänger" (Goethe)
(First stanza only)

"The Minstrel"[20]

"Was hör ich draußen vor dem Tor,
Was auf der Brücke schallen?
Laß den Gesang vor unserm Ohr
Im Saale wiederhallen!"
Der König sprach's, der Page lief;
Der Knabe kam, der König rief:
"Laßt mir herein den
    Alten!"

"What hear I outside the gate,
What on the bridge sounds?
Let that song for our ears
In the hall echo!"
So the king said it, the page ran;
The page returned, the king cried:
"Let be to me admitted the
    old man!"

"Der Tod, das ist die kühle Nacht"
(Heine)

"Death That Is the Cool Night"[21]

Der Tod, das ist die kühle Nacht,
Das Leben ist der schwüle Tag.

Death, that is the cool night,
Life is the sultry day.

Es dunkelt schon, mich schläfert,
Der Tag hat mich müd' gemacht.

Über mein Bett erhebt sich ein
    Baum,
D'rin singt die junge
    Nachtigall;
Sie singt von lauter Liebe,
Ich hör es, ich hör es sogar im
    Traum.

Falls dusk already, I am drowsy,
The day has me tired made.

Over my bed rises a
    tree,
In it sings the young
    nightingale;
She sings solely of love,
I hear it, even in
    dreams.

"Der Tod und das Mädchen"
(Claudius)

"Death and the Maiden"[22]

Das Mädchen:
Vorüber, ach, vorüber!
Geh, wilder Knochenmann!
Ich bin noch jung, geh', Lieber!
Und rühre mich nicht an.

Maiden:
Go by, oh, go bye!
Go harsh skeleton!
I am still young, Go, dear one!
And touch me not.

Der Tod:
Gib deine Hand, du schön und
    zart Gebild!
Bin Freund und komme nicht zu
    strafen.
Sei guten Muts! Ich bin nicht wild,
Sollst sanft in meinen Armen
    schlafen!

Death:
Give your hand, you fair and
    gentle thing!
(I) am a friend and come not to
    punish.
Be of good cheer, I am not harsh,
You shall gently in my arms
    sleep!

"Der Wanderer"
(Friedrich Schlegel)

"The Wanderer"[23]

Wie deutlich des Mondes Licht
Zu mir spricht,
Mich beseelend zu der Reise:
"Folge treu dem alten Gleise,
Wähle keine Heimat nicht.
Ew'ge Plage
Bringen sonst die schweren Tage.
Fort zu andern
Sollst du wechseln, sollst du
    wandern
Leicht entfliehend jeder Klage."

How clearly the moon's light
To me speaks,
Me inspiring on my journey:
"Follow faithfully the old track,
Choose no home at all.
Eternal torment
Bring otherwise bad times.
Forth to others
Will you turn, will you
    move on
Lightly casting off all grief."

Dichterliebe, excerpts (Heine)
No. 1

Poet's Love [24]

Im wunderschönen Monat Mai
Als alle Knospen sprangen,
Da ist in meinem Herzen
Die Liebe aufgegangen.

In the wondrous month of May,
When all buds were bursting open,
Then was my heart
With love filled.

Im wunderschönen Monat Mai,
Als alle Vögel sangen,
Da hab' ich ihr gestanden
Mein Sehnen und Verlangen.

In the wondrous month of May,
When all birds were singing,
Then have I to her confessed
My longing and desire.

No. 2

Aus meinen Tränen sprießen
Viel blühende Blumen hervor,
Und meine Seufzer werden
Ein Nachtigallenchor.

From my tears burst
Many full-blown flowers forth,
And my sighs become
A nightingale chorus.

Und wenn du mich lieb hast,
Kindchen,
Schenk' ich dir die Blumen all',
Und vor deinem Fenster soll
klingen
Das Lied der Nachtigall.

And if you love me,
child,
Give I you the flowers all,
And at your window shall
sound
The song of the nightingale.

No. 3

Die Rose, Die Lilie, die Taube, die
Sonne,
Die liebt' ich einst alle in
Liebeswonne.
Ich lieb' sie nicht mehr, ich liebe
alleine
Die Kleine, die Feine,
Die Reine, die Eine;
Sie selber, aller Liebe Wonne.
Ist Rose und Lilie und Taube und
Sonne.
Ich liebe alleine
Die Kleine, Die Feine, Die Reine,
die Eine.

The rose, the lily, the dove, the
sun,
These loved I once all in love's
delight.
I love them no more, I love
alone
The small one, the fine one,
The pure one, the only one;
She alone, of all love delight,
Is rose and lily and dove and
sun.
I love alone
The small one, the fine one, the
pure one, the only one.

No. 4

Wenn ich in deine Augen seh',
So schwindet all' mein Leid und
Weh;

When I into your eyes look,
So flies all my pain and sorrow;

Doch wenn ich küsse deinen
Mund,
So werd' ich ganz und gar gesund.

But when I kiss your
mouth,
Then I am wholly healed.

Wenn ich mich lehn' an deine
Brust,
Kommt's über mich wie
Himmelslust;
Doch wenn du sprichst: ich liebe
dich!
So muß ich weinen bitterlich.

When I recline upon your
breast,
Comes it over me like
heavenly bliss;
But when you say: I love
you!
Then must I weep bitterly.

No. 6

Im Rhein, im heiligen Strome,
Da spiegelt sich in den Well'n
Mit seinem großen Dome,
Das große, heilige Köln.

In the Rhine, in the holy river,
There mirrors itself in the waves,
With its great cathedral,
The great, holy Cologne.

Im Dom da steht ein Bildnis,

Auf goldenem Leder gemalt;
In meines Lebens Wildnis
Hat's freundlich hineingestrahlt.

In the cathedral there stands a
picture,
On gilded leather painted;
Into my life's wilderness
Has it cheerfully cast rays.

Es schweben Blumen und Eng'lein
Um unsre liebe Frau;
Die Augen, die Lippen, die
Wänglein,
Die gleichen der Liebsten genau.

Float flowers and angels
About our dear Lady;
The eyes, the lips, the little
cheeks,
They resemble my love exactly.

No. 7

Ich grolle nicht, und wenn das
Herz auch bricht.
Ewig verlor'nes Lieb! Ich grolle
nicht.
Wie du auch strahlst in
Diamantenpracht,
Es fällt kein Strahl in deines
Herzens Nacht,
Das weiß ich längst.

I complain not, even if my
heart also breaks.
Eternally lost love! I complain
not.
Even as you shine in diamond
splendor,
Falls no ray into your
heart's night,
That have I known long.

Ich grolle nicht, und wenn das
Herz auch bricht.
Ich sah dich ja im Traume,
Und sah die Nacht in deines
Herzens Raume,

I complain not, even if my
heart also breaks.
I saw you indeed in a dream,
And saw the night in your
heart's space,

Und sah die Schlang', die dir am Herzen frißt,	And saw the snake, which at your heart eats,
Ich sah, mein Lieb, wie sehr du elend bist.	I saw, my love, how very you sick are.
Ich grolle nicht.	I complain not.

No. 13

Ich hab' im Traum geweinet,	I in a dream wept,
Mir träumt', du lägest im Grab.	I dreamt you lay in the grave.
Ich wachte auf, und die Träne	I awoke, and the tear
Floß noch von der Wange herab.	Flowed still down my cheek.
Ich hab' im Traum geweinet,	I in a dream wept,
Mir träumt', du verließest mich.	I dreamt, you left me.
Ich wachte auf, und ich weinte	I awoke, and I wept
Noch lange bitterlich.	Long after bitterly.
Ich hab' im Traum geweinet,	I in a dream wept,
Mir träumte, du wär'st mir noch gut.	I dreamt you me still loved.
Ich wachte auf, und noch immer	I awoke, and still
Strömt meine Tränenflut.	Flows my flood of tears.

"Die Forelle" (Schubart)   "The Trout" [25]

In einem Bächlein helle,	In a brooklet crear,
Da schoß in froher Eil'	There shot in lively haste
Die launische Forelle	The playful trout
Vorüber wie ein Pfeil.	By like an arrow.
Ich stand an dem Gestade	I stood on the bank
Und sah in süßer Ruh'	And saw in sweet contentment
Des muntern Fischleins Bade	The happy fish's bath
Im klaren Bächlein zu.	In the clear brooklet.
Ein Fischer mit der Rute	A fisherman with his rod
Wohl an dem Ufer stand,	Indeed on the bank stood,
Und sah's mit kaltem Blute,	And saw it with cold blood,
Wie sich das Fischlein wand.	How the fish turned.
Solang' dem Wasser Helle,	As long as to the water's clarity,
So dacht' ich, nicht gebricht,	So thought I is not broken,
So fängt er die Forelle	Then catches he the trout
Mit seiner Angel nicht.	With his hook not.
Doch endlich ward dem Diebe	But finally was for the thief
Die Zeit zu lang. Er macht	The time too long. He made
Das Bächlein tückisch trübe,	The brooklet deceptively murky,

Und eh' ich es gedacht,
So zuckte seine Rute,
Das Fischlein zappelt d'ran.
Und ich mit regem Blute
Sah die Betrog'ne an.

And before I it thought,
So twitched his rod,
The little fish flopped on it.
And I with heated blood
Saw the betrayed one.

"Die Lotosblume" (Heine)

"The Lotus Flower"[26]

Die Lotosblume ängstigt
Sich vor der Sonne Pracht,
Und mit gesenktem Haupte
Erwartet sie träumend die Nacht.

The lotus-flower fears
Itself before the sun's splendor,
And with bowed head
Awaits she, dreaming, the night.

Der Mond, der ist ihr Buhle,
Er weckt sie mit seinem Licht,
Und ihm entschleiert sie
　freundlich
Ihr frommes Blumengesicht.

The moon, he is her lover,
He awakens her with his light,
And to him unveils she
　gladly
Her innocent flower-like face.

Sie blüht und glüht und leuchtet,

She blooms and glows and
　gleams,

Und starret stumm in die Höh';
Sie duftet und weinet und zittert

And gazes silently toward the sky;
She is perfumes and weeps and
　trembles

Vor Liebe und Liebesweh.

With love and love's pain.

"Die Mainacht" (Hölty)

"May Night"[27]

Wann der silberne Mond durch
　die Gesträuche blinkt,
Und sein schlummerndes Licht
　über den Rasen streut,
Und die Nachtigall flötet,
Wandl' ich traurig von Busch zu
　Busch.

When the silver moon through
　the shrubs shines,
And its slumbering light over the
　grass scatters,
And the nightingale flutes,
Wander I sadly from bush to bush.

Überhüllet von Laub girret ein
　Taubenpaar
Sein Entzücken mir vor; aber ich
　wende mich,
Suche dunklere Schatten,
Und die einsame Träne rinnt.

Concealed by foliage coo a
　pair of doves
Their ecstasy before me; but I
　turn away,
Seek deeper shadows,
And a solitary tear flows.

Wann, o lächelndes Bild, welches
　wie Morgenrot

When, o smiling image, that like
　the sunrise

Durch die Seele mir strahlt, find ich auf Erden dich?	Through my soul streams finds, I on earth you?
Und die einsame Träne	And the solitary tear
Bebt mir heißer die Wang herab!	Trembles the hotter my cheek down!

Die schöne Müllerin (Müller)
No. 2
"Wohin?"

The Miller's Beautiful Daughter [28]

"Whither?"

Ich hört' ein Bächlein rauschen	I heard a brooklet murmur
Wohl aus dem Felsenquell,	(Indeed) from its rocky spring,
Hinab zum Tale rauschen	Downward into the valley splashing
So frisch und wunderhell.	So fresh and wonderfully bright.
Ich weiß nicht, wie mir wurde,	I know not, what to me occurred
Nicht, wer den Rat mir gab,	Nor, who the advice to me gave,
Ich mußte auch hinunter	I had to (go) down
Mit meinem Wanderstab.	With my walking stick.
Hinunter and immer weiter	Downward and always onward
Und immer dem Bache nach,	And always the brook following,
Und immer frischer rauschte	And always more freshly babbling,
Und immer heller der Bach.	And always more brightly, the brook.
Ist das denn meine Straße?	Is that then my way?
O Bächlein, sprich, wohin?	Oh brooklet, tell, whereto?
Du hast mit deinem Rauschen	You have with your babbling
Mir ganz berauscht den Sinn.	To me wholly confused my mind.
Was Sag' ich denn vom Rauschen?	Why speak I then of the babbling?
Das kann kein rauschen sein:	That cannot babbling be:
Es singen wohl die Nixen	Sing certainly the water spirits
Tief unten ihren Reihn.	In the deep their round.
Laß singen, Gesell, laß rauschen,	Let sing, friend, let babble,
Und wandre fröhlich nach!	And follow happily!
Es gehn ja Mühlenräder	Turn indeed the mill-wheels
In jedem klaren Bach!	In every clear brook!

No. 5
"Am Feierabend"

"When Work Is Over"

Hätt' ich tausend arme zu rühren!	Has I a thousand arms to move!
Könnt ich brausend die Räder führen!	Could I noisily the mill-wheels drive!

Könnt' ich wehen durch alle
   Haine!
Könnt' ich drehen alle Steine!
Daß die schöne Müllerin
Merkte meinen treuen Sinn!

Ach! wie ist mein Arm so schwach!
Was ich hebe, was ich trage,
Was ich schneide, was ich schlage,
Jeder Knappe tut mir's nach.

Und da sitz' ich in der großen
   Runde,
In der stillen, kühlen Feierstunde,
Und der Meister spricht zu Allen:
"Euer Werk hat mir gefallen";
Und das liebe Mädchen sagt
Allen eine gute Nacht.

No. 6
"Der Neugierige"

Ich frage keine Blume,
Ich frage keinen Stern;
Sie können mir allen nicht sagen,
Was ich erführ' so gern.

Ich bin ja auch kein Gärtner,
Die Sterne stehn zu hoch;
Mein Bächlein will ich fragen,
Ob mich mein Herz belog.

O Bächlein meiner Liebe,
Wie bist du heut' so stumm!
Will ja nur Eines wissen,
Ein Wörtchen um und um,

"Ja," heißt das eine
   Wörtchen,
Das and're heißet "Nein,"
Die beiden Wörtchen schließen
Die ganze Welt mir ein.

O Bächlein meiner Liebe,
Was bist du wunderlich!
Will's ja nicht weiter sagen,
Sag', Bächlein, liebt sie mich?

Could I blow through every
   wood!
Could I turn all stones!
So that the beautiful miller maid
Would notice my true sense!

Ah! How is my arm so weak!
What I lift, what I carry,
What I cut, what I hit,
Every apprentice can do just as
   well (after me).

And there sit I in the large
   circle,
In the quiet, cool hour of rest,
And the master says to all:
"Your work has pleased me";
And the dear maiden says
To all a good night.

"The Inquisitive One"

I ask no flower,
I ask no star;
They can to me all not say,
What I would learn so gladly.

I am indeed no gardner,
The stars are too high;
My brooklet will I ask,
If to me my heart lied.

Oh brooklet of my love,
How are you today so mute!
Want (I) only one thing to learn,
One word over and over,

"Yes," is the one
   little word,
The other is "No,"
The two little words contain
The whole world to me.

O brooklet of my love,
How are you strange!
Will it not (I) repeat,
Say, brooklet, loves she me?

No. 8
"Morgengruß"

"Morning Greeting"

Guten Morgen, schöne
  Müllerin!
Wo steckst du gleich das
  Köpfchen hin,
Als wär' dir was
  geschehen?
Verdrießt dich denn mein Gruß so
  schwer?
Verstört dich denn mein Blick so
  sehr?
So muß ich wieder gehen.

Good morning, lovely
  miller maid!
Where withdraw you immediately
  your head,
As if to you something
  had happened?
Annoys you then my greeting so
  heavily?
Bothers you then my glance so
  deeply?
Then must I away go.

O laß mich nur von ferne stehn,
Nach deinem lieben Fenster sehn,
Von ferne, ganz von ferne!
Du blondes Köpfchen, komm
  hervor!
Hervor aus eurem runden Tor,
Ihr blauen Morgensterne!

Oh let me only far off stand,
At your dear window look,
From far, from very far!
You little blond head, come
  forth!
Forth out of your round gate,
Your blue morning stars!

Ihr schlummertrunk'nen Äugelein,
Ihr taubetrübten
  Blümelein,
Was scheuet ihr die Sonne?
Hat es die Nacht so gut gemeint,
Daß ihr euch schielßt und bückt

Your drunk with sleep little eyes,
Your dew drunken
  little flowers,
Why avoid you the sun?
Has the night so kind been,
That you yourself close and lower
  and weep

Nach ihrer stillen Wonne?

For its quiet bliss?

Nun schuttelt ab der Träume Flor,
Und hebt euch frisch und
  frei empor
In Gottes hellen Morgen!
Die Lerche wirbelt in der Luft;
Und aus dem tiefen Herzen ruft

Now shake off dreams's veil,
And arise fresh and
  free
In God's bright morning!
The lark trills in the sky;
And from the depth of the heart
  calls

Die Liebe, Leid und Sorgen.

Love, sorrows, and cares.

No. 11
"Mein"

"Mine"

Bächlein, laß dein Rauschen sein!
Räder, stellt eu'r Brausen ein!
All ihr muntern Waldvögelein,

Brooklet, cease your noise!
Wheels, stop your roaring!
All you cheery little forest birds,

Größ und klein,
Endet eure Melodein.
Durch den Hain
Aus und ein
Schalle heut' ein Reim allein:
Die geliebte Müllerin ist mein!
Mein!
Frühling, sind das alle deine
    Blümelein?
Sonne, hast du keinen heller'n
    Schein?
Ach so muß ich ganz allein,
Mit dem seligen Worte mein,
Unverstanden in der weiten
    Schöpfung sein!

Large and small,
End your melodies.
Through the wood,
In and out
Echos today one rhyme only:
The beloved miller maid is mine!
Mine!
Spring, are those all your little
    flowers?
Sun, have you no brighter
    shine?
Ah, then must I all alone,
With the blessed word of mine,
Uncomprehended in all of
    creation be!

No. 16
"Die Liebe Farbe"

"The Beloved Color"

In Grün will ich mich kleiden,
In grünen Tränenweiden,
Mein Schatz hat's Grün so
    gern.
Will suchen einen Zypressenhain,
Eine Heide von grünen
    Rosmarein,
Mein Schatz hat's Grün so
    gern.

In green will I myself dress,
In green weeping willow,
My sweetheart likes green so
    much.
Will seek out a grove of cypress,
A heath of green
    rosemary,
My sweetheart likes green so
    much.

Wohlauf zum fröhlichen Jagen!
Wohlauf durch Heid' und
    Hagen!
Mein Schatz hat's Jagen so
    gern!
Das Wild, das ich jage, das ist der
    Tod,
Die Heide, die heiß' ich die
    Liebesnot,
Mein Schatz hat's Jagen so
    gern.

Up to the cheery hunt!
Up through the heath and
    bramble!
My sweetheart likes hunting so
    much!
The prey, that I hunt, that is
    death,
The heath, that call I the
    lack of love,
My sweetheart likes hunting so
    much.

Grabt mir ein Grab im Wasen,
Deckt mich mit grünem Rasen!
Mein Schatz hat's Grün so gern.
Kein Kreuzlein schwarz, kein
    Blümlein bunt,

Dig me a grave in the meadow,
Cover me with green grass!
My sweetheart likes green so much.
No little cross of black, no little
    flower colorful,

Grün, alles grün, so rings und
  rund!
Mein Schatz hat's Grün so gern.

Green, everything green, all
  around!
My sweetheart likes green so much.

No. 19
"Der Müller und der Bach"

"The Miller and the Brook"

Der Müller:
Wo ein treues Herze
In Liebe vergeht,
Da welken die Lilien
Auf jedem Beet;

The Miller:
Where a true heart
Of love dies,
There wither the lilies
In every flower beds;

Da muß in die Wolken
Der Vollmond gehn,
Damit seine Tränen
Die Menschen nicht sehen;

Then must in the clouds
The full moon go,
So that its tears
Men do not see;

Da halten die Englein
Die Augen sich zu
Und schluchzen und singen
Die Seele zur Ruh'.

Then hold shut the little angels
Their eyes
And sob and sing
The soul to rest.

Der Bach:
Und wenn sich die Liebe
Dem Schmerz entringt,
Ein Sternlein, ein neues,
Am Himmel erblinkt;

The Brook:
And when love
From sorrow escapes,
A little star, a new one,
In the sky twinkles;

Da springen drei Rosen,
Halb rot und halb weiß,
Die welken nicht wieder,
Aus Dornenreis.

There sprout three roses,
half red and half white,
Which wither no more,
Among the thorns.

Und die Englein schneiden
Die Flügel sich ab,
Und gehn alle Morgen
Zur Erde hinab.

And the little angels cut
Their wings off,
And go every morning
To Earth down.

Der Müller:
Ach Bächlein, liebes Bächlein,
Du meinst es so gut:
Ach Bächlein, aber weißt du
Wie Liebe tut?

The Miller:
Oh, brooklet, dear brooklet,
You mean so well:
Oh brooklet, but know you
What love does?

Ach unten, da unten,
Die kühle Ruh'!
Ach Bächlein, liebes Bächlein,
So singe nur zu.

Oh, under, there under,
Is cool rest!
Oh brooklet, dear brooklet,
Just sing on.

Die Winterreise (Müller)
No. 1
"Gute Nacht"

Fremd bin ich eingezogen,
Fremd zieh' ich wieder aus.
Der Mai war mir gewogen
Mit manchem Blumenstrauß.
Das Mädchen sprach von Liebe,
Die Mutter gar von
  Eh'—
Nun ist die Welt so trübe,
Der Weg gehüllt in Schnee.

Ich kann zu meiner Reisen
Nicht wählen mit der Zeit:
Muß selbst den Weg mir weisen
In dieser Dunkelheit.
Es zieht ein Mondenschatten
Als mein Gefährte mit,
Und auf den weißen Matten
Such' ich des Wildes Tritt.

Was soll ich länger weilen,
Daß man mich trieb hinaus?
Laß irre Hunde heulen
Vor ihres Herren Haus!

Die Liebe liebt das Wandern,
Gott hat sie so gemacht—
Von einem zu dem andern—
Fein Liebchen, gute Nacht!

Will dich im Traum nicht stören,
Wär' schad' um deine Ruh',
Sollst meinen Tritt nicht hören—
Sacht, sacht die Türe zu!
Schreib' im Vorübergehen
An's Tor dir gute Nacht,
Damit du mögest sehen,
An dich hab' ich gedacht.

No. 5

"Der Lindenbaum"

Am Brunnen vor dem Tore,

Winter's Journey[29]

"Good Night"

A stranger I arrived,
A stranger leave I again.
May was to me kind
With many a bouquet.
The girl spoke of love,
The mother even of
  marriage—
Now is the world so dreary,
The path covered with snow.

I can for my journey
Not choose the time:
Must myself the way find
In this darkness.
Moves a moon-shadow
As my travel companion,
And on the white fields
Search I for animal tracks.

Why should I longer stay,
That one me drives out?
Let mad dogs howl
Before their master's house!

Love loves to travel,
God has it so made—
From one to the other—
Fine beloved, good night!

Will (I) you in dream not disturb,
(It) would be bad for your rest,
Must my step not hear—
Quietly the door closed!
Write (I) in passing
On your gate good night,
So that you may see,
Of you have I thought.

"The Linden Tree"

By the well outside the gate,

Da steht ein Lindenbaum;
Ich träumt' in seinem Schatten
So manchen süßen Traum.

There stands a linden tree;
I dreamed in its shadow
So many a sweet dream.

Ich schnitt in seine Rinde
So manches liebe Wort;
Es zog in Freud' und Leide
Zu ihm mich immer fort.

I cut in its bark
So many a loving word;
It drew in joy and sorrow
To itself me continually.

Ich mußt' auch heute wandern
Vorbei in tiefer Nacht,
Da hab' ich noch im Dunkel
Die Augen zugemacht.

I had also today to go
By there in the dark of night,
Then have I even in the dark
My eyes closed.

Und seine Zweige rauschten,
Als riefen sie mir zu:
Komm her zu mir, Geselle,
Hier find'st du deine Ruh'!

And its branches rustled,
As if called they to me:
Come here to me, friend,
Here find you your peace!

Die kalten Winde bliesen
Mir grad' in's Angesicht,
Der Hut flog mir vom Kopfe,
Ich wendete mich nicht.

The cold winds blew
(To me) directly in the face,
My hat flew off my head,
I turned back not.

Nun bin ich manche Stunde
Entfernt von jenem Ort,
Und immer hör' ich's rauschen:
Du fändest
    Ruhe dort!

Now am I several hours
Distanced from that place,
And still hear I it rustle:
You would have found
    rest there!

No. 6
"Wasserflut"

"Flood Waters"

Manche Trän' aus meinen Augen
Ist gefallen in den Schnee;
Seine kalten Flocken saugen
Durstig ein das heiße Weh.

Many a tear from my eyes
Has fallen in the snow;
Its cold flakes absorb
Thirstily the hot pain.

Wenn die Gräser sprossen wollen,
Weht daher ein lauer Wind,
Und das Eis zerspringt in
    Schollen
Und der weiche Schnee zerrinnt.

When grasses to sprout want,
Blows this way a warm wind,
And the ice breaks apart into
    pieces
And the soft snow melts.

Schnee, du weißt von meinem
    Sehnen;
Sag', wohin doch geht dein Lauf?
Folge nach nur meinen Tränen,

Snow, you know of my
    longing;
Say, whereto is your course?
Follow only my tears,

Nimmt dich bald das Bächlein auf.	Will take you soon the brooklet up
Wirst mit ihm die Stadt	(You) will with it the town
durchziehen,	flow through,
Munt're Straßen ein und aus;	Cheerful streets in and out;
Fühlst du meine Tränen glühen,	Feel you my tears glow,
Da ist meiner Liebsten Haus.	There is my beloved's house.

No. 7
"Auf dem Flusse"   "On the Stream"

Der du so lustig rauschtest,	Who you so merrily rippled,
Du heller, wilder Fluß,	You bright, boisterous stream,
Wie still bist du geworden,	How silent have you become,
Gibst keinen Scheidegruß.	Give no farewell.

Mit harter, starrer Rinde	With a hard, stiff crust
Hast du dich überdeckt,	Have you yourself covered,
Liegst kalt und unbeweglich	Lie cold and motionless
Im Sande ausgestreckt.	In the sand outstretched.

In deine Decke grab' ich	In your cover dig I
Mit einem spitzen Stein	With a sharp stone
Den Namen meiner Liebsten	The name of my beloved
Und Stund' und Tag hinein:	And hour and date (into it):

Den Tag des ersten Grußes,	The day of the first greeting,
Den Tag, an dem ich ging,	The day on which I left,
Um Nam' und Zahlen windet	Around name and dates winds
Sich ein zerbrochner Ring.	A broken ring.

Mein Herz, in diesem Bache	My heart, in this brook
Erkennst du nun dein Bild?	Recognize you now your image?
Ob's unter seiner Rinde	If under its crust
Wohl auch so reißend schwillt?	Indeed also so wildly it swells?

No. 24
"Der Leiermann"   "The Organ Grinder"

Drüben hinter'm Dorfe	Over there behind the village
Steht ein Leiermann,	Stands an organ grinder,
Und mit starren Fingern	And with stiff fingers
Dreht er was er kann.	Plays he, what he can.

Barfuß auf dem Eise	Barefoot on the ice
Swankt er hin und her;	Totters he to and fro;
Und sein kleiner Teller	And his little dish
Bleibt ihm immer leer.	Remains for him always empty.

Keiner mag ihn hören,
Keiner sieht ihn an;
Und die Hunde knürren
Um den alten Mann.

No one wants him to hear,
No one looks at him;
And the dogs growl
Around the old man.

Und er läßt es gehen
Alles, wie es will,
Dreht, und seine Leier
Steht ihm nimmer still.

And he lets go
Everything, as it will,
Grinds, and his organ
Stays never quiet.

Wunderlicher Alter,
Soll ich mit dir gehn?
Willst zu meinen Liedern
Deine Leier drehn?

Marvelous old man,
Should I with you go?
Wish you to my songs
To your hurdy-gurdy grind?

"Du bist die Ruh" (Rückert)

"You Are Repose"[30]

Du bist die Ruh,
Der Friede mild,
Die Sehnsucht du,
Und was sie stillt.

You are repose,
The gentle peace,
Longing (are) you,
And what it quiets.

Ich weihe dir
Voll Lust und Schmerz
Zur Wohnung hier
Mein Aug und Herz.

I dedicate to you,
Full of joy and pain,
As a dwelling here,
My eye and heart.

Kehr ein bei mir
Und schließe du
Still hinter dir
Die Pforte zu.

Come in to me
And close you
Softly behind you
The gate.

Treib andern Schmerz
Aus dieser Brust!
Voll sei dies Herz
Von deiner Lust.

Drive other pain
From this breast.
Full be this heart
Of your joy.

Dies Augenzelt,
Von deinem Glanz
Allein erhellt,
O füll es ganz!

The temple of these eyes,
By your gleam
Alone is lit,
Oh fill it completely!

"Du bist wie eine Blume" (Heine)

"You Are Like a Flower"[31]

Du bist wie eine Blume
So hold und schön und rein;
Ich schau dich an, und Wehmut
Schleicht mir ins Herz hinein.

You are like a flower
So sweet and fair and pure;
I gaze at you, and melancholy
Steals to me into my heart.

Mir ist, als ob ich die Hände
Aufs Haupt dir legen
  sollt,
Betend, daß Gott dich erhalte
So rein und schön und hold.

To me it is as if my hands
Upon the head of you (I) lay
  should,
Praying that God you preserve
So pure and fair and sweet.

"Einsamkeit" (Goethe)

"Solitude"[32]

Die ihr Felsen und Bäume
  bewohnt, o heilsame Nymphen,
Gebet jeglichem gern, was er im
  stillen begehrt!

You who rocks and trees
  inhabit, o healing nymphs,
Give to each gladly what he
  silently desires!

Schaffet dem Traurigen Trost,
  dem Zweifelhaften Belehrung
Und dem Liebenden gönnt,
  daß ihm begegne sein Glück.

Bring to the sad Solace,
  to the uncertain counsel
And to the lover grant, that to
  him comes his happiness.

Denn euch gaben die Götter, was
  sie den Menschen versagten,
Jeglichem, der euch vertraut,
  tröstlich und hilfreich zu sein.

For to you gave the gods, what
  they to men denied,
To each, who you trust, comforting
  and helpful to be.

"Er ist's" (Mörike)

"(Spring) It Is"[33]

Frühling läßt sein blaues Band
Wieder flattern durch die
  Lüfte;
Süße, wohlbekannte Düfte
Streifen ahnungsvoll
  das Land.

Spring lets its blue ribbon
Once more flutter through the
  air;
Sweet, familiar fragrances
Drift full of foreboding through
  the land.

Veilchen träumen schon,
Wollen balde kommen.
Horch, von fern ein leiser
  Harfenton!
Frühling, ja du bists!
Dich habb' ich vernommen!

Violets dream as yet,
Want soon to arrive.
Hark, from afar a soft
  harp!
Spring, yes you it is!
You have I heard!

"Erlkönig" (Goethe)

"Erlking" (King of the Alders)[34]

Wer reitet so spät durch Nacht
  und Wind?
Es ist der Vater mit seinem Kind;

Who rides so late through
  night and wind?
It is the father with his child;

Er hat den Knaben wohl in dem
Arm,
Er faßt ihn sicher, er hält ihn
warm.

He has the boy secure in his
arm,
He holds him safe, he holds him
warm.

"Mein Sohn, was birgst du so
bang dein Gesicht?"—
"Siehst, Vater, du den Erlenkönig
nicht?"
Den Erlenkönig mit Kron' und
Schweif?"—
"Mein Sohn, es ist ein
Nebelstreif."—

"My son, why hide you so
fearfully your face?"—
"See, father, you the Erlking
not?
The Erlking, with crown and
robes?"—
"My son, it is a
band of mist."—

"Du liebes Kind, komm, geh mit
mir!
Gar schöne Spiele spiel ich mit
dir;
Manch bunte Blumen sind an
dem Strand,
Meine Mutter hat manch gülden
Gewand."

"You lovely child, come, go with
me!
Really lovely games play I with
you;
Many colorful flowers are on
the shore,
My mother has much golden
finery."

"Mein Vater, mein Vater, und
hörest du nicht,
Was Erlenkönig mir leise
verspricht?"—
"Sei ruhig, bleibe ruhig, mein
Kind:
In dürren Blättern säuselt der
Wind."—

"My father, my father, and hear
you not,
What Erlking to me softly
promises?"—
"Be calm, stay calm, my
child:
In dry leaves rustles the
wind."

"Willst, feiner Knabe, du mit mir
gehn?
Meine Töchter sollen dich warten
schön;
Meine Töchter führen den
nächtlichen Reihn
Und wiegen und tanzen und
singen dich ein."

"Will, fine boy, you with me
go?
My daughters shall on you wait
beautifully;
My daughters lead the nightly
round
And rock and dance and sing you
to sleep."

"Mein Vater, mein Vater, und
siehst du nicht dort
Erlkönigs Töchter am düstern
Ort?"—

"My father, my father, and
see you not there
Erlking's daughters in the
shadowy place?"—

"Mein Sohn, mein Sohn, ich seh'
  es genau;
Es scheinen die alten Weiden so
  grau."—
"Ich liebe dich, mich reizt deine
  schöne Gestalt.
Und bist du nicht willig, so brauch
  ich Gewalt."
"Mein Vater, mein Vater, jetzt faßt
  er mich an!
Erlkönig hat mir ein Leid's
  getan!"—

Dem Vater grausets; er reitet
  geschwind,
Er hält in Armen das ächzende
  Kind,
Erreicht den Hof mit Mühe und
  Not:
In seinen Armen das Kind war tot.

"My son, my son, I see
  it clearly;
Shine the old willows so
  grey."—
"I love you, I am excited by your
  beautiful figure.
And if you not willing be, then use
  I force."
"My father, my father, now grabs
  he me!
Erlking has to me a harm
  done!"—

The father shudders; he rides
  swiftly,
He hold in his arms the suffering
  child,
Reaches the courtyard with great
  distress:
In his arms the child was dead.

"Erster Verlust" (Goethe)

Ach, wer bringt die schönen
  Tage,
Jene Tage der ersten Liebe,
Ach, wer bringt nur eine Stunde
Jener holden Zeit zuruck!

Einsam nähr ich meine Wunde,
Und mit stets erneuter Klage
Traur ich ums verlorne Glück.

Ach, wer bringt die schönen Tage,
Jene holde Zeit zurück.

"First Loss"[35]

Oh, who will bring the fair
  days,
Those days of first love,
Oh, who will bring but one hour
Of that sweet time back!

Lonely, I feed my wound,
And with ever-renewed lament
Mourn I the lost happiness.

Oh, who will bring the fair days,
That sweet time back!

Frauenliebe und -Leben
(von Chamisso)

No. 1

Seit ich ihn gesehen,
Glaub' ich blind zu sein;
Wo ich hin nur blicke,
Seh' ich ihn allein;
Wie im wachen Traume

Woman's Love and Life[36]

Since I him have seen
Believe I blind to be;
Wherever I but look,
See I him alone;
As in a waking dream

Schwebt sein Bild mir vor,
Taucht aus tiefstem Dunkel
Heller nur empor.

Hovers his image before me,
Rising out of the deepest darkness
Ever more brightly.

Sonst ist licht–und farblos
Alles um mich her,
Nach der Schwester Spiele
Nicht begehr' ich mehr,
Möchte lieber weinen
Still im Kämmerlein;
Seit ich ihn gesehen,
Glaub' ich blind zu sein.

Else is light- and colorless
Everything around me,
For my sisters' games
Do not long I anymore,
Would (I) rather to weep
Quietly in my little room;
Since I him have seen,
Believe I blind to be.

"Ganymed" (Goethe)

"Ganymede"[37]

Wie im Morgenglanze
Du rings mich anglühst,
Frühling, Geliebter!
Mit tausendfacher Liebeswonne
Sich an mein Herz drängt
Deiner ewigen Wärme
Heilig Gefühl,
Unendliche Schöne!
Daß ich dich fassen möcht'
In diesen Arm!

As in morning splendor
You around me glow,
Spring, beloved!
With thousandfold ecstasy of love
On my heart presses
Of your eternal warmth
Holy feeling,
Unending beauty!
That I you clasp might
In this arm!

Ach, an deinem Busen
Lieg' ich und Schmachte,
Und deine Blumen, dein Gras
Drängen sich an mein Herz.
Du kühlst den brennenden
Durst meines Busens,
Lieblicher Morgenwind!
Ruft drein die Nachtigall
Liebend nach mir aus dem
    Nebeltal.

Ah, on your breast
Lie I (would) and languish,
And your flowers, your grass
Press on my heart.
You cool the burning
Thirst of my bosom,
Dear morning wind!
Calls hither the nightingale
Lovingly to from the
    misty valley.

Ich komm', ich komme.
Wohin, Ach, wohin?

I come, I come.
Where, oh, where?

Hinauf! Hinauf strebt's,
Es schweben die Wolken
Abwärts, die Wolken
Neigen sich der sehnenden Liebe.
Mir! Mir!

Upward! upward struggles (it),
Float the clouds
Downwards, the clouds
Bow before the longing love.
To me, to me!

In eurem Schoße
Aufwärts!
Umfangend umfangen!
Aufwärts an deinen Busen,
Alliebender Vater!

In your lap
Upwards!
Embracing, embraced!
Upwards to your breast,
All-loving father!

"Gesang Weylas" (Mörike)

"Weyla's Song"[38]

Du bist Orplid, mein Land!
Das ferne leuchtet;
Vom Meere dampfet dein
    besonnter Strand
Den Nebel, so der Götter Wange
    feuchtet.

You are Orplid, my land!
Which distant gleams;
From the sea steams your sunny
    shore
The mist, which the gods' cheeks
    bedews.

Uralte Wasser steigen
Verjüngt um deine Hüpfen,
    Kind!
Vor deiner Gottheit beugen
Sich Könige, die deine Wärter sind.

Ancient waters rise
Renewed around your waist,
    child!
Before your divinity bow
Kings, who your attendants are.

Gesänge des Harfners (Goethe)
No. 1

The Harper's Songs [39]

Wer sich der Einsamkeit ergibt,
Ach! der ist bald allein;
Ein jeder lebt, ein jeder liebt
Und läßt ihn seiner Pein.

Who himself to loneliness gives,
Ah, he is soon alone;
Each one lives, each one loves
And leaves him to his pain.

Ja! Laßt mich meiner Qual!
Und kann ich nur einmal
Recht einsam sein,
Dann bin ich nicht allein.

Yes! leave me to my torment!
And can I but once
Truly lonely be,
Then (will) be I not alone.

Es schleicht ein Liebender
    lauschend sacht,
Ob seine Freundin allein?
So überschleicht bei Tag und
    Nacht
Mich Einsamen die Pein,
Mich Einsamen die Qual.
Ach, werd ich erst einmal
Einsam im Grabe sein,
Da läßt sie mich allein!

Steals a lover
    listening softly,
If his beloved (is) alone?
So, steals by day and
    night
Upon me lonely one the pain,
Upon me lonely one, the torment.
Ah, when I shall at last
Lonely in my grave to be,
Then will it leave me alone!

"Gretchen am Spinnrade"
(Goethe)

"Gretchen at the Spinning
    Wheel"[40]

Meine Ruh' ist hin,
Mein Herz is schwer,
Ich finde sie nimmer
und nimmermehr.

My peace is gone,
My heart is heavy,
I shall find (peace) never
And never more.

Wo ich ihn nicht hab',
Ist mir das Grab,
Die ganze Welt
Ist mir vergällt.

Where I him do not have,
Is to me a grave,
The entire world
Is for me poisoned.

Mein armer Kopf
Ist mir verrückt,
Mein armer Sinn
Ist mir zerstückt.

My poor head
Is to me crazed,
My poor mind
Is to me destroyed.

Nach ihm nur schau' ich
Zum Fenster hinaus,
Nach ihm nur geh' ich
Aus dem Haus.

For him only gaze I
From the window,
For him only go I
From the house.

Sein hoher Gang,
Sein' edle Gestalt,
Seines Mundes Lächeln,
Seiner Augen Gewalt.

His superior walk,
His noble air,
His mouth's smile,
His eyes' power.

Und seiner Rede
Zauberfluß,
Sein Händedruck,
Und ach, sein Kuß!

And his words's
Magic flow,
His hand's press,
And ah, his kiss!

Mein Busen drängt
Sich nach ihm hin.
Ach dürft ich fassen
Und halten ihn,

My heart craves
For him,
Oh might I clasp
And hold him,.

Und küssen ihn,
So wie ich wollt,
An seinen Küssen
Vergehen sollt!

And kiss him,
Just as I liked,
From his kisses
Expire (I) should!

"Heimweh" (Eichendorff)
(Last stanza)

"Homecoming"[41]

Der Morgen, das ist meine Freude!   Dawn, that is my delight!

Da steig' ich in stiller
  Stund'
Auf den höchsten Berg in die
  Weite,
Grüß dich, Deutschland, aus
  Herzensgrund!

Then I climb at peaceful
  hour
On the highest mountain in the
  distance,
I greet you, Germany, from my
  heart's depth!

"Ich atmet' einen linden Duft"
(Rückert)

"I Breathed a Gentle Fragrance"[42]

Ich atmet' einen linden Duft.
Im Zimmer stand
Ein Zweig der Linde,
Ein Angebinde
Von lieber Hand.
Wie lieblich war der
  Lindenduft!
Wie lieblich ist der
  Lindenduft!

I breathed a gentle fragrance.
In the room stood
A sprig of linden,
A gift
Of a dear hand.
How lovely was the linden
  fragrance!
How lovely is the linden
  fragrance!

Das Lindenreis
Brachst du gelinde:
Ich atme' leis
Im Duft der Linde
Der Liebe linden Duft.

That sprig of lime,
Broke you tenderly;
I breathe softly
In the fragrance of lime
Love's gentle fragrance.

"Im Frühling" (Schulze)

"In Spring"[43]

Still sitz ich an des Hügels Hang,
Der Himmel ist so klar,
Das Lüftchen spielt im grünen
  Tal,
Wo ich beim ersten
  Frühlingsstrahl
Einst, ach so glücklich war.
Wo ich an ihrer Seite ging
So traulich und so nah,
Und tief im dunklen
  Felsenquell
Den schönen Himmel blau und
  hell
Und sie im Himmel sah.

Silent, sit I on the hillside,
Heaven is so clear,
The breezes play in the green
  valley,
Where I in the first gleam of
  spring,
Once, ah, so happy was.
Where I at her side walked
So fondly and so close,
And deep in the dark rocky
  spring
The fair heavens blue and
  bright
And her in the heavens saw.

Sieh, wie der bunte Frühling
  schon

See, how the colorful spring
  already

Aus Knosp' und Blüte blickt!
Nicht alle Blüten sind mir gleich,
Am liebsten pflückt ich von dem
    Zweig,
Von welchem sie gepflückt!

Den alles ist wie damals noch,
Die Blumen, das Gefild;
Die Sonne scheint nicht minder
    hell,
Nicht minder freundlich
    schwimmt im Quell
Das blaue Himmelsbild.

Es wandeln nur sich Will und
    Wahn,
Es wechseln Lust und Streit,
Vorüber flieht der Liebe Glück,
Und nur die Liebe bleibt zurück,
Die Lieb' und ach, das Leid.

O wär ich doch ein Vöglein nur
Dort an dem Wiesenhang,
Dann blieb ich auf den Zweigen
    hier,
Und säng ein süßes Lied von ihr,
Den ganzen Sommer lang.

"Immer leiser wird mein
    Schlummer" (Lingg)

Immer leiser wird mein
    Schlummer,
Nur wie Schleier liegt mein
    Kummer
Zitternd über mir.
Oft im Traume hör' ich dich
Rufen drauß vor meiner Tür,
Niemand wacht und öffnet
    dir,
Ich erwach und weine bitterlich.
Ja, ich werde sterben müssen,
Eine and're wirst du küssen,
Wenn ich bleich und kalt.
Eh' die Maienlüfte wehn,

From bud and blossom peeks!
Not all blossoms are to me alike,
I prefer to pick from that
    branch,
From which she has picked!

For all is as it was then,
The flowers, the fields
The sun shines not less
    brightly,
No less kindly bathes in the
    stream
The blue image of heaven.

Change only will and
    delusion,
Alternate joy and strife,
Gone flies love's happiness,
And only love remains,
Love, and, ah, sorrow.

O, were I a tiny bird only
There on the meadow's bank,
Then I would stay on the branches
    here,
And sing a sweet song of her,
All the summer long.

"Ever Lighter Grows my
    Slumber"[14]

Ever lighter becomes my slumber,

Only like a veil lie my sorrows

Trembling over me.
Often in my dreams hear I you
Calling outside my door,
No one wakes and opens
    for you,
I awaken and weep bitterly.
Yes, I shall die must,
Another will you kiss,
When I (am) pale and cold.
Ere May breezes blow,

Eh' die Drossel singt im Wald:
Willst du mich noch einmal sehn,
Komm, o komme bald!

Ere the thrush sings in the wood:
Would you me just once more see,
Come, oh come soon!

"Iphigenia" (Mayrhofer)
(first stanza)

"Iphigenia"[45]

Blüht denn hier an Tauris
    Strande
Keine Blum' aus Hellas Land?
Weht kein milder Segenshauch
Aus den lieblichen Gefilden,
Wo Geschwister mit mir
    spielten?—
Ach, mein Leben ist ein Rauch!

Bloom then here on the Tauris
    shore
No flower from the Grecian land?
Blows no gentle breath of blessing
From the blessed fields,
Where my sisters with me
    played?—
Ah, my life is but smoke!

"Italienischesliederbuch"
(trans. Heyse)
No. 1

"Italian Songbook"[46]

Auch kleine Dinge können uns
    entzücken,
Auch kleine Dinge können teuer
    sein.
Bedenkt, wie gern wir uns mit
    Perlen schmücken;
Sie werden schwer bezahlt und
    sind nur klein.
Bedenkt, wie klein ist die
    Olivenfrucht,
Und wird um ihre Güte doch
    gesucht.
Denkt an die Rose nur, wie klein
    sie ist,
Und duftet doch so lieblich, wie
    ihr wißt.

Even small things may us
    delight,
Even small things may precious
    be.
Think, how gladly we ourselves in
    pearls bedeck;
They are for much sold and are
    only small.
Think, how small is the
    olive fruit,
And for its virtue is yet
    sought.
Think of the rose only, how small
    it is,
And smells yet so sweet, as
    you know.

No. 2

Mir ward gesagt, du reisest in die
    Ferne.
Ach, wohin gehst du, mein
    geliebtes Leben?
Den Tag, an dem du scheidest,
    wüßt' ich gerne;

To me was told, you are traveling
    afar.
Ah, where go you, my
    dearest life?
The day, on which you depart,
    knew I gladly;

Mit Tränen will ich das Geleit dir
geben.
Mit Tränen will ich deinen Weg
befeuchten—
Gedenk' an mich, und Hoffnung
wird mir leuchten!
Mit Tränen bin ich bei dir
allerwärts—
Gedenk' an mich, vergiß es nicht,
mein Herz!

With tears will I escort to you
give
With tears will I your path
moisten—
Think of me, and hope
will on me shine!
With tears I am with you
everywhere—
Think of me, forget it not, my
heart!

No. 19

Wir haben beide lange Zeit
geschwiegen,
Auf einmal kam uns nun die .
Sprache wieder.
Die Engel, die herab vom Himmel
fliegen,
Sie brachten nach dem Krieg den
Frieden wieder.
Die Engel Gottes sind
herabgeflogen,
Mit ihnen ist der Frieden
eingezogen.
Die Liebesengel kamen über
Nacht
Und haben Frieden meiner Brust
gebracht.

No. 19

We have both long been
silent,
Suddenly returned to us
speech again.
The angels, who down from
heaven fly,
They brought after the war
peace again.
The angels of God have
flown down,
With them peace has
arrived.
The angels of love came by
night
And have peace to my breast
brought.

No. 20

Mein Liebster singt am Haus im
Mondenscheine,
Und ich muß lauschend hier im
Bette liegen.
Weg von der Mutter wend ich
mich und weine;
Blut sind die Tränen, die mir
nicht versiegen.
Den breiten Strom am Bett hab'
ich geweint,
Weiß nicht vor Tränen, der
Morgen scheint.
Den breiten Strom am Bett weint
ich vor Sehnen;

No. 20

My lover sings by the house in the
moonlight,
And I must listening here in
bed lie.
Away from my mother turn I and
weep;
Bloody are the tears, which for me
do not dry up.
The broad stream by the bed
have I wept,
Know not for tears if the
morning dawns.
The broad stream by the bed
wept I from yearning;

Blind haben mich gemacht die
   blutgen tränen.

No. 34

Und steht Ihr früh am Morgen
   auf vom Bette,
Scheucht Ihr vom Himmel alle
   Wolken fort;
Die Sonne lockt Ihr auf die
   Berge dort;
Und Engelein erscheinen um die
   Wette
Und bringen Schuh' und Kleider
   Euch sofort.
Dann, wenn Ihr ausgeht in die
   heil'ge Mette,
So zieht Ihr alle Menschen mit
   Euch fort,
Und wenn Ihr naht der
   benedeiten Stätte,
So zündet Euer Blick die
   Lampen an.
Weihwasser nehmt Ihr, macht des
   Kreuzes Zeichen
Und netzet Eure weiße Stirn
   sodann
Und neiget Euch und beugt die
   Knie ingleichen—
O wie holdselig steht Euch
   alles an!
Wie hold und selig hat Euch Gott
   begabt,
Die Ihr der Schönheit Kron'
   empfangen habt!
Wie hold und selig wandelt Ihr im
   Leben;
Der Schönheit Palme ward an
   Euch gegeben.

No. 46

Ich hab' in Penna einen Liebsten
   wohnen,
In der Maremmenebne' einen
   andern,

Blinded have me made the
   bloodfilled tears.

No. 34

And arise you early in the
   morning from bed,
Banish you from the Heavens all
   clouds away;
You lure the sun onto the
   hills there;
And cherubs appear as in a
   race
And bring shoes and clothes
   to you immediately.
Then, when you go out to Holy
   Mass,
(So doing) draw you all people
   with you along,
And when you approach the
   blessed place,
Then kindles your gaze the
   holy lights.
Holy water take you, make the
   cross's sign,
And dampen your white forehead
   then
And bow you and bend the
   knee as well—
Oh, how blessed is about you
   everything!
How dearly and blessedly has you
   God gifted,
That you the crown of beauty
   received have!
How dearly and blessedly go you
   through life;
The prize for beauty was to you
   bestowed.

No. 46

I have in Penna one lover
   living,
In the Maremma plains
   another,

Einen im schönen Hafen von
　Ancona,
Zum vierten muß ich nach Viterbo
　wandern;
Ein and'rer wohnt in Casentino
　dort,
Der nächste lebt mit mir am
　selben Ort,
Und wieder einen hab' ich in
　Magione,
Vier in La Fratta, zehn in
　Castiglione!

One in the lovely harbor of
　Ancona,
To the fourth must I to Viterbo
　go;
Another lives in Casentino
　there,
The next lives with me in the
　same place,
And again one have I in
　Magione,
Four in La Fratta, ten in
　Castiglione!

"Klage an den Mond" (Hölty)

"Lament to the Moon"[17]

Dein Silber schien
Durch Eichengrün,
Das Kühlung gab,
Auf mich herab,
O Mond, und lachte Ruh'
Mir frohem Knaben zu.

Your silver shone
Through the oaks of green,
That cool shade gave,
On me down,
O moon, and smiled peace
On me, a happy youth.

Wenn jetzt dein Licht
Durch's Fenster bricht,
Lacht's keine Ruh'
Mir Jüngling zu,
Sieht's meine Wange blaß,
Mein Auge thränennaß.

When now your light
Through the window breaks,
Smiles it no peace
On me, a young man,
Sees it my cheeks pale,
My eye moist with tears.

Bald, lieber Freund,
Ach bald bescheint
Dein Silberschein
Den Leichenstein,
Der meine Asche birgt,
Des Jünglings Asche birgt!

Soon, dear friend,
Ah soon will shine
Your silver light
On the tombstone
That my ashes shelters,
The young man's ashes shelters.

"Kurze Fahrt" (Eichendorff)

"Short Journey"[18]

Posthorn, wie so keck und fröhlich
Brachst du einst den
　Morgen an,
Vor mir lag's so frühlingsselig,
Daß ich still auf Lieder sann.

Posthorn, how bold and merry
Introduced you once the
　morning,
Before me lay such spring bliss,
That I silently of songs thought.

Dunkel rauscht es schon im Walde,
Wie so abendkühl wird's hier,
Schwager, stoß ins Horn—wie
     balde
Sind auch wir im Nachtquartier!

Darkly murmurs it still the forest,
How evening-cool grows it here,
Coachman, sound your horn—
     how soon
Are lodged too we for the night!

"Lebe wohl!" (Mörike)

"Farewell"[49]

"Lebe wohl"—Du fühlest nicht,
Was es heißt, dies Wort der
     Schmerzen;
Mit getrostem Angesicht
Sagtest du's und leichtem Herzen.

"Farewell"—You feel not,
What it means, this word of
     pains;
With benign expression
You said it and (with) light heart.

"Lebe wohl!"—Ach
     tausendmal
Hab' ich mir es vorgesprochen,
Und in nimmersatter Qual
Mir das Herz damit gebrochen!

"Farewell"—Oh,
     a thousand times
Have I to myself it said,
And in insatiable torment
My heart with it broken!

"Leiden der Trennung" (von Collin)

"Sorrows of Separation"[50]

Vom Meere trennt sich die Welle,
Und seufzet durch Blumen im
     Thal,
Und fühlet, gewiegt in der Quelle,
Gebannt in dem Brunne, nur
     Qual!
Es sehnt sich die Welle
In lispelnder Quelle,
Im murmelnden Bache,
Im Brunnengemache,
Zum Meer, zum Meer,
Von dem sie kam,
Von dem sie Leben nahm,
Von dem, des Irrens matt und
     müde,
Sie süsse Ruh' verhofft und Friede.

From the sea separates the wave,
And sighs amid the flowers in the
     valley,
And feels, cradled in the spring
Confined in the well, only
     torment!
Longs the wave
In the whispering spring,
In the murmuring stream,
In the well-chamber,
For the sea
From which it came,
From which it life took,
From which, from wandering
     faint and weary,
For sweet rest it hopes and peace.

"Leise zieht durch mein Gemüt"
(Heine)

"Gently Goes through My Soul"[51]

Leise zieht durch mein Gemüt
Liebliches Geläute.

Gently goes through my soul
Sweet ringing.

Klinge, kleines Frühlingslied,
Kling hinaus ins Weite.

Kling hinaus, bis an das Haus,
Wo die Blumen sprießen.
Wenn du eine Rose schaust,
Sag', ich laß' sie grüßen.

Sound, tiny song of spring,
Sound out far and wide.

Ring out as far as the house,
Where the flowers bloom.
If you a rose should see,
Say I send it greeting.

"Liebst du um Schönheit"
(Rückert)

"If You Love for Beauty"[52]

Liebst du um Schönheit, O nicht
  mich liebe!
Liebe die Sonne, sie trägt ein
  gold'nes Haar.

Liebst du um Jugend, o nicht
  mich liebe!
Liebe den Frühling, der jung ist
  jedes Jahr!

Liebst du um Schätze, O nicht
  mich liebe!
Liebe die Meerfrau, sie hat viel
  Perlen klar!

Liebst du um Liebe, o ja mich
  liebe!
Liebe mich immer; dich lieb' ich
  immerdar!

If you love for beauty, Oh, don't
  me love!
Love the sun, she wears
  golden hair.

If you love for youth, Oh, don't
  me love!
Love the Spring, which young is
  every year.

If you love for treasures, Oh, don't
  me love!
Love the mermaid, she has many
  pearls clear!

If you love for love, oh, yes, me
  love!
Love me always; you love I
  forever!

"Lied eines Schiffers an die
  Dioskuren" (Mayrhofer)

"Sailor's Song to the Dioscuri"[53]

Dioskuren, Zwillingssterne,
Die ihr leuchtet meinem Nachen,
Mich beruhigt auf dem Meere
Eure Milde, euer
  Wachen.

Wer auch fest in sich
  begründet,
Unverzagt dem Sturm begegnet,
Fühlt sich doch in euren Strahlen
Doppelt mutig und gesegnet.

Dieses Ruder, das ich schwinge,

Dioscuri, twin stars,
That you illuminate my boat,
Me calms on the sea
Your gentleness, your
  watchfulness.

He who also firmly is settled in
  himself,
Undaunted the storm faces,
Feels as well in your beaming
Doubly courageous and blest.

This tiller, which I swing,

Meeresfluten zu zerteilen,
Hänge ich, so ich geborgen,
Auf an eures Tempels Säulen,
Dioskuren, Zwillingssterne.

Sea waters to part,
Hang I, if I am protected,
Up on your temple's columns,
Dioscuri, twin stars.

Liederkreis (Eichendorff)
No. 1
"In der Fremde"

Song Cycle [34]

"In the Foreign Land"

Aus der Heimat hinter den
  Blitzen rot
Da kommen die Wolken her,
Aber Vater und Mutter sind lange
  tot,
Es kennt mich dort keiner
  mehr.

From the homeland behind the
  lightening red
There approach clouds,
But father and mother are long
  dead
No one remembers me there no
  more.

Wie bald, wie bald kommt die
  stille Zeit,
Da ruhe ich auch, und über mir
Rauschet die schöne
  Waldeinsamkeit,
Und keiner mehr kennt mich
  auch hier.

How soon, how soon comes the
  quiet time,
There rest I also, and over me
Murmurs the beautiful
  loneliness of the forest
And no one knows me anymore
  here.

No. 3
"Waldesgespräch"

"Wood Dialog"

"Es ist schon spät, es ist schon
  kalt;
Was reitest du einsam durch den
  Wald?
Der Wald ist lang, du bist allein;
Du schöne Braut, ich führ' dich
  heim."—

"It is already late, it is already
  cold;
Why ride you alone through the
  wood?
The wood is long, you are alone;
You lovely bride, I'll lead you
  home."—

"Groß ist der Männer Trug und
  List,
Vor Schmerz mein Herz
  gebrochen ist,
Wohl irrt das Waldhorn her und
  hin,
O flieh'! Du weißt nicht, wer ich
  bin!"—

"Great is men's deception and
  trickery,
From sorrow my heart
  broken is,
Indeed wanders the hunting horn
  to and fro,
Oh, flee! You know not who I
  am!"—

"So reich geschmückt ist Roß und
  Weib,

"So richly adorned is horse and
  woman,

So wunderschön der junge
  Leib,
Jetzt kenn' ich dich—Gott steh'
  mir bei!
Du bist die Hexe Lorelei!"—

So wonderfully lovely the young
  body,
Now recognize I you—God be
  with me!
You are the witch, Lorelei!"—

"Du kennst mich wohl—vom
  hohen Stein,
Schaut still mein Schloß tief in
  den Rhein.
Es ist schon spät, es ist schon kalt,
Kommst nimmermehr aus diesem
  Wald."

"You know me well—from the
  lofty rock,
Looks quietly my castle far down
  to the Rhine.
It is already late, it is already cold,
Come (you) never again out of
  this wood."

No. 5
"Mondnacht"

"Moonlit Night"

Es war, als hätt' der Himmel
Die Erde still geküßt,
Daß sie im Blütenschimmer
Von ihm nun träumen müßt.

It was as if had the heavens
The earth softly kissed,
So that it in blossom's shimmer,
Of him now dream must.

Die Luft ging durch die Felder,
Die Ähren wogten sacht,
Es rauschten leis' die Wälder,
So sternklar war die Nacht.

The breeze ran though the fields,
The ears of corn swayed gently,
Rustled faintly the woods,
So starry clear was the night.

Und meine Seele spannte
Weit ihre Flügel aus,
Flog durch die stillen Lande,
Als flöge sie nach Haus.

And my soul spread
Wide its wings,
Flew over the silent land,
As if it flew toward home.

No. 6
"Schöne Fremde"

"Beautiful Foreign Land"

Es rauschen die Wipfel und
  schauern,
Als machten zu dieser Stund'
Um die halbversunkenen Mauern
Die alten Götter die Rund.

Murmur the treetops and
  shiver,
As though make at this hour
Around the half-sunken walls
The old gods the circle.

Hier hinter den Myrtenbäumen
In heimlich dämmernder Pracht,
Was sprichst du wirr wie in
  Träumen
Zu mir, phantastische Nacht?

Here, beyond the myrtles,
In secretly darkening splendor,
What whisper you confused as in
  dreaming
To me, fantastic night?

Es funken auf mich alle Sterne
Mit glühendem Liebesblick,
Es redet trunken die Ferne
Wie von künftigem, großen
    Glück.

Sparkle on me all stars
With glowing look of love,
Speaks drunkenly the distance
As if about future, great
    happiness.

No. 7
"Auf einer Burg"

"In a Castle"

Eingeschlafen auf der Lauer
Oben ist der alter Ritter;
Drüber gehen Regenschauer,
Und der Wald rauscht
    durch das Gitter.

Asleep in his lookout
Up there is the old knight;
Overhead go rain squalls
And the forest rustles durch
    through the lattice.

Eingewachsen Bart und Haare
Und versteinert Brust und
    Klause,
Sitzt er viele hundert Jahre
Oben in der stillen Krause.

Grown inward beard and hair
And turned to stone breast and
    ruffle,
Sits he many hundred years
Up there in the quiet cell.

Draußen ist es still und friedlich,
Alle sind ins Tal gezogen,
Waldesvögel einsam singen
In den leeren Fensterbogen.

Outside is it quiet and peaceful,
Everyone has to the valley moved,
Wood birds lonely sing
In the empty window arches.

Eine Hochzeit fährt da unten
Auf dem Rhein im Sonnescheine,
Musikanten spielen munter,
Und die schöne Braut, die weinet.

A wedding goes by down there
On the Rhine in the sunshine,
Musicians play merrily,
And the lovely bride, she weeps.

Liederkreis (Heine)
No. 5

Song Cycle[35]

Schöne Wiege meiner Leiden,
Schönes Grabmal meiner Ruh',
Schöne Stadt, wir müssen
    scheiden,—
Lebe wohl, ruf' ich dir zu.

Beautiful cradle of my sorrows,
Beautiful tombstone of my peace,
Beautiful city, we must
    part,—
Farewell, call I to you.

Lebe wohl, du heil'ge Schwelle,
Wo da wandelt Liebchen
    traut;
Lebe wohl, du heil'ge Stelle,
Wo ich sie zuerst geschaut!

Farewell, you sacred threshhold,
Where there wandered beloved
    dear;
Farewell, you sacred place,
Where I her first saw!

Hätt' ich dich doch nie geseh'n,
Schöne Herzenskönigin!

Had I you never seen,
Beautiful heart's queen!

Nimmer wär' es dann geschehen,	Never would it then have happened,
Daß ich jetzt so elend bin.	That I now so suffering am.
Nie wollt' ich dein Herze rühren,	Never wanted I your heart to touch,
Liebe hab' ich nie erfleht;	Love have I never begged for;
Nur ein stilles Leben führen	Only a quiet life to lead
Wollt' ich, wo dein Odem weht.	Wanted I, where your breath blows.
Doch du drängst mich selbst von hinnen;	But you drive me away from here;
Bitt're Worte spricht dein Mund;	Bitter words speak your mouth;
Wahnsinn wühlt in meinen Sinnen,	Insanity stirs in my senses,
Und mein Herz ist krank und wund.	And my heart is sick and wounded.
Und die Glieder, matt und träge,	And my limbs, tired and slow,
Schlepp' ich fort am Wanderstab,	Drag I forth on my staff,
Bis mein müdes Haupt ich lege	Until my tired head I lay
Ferne in ein kühles Grab.	Far away in a cool grave.

"Litanei" (Jacobi) (Two verses)	"Litany"[56]
Ruhn in Frieden alle Seelen,	Rest in peace, all souls
Die vollbracht ein banges Quälen,	Who, completed an anxious torment,
Die vollendet süßen Traum,	Who ended sweet dream,
Lebenssatt, geboren kaum,	Weary of life, born scarcely,
Aus der Welt hinüberschieden:	From this world departed:
Alle Seelen ruhn in Frieden!	All souls, rest in peace!
Und die nie der Sonne lachten,	And who never in the sun laughing,
Unterm Mond auf Dornen wachten,	Under the moon on thorns kept watch,
Gott, im reinen Himmelslicht,	God, in the pure light of heaven,
Einst zu sehn vom Angesicht:	Once to see face to face:
Alle, die von hinnen schieden,	All who have hence departed,
Alle Seelen ruhn in Frieden!	All souls, rest in peace!

"Meeres Stille" (Goethe)	"Sea Calm"[57]
Tiefe Stille herrscht im Wasser	Deep calm rules the water

Ohne Regung ruht das Meer,
Und bekümmert sieht der Schiffer
Glatte Fläche ringsumher.
Keine Luft von keiner Seite!
Todesstille fürchterlich!
In der ungeheuern Weite
Reget keine Welle sich.

Without motion, rests the sea,
And troubled sees the sailor
Smooth flatness all around.
No wind from any quarter!
Deadly calm dreadful!
In the vast expanse
Stirs no wave.

"Mondenschein" (Heine)

Nacht liegt auf den fremden
    Wegen,
Krankes Herz und müde
    Glieder;—
Ach, da fließt, wie stiller
    Segen,
Süßer Mond, dein Licht
    hernieder.

Süßer Mond, mit deinen Strahlen
Scheuchest du das nächt'ge
    Grauen;
Es zerrinen meine Qualen,
Und die Augen übertauen.

"Moonlight"[58]

Night lies on the unfamiliar
    ways,
Sick heart and tired
    limbs;—
Ah, there streams, as a silent
    blessing,
Sweet moon, your light
    down.

Sweet moon, with your beams
Drive you away night's
    horror;
Vanish my torments,
And my eyes melt into tears.

"Morgen!" (Mackay)

Und morgen wird die Sonne
    wieder scheinen
Und auf dem Wege, den ich
    gehen werde,
Wird uns, die Glücklichen, sie
    wieder einen
Inmitten dieser Sonnenatmenden
    Erde . . .

Und zu dem Strand, dem weiten,
    wogenblauen,
Werden wir still und langsam
    niedersteigen,
Stumm werden wir uns in die
    Augen schauen,
Und auf uns sinkt des Glückes
    stummes Schweigen . . .

"Tomorrow"[59]

And tomorrow will the sun again
    shine,
And on the path that I
    take shall,
Will us, the happy ones, they
    again unite
Upon this sun-breathing
    earth . . .

And to the shore, to the broad,
    blue-waved,
Shall we quiet and slow
    descend,
Silent will we into each other's
    eyes gaze,
And on us sinks joy's
    speechless silence . . .

"Nachtstück" (Mayrofer)
(First stanza only)

"Nocturne"[60]

Wenn über Berge sich der Nebel
    breitet,
Und Luna mit Gewölken
    kampft,
So nimmt der Alte seine Harfe,
    und schreitet,
Und singt waldeinwärts und
    gedämpft: . . .

When over the mountains the
    mist spreads
And moon with the clouds
    struggles,
Takes the old man his harp and
    strides,
And sings into the forest and
    quietly: . . .

"Nachtviolen" (Mayrhofer)

"Night's Violets"[61]

Nachtviolen,
Dunkle Augen, seelenvolle,
Selig ist es, sich versenken
In dem samtnen Blau.

Night's violets,
Dark-eyed, soulful,
Blissful is it to plunge
In your velvety blue.

Grüne Blätter streben freudig,
Euch zu hellen, euch zu
    schmücken;
Doch ihr blicket ernst und
    schweigend
In die laue Frühlingsluft.

Green leaves strive joyously,
You to brighten, you to
    adorn;
But, you gaze earnest and
    silent
Into the mild spring air.

Mit erhabnen Wehmutsstrahlen
Trafet ihr mein treues Herz,
Und nun blüht in stummen
    Nächten
Fort die heilige Verbindung.

With sublime melancholy beams
Touch you my loyal heart,
And now blossoms in muted
    nights,
Forth the sacred bond.

"Nachtzauber" (Eichendorff)

"Night Magic"[62]

Hörst du nicht die Quellen gehen
Zwischen Stein und Blumen weit
Nach den stillen Waldesseen,
Wo die Marmorbilder stehen,
In der schönen Einsamkeit?
Von den Bergen sacht hernieder,
Weckend die uralten Lieder,
Steigt die wunderbare Nacht,
Und die Gründe glänzen wieder,
Wie du's oft im Traum
    gedacht.

Hear you not the brooks running
Amongst stones and flowers afar
Toward silent forest lakes,
Where the marble statues stand,
In the beautiful solitude?
From the mountains gently down,
Stirring the ancient songs,
Falls the wondrous night,
And the valleys gleam again,
As you it often in dreams
    imagined.

Kennst die Blume du, entsprossen	Know the flower you, sprung forth
In dem mondbeglänzten Grund?	In the moonlit valley?
Aus der Knospe, halb erschlossen,	Out from its bud half open,
Junge Glieder blühend sprossen,	Young limbs have blossomed,
Weiße Arme, roter Mund,	White arms, red mouth,
Und die Nachtigallen schlagen,	And nightingales warble,
Und rings hebt es an zu klagen,	And all around arises a lament,
Ach, vor Liebe todeswund,	Ah, by love wounded mortally,
Von versunknen schönen Tagen—	Of lost lovely days —
Komm, o komm zum stillen Grund!	Come, oh come to the silent place!

"Nähe des Geliebten" (Goethe)	"Nearness of the Beloved"[63]
Ich denke dein, wenn mir der	I think of you, when to me the
Sonne Schimmer	sun's shimmer
Vom Meere strahlt;	From the sea gleams;
Ich denke dein, wenn sich des	I think of you, when itself the
Mondes Flimmer	moon's light
In Quellen malt.	In springs depicts.
Ich sehe dich, wenn auf dem	I see you, when on the distant
fernen Wege	path
Der Staub sich hebt;	The dust itself raises;
In tiefer Nacht, wenn auf dem	In the dark of night, when on the
schmalen Stege	narrow step
Der Wand'rer bebt.	The wanderer totters.
Ich höre dich, wenn dort mit	I hear you, when there with
dumpfen Rauschen	muted roar
Die Welle steigt.	The wave rises.
Im stillen Hain, da geh' ich oft	In the quiet grove, there go I
zu lauschen,	often to listen,
Wenn alles schweigt.	When all is quiet.
Ich bin bei dir; du sei'st auch noch	I am with you; (even if) you are so
so ferne,	far away,
Du bist mir nah!	You are to me near!
Die Sonne sinkt, bald leuchten	The sun sinks, soon light for me
mir die Sterne;	the stars;
O wärst du da!	Oh, were you here!

"O wüßt ich doch den Weg zurück"	"Oh, If I But Knew the Way
(Groth)	Back"[64]
O wüßt ich doch den Weg zurück,	Oh, if I but knew the way back,

Den lieben Weg zum Kinder -land! O warum sucht ich nach dem Glück Und ließ der Mutter Hand?	The sweet way back to childhood land! Oh why sought I for happiness And left the mother's hand?
O wie mich sehnet auszuruhn, Von keinem Streben aufgeweckt, Die müden Augen zuzutun, Von Liebe sanft bedeckt!	Oh, how I long to take rest, By no striving aroused, My weary eyes to close, In love softly covered!

Und nichts zu forschen,
  nichts zu spähn,
Und nur zu träumen leicht und
  lind;
Der Zeiten Wandel nicht zu
  sehn,
Zum zweiten Mal ein Kind!
	And nothing to seek,
	  nothing to watch for,
	And only to dream lightly and
	  gently;
	The time's changing not to
	  see,
	For a second time a child!

O zeig mir doch den Weg zurück, Den lieben Weg zum Kinder -land! Vergebens such ich nach dem Glück, Ringsum ist öder Strand!	Oh show me then the way back, The sweet way back to childhood land! In vain seek I for happiness, Around is desolate shore!

"Schäfers Klagelied" (Goethe)	"Shepherd's Song of Complaint"[65]
Da droben auf jenem Berge, Da steh ich tausendmal, An meinem Stabe gebogen, Und schaue hinab in das Tal.	Up there on that mountain, There stand I a thousand times, Over my staff bowed, And gaze down into the valley.

Dann folg' ich der weidenden
  Herde,
Mein Hündchen bewahret mir
  sie.
Ich bin herunter gekommen
Und weiss doch selber nicht wie.
Da stehet von schönen
  Blumen
Die ganze Wiese so voll.
Ich breche sie, ohne zu wissen,
Wem ich sie geben soll.
	Then follow I the grazing
	  herd,
	My little dog watches for me
	  them.
	I have descended
	And know nevertheless not how.
	There stands of beautiful
	  flowers
	The whole meadow so full.
	I pick them, without knowing,
	To whom I them give should.

Und Regen, Sturm und Gewitter
Verpass ich unter dem Baum.
Die Türe dort bleibet verschlossen;
Denn alles ist leider ein
    Traum.

And rain, storm, and bad weather
Endure I under a tree.
The door there remains closed;
For everything is painfully a
    dream.

Es stehet ein Regenbogen
Wohl über jenem Haus!
Sie aber ist weggezogen,
Und weit in das Land hinaus.

There is a rainbow
Indeed over that house!
She, however, has moved away,
And far away in the country.

Hinaus in das Land und, weiter
Veilleicht gar über die See,
Vorüber, ihr Schafe, vorüber!
Dem Schäfer ist gar so weh.

Out in the country, and farther
Perhaps even over the ocean,
On, you sheep, on,
The shepherd is so very hurt.

Spanischesliederbuch
(trans. Geibel & Heyse)
Weltliche Lieder No. 2

Spanish Songbook

Secular Songs, No. 2

"In dem Schatten meiner Locken"

"In the Shadow of My Curls"[66]

In dem Schatten meiner Locken
Schlief mir mein Geliebter ein.
Weck' ich ihn nun auf? Ach nein.

In the shadow of my curls
Asleep on me my lover fell.
Wake I him now up? Ah, no.

Sorglich strählt' ich meine krausen
Locken täglich in der Frühe;
Doch umsonst ist meine Mühe,
Weil die Winde sie zersausen.

Carefully combed I my tangled
Curls daily in the morning;
But in vain is my work,
Because the breezes them rumple.

Lockenschatten, Windessausen,
Schläferten den Liebsten ein;
Weck' ich ihn nun auf! Ach nein.

Tresses' shadow, wind's rumpling,
Fell asleep my love;
Wake I him now up? Ah, no.

Hören muß ich, wie ihn gräme,
Daß er schmachtet schon so
    lange,
Daß ihm Leben geb' und nehme
Diese meine braune Wange.
Und er nennt mich seine
    Schlange;
Und doch schlief er bei mir ein.
Weck' ich ihn nun auf? Ach nein.

Hear must I, how him torments,
That he languishes already so
    long,
That (for) him life gives and takes
This, my brown cheek.
And he calls me his
    snake;
And still sleeps he next to me.
Wake I him now up? Ah, no.

"Ständchen" (Kugler)

Der Mond steht über dem
    Berge,
So recht für verliebte Leut;
Im Garten rieselt ein
    Brunnen,
Sonst stille weit und breit.

Neben der Mauer im Schatten,
Da steh'n der Studenten drei,
Mit Flöt' und Geig' und Zither,
Und singen und spielen dabei.

Die Klänge schleichen der
    Schönsten
Sacht in den Traum hinein;
Sie schaut den blonden Geliebten,
Und lispelt: "Vergiß nicht mein!"

Ständchen (von Schack)

Mach auf, mach auf doch leise,
    mein Kind,
Um keinen vom Schlummer zu
    wecken.
Kaum murmelt der Bach, kaum
    zittert im Wind
Ein Blatt an den Büschen und
    Hecken.
D'rum leise, mein Mädchen, daß
    nichts sich regt;
Nur leise die Hand auf die
    Klinke gelegt.

Mit Tritten, wie Tritte der Elfen so
    sacht,
Um über die Blumen zu hüpfen,
Flieg' leicht hinaus in die
    Mondscheinnacht,
Zu mir in den Garten zu schlüpfen.
Rings schlummern die Blüten am
    rieselnden Bach
Und duften im Schlaf; nur die
    Liebe ist wach.

"Serenade" [67]

The moon stands over the
    mountain,
So right for in-love people.
In the garden ripples a
    fountain,
Else quiet far and wide.

By the wall in the shadows,
There stand students three,
With flute and violin and zither,
And sing and play along.

The sounds slip to the
    most beautiful one
Gently into her dream;
She gazes at the blond beloved,
And whispers: Forget not me!

Serenade [68]

Open up, open up, but softly, my
    child,
In order no one from sleep to
    awaken.
Scarcely murmurs the brook,
    scarcely trembles in the wind
A leaf in the bushes and
    hedges.
Therefore quietly, my girl, so that
    nothing stirs;
Only quietly your hand on the
    latch laid.

With steps, like the steps of elves
    so gentle,
In order over the flowers to hop,
Fly lightly out into the moonlight
    night,
To me in the garden to slip.
All around slumber the flowers by
    the rustling brook
And fragrant in sleep; only love is
    awake.

Sitz' nieder; hier dämmert's
   geheimnisvoll,
Unter den Lindenbäumen.
Die Nachtigall, uns zu Häupten
   soll,
Von uns'rer Küssen träumen
Und die Rose, wenn sie am
   Morgen erwacht,
Hoch glühn von den
   Wonneschauern der Nacht.

Sit down; here darkens it
   mysteriously,
Under the linden trees.
The nightingale at our heads
   shall,
Of our kisses dream.
And the rose, when it tomorrow
   awakens,
Brightly gleam from the trembling
   raptures of the night.

"Trost in Tränen" (Goethe)
  (One of four verses)

"Comfort in Tears"[69]

Wie kommts, daß du so traurig bist,
Da alles froh erscheint?
Man sieht dirs an den Augen an,
Gewiß du hast geweint.

How comes it that you so sad are,
When all happy seems?
One can see from your eyes,
Certainly, you have been weeping.

"Und hab' ich einsam auch geweint
So ist's mein eigner Schmerz,
Und Tränen fließen gar so süß,
Erleichtern mir das Herz."

"And have I alone also wept,
So is it my own distress,
And tears flow so very sweetly,
Easing to me my heart."

"Verborgenheit" (Mörike)

"Obscurity"[70]

Laß, o Welt, o laß mich sein!
Locket nicht mit Liebesgaben,
Laßt dies Herz alleine haben
Seine Wonne, seine Pein!

Leave, o world, o leave me be!
Tempt me not with love's gifts
Leave this heart alone to have
Its bliss, its agony!

Was ich traure, weiß ich nicht,
Es ist unbekanntes Wehe;
Immerdar durch Tränen sehe
Ich der Sonne liebes Licht.

Why I grieve, know I not,
It is unknown grief;
All the time through tears see
I the sun's lovely light.

Oft bin ich mir kaum
   bewußt,
Und die helle Freude zücket
Durch die Schwere, so mich
   drücket
Wonniglich in meiner Brust.

Often am I of myself scarcely
   aware,
And the pure joy flashes
Through the heaviness, so to me
   presses
Blissful in my heart.

Laß, o Welt, o laß mich sein!
Locket nicht mit
   Liebesgaben,

Leave, o world, o leave me be!
Tempt me not with
   gifts of love,

Laßt dies Herz alleine haben
Seine Wonne, seine Pein!

Leave this heart alone to have
Its bliss, its agony!

"Vergebliches Ständchen"
(Lower Rhine Folksong)

"Vain Serenade"[71]

"Guten Abend, mein Schatz, guten
    Abend, mein Kind!
Ich komm' aus Lieb' zu dir;
Ach, mach' mir auf die Tür,
Mach' mir auf die Tür!"

"Good evening, my dear, Good
    evening, my child!
I come out of love for you;
Ah, open for me the door!
Open for me the door!"

"Mein Tür ist verschlossen, ich laß'
    dich nicht ein,
Mutter, die rät' mir klug,
Wär'st du herein mit Fug,
Wär's mit mir vorbei!"

"My door is locked, I admit
    you not,
Mother advises my wisely,
Were you in here by right,
Would it be over with me!"

"So kalt ist die Nacht, so eisig der
    Wind;
Daß mir das Herz erfriert,
Mein Lieb' erlöschen wird,
Öffne mir, mein Kind!"

"So cold is the night, so icy the
    wind;
That my heart will freeze,
My love go out will,
Open up for me, my child!"

"Löschet dein' Lieb', laß sie
    löschen nur,
Löschet sie immerzu,
Geh' heim zu Bett, zur Ruh'!
Gute Nacht, mein Knab'!"

"If your love is extinguished, let it
    go out,
Extinguish it ceaselessly,
Go home to bed, to rest!
Good night, my boy!"

"Verklärung" (Alexander Pope)
(First verse only)

"Transfiguration"[72]

Lebensfunke, vom Himmel
    entglüht,
Der sich loszuwinden müht,
Zitternd, kühn, vor Sehnen
    leidend,
Gern und doch mit Schmerzen
    scheidend!

Spark of life, from heaven
    kindled,
That to wrench itself away toils,
Trembling, brave, longing
    enduring,
Gladly and yet in agony,
    departing!

"Verschwiegene Liebe"
(Eichendorff)

"Silent Love"[73]

Über Wipfel und Saaten
In den Glanz hinein—

Over trees and grain fields
Into the gleam—

Wer mag sie erraten,	Who may them guess,
Wer holte sie ein?	Who retrieves them?
Gedanken sich wiegen,	Thoughts sway,
Die Nacht ist verschwiegen,	The night is silent,
Gedanken sind frei.	Thoughts are free.
Errät es nur eine,	Guess it only one,
Wer an sie gedacht	Who of her has thought
Beim Rauschen der Haine,	As murmur the woods,
Wenn niemand mehr wacht	When no one anymore watches
Als die Wolken, die fliegen—	When the clouds that soar—
Mein Lieb ist verschwiegen	My love is silent
Und schön wie die Nacht.	And beautiful as the night.

"Wanderers Nachtlied I" (Goethe)	"Wanderers Nightsong I"[74]
Über allen Gipfeln	Over every summit
Ist Ruh,	Is peace,
In allen Wipfeln	In all treetops
Spürest du	Detect you
Kaum einen Hauch;	Scarce a breath;
Die Vögelein schweigen im	The little birds are quiet in the
Walde.	woods.
Warte nur, balde	Wait now, soon
Ruhest du auch.	Rest you also.

"Wanderers Nachtlied II" (Goethe)	"Wanderer's Nightsong II"[75]
Der du von dem Himmel bist,	You who from heaven are,
Alles Leid und Schmerzen stillest,	(Who) all pain and sorrow ease,
Den, der doppelt elend	To the one who doubly wretched
ist,	is,
Doppelt mit Erquickung füllest,	Doubly with fresh vigour fill,
Ach, ich bin des Treibens müde!	Ah, I am of restless life tired!
Was soll all der Schmerz und Lust?	What is all this pain and joy?
Süßer Friede,	Sweet peace,
Komm, ach, komm in meine Brust!	Come, ah come into my breast!

"Widmung" (Rückert)	"Dedication"[76]
Du meine Seele, du mein Herz,	You my soul, you my heart,
Du meine Wonn', o du mein	You my bliss, O you my
Schmerz,	pain,
Du meine Welt, in der ich lebe,	You my world, in which I live,

Mein Himmel du, darein ich
schwebe,
O du mein Grab, in das hinab
Ich ewig meinen Kummer gab.

Du bist die Ruh, du bist der
Frieden
Du bist vom Himmel mir
beschieden.
Daß du mich liebst, macht mich
mir wert,
Dein Blick hat mich vor mir
verklärt,
Du hebst mich liebend über
mich,
Mein guter Geist, mein beß'res Ich!

My heaven you, into which I
float,
O you my grave, into which
I forever my grief consigned.

You are repose, you are the
peace
You are from Heaven on me
bestowed.
That you me love, gives me my
worth,
Your glance has me in mine
transfigured,
You raise me lovingly above
myself,
My good spirit, my better self!

"Wie Melodien zieht es mir"
(Groth)

"As Melodies Steal to Me"[71]

Wie Melodien zieht es
Mir leise durch den Sinn,
Wie Frühlingsblumen blüht es
Und schwebt wie Duft dahin.

Doch kommt das Wort und faßt es
Und führt es vor das Aug',
Wie Nebelgrau erblaßt es
Und schwindet wie ein Hauch.

Und dennoch ruht im Reime
Verborgen wohl ein Duft,
Den mild aus stillem Keime
Ein feuchtes Auge ruft.

As melodies steal
To me softly through the mind,
As spring flowers blooms it
And floats like a scent away.

But comes the word and seizes it
And brings it before the eye,
As the grey of mist pales it
And vanishes like a breath.

And yet reposes in rhyme
Concealed a scent,
Which gently out of silent bud
A moist eye summons.

"Wiegenlied" (Claudius?)

"Cradle Song"[78]

Schlafe, holder, süßer Knabe,
Leise wiegt dich deiner Mutter
Hand;
Sanfte Ruhe, milde Labe
Bringt dir schwebend dieses
Wiegenband.

Schlafe in dem süßen Grabe,

Sleep, dear, sweet boy,
Gently rocks you your mother's
hand;
Gentle rest, soft comfort
Brings you swaying this cradle
strap.

Sleep in the sweet grave,

Noch beschützt dich deiner
  Mutter Arm,
Alle Wünsche, alle Habe
Fast sie lebend, alle liebe-
  warm.

Yet protects you your
  mother's arm,
All wishes, all possessions
Holds she lovingly, all loving
  warmth.

Schlafe in der Flaumen Schoße,
Noch umtönt dich lauter
  Liebeston,
Eine Lilie, eine Rose,
Nach dem Schlafe werd' sie dir
  zum Lohn.

Sleep in the down lap,
Still rings around you pure
  notes of love.
A lily, a rose,
After sleep shall they be to you
  reward.

"Wiegenlied" (Dehmel)

"Cradle Song"[79]

Träume, träume' du mein süßes
  Leben,
Von dem Himmel, der die Blumen
  bringt,
Blüten schimmern da, die
  leben
Von dem Lied, das deine Mutter
  singt.

Dream, dream, my sweet
  life
From heaven, which flowers
  bring,
Blossoms shimmer there, that
  live
From the song that your mother
  sings.

Träume, träume, Knospe meiner
  Sorgen,
Von dem Tage, da die Blume
  sproß;
Von dem hellen Blütenmorgen,

Dream, dream bud of my
  sorrows,
Of the day when the flower
  opened;
Of the shining blossoming
  morning,

Da dein Seelchen sich der Welt
  erschloß.

When your little soul to the world
  opened.

Träume, träume, Blüte meiner
  Liebe,
Von der stillen, von der heil'gen
  Nacht,
Da die Blume seiner Liebe
Diese Welt zum Himmel mir
  gemacht.

Dream, dream, blossom of my
  love,
Of the still, of the holy
  night
When the flower of his love
This world into my heaven
  made.

"Wiegenlied"
(Des Knaben Wunderhorn)

"Cradle Song"[80]
(The Boy's Magic Horn)

Guten Abend, gut' Nacht,

Good night, good night,

Mit Rosen bedacht,
Mit Näglein besteckt,
Schlupf unter die Deck:
Morgen früh, wenn Gott will,
Wirst du wieder geweckt.

Guten Abend, gut Nacht,
Von Englein bewacht,
Die zeigen im Traum
Dir Christkindleins Baum:
Schlaf nun selig und süß,
Schlau im Traum's Paradies.

With roses covered,
With carnations adorned,
Slip under your quilt:
By morning early, if God wills,
Will you again be awakened.

Good night, good night,
By angels watched,
They show in dreams
The Christ-child's tree:
Sleep now happy and sweet,
See in your dreams Heaven.

Notes to Appendix I

1. Set by Franz as op. 16, no. 4.
2. Set by Gustav Mahler, ca. 1880–83.
3. Set by Strauss as op. 10, no. 8, 1882–1883. A mignonette is a fragrant flowering plant.
4. Set by Robert Schumann as op. 35, no. 12 in 1840.
5. Set by Zelter in 1812 and Schubert twice, as D. 259 in 1815 and D. 296 in 1819(?).
6. Set by Wolf in 1888.
7. Set by Schubert in 1817 as op. 88, no. 4, D 547.
8. Set by Brahms in 1858 as op. 19, no. 5 and Wolf in 1888.
9. Set by Schubert in 1823 as op. 72, D. 774.
10. Set by Wolf in 1888.
11. Set by Franz as op. 5, no. 1 and Wolf in 1878.
12. From Walter Scott's *The Lady of the Lake.* The song is alternatively called "Ellen's Gesang III;" it was set by Schubert as op. 52, no. 6, D. 839 in 1825.
13. Set by Wolf in 1888.
14. Set by Reichardt in 1809, Zelter in 1810, and Wolf in 1888.
15. Set by Robert Schumann as op. 64, no. 2 in 1841–1847 and Wolf in 1888.
16. Set by Schubert in 1817 as D. 545.
17. Set by Wolf in 1886 and Reger as op. 70, no. 2 in 1902–1903.
18. Set by Schubert as D. 932 in 1827.
19. Set by Schubert as op. 92, no. 1, D. 794 in 1822.
20. Set by Schubert in 1815, D. 149.
21. Set by Brahms as op. 96, no. 2 in 1884.
22. Set by Schubert in 1817 as op. 7, no. 3, D. 531.
23. Set by Schubert in ca. 1919, D. 649.
24. Set by Schumann as op. 48 in 1840.
25. Set by Schubert in ca. 1817, D. 550.
26. Set by Franz as op. 25, no. 1, and Schumann as op. 25, no. 7 in 1840.
27. Set by Schubert in 1815 as D. 194 and Brahms in 1864 as op. 43, no. 2.
28. Set by Schubert in 1823, D. 795.
29. Set by Schubert in 1827 as op. 89, D. 911.
30. Set by Schubert as op. 59, no. 3, D. 776 in 1823.
31. Set by Schumann as op. 25, no. 24 in 1840; Liszt in 1840; and Wolf in 1876.
32. Set by Schubert in 1818, D. 620.
33. Set by Schumann as op. 79, no. 24 in 1849 and Wolf in 1888.
34. Set by Schubert as op. 1, D. 328, in 1815 and Loewe as op. 1, no. 3 in 1818.
35. Set by Schubert in 1815, D. 226.

36. Set by Schumann as op. 42 in 1840; seven of the poems were also set by Loewe as op. 60.

37. Set by Schubert as op. 19, no. 3 in 1817, D. 544, and by Wolf in 1889.

38. Set by Wolf in 1888.

39. From Goethe's *Wilhelm Meister*, this poem was set by Schubert twice as D. 325 (1815) and D. 478 (1816); Schumann, as op. 98a, no. 2; and Wolf in 1888.

40. Set by Louis Spohr as op. 25, no. 3 in 1809 and Schubert as op. 2, D. 118, in 1814.

41. Set by Set by Wolf in 1888.

42. Set by Mahler in 1905.

43. Set by Schubert in 1826, D. 882.

44. Set by Brahms as op. 105, no. 2 in 1886.

45. Set by Schubert in 1817, D. 573.

46. Poetry compiled by Paul Heyse; Wolf set nos. 1–7 in 1890, nos. 8–22 in 1891, and nos. 23–46 in 1896.

47. Set by Schubert in 1816, D. 436.

48. This poem was not set by nineteenth-century composers.

49. Set by Wolf in 1888.

50. Set by Schubert in 1816, D. 509.

51. Set by Mendelssohn as op. 19a, no. 5 in 1830–1834.

52. Set by Clara Schumann as op. 37, no. 4 in 1840 and Gustav Mahler in 1905(?).

53. Set by Schubert as op. 65, no. 1, D. 360, in 1816 or 1822(?).

54. Set by Robert Schumann as op. 39 in 1840.

55. Set by Robert Schumann as op. 24 in 1840. Brahms set "In der Fremde" as op. 3, no. 5 in 1852–1853. In that song, Schumann changed several words, including the last line, which he set as: "Und keiner kennt mich mehr hier." Brahms used Schumann's text.

56. Set by Schubert in 1816, D. 343.

57. Set by Reichardt in c. 1809 and twice by Schubert in 1815: D. 215A and D. 216.

58. Set by Brahms as op. 85, no. 2 in 1879.

59. Set by Strauss in 1893–1894 as op. 27, no. 4 and Reger in 1902 as op. 66, no. 10.

60. Set by Schubert in 1819 as op. 36, no. 2, D. 672.

61. Set by Schubert in 1822, D. 752.

62. Set by Wolf in 1888.

63. Set by Zelter in 1808; Reichardt in 1809; and Schubert as op. 5, no. 2 in 1815, D. 162.

64. Set by Brahms as op. 63, no. 8 in 1874.

65. Set by Zelter in 1802; Reichardt in ca. 1809; and Schubert in 1814 as op. 3, no. 1, D. 121.

66. Set by Brahms as op. 6, no. 1 in 1852 and Wolf in 1889.

67. Set by Brahms as op. 106, no. 1 in 1886.

68. Set by Strauss as op. 17, no. 2 in 1885–1887.

69. Set by Zelter in 1803, Reichardt in ca. 1809; Schubert in 1814, D. 120; and Brahms as op. 48, no. 5 in 1858.

70. Set by Franz as op. 28, no. 5 and Wolf in 1888.

71. Set by Brahms as op. 84, no. 4 in 1881.

72. Set by Schubert in 1813, D. 59.

73. Set by Wolf in 1888.
74. Set by Schubert in 1815, D. 224.
75. Set by Schubert in ca. 1822, D. 768.
76. Set by Schumann as op. 25, no. 1 *(Myrten)* in 1840.
77. Set by Brahms as op. 105, no. 1 in 1886.
78. Set by Schubert in 1816, D. 498.
79. Set by Strauss as op. 41, no. 1 in 1899 and Reger as op. 51, no. 3 in 1900.
80. Set by Brahms as op. 49, no. 4 in 1868.

Glossary

ACCENT   This term has two distinct meanings. In music theory and analysis, musical accent occurs in its simplest form through meter, where normal accents of strong vs. weak occur systematically. The term *accent* also is used to denote rhythmic emphasis through nonmetric means, such as "agogic accent," emphasis through change in register, dynamic, timbre, etc. The term *accent* is preferred to the more generic word *stress*, which means in our definition, simply, emphasis. In the performer's language, "accent" denotes a sharper attack on a pitch or pitches, in contrast to "stress," which denotes a softer attack.

AGOGIC   In music theory and analysis, rhythmic emphasis is achieved by stressing a normally weak beat, or using a note of long duration or the two devices combined. In performer's language, "agogic accent" denotes a hesitation or delay in articulating a note to give it more emphasis.

ALLITERATION   In poetry, the repetition of opening consonants to connect words together and create flow, as in "red, red rose."

AMBIGUITY   The term *ambiguous,* according to *Webster's New Universal Unabridged Dictionary,* means "having two or more possible meanings; being of uncertain signification; susceptible of different interpretations; hence, obscure, not clear, not definite; uncertain or vague." The word *ambiguous* is useful in discussing both instrumental moments of tension and musical depiction of poetic ambiguity. The musical depiction of poetic ambiguity is of special importance to *Lied* and opera performers but instrumental performers of nineteenth-century music also encounter musical ambiguity that creates musical tension and drama.

AMBIVALENCE   The term *ambivalence* expresses a vacillation between two conflicting desires or feelings; for example, the Romantic poet might be caught in a conflict of ambivalence by wishing to continue to live and at the same time yearning for peaceful death.

ANACRUSIS   Also called *upbeat,* this term refers to the weaker note that precedes a metrically stressed downbeat.

ANTECEDENT/CONSEQUENT PHRASE   A common two-phrase group where phrase 1 ends on a half cadence (V), and relies on phrase 2 to create closure on I. Phrase 2 then closes on a tonic through an authentic cadence. The two phrases may or may not be linked by common melodic or motivic material.

APPOGGIATURA (LABELED APP)   Also called accented incomplete neighbor (AIN); in this melodic figure an incomplete embellishing neighboring pitch occurs on a metrically stressed beat, often beat 1. The resolution to a structural pitch then occurs on a normally weak beat.

ARTICULATION   The term *articulation* within various musical languages refers to how musical phrases are shaped by such means as rhythmic gesture, metric placement, melodic contour, and harmonic cadence.

ASSONANCE   In poetry, a repetition of vowel sounds within verse that connects words and creates a flow, as in "high in the sky." Rhyming assonances often connect the interior of verses with their line endings, for example, "High in the sky in the/Light of Night."

AUGMENTATION   Repetition of a gesture or motive that takes twice as long, for example, a melodic idea in eighth notes that recurs in quarter notes. The opposite of augmentation is diminution. (*See* Dimunition.)

BAR FORM   A formal design AAB characterized by a repeated A section that does not recur at the song's end and thus does not provide one type of formal closure. This form is not that common in *Lieder*, but was later used extensively by Wagner in his operas.

BEAT   Recurring durational unit that is heard and felt throughout a work; the term is used synonymously with "pulse," and both denote a metronome-like tick that is perceived throughout, even in moments of silence.

CAESURA   In poetry, a break or pause in a line of verse, often in the middle of the line. The caesura results in a natural cessation of rhythmic progress. Various punctuations denote this, including a colon and a dash; in scansion, the caesura is indicated by | |.

CIRCULAR PROGRESSION   A phrase that begins and ends on the same harmony, for example, I–I or V–V. Such a phrase is called "prolongational."

CLOSED VOWEL   A closed vowel is the sound produced by making the mouth smaller when reproducing vowels, for example, the *e* in "be" is closed, while the *e* in "let" is open.

CLOSING PHRASE   A phrase that concludes with an authentic cadence, V–I. Such a phrase does not begin on I and is therefore "progressive" in nature.

CLOSURE   The term *closure* generally connotes the ending of a musical work, which, because of music's temporal nature, occurs gradually, through a variety of compositional techniques.

COMPOUND LINE   Where one melodic voice comprises melodic strands of several different registers and functions.

COMPOUND METER   A type of meter that incorporates two distinct types of grouping, the number of beats per bar and the number of subdivisions per beat. The most common form of compound meter is 6/8; its six eighth notes are divided into two beats per bar, each beat subdivided into three eighths. Other compound meters are 9/8, 12/8, and 6/4.

CONJUNCT   Melodic motion by step, in contrast to motion by leap (disjunct). (*See* Disjunct.)

COUPLET   In poetry, two lines of verse, that often rhyme and have the same length, and are considered a self-contained unit.

CRESCENDO   A steady increase in dynamic level.

DA CAPO   In musical form, return to the beginning.

DECEPTIVE CADENCE   The deceptive cadence, V–vi (or V–♭VI), usually defers resolution from V to I; an authentic cadence then follows with true tonal closure. This cadence creates a unique form of harmonic tension, as the expected closure is denied; it is effective in both texted and instrumental genres.

DECRESCENDO   Gradual decrease in dynamic level.

DÉNOUEMENT   A French term usually applied to drama that denotes a period of resolution toward the work's ultimate conclusion that follows a point of extreme intensity or climax.

DICHOTOMY   A division of something into two contradictory parts, for example, real and unreal.

DIMINUENDO   Gradual decrease in dynamics.

DIMINUTION   The transformation of a melodic gesture or motive so that it moves faster than the original, for example, a gesture or motive in half notes is repeated in quarter notes. The opposite of diminution is augmentation. (*See* Augmentation.)

DIRECTIONAL TONALITY   An unusual form of double tonality where a work begins in one key and concludes in another. This radical tonal design was explored by several composers of the nineteenth century; Schubert and Wolf composed the most *Lieder* using directional tonality, where double tonality helped convey most vividly the poetic text.

DISJUNCT   Melodic motion by leap, as compared to motion by step. (*See* Conjunct.)

DOWNBEAT   The first beat of each bar that is the most strongly accented beat irrespective of the meter.

DUPLE METER   One of the simple meters where the bar is subdivided into two or four beats. The most common forms of duple meter are 2/4 and 4/4; in 2/4 there are two quarter notes per bar, in 4/4 there are four quarters per bar. The downbeat is always the most accented beat in both 2/4 and 4/4; in 4/4 beat 3 has an accent that is stronger than beats 2 and 4, but not as strong as beat 1.

DUPLET   In music, a group of two notes to be played in the time of three; this creates rhythmic tension similar to the more usual triplets played in one or two beats.

DURATION   A term that measures the amount of time a musical event is sustained ("how long it lasts"). Longer pitches tend to reinforce the prevailing meter by beginning on strong beats, for example, the downbeat. Longer notes beginning on weaker beats are called "agogic accents."

DURCHKOMPONIERT   German term for the *Lied* through composed form, where there are no sectional repetitions. The form is used to set poems that convey a particular story or poetic progression and musical coherence is achieved by motivic reiteration.

ELISION   Also known as overlap, this term refers to a phrase structure where the end of one phrase coincides with the beginning of another; this overlap usually occurs on a downbeat, often on the tonic harmony.

EMBELLISHED HALF CADENCE   A strong arrival on V that is enhanced by being approached by its dominant, V of V. This emphasis on the half cadence is often misunderstood to be a tonicization, as if a change in key has occurred.

EMBELLISHING   A pitch or chord whose function is to ornament a more important structural pitch or chord; common embellishing functions are neighboring (N), passing (P), or chordal skip (CS). Embellishing elements may resolve to structural ones immediately or eventually over a period of time.

ENHARMONIC PUNS   Pitches that have the same sound but different spellings and functions (for example, F♯ and G♭); these pitches often facilitate key changes.

ENHARMONIC REINTERPRETATION   Pitches that have the same sound but, as suggested by different spellings, have different functions, often in different tonalities.

ENJAMBMENT   In poetry, the connection between two lines when a line of verse does not stop, but flows naturally into the next line without any pause. This is the opposite of end-stopped verse, where a line stops at the right-hand end because of some form of punctuation.

ENLIGHTENMENT   Eighteenth-century European philosophical movement characterized by rationalism and orderliness.

END-RHYME   In poetry, the rhyming of line endings that connects lines through rhyming patterns. Typical end-rhyme patterns are *abab* and *abba*.

END-STOPPED   In poetry, a line of verse that stops naturally at the right-hand end because of some form of punctuation. This contrasts with enjambment, where one line flows naturally into the next without pause.

EXPANSION   In general, *expansion* means enlarging something to increase its size and/or complexity. The term is used most often in the context of phrase structure, where an expansion denotes the enlarging of a phrase by adding one or more measures either at the phrase beginning, middle, or ending.

FOOT   *See* Metric Foot.

FLORID   This term refers to melodic lines characterized by ornaments or embellishments; this style is often contrasted by parlando melodic style, which is more like actual speech.

GENDER STUDIES   Recent area of scholarly research that questions whether the gender of a composer, writer, etc. influences the creative process in the areas of harmonic and tonal usage, formal design, melodic and motivic usage, rhythmic and metric features, etc. This area of study also attempts to bring to the fore creative works that have previously been dismissed or ignored simply because they were composed or written by a woman. As a result of gender studies, the music of many superb women composers has become available, including *Lieder* by Clara Schumann, Fanny Mendelssohn Hensel, Josephine Lang, and Alma Mahler, among others.

GROUPING   Combining pitches into rhythmic patterns or gestures. This happens both on the surface level of music and on deeper levels of musical structure where pitches are grouped by rhythmic relationship over longer spans of time. A *quintuplet* is a grouping of five pitches within a beat, while pitches heard on successive downbeats constitute a grouping of metric accents within a phrase.

HARMONIC RHYTHM   Rate of harmonic change over time; for example, a harmonic change every measure or a change every beat.

HEMIOLA   An alteration in metric pattern where systematic accenting of normally weak beats temporarily changes the meter. This often occurs when 2/4 becomes 3/4 or the reverse. Hemiola creates rhythmic and metric tension and often occurs just prior to a strong arrival on V.

HIERARCHY   A system of relationships among pitches, chords, keys, beats, phrases, etc. where one element is perceived to be more important than the others. The remaining elements also might be considered more or less important in relation to one another. For example, the tonic is the most important chord and key, the dominant second most important. In 4/4, the downbeat is the strongest beat, beat 3 is the next strongest, and beats 2 and 4 are the weakest.

HOMOPHONY   A texture in which all parts move in the same rhythm; this kind of texture is also called *chordal* or *homorhythmic.*

IMAGE   In poetry, a representation of something that renders an idea more vivid and that places the idea within a rich and expressive context, for example, the image of the beloved as a delicate flower.

IMPLICIT TONALITY   A section of a piece where a tonality is suggested, by its dominant, vii^{o7} and other chords, but is not clearly established through a tonicization or modulation.

INTERIOR RHYME   A series of rhyming sounds (two or more) within a line, as in "Die Reine, die Feine, die Kleine." Interior rhyme includes but is not limited to the use of alliteration (repeated consonances between words: d . . . d . . . d) and assonance (repeated vowel sounds between words: eine . . . eine . . . eine) to create rhymes within lines, either as opposed to or in conjunction with rhymes at the line endings.

INTERPOLATION   In general, *interpolation* refers to adding something to expand a given form, for example, adding extra notes to a melody. The term is most frequently used in the context of phrase structure, where as a device of phrase extension or expansion, added measures occur within a phrase, as opposed to at the phrase's beginning or ending.

IRONY   An expression of one thing in order to convey another, for example, to say something you know to be untrue as a way of dramatizing that falsehood. An example would be a poet's saying "your love heals me" when in fact the poet remains hurt by the rejecting lover. Heine is a poet famous for his use of irony.

LEGATO   To be played without any perceptible interruption between notes, in contrast to staccato, where each note is separated by subtle shortening of note values.

LINEAR ANALYSIS   Analytical system based on the existence of a pitch hierarchy within tonal music; in melodic structure, the system determines a primary tone and traces how this pitch is embellished and supported harmonically. The term is often associated with theorist Heinrich Schenker.

LORELEI   A siren (or mermaid) in German legend whose singing on a rock in the Rhine lured sailors to shipwreck on the reefs; Lorelei thus symbolizes a charming or enticing woman who uses her charms to seduce men into danger.

MEDIATING MOTIVES Chromatic linear motives that facilitate the change from one key to another.

MELISMA An expressive melodic figure setting one syllable of text that is found in the florid vocal style. The term originates from Gregorian chant, where the melismatic style contrasts with syllabic style.

METAPHOR In poetry, a figure of speech in which one thing is spoken of as if it were something else; for example, a happy wanderer is described as a babbling brook.

METER The systematic arrangement of strong and weak beats into a recurring pattern. In music, simple meters are in duple—2/4 and 4/4—and triple—3/4 and 3/8. Compound meter involves more than one grouping, for example 6/8, with two beats to the bar, each beat having three eighths. For the definition of meter in poetic verse, *see* Poetic Meter.

METRIC FOOT A unit of syllables containing one stress or accent. Most verse contains several feet per line.

MODAL MIXTURE The selective use of elements from the opposite mode, most often pitches of minor, ♭6 and ♭3, within the major mode.

MODE OF ADDRESS In poetry, the persona is the "voice" that speaks, for example, the poet, a figure in the poem who is quoted, or an element of nature that is personified. The mode of address, then, is the object or audience of the persona's utterance: the poet's persona might speak to a beloved or to nature (both are modes of address); the young man persona speaking aloud in nature might address a brook or springtime (both are modes of address); or the persona of the flower might muse aloud to herself or to a general listener who reads the poem (both are modes of address). *(See* Persona.)

MODIFIED STROPHIC A *Lied* form that involves some kind of variation within an otherwise simple strophic form. An example of such a variation would be recasting an entire stanza in the opposite mode.

MODULATION A lengthy section of music in a new key. Modulations differ from tonicizations in the length of time spent in the new key; tonicizations involve a brief musical period and modulations involve large sections.

MONOTONALITY A term suggested by Arnold Schoenberg that refers to the fact that despite modulations within tonal music, most works begin and end in one key.

MORDENT A lower-neighbor figure originating from Renaissance and Baroque performance practice; once indicated by a specific notational device, it came to be written out explicitly in the late eighteenth and nineteenth centuries.

MOTIVE   A small melodic element that is readily identifiable and is repeated systematically; it can recur with or without distinctive rhythmic identity and can recur in transformed forms: inverted, retrograde, retrograde inversion, etc. Motives occur in two categories: *untransposed* (same pitches) vs. *transposed* (different pitches) and *diatonic* (no chromatic pitches) vs. *chromatic* (some chromatic pitches).

MOTIVIC ANALYSIS   Analytical system that traces motivic repetition; the most common tonal motives are neighbor notes (N), thirds (3rd), and perfect fourths (P4).

MOTIVIC PARALLELISM   A motive originally heard as a brief linear element recurs over a longer time span and/or within the harmonic domain.

MOTIVIC TRANSFORMATION   The term is used in two ways. The most simple way denotes repetition of motives in altered states: inverted, backward, transposed, etc. The more complex use of the term denotes a change in the function of a motive within a new musical context, for example, a N figure becomes part of a P figure.

ONOMATOPOEIA   In poetry, the use of a word because its sound conveys its meaning, for example, the English words "buzz" and "hum" and the German words "Stille" and "Ruh."

OPEN VOWEL   An open vowel sound results from forming a more relaxed, more open mouth while pronouncing vowels, for example, the *o* in "lot" is open, while the *o* in "open" is closed.

OPENING PROGRESSION   A phrase that ends on a half cadence, thus requiring another phrase to return to I. Such a phrase is "progressive" in nature.

PARADOX   Something that is inherently self-contradictory and thus seems false, for example, the poet who finds love and feels pain.

PARALLEL MODE PAIR   A pair of major and minor modes that has the same tonic but differ in scale degrees $\hat{3}$, $\hat{6}$, and $\hat{7}$.

PARLANDO   Melodic style that simulates speech, one note per syllable of text. This often occurs in rapid tempo and is the opposite of florid melodic style. The "spoken speech" of parlando style is not to be confused with the recitative style, which creates a "musical speech" that captures verbal inflection.

PERIOD   This term has for years been synonymous with the antecedent/consequent phrase pair where one phrase (the antecedent) ends in a half cadence and is followed by a second phrase (the consequent) that concludes on the tonic. Recent theorists have broadened the term to denote other kinds of phrase groupings.

PERSONA   The term persona denotes "who is speaking," what voice a performer articulates; the concept also considers what is called the mode of address: to whom that voice speaks. In *Lieder* the pianist's voice or persona may differ from that of the singer, the various voices expressing different parts of the poetic text. In instrumental music, meanwhile, various musical gestures and expressions also can assume personas, and these "voices" may differ between treble and bass and among members of an ensemble. *(See* Mode of Address.)

PERSONIFICATION   A term associated with poetry and other literary forms wherein something inanimate (for example, a tree or brook) is endowed with human qualities: the tree weeps or the brook laughs.

PHRASE   A musical statement that is more or less self-contained in the way a sentence of prose is within a paragraph.

PHRASE EXPANSION OR EXTENSION   A phrase of a particular length, for example, the common four-bar phrase, is lengthened by, say, two additional bars to create a six-bar phrase. Extensions can occur at the beginning of a phrase, in the middle, or at the phrase ending.

PHRASE INTERPOLATION   The lengthening of a phrase in which the additional bars are added to the internal portion, as opposed to the phrase beginning or ending.

PHRASE OVERLAP   Two phrases overlap or are elided when the second phrase begins at the same time (on the same beat) as the first ends. This overlap usually occurs on a downbeat, often on the tonic harmony. (*See* Elision.)

PHRASE STRUCTURE   The term used to denote the complete design of phrase usage in a work. Usually it involves finding phrase "norms" and where these phrase lengths recur or are either shortened (by phrase contraction) or lengthened (by phrase expansion or interpolation).

PLAGAL CADENCE   A IV–I cadence. This cadence does not use the tonality-defining V, and is not as strong a closing gesture; it often occurs after a strong authentic cadence, as part of a larger cadential phrase. The plagal cadence often conveys particular poetic sentiments, for example, the religious "Amen" ending.

POETIC METER   The rhythmic patterns of words within lines of poetry. The five basic meters are: in duple, iambic ($\smile$ /) and trochaic (/ $\smile$); in triple, anapest ($\smile$ $\smile$ /) and dactylic (/ $\smile$ $\smile$); and the spondee (/). A single unit of meter is called a "foot" and a change from a prevailing meter is called a "substitution."

POETIC PROGRESSION   The flow of a poet's thoughts or feelings as they evolve over the time of a poem. This includes the poet's experience of the outer world of nature and other people as well as the poet's inner personal experience.

PRIMARY TONE   A concept adapted from Heinrich Schenker that asserts that one pitch of the tonic triad, usually $\hat{3}$ or $\hat{5}$, is the most important melodic pitch of a section or an entire piece. This tone receives metric emphasis and often initiates and concludes phrases; in addition, much melodic activity involves pitches and gestures that embellish the primary tone, for example, with Ns, thirds (linear or disjunct), and the like.

PROGRESSION   In general, the term *progression* expresses musical motion, harmonic and melodic, from one place to another over time. Progressive music contrasts with prolongational music, which essentially remains in one place over time.

PROLONGATION   In general, the term means a structural pitch or harmony that continues to be in effect over a long period of time despite intervening, less important — embellishing — pitches or harmonies. In contrast to the movement from one place to another in music that progresses, prolongational music essentially remains in the same place over time.

PULSE   Similar to the term *beat,* pulse denotes the durational unit that recurs like a metronomic tick throughout a work, even in moments of silence.

PUN   A literary pun is a word used, sometimes humorously, to emphasize its two different meanings, for example, a bass voice is basically low; both oranges and bells have peels/peals. A musical pun is a pitch that has two different functions, each in a different key, for example, the B♮ in C minor is reinterpreted as a C♭ in a♭ minor.

RANGE   The term *range* generally means the normal span of possible pitches for given voices or instruments. In *Lied* study, it is used to specify the span of pitches used by the singer and the accompanist within a given song.

RECAPITULATION   This term denotes a large-scale "reprise" that occurs most often in instrumental sonata forms. The term *reprise* is more appropriate for *Lied* form. *(See* Reprise.)

RECITATIVE   A vocal style designed to imitate and emphasize the natural inflections of speech. This style flourished in early music from Gregorian chant through Baroque religious music and opera. Richard Wagner, who criticized the stereotyped parlando recitative of Italian opera, created a different form of the style: a highly dramatic and expressive recitative style that characterized his "unending melody." Wolf, who modeled his music after that of Wagner, also used this new form of recitative.

REFRAIN A usually small musical idea that recurs systematically throughout a work, thus providing a special kind of formal repetition.

RELATIVE MAJOR/MINOR PAIR A pair of major and minor modes that shares the same key signature and scale and many harmonies but with different tonics. The relative major commonly is the tonal polarity of a work in minor and shifting between the minor and the relative major occurs readily in many different ways throughout the literature.

REPRISE A return to opening material and, usually, tonality that signals the imminent conclusion of a work.

RITARD A gradual slowing down of speed, often occurring at cadences.

RONDO A formal design where an opening A section recurs systematically after two or more contrasting sections: ABACA.

RUBATO Use of an elastic, flexible tempo involving slight *accelerandos* and *ritardandos* to enhance musical expression. *Rubato* is an instrument of interpretation that requires careful consideration of maintaining an overall tempo; this usually necessitates a balance of slowing down and speeding up to remain in sync with the overall tempo of a given work.

SCANSION In poetry, the determination of a poem's metric design by tracing patterns of various meters and substitutions.

SEHNSUCHT German word for yearning; romantic yearning *(romantische Sehnsucht)* often connotes longing for the unattainable or for peaceful death.

SIMILE In poetry, a figure of speech where something is compared to something else; for example, my love is *like* a red, red rose.

STACCATO A style characterized by separate articulation of each note, usually done by shortening each pitch enough to clearly articulate and separate it from the next. This contrasts with legato style, which aims to create no separation from note to note.

STANZA In poetry, a group of lines (usually four or more) forming one of the divisions of a poem; the stanza usually recurs with all its formal characteristics such as number of lines and use of meter and rhyme. The word "strophe" often is used as a synonym.

STIMMUNG A German word that connotes a single overriding mood or psychological state that pervades an entire poem. The word's application to German Romantic poetry derives from an earlier meaning of tuning musical instruments. The concept can be applied to some but not all poetry of the period and is most readily associated with the lyrics of Eichendorff.

STRESS   In music theory and analysis, *stress* describes general musical emphasis; this is not to be confused with the term *accent* which denotes emphasis through meter or various rhythmic devices, such as syncopation or agogic emphasis, etc. In performer's language, stress denotes a type of attack that is less sharp than an accent, which is a sharper attack.

STROPHIC FORM   A common formal design in *Lieder* where the same music sets several verses with little or no alterations. This form was commonly used by Schubert's predecessors, and while Schubert used it often, he enlarged upon the whole-scale repetition by including elements of tension and ambiguity that could convey changes in text more flexibly and that encouraged repeated hearings.

STRUCTURAL   A pitch or chord whose importance is clear and emphasized by rhythm, meter, tonal context, and the like. Structural elements are usually ornamented by embellishing pitches and chords of less value, like Ns, Ps, CSs, etc. *(See* Embellishing)

STURM UND DRANG   Storm and Stress movement in eighteenth-century German culture that led away from the Enlightenment and toward the Romantic period. The period was characterized by increased intensity and emotionalism.

SUBSTITUTION   In poetry, a metric pattern that is used in place of the expected one. Substitution occurs to underscore a particular word or phrase and to create rhythmic and metric changes that convey poetic shifts, for example, acceleration or deceleration.

SUSPENSION   Melodic figure where an embellishing pitch occurs on a strong beat; the suspension has three parts: (1) preparation, a consonant pitch occurring on a weak beat held over to become (2) a dissonant suspension on a strong beat, that is followed by (3) a resolution, usually down a step, on the next, weak beat.

SYLLABIC   Melodic style using one note per syllable of text. This is a simpler version of the parlando and recitative styles and contrasts directly with florid melody.

SYMBOL   In poetry, the use of a word to convey a larger meaning. For example, the nightingale ("Die Nachtigall") is used in German Romantic poetry to express a longing for lost or unattainable love.

SYNCOPATION   The disruption of "normative" metric accents by stressing a normally weak beat. This can be done by a simple accent, by holding a note over a bar (as in a suspension) or by using rests on normally strong beats.

SYNTAX   The term *syntax* is useful when talking about music as a temporal language. In general, syntax refers to the structure — or ordering —

of words in a phrase, clause, or sentence of prose; in the present context, syntax denotes the ordering of musical elements (pitch, chord, rhythm) in a phrase or section of music.

TEMPO   The pace of a piece of music over time, usually suggested by tempo indications (for example, *presto, andante*) and often influenced by other factors, such as texture, figuration, performance difficulty, and issues of expressivity.

TEMPORALITY   A general term denoting the concerns of time in musical performance. The issues incorporated here are those of tempo, rhythm, and meter, and the interpretative decisions performers make about the flow of music through time.

TERNARY   A three-part form usually with an ABA or ABA' design. This form occurs in many *Lieder* and was favored by Brahms in particular because of its use of one large contrasting section (B) and a large-scale reprise of the opening A section for formal balance and closure.

TESSITURA   In contrast to range, which denotes all pitches occuring in a performer's part, this term denotes the pitch level where a voice stays most of the time.

TEXTURE   This term has several meanings. In its most general use, it refers to the relative density or sparseness of a piece. In another common use, it refers to the way different parts combine, as in melody and accompaniment, homophonic, polyphonic or contrapuntal, etc.

THROUGH COMPOSED   The English translation for *durchkomponiert*, the term used to denote the formal design where a *Lied* has virtually no repetition but rather sets a poem with a clear story or a forward-moving poetic progression. Musical coherence sometimes is created by motivic repetition.

TIMBRE   The distinction of pitches by their color. Oboes sound different from horns, for example, and string timbre is different from piano timbre. In vocal writing, the singer can alter the timbre of the voice to give it a brighter or darker sound, as well as a lighter or heavier one. These are important expressive devices used by singers to convey nuances of the poetic text as well as to vary and dramatize the melodic line itself.

TONAL POLARITY   Within tonal music, a second tonality occurs that contrasts with and maintains tension with the opening, prevailing tonic. In early common-practice tonality, the most common tonal polarity with a major tonic was the key of the dominant while that with a minor tonic was the key of the relative major. Later in the nineteenth century, composers created tonal polarities and tensions with other, often less closely related keys such as tonalities a chromatic third apart.

TONAL REPRISE   The return of the tonic late in a work, usually after an emphasized dominant, that signals the end of any tonal contrasts or polarities and the beginning of the work's closing section.

TONIC/DOMINANT AXIS   The concept that most tonal music is based on the primary relationship between I and V, where the tonic is the harmonic and tonal anchor and the dominant is the chord or key that confirms the tonic through cadences and the tonal polarity I–V.

TONICIZATION   A brief change of key. Tonicizations differ from modulations in terms of duration—tonicizations involve short periods of time and modulations involve longer musical sections.

TRIPLE METER   Meter where the bar is divisible into three beats. In 3/4 time the bar is composed of three quarter notes, and in 3/8 meter there are three eighth notes per bar. Common triple meters are 3/4 and 3/8.

Selected Bibliography

On German Romanticism and German Romantic Poetry

Abraham, Gerald, ed. *Romanticism (1830–1890).* The New Oxford History of Music, vol. 9. Oxford and New York: Oxford University Press, 1990.

Barzun, Jacques. *Classic, Romantic, and Modern.* Rev. ed. Chicago: University of Chicago Press, 1975.

Boyle, Nicholas. *Goethe: The Poet and the Age.* Oxford and New York: Oxford University Press, 1991.

Chapple, Gerald, Frederick Hall, and Hans Schulte, eds. *The Romantic Tradition: German Literature and Music in the Nineteenth Century.* Lanham, Md.: University Press of America, 1991.

Cottrell, Alan P. *Wilhelm Müller's Lyrical Song Cycles: Interpretations and Texts.* Chapel Hill: University of North Carolina Press, 1970.

Dahlhaus, Carl. *Between Romanticism and Modernism: Four Studies in the Later Nineteenth Century.* Translated by Mary Whittall. Berkeley and Los Angeles: University of California Press, 1980.

Garland, Henry, and Mary Garland. *Oxford Companion to German Literature.* 2d ed. Oxford and New York: Oxford University Press, 1986.

Glaser, Hermann, ed. *The German Mind of the Nineteenth Century: A Literary and Historical Anthology.* New York: Continuum Press, 1981.

Hauser, Arnold. *The Social History of Art.* 4 vols. Translated by Stanley Godman. New York: Vintage Books, 1951.

Hollander, John. *Rhyme's Reason: A Guide to English Verse.* New Haven: Yale University Press, 1981.

Kaufmann, Walter. *From Shakespeare to Existentialism.* Freeport, N.Y.: Books for Libraries Press, 1971.

Lanham, Richard A. *A Handlist of Rhetorical Terms.* 2d ed. Berkeley and Los Angeles: University of California Press, 1991.

Lennenberg, Hans. "Classic and Romantic: The First Usage of the Terms." *Musical Quarterly* 78 (1994): 610–25.

Peucker, Brigitte. *Lyric Descent in the German Romantic Tradition.* New Haven: Yale University Press, 1987.

———. "Poetic Descent in Eichendorff's Lyric." *Germanic Review* 56/3 (1982): 98–106.

Prawer, Siegbert S. *Heine, the Tragic Satirist.* Cambridge: Cambridge University Press, 1961.

———, ed. *The Romantic Period in Germany: Essays by Members of the London University Institute of Germanic Studies.* London: Weidenfeld & Nicolson, 1970.

Preminger, Alex, ed. *Princeton Encyclopedia of Poetry and Poetics.* Princeton: Princeton University Press, 1974.

Smith, Barbara H. *Poetic Closure: A Study of How Poems End.* Chicago: University of Chicago Press, 1968.

Temperley, Nicholas, ed. *The Romantic Age, 1800–1914.* London: Athlone Press, 1981.

Thalmann, Marianne. *The Literary Sign Language of German Romanticism.* Translated by Harold A. Basilius. Detroit, Mich.: Wayne State University Press, 1972.

Turco, Lewis. *The New Book on Forms: A Handbook of Poetics.* Hanover, N.H.: University Press of New England, 1986.

Weimar, Karl S., ed. *German Language and Literature: Seven Essays.* Englewood Cliffs, N.J.: Prentice-Hall, 1974.

Wilkinson, Elizabeth. "Goethe's Poetry." *German Life and Letters* 2 (1949): 316–29.

Collected Editions

Brahms, Johannes. *Sämtliche Werke.* Vols. 24–26: *Lieder und Gesänge für eine Singstimme mit Klavierbegleitung.* Edited by Eusebius Mandyczewski. Leipzig: Breitkopf & Härtel, 1926.

Mahler, Gustav. *Sämtliche Werke: Kritische Gesamtausgabe.* Herausgegeben von der Internationalen Gustav Mahler Gesellschaft, Wien, c. 1960.

Schubert, Franz. *Werke: Erste Kritisch durchgesehene Gesamtausgabe.* Ser. 20, *Lieder und Gesänge.* Edited Eusebius Mandyczewski. Leipzig: Breitkopft & Härtel, 1894–97.

Schubert, Franz. *Neue Ausgabe Sämtlicher Werke.* Ser. 4, *Lieder.* Edited by Walther Dürr. Kassel and New York: Bärenreiter, 1964–.

Schumann, Robert. *Werke.* Edited by Clara Schumann. Leipzig: Breitkopf & Härtel, 1882–87.

Strauss, Richard. *Sämtliche Werke in Wiedergabe der Originaldrucke.* Edited by Ernst Hilmar. Tutzing: Hans Schneider, 1987–.

Wagner, Richard. *Werke: Erste kritisch revidierte Gesamtausgabe.* Vol. 1: *Lieder und Gesänge.* Edited by Michael Balling. Leipzig: Breitkopf & Härtel, 1912–c. 1929.

Wolf, Hugo. *Sämtliche Werke: Kritische Gesamtausgabe.* Edited by Hans Jancik. Vienna: Döblinger, Musikwissenschaftlicher Verlag, 1960.

Recommended Text Translations

Fischer-Dieskau, Dietrich, ed. and comp. *The Fischer-Dieskau Book of Lieder:*

The Original Texts of over Seven Hundred and Fifty Songs. Translated by George Bird and Richard Stokes. New York: Limelight Editions,1984.

Miller, Philip L., ed. and trans. *The Ring of Words.* New York: Norton, 1973.

Prawer, Siegbert S., ed. and trans. *The Penguin Book of Lieder.* Baltimore: Penguin Books, 1964.

Wigmore, Richard, ed. and trans. *Schubert: The Complete Song Texts.* New York: Schirmer, 1988.

On Words and Music

Barzun, Jacques. *Critical Questions on Music and Letters, Culture and Biography, 1940–1980.* Edited by Bea Friedland. Chicago: University of Chicago Press, 1982.

Berman, Laurence, ed. *Words and Music: The Scholar's View.* Cambridge: Harvard University Press, 1972.

Bonds, Mark Evan. *Wordless Rhetoric: Musical Form and the Metaphor of the Oration.* Cambridge: Harvard University Press, 1991.

Booth, Mark. *The Experience of Songs.* New Haven: Yale University Press, 1981.

Cone, Edward T. *The Composer's Voice.* Berkeley and Los Angeles: University of California Press, 1974.

———. "Words into Music: The Composer's Approach to the Text." In *Music: A View from Delft.* Edited by Robert P. Morgan, 115–23. Chicago: University of Chicago Press, 1989.

Hoffmann, E. T. A. *E. T. A. Hoffmann's Msucial Writings: "Kreisleriana," "The Poet and the Composer," and Music Criticism.* Translated by Martyn Clarke and edited by David Charlton. Cambridge: Cambridge University Press, 1989.

Ivey, Donald. *Song: Anatomy, Imagery, and Styles.* New York: Free Press, 1970.

Jonas, Oswald, "The Relation of Word and Tone." In *Introduction to the Theory of Heinrich Schenker: The Nature of the Musical Work of Art.* Rev. ed. Edited by John Rothgeb, 149–61. New York: Longman, 1982.

Kivy, Peter. *The Corded Shell: Reflections on Musical Expression.* Princeton: Princeton University Press, 1980.

———. *Sound and Semblance: Reflections on Musical Representation.* Princeton: Princeton University Press, 1984.

Kramer, Lawrence. *Music and Poetry: The Nineteenth Century and After.* Berkeley and Los Angeles: University of California Press, 1984.

Kramer, Richard. "Schubert's Heine." *19th Century Music* 8 (1985): 213–25.

Langer, Susanne K. *Feeling and Form.* New York: Scribner, 1953.

McAdams, Stephen, and Irene Deliége, eds. *Music and the Cognitive Sciences.* London: Harwood Academic Publishers, 1989.

Marshall, H. Lowen. "Symbolism in Schubert's *Winterreise.*" *Studies in Romanticism* 12 (1973): 607–32.

Maus, Fred Everett. "Agency in Instrumental Music and Song." *College Music Symposium* 29 (1989): 31–43.

Mosley, David L. *Gesture, Sign, and Song: An Interdisciplinary Approach to Schumann's Liederkreis, Op. 39.* New York: P. Lang, 1990.

Plantinga, Leon. *Schumann as Critic.* New Haven: Yale University Press, 1967.

Reed, John. *The Schubert Song Companion.* Manchester: Manchester University Press, 1985.

Robinson, Paul A. "The Self and Nature: Franz Schubert's *Die schöne Müllerin* and *Winterreise.*" Chapter 2 in *Opera and Ideas: From Mozart to Strauss.* New York: Harper & Row, 1985.

Scher, Steven Paul, ed. *Music and Text: Critical Inquiries.* Cambridge: Cambridge University Press, 1992.

Schochow, Maximilian, and Lilly Schochow. *Franz Schubert: Die Texte seiner einstimmig komponierten Lieder und ihre Dichter.* 2 vols. Hildesheim, N.Y.: Georg Olms, 1974.

Temperley, Nicholas. *English Songs, 1800–1860.* Musica Britannica, 43. London: Stainer & Bell, 1979.

Thym, Jurgen, and Ann Fehn. "Who Is Speaking? Edward T. Cone's Concept of Persona and Wolfgang von Schweinitz's Settings of Poems by Sarah Kirsch." *Journal of Musicological Research* 11 (1991): 1–31.

Wagner, Richard. *On Music and Drama.* Translated by H. Ashton Ellis. London: Gollancz, 1964. Reprint, Lincoln: University of Nebraska Press, 1992.

Winn, James. *Unsuspected Eloquence: A History of the Relations Between Poetry and Music.* New Haven: Yale University Press, 1981.

Biographical Works

Abraham, Gerald, ed. *the Music of Schubert,* New York: Norton, 1947.

————, ed. *Schumann: A Symposium.* Rev. ed. Westport, Conn.: Greenwood Press, 1977.

Bozarth, George. "Brahms's *Liederjahr* of 1868." *Music Review* 44 (1983): 208–22.

Brown, Maurice J. *Essays on Schubert.* New York: St. Martin's Press, 1966.

————. *Schubert: A Critical Biography.* Rev. ed. London: Macmillan, 1977.

————, and Eric Sams. *The New Grove Schubert.* London: Macmillan, 1982.

Cooke, Deryck, Heinz Becker, John Clapham, and Eric Sams. *The New Grove Late Romantic Masters: Bruckner, Brahms, Dvorak, Wolf.* London: Macmillan, 1985.

Deathridge, John, and Carl Dahlhaus. *The New Grove Wagner.* London: Macmillan, 1984.

Deutsch, Otto Erich. *Schubert: Memoirs by His Friends.* Translated by Rosamond Ley and John Nowell. London: Adam & Charles Black, 1958.

————. *The Schubert Reader: The Life of Franz Schubert in Letters and Documents.* Translated by Eric Blom. New York: Norton, 1947.

Einstein, Alfred. *Schubert: A Musical Portrait.* Oxford and New York: Oxford University Press, 1951.

Fischer-Dieskau, Dietrich. *Schubert's Songs: A Biographical Study.* Translated by Kenneth S. Whitton. New York: Knopf, 1977.

Frisch, Walter, ed. *Brahms and His World.* Princeton: Princeton University Press, 1990.

Gal, Hans. *Johannes Brahms: His Work and Personality.* Translated by Joseph Stein. Westport, Conn.: Greenwood Press, 1977.

Geiringer, Karl. *Brahms: His Life and Work.* Enlarged ed. New York: Da Capo Press, 1982.

Gilliam, Bryan, ed. *Richard Strauss and His World.* Princeton: Princeton University Press, 1992.

Hillmar, Ernst. *Franz Schubert in His Time.* Translated by Reinhard G. Pauly. Portland, Ore.: Amadeus Press, 1988.

Millington, Barry, ed. *The Wagner Compendium: A Guide to Wagner's Life and Music.* New York: Schirmer, 1992.

Mitchell, Donald. *Gustav Mahler: The Early Years.* Rev. ed. Berkeley and Los Angeles: University of California Press, 1980.

————. *Gustav Mahler: The Wunderhorn Years.* Boulder, Co.: Westview Press, 1976.

Musgrave, Michael, ed. *Brahms 2: Biographical, Documentary, and Analytical Studies.* Cambridge: Cambridge University Press, 1987.

————. *The Music of Brahms.* London: Routledge & Kegan Paul, 1985.

Newman, Ernest. *Hugo Wolf.* London: Methuen, 1907.

Osborne, Charles. *Schubert and His Vienna.* New York: Knopf, 1985.

Pascall, Robert, ed. *Brahms: Biographical, Documentary, and Analytical Studies.* Cambridge: Cambridge University Press, 1983.

Pleasants, Henry, ed. *The Musical World of Robert Schumann: A Selection from His Own Writings.* New York: St. martin's Press, 1965.

————, ed. and trans. *The Music Criticism of Hugo Wolf.* New York: Holmes & Meier, 1978.

Reed, John. *Schubert: The Final Years.* New York: St. Martin's Press, 1972.

Temperley, Nicholas, Gerald Abraham, and Humphrey Searle. *The New Grove Early Romantic Masters I: Chopin, Schumann, Liszt.* New York: Norton, 1985.

Todd, R. Larry, ed. *Mendelssohn and His World.* Princeton: Princeton University Press, 1992.

————, ed. *Schumann and His World.* Princeton: Princeton University Press, 1994.

Walker, Alan, ed. *Robert Schumann: The Man and His Music.* Rev. ed. London: Barrie & Jenkins, 1976.

On German Lieder

Agawu, V. Kofi. "On Schubert's 'Der greise Kopf'." *In Theory Only* 8/6 (1985): 7–16.

———. "Schubert's Harmony Revisited: The Songs 'Du liebst mich nicht' and 'Dass Sie hier geswesen'." *Journal of Musicological Research* 9 (1989): 23–42.

———. "Structural 'Highpoints' in Schumann's *Dichterliebe.*" *Music Analysis 3* (1984): 159–80.

———. "Theory and Practice in the Analysis of the 19th Century *Lied.*" *Music Analysis* 11 (1992): 3–36.

Atlas, Raphael. "Enharmonic Trompe-l'oreille: Reprise and the Disguised Seam in 19th-Century Music." *In Theory Only* 10/6 (1988): 15–36.

Barthes, Roland. "The Romantic Song." In *The Responsibility of Forms: Critical Essays on Music, Art, and Representation.* Translated by Richard Howard, 286–92. New York: Hill & Wang, 1985

Berry, Wallace T. "Text and Music in *The Alto Rhapsody.*" *Journal of Music Theory* 27 (1983): 239–54.

Boylan, Paul. "The Lieder of Hugo Wolf: Zenith of the German Art Song." Ph.D. diss., University of Michigan, 1968.

Bozarth, George. "Brahms's *Lieder ohne Worte:* The 'Poetic' Andantes of the Piano Sonatas." In *Brahms Studies: Analytical and Historical Perspectives.* Edited by George Bozarth, 345–78. Oxford: Oxford University Press, Clarendon Press, 1990.

Branscombe, Peter. "Schubert and the Melodrama." *Schubert Studies: Problems of Style and Chronology.* Edited by Eva Badura-Skoda and Peter Branscombe, 105–42. Cambridge: Cambridge University Press, 1982.

Brauner, Charles S. "Irony in the Heine *Lieder* of Schubert and Schumann." *Musical Quarterly* 67 (1981): 261–81.

Braus, Ira. "Brahms's *Liebe und Fruhling II,* Op. 3, No. 3: A New Path to the Artwork of the Future?" *19th Century Music* 10 (1986): 135–56.

Brody, Elaine, and Robert A. Fowkes. *The German Lied and Its Poetry.* New York: New York University Press, 1971.

Brown, Maurice J. *Schubert Songs.* Seattle: University of Washington Press, 1969.

Cacioppo, Curt. "Poem to Music: Schumann's 'Mondnacht' Setting." *College Music Symposium* 30 (1990): 46–56.

Capell, Richard. *Schubert's Songs.* 3d ed. Old Woking, Surrey: Gresham Press, 1973.

Cone, Edward T. "On the Structure of *Ich folge dir.*" *College Music Symposium* 5 (1965): 77–87.

Daverio, John. "Schumann's *Im Legendenton* and Friedrich Schlegel's *Arabeske.*" *19th Century Music* 11 (1987): 150–63.

———. "The *Wechsel der Töne* in Brahms's *Schicksalslied.*" *Journal of the American Musicological Society* 46 (1993): 84–13.

Dill, Heinz J. "Romantic Irony in the Works of Robert Schumann." *Musical Quarterly* 73 (1989): 172-95.

Dürr, Walther. "Schubert's Songs and Their Poetry: Reflections on Poetic Aspects of Song Composition." In *Schubert Studies: Problems of Style and Chronology*. Edited by Eva Badura-Skoda and Peter Branscombe, 1–24. Cambridge: Cambridge University Press, 1982.

Fehn, Ann C., and Rufus Hallmark. "Text and Music in Schubert's Pentameter Lieder: A Consideration of Declamation." In *Studies in the History of Music*. Vol. 1, *Music and Language*. New York: Broude Brothers, 1983.

———. "Text Declamation in Schubert's Settings of Pentameter Poetry." *Zeitschrift für Literaturwissenshaft und Linguistik* 9/34 (1979): 80–111.

Feil, Arnold. *Franz Schubert: Die schöne Müllerin, Winterreise*. Translated by Ann C. Sherwin. Portland, Ore.: Amadeus Press, 1988.

———. "Rhythm in Schubert: Some Practical Problems: Critical Analysis, Critical Edition, Critical Performance." *Schubert Studies: Problems of Style and Chronology*. Edited by Eva Badura-Skoda and Peter Branscombe, 327–46. Cambridge: Cambridge University Press, 1982.

———. "Two Analyses: *Im Dorfe,* from *Winterreise* and *Moment Musical* in F Minor, Op. 94/3 (D. 780)." Translated by Walter Frisch. *Schubert: Critical and Analytical Studies*. Edited by Walter Frisch, 116–25. Lincoln: University of Nebraska Press, 1986.

Fellinger, Imogen. "Cyclic Tendencies in Brahms Song Collections." In *Brahms Studies: Analytical and Historical Perspectives*. Edited by George Bozarth, 379–90. Oxford: Clarendon Press, 1990.

Finscher, Ludwig. "Brahms Early Songs: Poetry vs. Music." In *Brahms Studies: Analytical and Historical Perspectives*. Edited by George Bozarth, 331–44. Oxford: Oxford University Press, Clarendon Press, 1990.

Flothius, Marius. "Schubert Revises Schubert." In *Schubert Studies: Problems of Style and Chronology*. Edited by Eva Badura-Skoda and Peter Branscombe, 61–84. Cambridge: Cambridge University Press, 1982.

Forbes, Elliot. "*Nur wer die Sehnsucht kennt:* An Example of a Goethe Lyric Set to Music." In *Words and Music: The Scholar's View*. Edited by Laurence Berman, 59–82. Cambridge:Harvard University Press, 1971.

Forte, Allen. "Motive and Rhythmic Contour in *The Alto Rhapsody*." *Journal of Music Theory* 27 (1983): 255–71.

Frisch, Walter. "Schubert's *Nähe des Geliebten* (D. 162): Transformation of the Volkston." In *Schubert: Critical and Analytical Studies*. Edited by Walter Frisch, 175–99. Lincoln: University of Nebraska Press, 1986.

———. "Song and Chamber Music, 1864–1879." Chapter 4 in *Brahms and the Principle of Developing Variation*. Berkeley and Los Angeles: University of California Press, 1984.

Gal, Hans. *Franz Schubert and the Essence of Melody*. London: Victor Gollancz, 1974.

Georgiades, Thrasybulos. "Lyric as Musical Structure: Schubert's *Wandrers Nachtlied* ("Über allen Gipfeln," D. 768)." In *Schubert: Critical and Analytical Studies*. Edited by Walter Frisch, 74–103. Lincoln: University of Nebraska Press, 1986.

Hallmark, Rufus. *The Genesis of Schumann's Dichterliebe: A Source Study.* Ann Arbor: UMI Research Press, 1979.

———, ed. *Nineteenth-Century German Lieder: Studies in Musical Genres and Repertories.* New York: Schirmer, 1995.

———. "The Rückert *Lieder* of Robert and Clara Schumann," *19th Century Music* 14 (1990): 3–30.

———. "Schubert's '*Auf dem Strom*'." In *Schubert Studies: Problems of Style and Chronology.* Edited by Eva Badura-Skoda and Peter Branscombe, 25–46. Cambridge: Cambridge University Press, 1982.

Hirsch, Marjorie Wing. *Schubert's Dramatic Lieder.* Cambridge: Cambridge University Press, 1993.

Horton, Charles T. "A Structural Function of Dynamics in Schumann's *Ich grolle nicht*." *In Theory Only* 4/8 (1979): 30–46.

Jackson, Timothy. "Schubert's Revisions of '*Der Jüngling und der Tod*', D. 545a–b, and '*Meeresstille*', D.216a–b." *Musical Quarterly* 75 (1991): 336–61.

Kerman, Joseph. "*An die ferne Geliebte.*" In *Beethoven Studies.* Edited by Alan Tyson, 123–57. New York: Norton, 1973.

———. "A Romantic Detail in Schubert's *Schwanengesang*." In *Schubert: Critical and Analytical Studies.* Edited by Walter Frisch, 48–64. Lincoln: University of Nebraska Press, 1986.

Komar, Arthur, ed. *Schumann: "Dichterliebe."* New York: Norton, 1971.

Kramer, Lawrence. "The Schubert Lied: Romantic Form and Romantic Consciousness." In *Schubert: Critical and Analytical Studies.* Edited by Walter Frisch, 200–237. Lincoln: University of Nebraska Press, 1986.

———. "Decadence and Desire: The Wilhelm Meister Songs of Wolf and Schubert." *19th Century Music* 10 (1987): 229–42.

Kramer, Richard. *Distant Cycles: Schubert and the Conceiving of Song.* Chicago: University of Chicago Press, 1994.

———. "Distant Cycles: Schubert, Goethe and the *Entfernte*." *Journal of Musicology* 6 (1988): 3–26.

———. "Schubert's Heine." *19th Century Music* 8 (1985): 213–25.

Krebs, Harald. "Some Addenda to McNamee's Remarks on '*Erlkönig*'." *Music Analysis* 7 (1988): 53–57.

Laitz, Steven. "Pitch-class Motive in the Songs of Franz Schubert: The Submediant Complex." Ph.D. diss., University of Rochester, 1992.

Lewin, David. "Schubert: *Auf dem Flusse.*" *19th Century Music* 6 (1982): 47–59.

Lewis, Christopher. "Text, Time, and the Tonic: Aspects of Patterning in the Romantic Cycle." *Integral* 2 (1988): 37–74.

Lockwood, Lewis. "Beethoven's Sketches for *Sehnsucht*, WoO 146." In *Beethoven Studies.* Edited by Alan Tyson, 97–122. New York: Norton, 1973.

McCreless, Patrick. "Song Order in the Song Cycle: Schumann's *Liederkreis*, Op. 39," *Music Analysis* 5 (1986) 8–11.

McKinney, Thomas R. "Harmony in the Songs of Hugo Wolf." Ph.D. diss., University of North Texas State, 1989.

McNamee, Ann K. "The Introduction in Schubert's Lieder." *Music Analysis* 4 (1985): 95–106.

Marston, Nicholas. "'*Im Legendenton*': Schumann's 'Unsung Voice'." *19th Century Music* 16 (1993) 227–41.

Meister, Barbara. *An Introduction to the Art Song*. New York: Taplinger, 1980.

Neumeyer, David. "Organic Structure and the Song Cycle: Another Look at Schumann's *Dichterliebe*." *Music Theory Spectrum* 4 (1982): 92–105.

Newcomb, Anthony. "Structure and Expression in a Schubert Song: Noch einmal *Auf dem Flusse* zu hören." In *Schubert: Critical and Analytical Studies*. Edited by Walter Frisch, 153–74. Lincoln: University of Nebraska Press, 1986.

Sams, Eric. *The Songs of Hugo Wolf*. London: Methuen, 1961.

———. *Brahms Songs*. Seattle: University of Washington Press, 1972.

———. *The Songs of Robert Schumann*. 2d ed. London: Eulenburg, 1975.

Schaeffer, Erwin. "Schubert's *Winterreise*." Translated by Harold Spivacke. *Musical Quarterly* 24 (1938): 37–57.

Schroeder, David. "Schubert the Singer." *Music Review* 49 (1988): 254–66.

Smeed, J. W., ed. *Famous Poets, Neglected Composers: Songs to Lyrics by Goethe, Heine, Möricke, and Others*. Recent Researches in the Music of the Nineteenth and Early Twentieth Centuries, vol. 10. Madison: A-R Editions, 1992.

Stein, Deborah. "The Expansion of the Subdominant in the Late Nineteenth Century." *Journal of Music Theory* 27/2 (1983): 153–80.

———. *Hugo Wolf's Lieder and Extensions of Tonality*. Ann Arbor: UMI Research Press, 1985.

———. "Schubert's '*Erlkönig*': Motivic Parallelism and Motivic Transformation." *19th Century Music* 13 (1989) 145–58.

———. "Schubert's '*Die Liebe hat gelogen*': The Deception of Mode and Mixture" *Journal of Musicological Research* 9/4 (1989): 109–31.

Stein, Jack. *Poem and Music in the German Lied from Gluck to Hugo Wolf*. Cambridge: Harvard University Press, 1971.

———. "Poem and Music in Hugo Wolf's Mörike Songs." *Musical Quarterly* 55 (1967): 22–38.

———. "Schubert's Heine Songs." *Journal of Aesthetics and Art Criticism* 24 (1966) 559–66.

———. "Was Goethe Wrong about the Nineteenth-Century Lied? An Explanation of the Relation of Poem and Music." Publications of the *Modern Language Association* 77/3 (1962): 232–39.

Swent, Jeannette. "Register as a Structural Element in Schubert's *Die schöne Müllerin* and *Winterreise*." Ph.D. diss., Yale University, 1984.

Thym, Jurgen, ed. *One Hundred Years of Eichendorff Songs*. Recent Researches in the Music of the Nineteenth and Early Twentieth Centuries, vol. 5. Madison: A-R Editions, 1983.

———. "The Solo Song Settings of Eichendorff's Poems by Schumann and Wolf." Ph.D. diss., Case Western Reserve University, 1974.

Tovey, Donald F. "Franz Schubert." In *Essays and Lectures on Music.* London: Oxford University Press, 1949.

Turchin, Barbara. "The Nineteenth-Century *Wanderlieder* Cycle." *Journal of Musicology* 5 (1987): 498–526.

———. "Robert Schumann's Song Cycles: The Cycle within the Song." *19th Century Music* 8 (1985): 231–44.

———. "Robert Schumann's Song Cycles in the Context of the Nineteenth-Century *Liederkreis.*" Ph.D. diss., Columbia University, 1981.

Walsh, Stephen. *The Lieder of Schumann.* New York: Praeger, 1972.

Whitton, Kenneth. *Lieder: An Introduction to German Song.* London: Julia MacRae Books, 1984.

Wolff, Christoph. "Schubert's 'Der Tod und das Madchen': Analytical and Explanatory Notes on the Song D. 531 and the Quartet D. 810." In *Schubert Studies: Problems of Style and Chronology.* Edited by Eva Badura-Skoda and Peter Branscombe, 143–71. Cambridge: Cambridge University Press, 1982.

Youens, Susan. *Hugo Wolf: The Vocal Music.* Princeton: Princeton University Press, 1992.

———. "Poetic Rhythm and Musical Metre in Schubert's *Winterreise.*" *Music and Letters* 65 (1984): 28–40.

———. *Retracing a Winter's Journey: Schubert's Winterreise.* Ithaca, N.Y.: Cornell University Press, 1991.

———. Retracing a Winter Journey: Reflections on Schubert's *Winterreise.*" *19th-Century Music* 9 (1985): 128–35.

———. "*Wegweiser* in *Winterreise.*" *Journal of Musicology* 5 (1987): 357–79.

———. "*Winterreise:* In the Right Order." *Soundings* 13 (1985): 41–50.

On Rhythm and Meter

Basic References

Barry, Barbara. *Musical Time: The Sense of Order.* Stuyvesant, N.Y.: Pendragon Press, 1990.

Cone, Edward T. *Musical Form and Musical Performance.* New York: Norton, 1968.

Cooper, Grosvenor, and Leonard B. Meyer. *The Rhythmic Structure of Music.* Chicago: University of Chicago Press, 1960.

Epstein, David. *Shaping Time: Music, the Brain, and Performance.* New York: Schirmer, 1994.

Kramer, Jonathan. *The Time of Music.* New York: Schirmer, 1988.

Lehrdahl, Fred, and Ray Jackendoff. *A Generative Theory of Tonal Music.* Cambridge: MIT Press, 1983.

Lester, Joel. *The Rhythms of Tonal Music.* Carbondale: Southern Illinois University Press, 1986.

Rothstein, William. *Phrase Structure in Tonal Music.* New York: Schirmer, 1989.

Additional Theoretical and Analytical Studies of Rhythm

Benjamin, William. "A Theory of Musical Meter." *Music Perception* 1 (1984): 355–413.

Berry, Wallace T. "Metric and Rhythmic Articulation in Music." *Music Theory Spectrum* 7 (1985): 7–33.

Cinnamon, Howard. "New Observations on Voice Leading, Hemiola, and Their Roles in Tonal and Rhythmic Structures in Chopin's Prelude in B Minor, Op. 28, No. 6." *Integral* 6 (1992): 66–106.

Cohn, Richard. "Dramatization of Hypermetric Conflicts in the Scherzo of Beethoven's Ninth Symphony." *19th-Century Music* 15 (1992): 22–40.

Epstein, David. "Brahms and the Mechanisms of Motion: The Composition of Performance." In *Brahms Studies: Analytical and Historical Perspectives.* Edited by George Bozarth, 191–228. Oxford: Clarendon Press, 1990.

———. "Tempo Relations." *Music Theory Spectrum* 7 (1985): 34–71.

Frisch, Walter. "The Shifting Bar Line: Metrical Displacement in Brahms." In *Brahms Studies: Analytical and Historical Perspectives.* Edited by George Bozarth, 139–64. Oxford: Oxford University Press, Clarendon Press, 1990.

Imbrie, Andrew. " 'Extra Measures' and Metrical Ambiguity in Beethoven." In *Beethoven Studies.* Edited by Alan Tyson, 44–66. New York: Norton, 1973.

Krebs, Harald. "Some Extensions of the Concepts of Metrical Consonance and Dissonance." *Journal of Music Theory* 31 (1987): 99–120.

———. "Dramatic Functions of Metrical Consonances and Dissonances in *Das Rheingold*." *In Theory Only* 10/5 (1988): 5–20.

Komar, Arthur. *Theory of Suspensions.* Princeton: Princeton University Press, 1971.

Lehrdahl, Fred and Ray Jackendorff. "On the Theory of Grouping and Meter." *Musical Quarterly* 67 (1981): 479–506.

———. "Toward a Formal Theory of Tonal Music." *Journal of Music Theory* 21 (1977): 111–71.

Lowinsky, Edward. "On Mozart's Rhythm." In *The Creative World of Mozart.* Edited by Paul Henry Lang, 31–55. New York: Norton, 1963.

Morgan, Robert P. "The Theory and Analysis of Tonal Rhythm." *Musical Quarterly* 64 (1978): 435–73.

———. "Rhythm and the Theory of Structural Levels." Ph.D. diss., Yale University, 1981.

Schachter, Carl. "Rhythm and Linear Analysis: A Preliminary Study." *Music Forum* 4 (1976): 281–334.

———. "Rhythm and Linear Analysis: Aspects of Meter." *Music Forum* 6 (1978): 1–59.

———. "Rhythm and Linear Analysis: Durational Reduction." *Music Forum* 5 (1980): 197–232.

Yeston, Maury. *The Stratification of Musical Rhythm.* New Haven: Yale University Press, 1976.

On Harmony and Form

Aldwell, Edward, and Carl Schachter. *Harmony and Voice Leading.* 2d ed. New York: Harcourt Brace Jovanovich, 1979.

Berry, Wallace T. *Form in Music.* Englewood Cliffs, N.J.: Prentice-Hall, 1966.

Green, Douglass M. *Form in Tonal Music: An Introduction to Analysis.* 2d ed. New York: Holt, Rinehart & Winston, 1979.

Kostka, Stefan, and Dorothy Payne. *Tonal Harmony.* 2d ed. New York: McGraw-Hill, 1989.

Lester, Joel. *Harmony in Tonal Music.* New York: Knopf, 1982.

Piston, Walter, with Mark DeVoto. *Harmony.* 5th ed. New York: Norton, 1987.

On General Music History, Theory, and Analysis

Abbate, Carolyn. *Unsung Voices: Opera and Musical Narrative in the Nineteenth Century.* Princeton: Princeton University Press, 1991.

———. "What the Sorcerer Said." *19th Century Music* 12 (1989): 221–30.

Abraham, Gerald. *A Hundred Years of Music.* 4th ed. London: Duckworth, 1974.

Agawu, V. Kofi. *Playing with Signs: A Semiotic Interpretation of Classic Music.* Princeton: Princeton University Press, 1991.

Bailey, Robert, ed. *Wagner: Prelude and Transfiguration from "Tristan and Isolde."* New York: Norton, 1985.

———. "Musical Language and Structure in the Third Symphony." In *Brahms Studies: Analytical and Historical Perspectives.* Edited by George Bozarth, 405–22. Oxford: Oxford University Press, Clarendon Press, 1990.

———. "The Structure of the *Ring* and Its Evolution." *19th Century Music* 1 (1977): 48–61.

Bent, Ian, with William Drabkin. *Analysis.* New York: Norton, 1987.

Berry, Wallace T. *Structural Functions in Music.* Englewood Cliffs, N.J.: Prentice-Hall, 1976.

Blume, Friedrich. *Classic and Romantic Music: A Comprehensive Survey.* Translated by M. D. Herter Norton. London: Faber & Faber, 1972.

Botstein, Leon. "Brahms and Nineteenth-Century Painting." *19th Century Music* 14 (1990): 154–68.

Cone, Edward T. "Harmonic Congruence in Brahms." In *Brahms Studies: Analytical and Historical Perspectives.* Edited by George Bozarth, 165–90. Oxford: Oxford University Press, Clarendon Press, 1990.

Cook, Nicholas. *A Guide to Musical Analysis.* New York: Braziller, 1987.

Dahlhaus, Carl. *Nineteenth-Century Music.* Translated by J. Bradford Robinson. Berkeley and Los Angeles: University of California Press, 1989.

———. *Studies on the Origin of Harmonic Tonality.* Translated by Robert O. Gjerdingen. Princeton: Princeton University Press, 1990.

Darcy, Warren, *"Creatio ex nihilo:* The Genesis, Structure, and Meaning of the *Rheingold* Prelude." *19th Century Music* 12 (1989): 79–100.

Daverio, John. *Nineteenth-Century Music and the German Romantic Ideology.* New York: Schirmer, 1993.

Deutsch, Otto Erich. *Schubert: Thematic Catalogue of All His Works in Chronological Order.* New York: Norton, 1951.

Dunsby, Jonathan. *Structural Ambiguity in Brahms: Analytical Approaches to Four Works.* Ann Arbor: UMI Research Press, 1981.

———, and Arnold Whittall. *Music Analysis in Theory and Practice.* New Haven: Yale University Press, 1988.

Dürr, Walther. "Schubert and Johann Michael Vogl: A Reappraisal." *19th Century Music* 3 (1979): 126–40.

Einstein, Alfred. *Essays on Music.* New York: Norton, 1956.

———. *Music in the Romantic Era.* New York: Norton, 1947.

Epstein, David. *Beyond Orpheus: Studies in Musical Structure.* Cambridge: MIT Press, 1980.

Ferrara, Lawrence. *Philosophy and the Analysis of Music.* New York: Greenwood Press, 1991.

Hatten, Robert. "Interpreting Deception in Music." *In Theory Only* 12/5–6 (1992): 31–50.

Jensen, Eric Frederick. "Liszt, Nerval, and Faust." *19th Century Music* 6 (1982): 151–58.

Jordan, Roland, and Emma Kafalenos. "The Double Trajectory: Ambiguity in Brahms and Henry James." *19th Century Music* 13 (1989): 129–44.

Kallberg, Jeffrey. "The Rhetoric of Genre: Chopin's Nocturne in G Minor." *19th Century Music* 11 (1988): 238–61.

Kaplan, Richard. "Sonata Form in the Orchestral Works of Liszt: The Revolutionary Reconsidered." *19th Century Music* 8 (1984): 142–52.

Kinderman, William. "Dramatic Recapitulation in Wagner's *Götterdämmerung.*" *19th Century Music* 4 (1980): 101–12.

Knapp, Raymond. "The Finale of Brahms's Fourth Symphony: The Tale of the Subject." *19th Century Music* 13 (1989): 3–17.

Korsyn, Kevin. "Brahms Research and Aesthetic Ideology." *Music Analysis* 12 (1993): 89–102.

Kramer, Lawrence. "Haydn's Chaos, Schenker's Order, or, Hermeneutics and Musical Analysis: Can They Mix?" *19th Century Music* 16 (1992): 3–17.

———. "The Mirror of Tonality: Transitional Features of 19th-century Harmony." *19th Century Music* 4 (1981): 191–208.

Kramer, Richard. "*Gradus ad Parnassum:* Beethoven, Schubert, and the Romance of Counterpoint." *19th Century Music* 11 (1987): 107–20.

Krebs, Harald. "Alternatives to Monotonality in Early Nineteenth-Century Music." *Journal of Music Theory* 25 (1981): 1–16.

———. "Third Relations and Dominant." Ph.D. diss., Yale University, 1980.

Kross, Siegfried. "Thematic Structure and Formal Processes in Brahms's Sonata Movements." In *Brahms Studies: Analytical and Historical Perspectives.* Edited by George Bozarth, 423–44. Oxford: Oxford University Press, Clarendon Press, 1990.

Levenson, Irene Montefiore. "Smooth Moves: Schubert and Theories of Modulation in the 19th Century." *In Theory Only* 7/5–6 (1984): 35–53.

Lewin, David. "Amfortas's Prayer to Titurel and the Role of D in *Parsifal:* The Tonal Spaces of the Drama and the Enharmonic C♭/B." *19th Century Music* 7 (1984): 336–49.

———. "Brahms, His Past, and Modes of Music Theory." *Brahms Studies: Analytical and Historical Perspectives.* Edited by George Bozarth, 13–28. Oxford: Oxford University Press, Clarendon Press, 1990.

———. *Musical Form and Transformation: Four Analytic Essays.* New Haven: Yale University Press, 1993.

———. "Music Theory, Phenomenology, and Modes of Perception." *Music Perception* 3 (1986): 327–92.

Longyear, Rey M. *Nineteenth Century Romanticism in Music.* 2d ed. Englewood Cliffs, N.J.: Prentice-Hall, 1973.

McCreless, Patrick. "Ernst Kurth and the Analysis of the Chromatic Music of the Late Nineteenth Century." *Music Theory Spectrum* 5 (1983): 56–75.

McDonald, William E. "What does Wotan Know? Autobiography and Moral Vision in Wagner's *Ring.*" *19th Century Music* 15 (1991): 36–51.

———. "Words, Music, and Dramatic Development in *Die Meistersinger.*" *19th Century Music* 1 (1978): 246–60.

Maus, Fred Everett. "Introduction: *The Composer's Voice* as Music Theory." *College Music Symposium* 29 (1989): 1–7.

———. "Music as Drama." *Music Theory Spectrum* 10 (1988): 56–73.

———. "Music as Narrative." *Indiana Theory Review* 12/1–2 (1991): 1–24.

Meyer, Leonard B. *Emotion and Meaning in Music.* Chicago: University of Chicago Press, 1956.

———. *Music, the Arts, and Ideas.* Chicago: University of Chicago Press, 1967.

———. *Explaining Music: Essays and Explorations.* Berkeley and Los Angeles: University of California Press, 1973.

Monelle, Raymond. *Linguistics and Semiotics in Music.* Contemporary Music Studies, 5. London: Harwood Academic Publishers, 1992.

Morgan, Robert P. "Dissonant Prolongations: Theoretical and Compositional Precedents." *Journal of Music Theory* 20 (1976): 49–91.

Musgrave, Michael. "Schoenberg's Brahms." In *Brahms Studies: Analytical and Historical Perspectives.* Edited by George Bozarth, 123–38. Oxford: Oxford University Press, Clarendon Press, 1990.

Nattiez, Jean-Jacques. *Music and Discourse: Toward a Semiology of Music.* Translated by Carolyn Abbate. Princeton: Princeton University Press, 1990.

———. "Plot and Seriation in Music Analysis." *Music Analysis* 4 (1985): 107–18.

Newbould, Brian. "A Schubert Palindrome," *19th Century Music* 15 (1992): 207–14.

Newcomb, Anthony. "Schumann and Late Eighteenth-Century Narrative Strategies." *19th Century Music* 11 (1987): 164–74.

Ostwald, Peter F. "Florestan, Eusebius, Clara, and Schumann's Right Hand." *19th Century Music* 4 (1980): 17–31.

Newlin, Dika. *Bruckner, Mahler, Schoenberg.* New York: Norton, 1947.

Parkany, Stephen. "Kurth's Bruckner and the Adagio of the Seventh Symphony." *19th Century Music* 11 (1988): 262–81.

Plantinga, Leon. *Romantic Music: A History of Musical Style in Nineteenth-Century Europe.* New York: Norton, 1984.

Poznansky, Alexander. "Tchaikovsky's Suicide: Myth and Reality." *19th Century Music* 11 (1988): 199–220.

Proctor, Gregory. "Technical Bases of Nineteenth-Century Chromatic Tonality: A Study in Chromaticism." Ph.D. diss., Princeton University, 1978.

Rahn, John. "D-Light Reflecting: The Nature of Comparison." In *Brahms Studies: Analytical and Historical Perspectives.* Edited by George Bozarth, 399–404. Oxford: Oxford University Press, Clarendon Press, 1990.

Ratner, Leonard. *Classic Music: Expression, Form, and Style.* New York: Schirmer, 1980.

———. *Romantic Music: Sound and Syntax.* New York: Schirmer, 1992.

Rosen, Charles. "Brahms the Subversive." In *Brahms Studies: Analytical and Historical Perspectives.* Edited by George Bozarth, 105–22. Oxford: Oxford University Press, Clarendon Press, 1990.

———. *The Classical Style: Haydn, Mozart, Beethoven.* New York: Norton, 1971.

———. *The Romantic Generation.* Cambridge: Harvard University Press, 1995.

———. *Sonata Forms.* New York: Norton, 1980.

Samson, Jim. *Music in Transition: A Study of Tonal Expansion and Atonality, 1900–1920.* London: Dent, 1977.

Schachter, Carl. "Analysis by Key: Another Look at Modulation." *Music Analysis* 6 (1987): 289–318.

Schoenberg, Arnold. "Brahms the Progressive." In *Style and Idea.* Edited and translated by Leonard Stein, 398–441. Berkeley and Los Angeles: University of California Press, 1975.

———. *Fundamentals of Musical Composition.* Edited by Gerald Strang and Leonard Stein. London: Faber & Faber, 1967.

———. *Structural Functions of Harmony.* New York: Norton, 1954.

Scholes, Robert. "Language, Narrative, and Anti-Narrative." *Critical Inquiry* 7 (1980): 204–12.

Smith, Peter H. "Liquidation, Augmentation, and Brahms's Recapitulatory Overlaps." *19th Century Music* 17 (1994): 237–61.

Solomon, Maynard. "Schubert and Beethoven." *19th Century Music* 3 (1979): 114–225.

———. "Franz Schubert and the Peacocks of Benvenuto Cellini." *19th Century Music* 12 (1989): 193–206.

Temperley, Nicholas. "Schubert and Beethoven's Eight-Six Chord." *19th Century Music* 5 (1981): 142–54.

Webster, James. *Haydn's "Farewell" Symphony and the Idea of Classical Style*. Cambridge: Cambridge University Press, 1991.

Webster, James. "Schubert's Sonata Form and Brahms's First Maturity." *19th Century Music* 2 (1978): 18–35.

Westergaard, Peter. *An Introduction to Tonal Theory*. New York: Norton, 1975.

Whittal, Arnold. *Romantic Music: A Concise History from Schubert to Sibelius*. London: Thames & Hudson, 1987.

Wolff, Christoph. "Brahms, Wagner, and the Problem of Historicism in Nineteenth-Century Music." In *Brahms Studies: Analytical and Historical Perspectives*. Edited by George Bozarth, 7–12. Oxford: Oxford University Press, Clarendon Press, 1990.

Zuckerkandl, Victor. *The Sense of Music*. Princeton: Princeton University Press, 1959.

———. *Sound and Symbol: Music and the External World*. Princeton: Princeton University Press, 1956.

On Issues of Performance

Adler, Kurt. *The Art of Accompanying and Coaching*. New York: Da Capo Press, 1971.

Berry, Wallace T. *Musical Structure and Performance*. New Haven: Yale University Press, 1989.

Brendel, Alfred. *Musical Thoughts and Afterthoughts*. Princeton: Princeton University Press, 1976.

Copland, Aaron. *Music and Imagination*. Cambridge: Harvard University Press, 1952.

Cranmer, Philip. *The Technique of Accompaniment*. London: Dobson, 1970.

Desmond, Astra. *Schumann Songs*. Seattle: University of Washington Press, 1972.

Dunsby, Jonathan. "Guest Editorial: Performance and Analysis of Music." In *Music Analysis* 8 (1989): 5–20.

Emmons, Shirlee and Stanley Sonntag. *The Art of the Song Recital*. New York: Schirmer, 1979.

Fischer, George, and Judy Lochhead. "Analysis, Hearing, and Performance." *Indiana Theory Review* 14 (1993): 1–36.

Jefferson, Alan. *The Lieder of Strauss*. New York: Praeger, 1972.

Lehmann, Lotte. *Eighteen Song Cycles*. New York: Praeger, 1972.

———. *More than Singing: The Interpretation of Songs*. Rev. ed. Translated by Frances Holden. New York: Dover Publications, 1985.

Leinsdorf, Erich. *The Composer's Advocate: A Radical Orthodoxy for Musicians*. New Haven: Yale University Press, 1981.

Moore, Gerald. *Am I Too Loud?* New York: Macmillan, 1962.

———. *Farewell Recital*. London: Hamilton, 1978.

———. *Poet's Love: The Songs and Cycles of Schumann.* New York: Taplinger, 1981.

———. *Singer and Accompanist.* New York: Macmillan, 1954.

———. *The Unashamed Accompanist.* Rev. ed. London: Julia MacRae Books, 1984.

Moriarty, John. *Diction.* Boston: E. C. Schirmer, 1975.

Porter, Ernest G. *Schubert's Song Technique.* London: Dobson, 1961.

Reinhard, Thilo, ed. and trans. *The Singer's Schumann.* New York: Rosen Publishing Group, 1989.

Rolf, Marie, and Elizabeth West Marvin. "Analytical Issues and Interpretive Decisions in Two Songs by Richard Strauss." *Integral* 4 (1990): 67–104.

Schenker, Heinrich. "A Contribution to the Study of Ornamentation." Translated by Hedi Siegel. *Music Forum* 4 (1976): 1–140.

———. "The Largo of J. S. Bach's Sonata No. 3 for Unaccompanied Violin [BWV 1005]." Translated by John Rothgeb. *Music Forum* 4 (1976): 161–95.

———. "The Sarabande of J. S. Bach's Suite No. 3 for Unaccompanied Violoncello [BWV 1009]." Translated by Hedi Siegel. *Music Forum* 2 (1970): 274–82.

Schmalfeldt, Janet. "On the Relation of Analysis to Performance: Beethoven's Bagatelles Op. 126, Nos. 2 and 5." *Journal of Music Theory* 29 (1985): 1–31.

Schumann, Robert. *On Music and Musicians.* Rev. ed. Edited by Konrad Wolff and translated by Paul Rosenfeld. New York: McGraw Hill, 1982.

Sessions, Roger. *The Musical Experience of Composer, Performer, Listener.* Rev. ed. New York: Atheneum Press, 1962.

Spillman, Robert. *The Art of Accompanying.* New York: Schirmer, 1985.

———. *Sightreading at the Keyboard.* New York: Schirmer, 1990.

Wilcke, Eva. *German Diction in Singing.* New York: E. P. Dutton, 1930.

On Schenkerian Analysis

Beach, David. "The Current State of Schenkerian Research." *Acta Musicologica* 57 (1985): 275–307.

———. "A Schenker Bibliography." In *Readings in Schenker Analysis and Other Approaches.* Edited by Maury Yeston, 275–309. New Haven: Yale University Press, 1977.

———. "A Schenker Bibliography." *Journal of Music Theory* 23 (1979): 275–86.

Burkhart, Charles. "Schenker's 'Motivic Parallelism'." *Journal of Music Theory* 22 (1978): 145–75.

———. "Schenker's Theory of Levels and Musical Performance." *Aspects of Schenkerian Theory.* Edited by David Beach, 95–112. New Haven: Yale University Press, 1983.

Cadwallader, Allen, ed. *Trends in Schenkerian Research.* New York: Schirmer, 1990

Forte, Allen, and, Steven Gilbert. *Introduction to Schenkerian Analysis.* New York: Norton, 1982.

Jonas, Oswald. *Introduction to the Theory of Heinrich Schenker.* Translated and edited by John Rothgeb. New York: Longman, 1982.

Kalib, Sylvan. "Thirteen Essays from the Three Yearbooks *Das Meisterwerk in der Musik.*" 3 vols. Ph.D. diss., Northwestern University, 1973.

Katz, Adele. *Challenge to Music Tradition: A New Concept of Tonality.* New York: Knopf, 1945.

Rothstein, William, "The Americanization of Schenker." *In Theory Only* 9/1 (1986): 5–17.

———. "Heinrich Schenker as an Interpreter of Beethoven's Piano Sonatas," *19th Century Music* 8 (1984): 3–28.

Schenker, Heinrich. "Franz Schubert: 'Ihr Bild'." Translated by William Pastille. *Sonus* 6/2 (1986): 31–35.

Schenkerian Analysis and German Lieder

Clarkson, Austin. "Brahms, Op. 105/1: A Literary-Historical Approach." In *Readings in Schenker Analysis and Other Approaches.* Edited by Maury Yeston, 230–53. New Haven: Yale University Press, 1977.

Everett, Walter. "Grief in *Winterreise:* A Schenkerian Perspective." *Music Analysis* 9 (1990): 157–75.

Forte, Allen. "Schenker's Conception of Musical Structure." In *Readings in Schenker Analysis and Other Approaches.* Edited by Maury Yeston, 3–37. New Haven: Yale University Press, 1977.

Laufer, Edward. "Brahms, Op. 105/1: A Schenkerian Approach." In *Readings in Schenker Analysis and Other Approaches.* Edited by Maury Yeston, 254–74. New Haven: Yale University Press, 1977.

Schachter, Carl. "Motive and Text in Four Schubert Songs." *Aspects of Schenkerian Theory.* Edited by David Beach, 61–76. New Haven: Yale University Press, 1983.

On Women and Music, including Gender Studies

Barkin, Elaine. "Feminism Forum: either/other." *Perspectives of New Music* 30/2 (1992): 206–33 [with response from Susan McClary, 234–42].

Belsey, Catherine, and Jane Moore, eds. *The Feminist Reader: Essays in Gender and the Politics of Literary Criticism.* Oxford: Blackwell, 1989.

Block, Adrienne Fried, and Carl Neuls-Bates. *Women in American Music: A Bibliography of Music and Literature.* Westport, Conn.: Greenwood Press, 1979.

Bowers, Jane. "Feminist Scholarship and the Field of Musicology." *College Music Symposium* 29 (1989): 81–92; 30 (1990): 1–13.

———, and Judith Tick, eds. *Women Making Music*. Urbana: University of Illinois Press, 1986.

Briscoe, James, ed. *Historical Anthology of Music by Women*. Bloomington: Indiana University Press, 1989.

Chissell, Joan. *Clara Schumann: A Dedicated Spirit*. New York: Taplinger, 1983.

Citron, Marcia. *Gender and the Musical Canon*. Cambridge: Cambridge University Press, 1993.

———, ed. *The Letters of Fanny Hensel to Felix Mendelssohn*. New York: Pendragon Press, 1987.

Clément, Catherine. *Opera, or the Undoing of Women*. Translated by Betsy Wing. Minneapolis: University of Minnesota Press, 1988.

Code, Lorraine. *What Can She Know: Feminist Theory and the Construction of Knowledge*. Ithaca, N.Y.: Cornell University Press, 1991.

Cook, Susan C. "Women, Women's Studies, Music, and Musicology: Issues of Pedagogy and Scholarship." *College Music Symposium* 29 (1989): 93–100.

———, and Judy Tsou, eds. *Cecillia Reclaimed: Exploring Gender and Music*. Urbana: University of Illinois Press, 1993.

Eagleton, Mary, ed. *Feminist Literary Theory: A Reader*. Oxford: Blackwell, 1986.

Filler, Susan M. "A Composer's Wife as Composer: The Songs of Alma Mahler." *Journal of Musicological Research* 4 (1983): 427–41.

Gilligan, Carol. *In a Different Voice: Psychological Theory and Women's Development*. Cambridge: Harvard University Press, 1982.

Green, Mildred Denby. *Black Women Composers: A Genesis*. Boston: Twayne Publishers, 1983.

Jacobus, Mary. *Reading Woman: Essays in Feminist Criticism*. New York: Columbia University Press, 1986.

Kaufman, Linda, ed. *Gender and Theory: Dialogues on Feminist Criticism*. Oxford: Blackwell, 1989.

Koskoff, Ellen, ed. *Women and Music in Cross-Cultural Perspective*. New York: Greenwood Press, 1987.

Kravitt, Edward. "The Lieder of Alma Maria Schindler-Mahler." *Music Review* 49 (1988): 190–204.

Lewin, David. "Women's Voices and the Fundamental Bass." *Journal of Musicology* 10 (1992): 464–82.

Maus, Fred Everett. "Masculine Discourse in Music Theory." *Perspectives of New Music* 31/2 (1993): 264–93.

McClary, Susan. *Feminine Endings*. Minneapolis: University of Minnesota Press, 1991.

Neuls-Bates, Carol, ed. *Women in Music: An Anthology of Source Readings from the Middle Ages to the Present*. New York: Harper & Row, 1982.

Pasler, Jann. "Feminism Forum: Some Thoughts on Susan McClary's Feminine Endings." *Perspectives of New Music* 30/2 (1992): 202–05.

Pendle, Karin, ed. *Women and Music.* Bloomington: Indiana University Press, 1991.

Placksin, Sally. *American Women in Jazz.* New York: Seaview Books, 1982.

Reich, Nancy B. *Clara Schumann: The Artist and the Woman.* Ithaca, N.Y.: Cornell University Press, 1985.

———. "Louise Reichardt." In *Ars Musica, Musica Scientia: Festschrift Heinrich Hüschen.* Edited by Detlef Altenburg. Cologne: Gitarre und Laute, 1980.

———, ed. *Women's Studies, Women's Status.* CMS Report No. 5. Boulder, Co.: College Music Society, 1988.

Showalter, Elaine, ed. *The New Feminist Criticism: Essays on Women, Literature, and Theory.* New York: Pantheon Books, 1985.

Solie, Ruth A., ed. *Music and Difference.* Berkeley and Los Angeles: University of California Press, 1993.

———. "Whose Life? The Gendered Self in Schumann's *Frauenliebe* Songs." In *Music and Text: Critical Inquiries.* Edited by Steven Paul Scher, 219–40. Cambridge: Cambridge University Press, 1992.

Straus, Joseph N. *Music by Women for Study and Analysis.* Englewood Cliffs, N.J.: Prentice-Hall, 1993.

Tick, Judith. *American Women Composers before 1870.* Ann Arbor: UMI Research Press, 1983.

Zaimont, Judith, ed. *The Musical Woman: An International Perspective.* Westport, Conn.: Greenwood Press, 1983–85.

Repertory by Chapter

Key to locating scores

Schubert, 59 Favorite = F

Schubert, Goethe = G

Schubert cycles: *Die schöne Müllerin* = SM
    Winterreise = W

Schumann cycles: *Dichterliebe* =D;
    Frauenliebe und -Leben = FLL
    Liederkreis, Op. 39 = L39
    Liederkreis, Op. 24 = L24
    Myrthen = M

Wolf, *Italienischesliederbuch* = I

Wolf, *Spanischesliederbuch* = S

Wolf, *Goethelieder* = G

Wolf, *Mörikelieder* = M

All other scores are in Appendix V.

Chapter Three

Schubert
    "Ave Maria," D. 839 (F)
    "Der Leiermann," D. 911 (W)
    "Lied eines Schiffers," D. 360 (F)
    "Litanei," D. 343 (F)
    "Meeres Stille," D. 216 (G)
    "Wanderers Nachtlied I," D. 768 (G)
    "Wohin?," D. 795 (SM)

Schumann
    "In der Fremde," op. 39 (L39)
    "Seit ich ihn gesehen," op. 42 (FLL)

Brahms
    "Ständchen," op. 106, no. 1

Wolf
    "Ich hab' in Penna" (I)
    "Lebe wohl" (M)

Chapter Four

Schubert
    "Der Neugierige," D. 795 (SM)
    "Die Forelle," D. 550 (F)
    "Gretchen am Spinnrade," D. 118 (G)
    "Nähe des Geliebten," D. 162 (G)
    "Wanderers Nachtlied I" (G)
    "Wohin?" (SM)

Schumann
    "Die Rose, die Lilie," Op. 48 (D)
    "Im Rhein, im heiligen Strome," D. 48 (D)
    "Widmung," Op. 25 (M)

Brahms
    "Die Mainacht," Op. 43, no. 2

Wolf
    "Gesang Weylas" (M)

Strauss
    "Ständchen," Op. 17, no. 2

Chapter Five

Schubert
    "Der Lindenbaum," D. 911 (W)
    "Die Forelle" (F)
    "Erlkönig," D. 328 (G)
    "Gretchen am Spinnrade" (G)
    "Wohin?" (SM)

Schumann
    "Ich hab' im Traum geweinet," op. 48 (D)
    "Im Rhein, im heiligen Strome" (D)
    "Mondnacht," Op. 39 (L39)

Brahms
    "Die Mainacht"
    "Vergebliches Ständchen," op. 84, no. 4
    "Wie Melodien," op. 105, no. 1

Wolf
    "Auch kleine Dinge" (I)

"In dem Schatten" (S)
"Mein Liebster singt" (I)
"Mir ward gesagt" (I)

Strauss
"Allerseelen," op. 10, no. 8
"Morgen!" op. 27, no. 4

Chapter Six

Schubert
"Am Feierabend," D. 798 (SM)
"An den Mond," D. 259 (F)
"Ave Maria," D. 839 (F)
"Der Jüngling und der Tod," D. 545
"Der Lindenbaum," (W)
"Der Musensohn," D. 764 (G)
"Der Neugierige" (SM)
"Der Tod und das Mädchen," D. 531 (F)
"Die liebe Farbe," D. 798 (SM)
"Du bist die Ruh," D. 776 (F)
"Erster Verlust," D. 226 (G)
"Leiden der Trennung," D. 509
"Nachtviolen," D. 752
"Schäfers Klagelied," D. 121 (G)
"Meeres Stille" (G)
"Wasserfluth," D. 911 (W)
"Wiegenlied," D. 498 (F)

Schumann
"Ich grolle nicht," Op. 48 (D)
"Im wunderschönen Monat Mai," Op. 48 (D)
"In der Fremde" (L39)
"Widmung" (M)

Brahms
"Die Mainacht"
"Immer leiser," Op. 105, no. 2

Wolf
"Mir ward gesagt" (I)
"Und steht Ihr früh" (I)

Chapter Seven

Schubert
"An die Musik," D. 547 (F)

"Auf dem Wasser zu singen," D. 774 (F)
"Du bist die Ruh" (F)
"Erlkönig" (G)
"Im Frühling," D. 882 (F)
"Litanei" (F)
"Schäfers Klagelied" (G)

Wolf
"Auch kleine Dinge" (I)

Chapter Eight

Schubert
"Der Kreuzzug," D. 932 (F)
"Der Neugierige" (SM)
"Die liebe Farbe" (SM)
"Du bist die Ruh" (F)
"Erlkönig" (G)
"Gretchen am Spinnrade" (G)
"Im Frühling" (F)
"Meeres Stille" (G)
"Nachtviolen," D. 752 (F)
"Schäfers Klagelied" (G)
"Wanderers Nachtlied I" (G)

Schumann
"In der Fremde" (L39)
"Seit ich ihn gesehen" (FLL)

Brahms
"Die Mainacht"
"Heimweh II" ("O wüßt ich doch den Weg zurück")
"Immer leiser wird mein Schlummer"
"Wie Melodien zieht es mir"

Wolf
"Mir ward gesagt" (I)

Chapter Nine

Schubert
"Der Müller und der Bach," D. 798 (SM)
"Der Musensohn" (G)
"Die Forelle" (F)
"Erlkönig" (G)
"Ganymed," D. 544 (G)

"Gretchen am Spinnrade" (G)
"Gute Nacht," D. 911 (W)
"Klage an den Mond"
"Litanei" (F)
"Mein!" D. 798 (SM)
"Morgengruß," D. 798 (SM)
"Wanderers Nachtlied I" (G)
"Wiegenlied" (F)

Schumann
"In der Fremde" (L39)
"Schöne Wiege meiner Leiden" (L24)
"Waldesgespräch" (L39)
"Widmung" (M)

Brahms
"Die Mainacht"
"Vergebliches Ständchen," op. 84, no. 4

Wolf
"Auch kleine Dinge (I)
"Ich hab' in Penna" (I)
"Verborgenheit" (M)

Strauss
"Morgen!"

Chapter Ten

Schubert
"Die Mainacht," D. 194
"Wer sich der Einsamkeit ergibt," D. 478 (G)

Schumann, Clara
"Liebst du um Schönheit," op. 12, no. 4

Schumann, Robert
"In der Fremde" (L39)
"Wer sich der Einsamkeit ergibt," op. 98a

Brahms
"Die Mainacht"
"In der Fremde," op. 3, no. 5

Wolf
"Wer sich der Einsamkeit ergibt" (G)

Mahler, Gustav
"Liebst du um Schönheit" *(Rückertlieder)*

Scores Not Readily Accessible

REPERTORY FOR APPENDIX V

"Der Jüngling und der Tod," D. 545

("The Young Man and Death")

Franz Schubert   (Spaun)

"Die Mainacht," D. 194

("May Night")

Franz Schubert   (Hölty)

Wann der sil - ber - ne Mond durch die Ge - sträu - che blinkt, und sein
preis' ich dich dann, flö - ten - de Nach - ti - gall, weil dein
hül - let von Laub, gir - ret ein Tau - ben - paar sein Ent -
lä - chelndes Bild, welches wie Mor - gen - roth durch die

schlummerndes Licht ü - ber den Ra - sen streut, und die Nach - ti - gall flö -
Weib - chen mit dir woh - net in ei - nem Nest, ih - rem sin - gen - den Gat -
zü - cken mir vor; a - ber ich wen - de mich, su - che dunk - le - re Schat -
See - le mir strahlt, find' ich auf Er - den dich? Und die ein - sa - me Thrä -

tet,   wandl' ich trau - rig von Busch zu Busch.   Se - lig
ten   tau - send trau - li - che Küs - se giebt.   Ü - ber
ten,   und die ein - sa - me Thrä - ne rinnt.
ne   bebt mir hei - sser die Wang' her - ab.

Fine.

"Klage an den Mond," D. 436

("Lament to the Moon")

Franz Schubert   (Hölty)

"Leiden der Trennung," D. 509

("Sorrows of Separation")

Franz Schubert   (Collin)

mur _ melnden Ba _ che, im Brun _ nen_ge_ma _ che, zum Meer,   zum

Meer,   von dem   sie kam,   von   dem   sie   Le _ _ ben nahm, von

dem,   des Ir _ rens   matt und   mü _ de, sie sü _ _ sse Ruh' ver_

hofft und Frie _ de.

"Wer sich der Einsamkeit ergibt,", op. 98a, no. 6

("He Who Gives Himself to Loneliness")

Robert Schumann   (Goethe)

"Die Mainacht", op. 43, no. 2
("May Night")

Johannes Brahms   (Hölty)

Wann der sil – ber-ne

Mond durch die Ge-sträu-che blinkt und sein schlum-merndes Licht ü-ber den

Ra – sen streut, und die Nach – ti-gall flö – tet, wandl ich trau-rig von

Busch   zu   Busch.

ein - - sa - me Trä - - - - - - - - ne

rinnt.

dimin. ritard.

Wann, o lä - chelndes

Bild, wel - ches wie Mor - gen - rot durch die See - le mir

strahlt, find ich auf Er - - den dich?

"Heimweh II," op. 63, no. 8

("Homesickness")

Johannes Brahms   (Klaus Groth)

"Immer leiser wird mein Schlummer," op. 105, no. 2

("Ever Lighter Grows My Slumber")

Johannes Brahms

(Lingg)

"In der Fremde," op. 3, no. 5

("In the Foreign Land")

Johannes Brahms   (Eichendorff)

Hei . mat hin . ter den Bli . tzen rot, da kom.men die Wol . ken her.

A . ber Va . ter und Mut . ter sind lan . ge tot, es kennt mich dort kei . ner

"Ständchen," op. 106, no. 1

("Serenade")

Johannes Brahms   (Kugler)

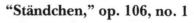

Die Klän.ge schleichen der Schön.sten sacht in den Traum hin . ein,

sie schaut den blon.den Ge . lieb . ten und lis . pelt: „Ver.

giß nicht mein!"

"Vergebliches Ständchen," op. 84, no. 4

("Vain Serenade") (Lower Rhine Folksong)

Johannes Brahms   (Kugler)

(Sie) Mein Tür ist ver-schlos-sen, ich laß dich nicht ein,

ich laß dich nicht ein; Mut-ter die

rät mir_ klug, wärst du her-ein mit_ Fug, wärs mit mir vor-bei,

wärs mit mir, wärs mit mir, wärs mit mir vor-bei!

(Er) So— kalt ist die Nacht, so ei . sig der Wind,

so ei . sig der Wind, daß mir das

Herz er . friert, mein Lieb er . lö . schen wird, öff . ne mir, mein Kind,

öff . ne mir,   öff . ne mir,   öff . ne mir, mein Kind!

(Sie) Lö schet dein Lieb, laß sie lö schen nur,

laß sie lö schen nur!   Lö schet sie im mer zu,

geh heim zu Bett, zur Ruh, gu te Nacht, mein Knab,   gu te Nacht,

gu te Nacht,   gu te Nacht, mein Knab!

"Wie Melodien," op. 105, no. 1
("As Melodies Steal to Me")

Johannes Brahms   (Klaus Groth)

Doch kommt das Wort und faßt es und führt es vor das

Aug, wie Ne-bel-grau er-blaßt es und schwin-det wie ein

Hauch, und schwin-det wie ein Hauch.

Und den-noch ruht im

"Wer sich der Einsamkeit ergibt"

("He Who Gives Himself to Loneliness")

Hugo Wolf

(Goethe)

"Lebe wohl"

("Farewell")

Hugo Wolf   (Mörike)

leich - tem Her - zen.
leave,   with glad - ness.

Le - be wohl!
Fare   thee well!

f immer gesteigerter

Ach tau - send - mal__ hab' ich mir es vor - ge - spro - chen,
Oh times a - gain__ to   my - self that word I've spok - en,

und   in nim - mer - sat - ter Qual____ mir das Herz da - mit ge-
thirs - ting e - ver more for   pain____ till   at   length my heart   is

bro - - chen!
brok - - en!

"Gesang Weylas"
("Weyla's Song")

Hugo Wolf

(Mörike)

"Liebst du um Schönheit," op. 12, no. 4
("If You Love for Beauty")

Clara Schumann (Rückert)

"Liebst du um Schönheit"
("If You Love for Beauty")

Gustav Mahler   (Rückert)

Index

9 780195 093285